Reinventing Data Protection?

Serge Gutwirth · Yves Poullet · Paul De Hert ·
Cécile de Terwangne · Sjaak Nouwt
Editors

Reinventing Data Protection?

Springer

Editors
Prof. Serge Gutwirth
Vrije Universiteit Brussel
Center for Law, Science
Technology & Society Studies (LSTS)
Pleinlaan 2
1050 Brussel
Belgium
serge.gutwirth@vub.ac.be

Prof. Yves Poullet
University of Namur
Research Centre for Information
Technology & Law
Rempart de la Vierge 5
5000 Namur
Belgium
yves.poullet@fundp.ac.be

Prof. Paul De Hert
Vrije Universiteit Brussel
Center for Law, Science
Technology & Society Studies (LSTS)
Pleinlaan 2
1050 Brussel
Belgium
paul.de.hert@vub.ac.be

Prof. Cécile de Terwangne
University of Namur
Research Centre for Information
Technology & Law
Rempart de la Vierge 5
5000 Namur
Belgium
cecile.deterwangne@fundp.ac.be

Dr. Sjaak Nouwt
Royal Dutch Medical Association (KNMG)
Mercatorlaan 1200
3528 BL Utrecht
Netherlands
s.nouwt@fed.knmg.nl
(formerly: TILT, Tilburg University, Netherlands)

ISBN 978-1-4020-9497-2 e-ISBN 978-1-4020-9498-9

DOI 10.1007/978-1-4020-9498-9

Library of Congress Control Number: 2009920948

Printed on acid-free paper

9 8 7 6 5 4 3 2 1

springer.com

Foreword by Karel De Gucht, Deputy Prime Minister and Minister of Foreign Affairs of Belgium

Twenty-first century world citizens are living at the crossroads of an ever expanding network of international trade-, investment-, travel-, communications- and knowledge flows. Modern societies find their dynamism in the free flow and competition of ideas and the free access to a wide range of information channels and pluralistic media.

Citizens discover new ways to develop their fundamental freedoms. Travelling across the globe – which a Minister for Foreign Affairs also does quite often – mobile ICT-technology allows us to stay abreast of developments at home or elsewhere. Credit cards – with microchips – also allow us to pay bills in virtually every hotel in the world.

MIT Professor Henry Jenkins has even developed the notion of '*twenty-first century literacy*', based on the ability to read and write but also digital skills to participate socially and collaboratively in the new media environment. These include: *instant messaging, Myspace, sampling, zines, mashups, Wikipedia, gaming and spoiling*.

Citizens in the developing world too use technological advancements to their maximal benefit. The introduction of mobile telecommunication in Sub-Saharan Africa is a good example. Faraway regions reconnect with their capital and the rest of the country, on which they often depend for the delivery of basic services. In many villages, citizens can either rent a mobile phone or make use of a collective mobile phone. The creation of a '*Virtual Souk*' on the Internet is another good example. Hundreds of craftsmen – in fact mostly women – in Morocco, Tunisia, Lebanon and Egypt suddenly gained direct access to the global market. Their sales volumes soared and their profit margins rose significantly.

These developments – often driven by new technologies – also bring along new threats for the individual citizen and for our modern, open society: such as identity theft, discriminatory profiling, continuous surveillance or deceit. That is why we must protect ourselves against the illegal use and the abuse of sensitive knowledge, technology and skills.

Within Europe, the individual's right to privacy is firmly embedded in the *European Convention on Human Rights and Fundamental Freedoms* of 1950. The Council of Europe reaffirmed these rights in 1981 when it adopted *Convention 108 for the protection of individuals with regard to the automatic processing of personal data*. Furthermore, the European Union established clear basic principles for the collection, storage and use of personal data by governments, businesses and other organizations or individuals in *Directive 95/46/EC* and *Directive 2002/58/EC on Privacy and Electronic communications*.

Nonetheless, the twenty-first century citizen – utilizing the full potential of what ICT-technology has to offer – seems to develop a *digital persona* that becomes increasingly part of his individual social identity. From this perspective, control over personal information is control over an aspect of the identity one projects in the world. The right to privacy is the freedom from unreasonable constraints on one's own identity.

Transaction data – both traffic and location data – deserve our particular attention. As we make phone calls, send e-mails or SMS messages, data trails are generated within public networks that we use for these communications. While traffic data are necessary for the provision of communication services, they are also very sensitive data. They can give a complete picture of a person's contacts, habits, interests, activities and whereabouts. Location data, especially if very precise, can be used for the provision of services such as route guidance, location of stolen or missing property, tourist information, etc. In case of emergency, they can be helpful in dispatching assistance and rescue teams to the location of a person in distress. However, processing location data in mobile communication networks also creates the possibility of permanent surveillance.

Because of the particular sensitivity of transaction data the EU adopted in March 2006 a *Directive on the retention of communication traffic data*. This Directive provides for an EU-wide harmonisation of the obligations on providers and for limits on retention periods from six months to two years. Use of traffic data for the purpose of police investigations of criminal offences is regulated by national law.

This brings me to the heart of the ongoing public debate about security and privacy, all too often presented as dichotomous rivals to be traded-off in a zero-sum game. However responsible liberal and democratic policy makers do not have the luxury to balance one against the other. Both are needed.

In a twenty-first century information society, the fundamental freedoms of the individual cannot be protected by opposing technological developments, nor by seeking to control the use of particular technologies or techniques. Such policy preferences reflect the determination of certain authoritarian regimes to cut their citizens off from the rest of the world. Reporters Without Borders published a list of 13 Internet black holes, among which were Belarus, Burma, Cuba, Iran, Syria, Tunisia and Uzbekistan. But China is also mentioned, as the *world's most advanced country in Internet filtering*.

Dan Solove has suggested that a more appropriate metaphor for Data Protection than Orwell's *Big Brother* is Kafka's *The Trial*. I tend to agree with him. The concern is of a *more thoughtless process of bureaucratic indifference, arbitrary error and dehumanization, a world where people feel powerless and vulnerable, without meaningful form of participation in the collection and use of their information*.

Recent academic literature (Taipale, NY Law School professor) highlights the potential of 'value sensitive technology development strategies in conjunction with policy implementations'. Privacy concerns are taken into account during design and development. Technical features can be built in to enable existing legal control mechanisms and related due process procedures for the protection of fundamental freedoms of the individual. Technical requirements to support such strategies include rule-based processing, selective revelation of personal data and strong credentials and audits.

The *particular privacy concerns* most implicated by employing advanced information technology for proactive law enforcement are primarily three. First, the *Chilling effect* or the concern that potential lawful behaviour would be inhibited due to potential surveillance. Two, the *Slippery slope* or the tendency to use powerful – but very intrusive – tools for increasingly pettier needs until, finally, we find ourselves in a situation of permanent surveillance. And three, the potential for *abuse or misuse*.

Programming code can never be law but code can bind what law, norms and market forces can achieve. Technology itself is neither the problem nor the solution. It presents certain opportunities and potentials that enable or constrain our public policy choices.

New technologies do not determine human fates: they rather alter the spectre of potentialities within which people act. An inter-disciplinary public debate is needed. Data protection is ultimately the shared responsibility of the individual, twenty-first century citizen, technology developers and policy makers together, next to that of data protection commissioners.

Karel De Gucht

Preface

In November 2007, the 'law and technology' research centres LSTS from the Vrije Universiteit Brussel, CRID from the University of Namur and TILT from Tilburg University co-organized the successful *Reinventing Data Protection?* conference in Brussels.[1] The conference gathered 150 people from all sectors of activities: universities, international, European and national administrations, companies, civil society associations, data protection authorities etc. and all were ready and interested to discuss the future of data protection in a society where information systems increasingly determine our destiny and shape our relations with our environment of humans and non-humans.

One of the roles of a university, *a fortiori* in the human sciences, is definitely to be a facilitator and stimulator of open and straightforward debates in a context of robust and tested knowledge. Such a role is certainly not neutral, since it urges all the stakeholders to revisit the genealogy and foundations of societal concepts and values in order to reshape and reframe political and societal discussion. Our explicit goal was to collectively re-initiate and invigorate the debate on data protection and its main concepts and objectives. In our opinion this debate is crucial and urgent, since our relationships with our physical or virtual co-humans, with the society as a whole and with things (that become 'intelligent') have drastically changed as a result of the introduction of powerful, ubiquitous and vital technologies in our lives. Since societies steadily reshape and rebuild themselves, it comes as no surprise that a tool such as data protection is in need of reinvention.

Let us shortly elaborate on the various reasons we had for initiating such debate.

1. **Why this debate**? At first glance it appears that data protection today receives more recognition, particularly from a legal perspective. The recently adopted EU Charter of Fundamental Rights erects data protection as a new fundamental right on an equal footing with the freedom of expression or the right to a fair trial. Also, more and more national constitutions are amended with a separate right to

[1] The conference was also co-organised and supported by the VUB instituut voor PostAcademische Vorming (iPAVUB) and the Vlaams-Nederlands Huis deBuren. It was further supported by the European Commission, the Fonds voor Wetenschappelijk Onderzoek (FWO) and the Fonds National de la Recherche Scientifique (FNRS).

data protection next to the more classical right to privacy. But beyond this formal recognition of a new constitutional right, a lot of interrogations remain. Is there a need to rethink the foundations of data protection in today's information society? What are the relationships between the 'old' constitutional right to privacy and its new counterpart, the constitutional right to protection of personal data?

The EU Charter of Fundamental Rights can, as Rodotà writes, be considered as the final point of a long evolution, separating privacy and data protection: from that point of view, the reinvention of data protection is ongoing, or more precisely, starting now.

In their former work De Hert and Gutwirth[2] described privacy and data protection as different but complementary fundamental rights. In order to devise accurate and effective privacy and data protection policies they must remain sharply distinguished. For these authors, by default, privacy law protects the opacity of the individual by prohibitive measures (non-interference), while data protection, also by default, calls for transparency of the processor of personal data enabling its control by the concerned individuals, states and special authorities. While privacy builds a shield around the individual, creating a zone of autonomy and liberty, data protection puts the activity of the processor in the spotlight, gives the individual subjective rights to control the processing of his/her personal data and enforces the processor's accountability. Opacity tools, such as privacy set *limits* to the interference of the power with the individuals' autonomy and as such, they have a strong normative nature, while transparency tools, such as data protection, tend to regulate accepted exercise of power by channelling, regulating and controlling. In their contribution De Hert and Gutwirth focus on the future of data protection, after its consecration as a fundamental right in the 2000 EU Charter of Fundamental Rights. Using Lessig's typology, the Charter should be regarded as a 'transformative constitution' rather than as a 'codifying constitution'. Of these two types, the transformative constitution is clearly the more difficult to realize, since it must act when the constitutional moment is over. This is a good reason to focus upon the current process of constitutionalisation of data protection by the European Court on Human Rights in Strasbourg and the Court of Justice of the European Communities in Luxemburg.

Next to this, Rouvroy and Poullet and Hosein endorse the need to enlarge and deepen the privacy debate: they see privacy as a prerequisite for a living and non discriminatory democracy. For Rouvroy and Poullet the fundamental right to privacy fosters the autonomic capabilities of individuals that are necessary for sustaining a vivid democracy, which notably presupposes the right to seclusion or to opacity. The importance of privacy today then derives from the support it provides for individuals to develop both reflexive autonomy allowing to resist

[2] De Hert P. and S. Gutwirth, 'Privacy, data protection and law enforcement. Opacity of the individual and transparency of power' (2006) in E. Claes, A. Duff & S. Gutwirth (eds), *Privacy and the criminal law*, Antwerp/Oxford, Intersentia, pp. 61–104.

social pressures to conform to dominant drifts and deliberative abilities allowing participation in deliberative processes.

Finally, the notion of human dignity is often invoked as the ultimate basis for the recognition of privacy. Several authors highlight that data protection legislation is grounded on important ethical values, human dignity being one of them. Identifying these values might help to correctly interpret data protection rules in a still changing context (Rodotà and Rouvroy and Poullet).

2. **Why this debate**? Our conference gave the floor to all stakeholders in the current process of reinvention of data protection. We considered this to be an urgent necessity because the new information society environment raises still more fundamental political, economical and ethical issues, which need to be addressed with tools and actions stemming from different horizons. Data subjects are not only concerned as (net)citizens, concerned about their fundamental liberties but also as adequately and inadequately profiled consumers and as monitored and tracked employees at the workplace and even at home. Data subjects claim for collective bargains and for being more associated and implied in the design of the information systems surrounding them. Data controllers are acting individually and collectively, ready to discuss with their counterparts, acting on behalf of data subjects.

   Building on previous work[3] Raab and Koops seek to develop a policy actor-based approach to data protection problems by looking into the actors' roles from empirical and normative standpoints, by considering actors' relationships to each other and to the instruments, by considering the levels or arenas in which they participate and by seeking greater clarity about the processes that are involved. They finish with some suggestions for adapting some of the roles within the cast of various actors, including the role of technology developers that may positively contribute to the future of privacy protection.

   Importantly, the EU Charter of Fundamental Rights has constitutionally endorsed the fundamental role of the data protection authorities (DPA's) not only to solve concrete litigations or to give opinions on specific draft legislations or decisions but above all to incite democratic debates on strategic and prospective issues and challenges and to feed the different actors' reflections. To bring those tasks to a good end, the data protection authorities must be enabled to act in complete independence. Hustinx convincingly shows that this independence is not only a question of legal and political status but it must be conquered through the provision of adequate means and with the support from other stakeholders.

3. **Why this debate**? Because we have to rethink and reinvent some of the concepts laid down by current data protection legislation.

   - Firstly, the different data protection legislations have been constructed upon concepts closely related to the nature of the data at stake (personal data v. non

[3] Bennet, C. and Raab, C. (2006) *The Governance of Privacy: Policy Instruments in Global Perspective* (2nd edn.), Cambridge, MA: MIT Press.

personal data; sensitive data v. non sensitive data). However, it has clearly become even more obvious that if the prime concern is the preservation of the citizen's autonomy, the concept of personal data turns out to be problematic and no longer seems to be appropriate: surveillance societies work with profiles and technology that are able to detect or predict behaviour without necessarily processing personal data. As regards the profiling techniques used both by public authorities and private companies, Hildebrandt denunciates their reductionism and opacity, which destroys any possibility of self-determination for the citizens. To her, the focus on personal data must be complemented with a persistent focus on the dynamic profiles that will soon have more impact on life than trivial or non-trivial data. Consequently, she holds a plea for the recognition of a right of access to profiles and of a right to contest the validity or the fairness of the application of a profile. To be effective, Hildebrandt contends, these rights need to be complemented with legal obligations for those that construct and apply profiles and they need to be inscribed in the technological infrastructure against which they aim to protect.

- Secondly, data protection legislation only takes into account a limited number of actors, focusing on data controllers and data subjects. But today technology and information systems are introducing new actors whose intervention create new risks: the terminal equipment producers and the infrastructure operators. How to address these new risks and how to assign an appropriate liability to these actors? Dinant points out that the Article 29 Working Group has recently stressed the 'responsibility for data protection from a societal and ethical point of view of those who design technical specifications and those who actually build or implement applications or operating systems'. This being said and proclaimed, is it socially acceptable that there is no well-defined legal liability for those actors?
- Thirdly, all data protection regulatory instruments, national legislation or international conventions, self-regulatory instruments or public regulations do implicitly refer to a common and universal list of minimal guarantees that already seem to have an universal character. Indeed, international privacy standards have already been defined for more than a quarter of a century, expressed in the OECD Guidelines and in the Council of Europe Convention 108. However, de Terwangne contends that the last international data protection instrument, the Asian-Pacific Economic Cooperation (APEC) Privacy Framework adopted in 2004, weakens these standards, even if it nevertheless expresses the expansion throughout the world of the concern about data protection. The development of the Internet has rendered this concern critical. ICT developments in general and the tremendous growth of their use in all human activities have also shown the necessity to enrich the fundamental data protection principles with additional principles meant to maintain the balance between the efficiency of the technological tools and the power of their users on one side and the rights and interests of the individuals, data subjects, on the other side.

- Fourthly, can we consider that the regulatory concepts of data protection legislation – consent and proportionality – put in place for limiting the data processors' right to collect and process information have to be renewed and rethought? Consent and proportionality indeed play a fundamental role for legitimizing their processing. Perhaps these concepts must be deeply renewed given, as Bygraeve and Shartum describe, that the 'consent' often turns out to be formal, rarely free and often unavoidable and that the principle of proportionality shows a persistent lack of teeth. Nevertheless, Brownsword fundamentally defends consent as a central concept in the data protection regime and he argues that data protection regimes should be based on right-based consent, rather than on duty-based confidentiality obligation. This is especially the case insofar as the information society evolves into an IT-enabling profiling community in which processing and profiling are carried out on a daily basis by much less visible operators. But for Brownsword there is more at hand: the option for a right-based approach, as opposed to dignitarian and utilitarian positions, fits into Europe's commitment to human rights: the consent of the right holders must stay as a cornerstone in data protection regime.
  Bygrave and Schartum explore if new forms of collective consent and new procedures to establish the proportionality of the data processing would be needed, since both consent mechanisms and the principle of proportionality suffer certain weaknesses. Mechanisms for *collective exercise of consent* are probably hard to realize under the present legal limitations. Yet the authors contend that collective consent could both bolster the position of the individual data subject towards data controllers and make proportionality as a principle guiding consent more likely.
  On this issue, Berkvens refers to the 'Consumer privacy Approach' adopted by certain recent new US-legislations: such an approach clearly favours collective agreements defining the conditions and modalities of the data processing. Such an approach would also recognise the importance of the consumer' education and information and lead to class actions that might enhance the effectiveness of data protection. Berkvens concludes by pleading for restarting the dialogue between the entrepreneur and the consumer.

4. **Why this debate**? How to face the new networked and global world wherein our relationships and actions become still more formatted by technological devices and a long list of diffuses economic, social and political interests? Undoubtedly, the normative instruments need to take into account such new characteristics through different means.

   - Attention must indeed be paid to ways to regulate privacy and data protection beyond the national borders. Self-regulation, for instance, offers methods to increase the effectiveness of data protection principles, such as labelling systems, privacy policies and Alternative Dispute Resolution mechanisms. Such ways offer credible complementary or alternative tools for the traditional legislative approach. The value of self regulatory instruments must nevertheless be assessed according to certain criteria such as the legitimacy of their authors (since it is quite clear that the more the different stakeholders are represented in the drafting and evaluating process of these instruments, the more it will be difficult to dispute them), the degree to which they substantially comply with the Fair Information Principles and their effectiveness and enforcement mechanisms.

- If technology constitutes the risk, technology might well also offer a solution for protecting privacy. Pursuing this idea, Winn underlines the attention paid by the data protection authorities to standardisation bodies and the need for these private or public institutions to dedicate sufficient consideration to the privacy requirement in the definition of the norms. She explores the costs and benefits of trying to integrate technical standards into European data protection laws as a possible strategy to enhance compliance and enforcement efforts. Accepting the discipline imposed by 'better regulation' principles and adopting new perspectives on the legitimacy of regulatory bodies, might increase the chances that ICT standards can be harmonized with data protection laws, which in turn might increase the practical impact of those laws. Dinant briefly demonstrates how the transclusive hyperlinks feature, embedded in recent browsers, permits Google to tap in real-time a substantial part of the clickstream of every individual surfing on the net, even if not using the Google search engine. The call for a value-sensitive design of terminal equipments and of the infrastructure is in line with a new broad approach far beyond the limits of the data protection legislation.
- Trudel suggests a new approach founded on risk management, which turns down any dogmatic vision, be it the legislative interventionist or the liberal one. He convenes all the different stakeholders to analyse the risks involved and to assign the adequate remedy at each level of the information systems. From that perspective the author describes a 'networked normativity', which should be built up in a transparent way.
- It also means that the laws guaranteeing privacy and enforcing data protection must evolve as to fit the technological and socio-political evolutions generating new threats for the individuals' capacity for 'self-development' of their personality. According to the German Constitutional Court's opinion the development of the data processing technologies obliges the State to revise and adapt the guarantees it provides to the individuals in order to protect and foster the capabilities needed to implement their right to freely self-determine their personality. In the circumstances of the day, the legal protections offered to the individuals' capabilities for self-development would probably need to address the specific threats accompanying the development of ubiquitous computing and ambient intelligence, as stated by Rouvroy and Poullet, Hildebrandt and Rodotà.

5. **Why this debate**? Certain specific privacy issues are particularly pertinent and should be focused upon.

- Firstly, privacy is most certainly a fundamental liberty but its protection might hinder other liberties or prejudice security interests. Szekely analyses the possible conflicts between freedom of expression and privacy. According to the author 'privacy' and 'freedom of information' are neither friends, nor foes of each other but complementary concepts. However, both concepts have conflicting areas and Szekely discusses these areas from two perspectives: the private life of the public servant and the information about collaborators of former (dictatorial) regimes that could constitute 'data of public interest'. Furthermore, both information privacy and freedom of information have been put at risk by the restrictions in the post-9/11 era. Szekely concludes by proposing the use of a checklist for decision-makers that could help to limit the restrictions of information privacy and freedom of information to the extent that is both necessary and sufficient but also reversible.
  Next to the freedom of information the claim for security is often evoked to justify interferences and restrictions of the citizens' liberties. The need to maintain the priority to our liberties and to consider security as an exception that might be invoked only under strict conditions, justifies the adoption at the EU level of a framework agreement, which applies the same concepts in the third and the second EU pillars as in the first pillar. However, Alonso-Blas does not favour such an approach. To her, data protection in the third pillar area should of course be based on the common principles established in Convention 108 and further developed in Directive 95/46/EC but requires a careful consideration of the specific nature of personal data processing in this sector. The particular features of police and judicial work need to be taken into account: in fact, there is a need for very clear and specific tailor-made rules for the diverse areas of activity within the third pillar field.
  For Nouwt to protect personal data in the third EU pillar adequately, it is important to tune the economic data protection approach by the EU with the human rights approach by the Council of Europe. This could and should result in a common approach for data protection within 'the two Europes' and perhaps even beyond.
- Secondly, the global dimension of the information society obliges all the countries to adopt common rules at an international level in order to effectively protect privacy and personal data. This has recently been requested not only by the World Summit of the Information Society (WSIS) in Tunis but also by Google. On that point, de Terwangne opposes two approaches, namely the APEC self-regulatory model and the EU legislative model. The recent Council of Europe Convention on Cybercrime – opened to the signature of all countries, with growing success – definitively demonstrates that it is possible to find solutions suiting all actors. While waiting for this international consensus, the solution proposed by article 25 of EU Directive 95/46/EC as regards the Transborder Data Flows has however been firmly criticised. In Kuner's opinion, this legal framework is inadequate, in both a procedural and substantive sense and needs reforming. Kuner describes the procedural problems in a very original and mathematical way, concluding that

> there are only 78 potential adequacy candidate countries and that it would take 130 years for these countries to be considered adequate. More substantially, the adequacy provisions are contained in a separate chapter in the Directive and are not part of the general rules on the lawfulness of the processing of personal data. Furthermore, it appears that in its adequacy decisions, the European Commission does not always require third countries to prohibit the transfer to non-adequate countries. Kuner concludes that for a number of reasons, an accountability or liability approach (accountability for the data controller) would be more efficient and effective than the adequacy standard.

As concluded by Burkert and by many of the contributions of this book, the constitutional acknowledgment of data protection as a fundamental right should be considered not only as an achievement but also and more important, as a new starting point. The recognition of the fundamental right to data protection is directed towards the future. It has a transformative stance and should create the opportunity of a dynamic participative, inductive and democratic process of 'networked' reinvention of data protection (rather than a contained and reductive legal exercise). We will be happy editors if the present book succeeds in contributing to the seizing of this opportunity.

In respect of the diversity of nationalities, disciplines and perspectives represented in this book, the editors and the publisher have left the choices concerning the use of reference systems and spelling to the authors of the contributions.

Serge Gutwirth
Yves Poullet
Paul De Hert
Cécile de Terwangne
Sjaak Nouwt

Contents

Part I Fundamental Concepts

1 **Data Protection in the Case Law of Strasbourg and Luxemburg: Constitutionalisation in Action** ... 3
P. De Hert and S. Gutwirth

2 **The Right to Informational Self-Determination and the Value of Self-Development: Reassessing the Importance of Privacy for Democracy** ... 45
Antoinette Rouvroy and Yves Poullet

3 **Data Protection as a Fundamental Right** ... 77
Stefano Rodotà

4 **Consent in Data Protection Law: Privacy, Fair Processing and Confidentiality** ... 83
Roger Brownsword

5 **The Concepts of Identity and Identifiablity: Legal and Technical Deadlocks for Protecting Human Beings in the Information Society?** ... 111
Jean-Marc Dinant

Part II The Actors

6 **Role of Trade Associations: Data Protection as a Negotiable Issue** ... 125
Jan Berkvens

7 **The Role of Data Protection Authorities** ... 131
Peter Hustinx

8 **The Role of Citizens: What Can Dutch, Flemish and English Students Teach Us About Privacy?** ... 139
Ronald Leenes and Isabelle Oomen

Part III Regulation

9 **Consent, Proportionality and Collective Power** ... 157
Lee A. Bygrave and Dag Wiese Schartum

10 **Is a Global Data Protection Regulatory Model Possible?** ... 175
Cécile de Terwangne

11 **Technical Standards as Data Protection Regulation** ... 191
Jane K. Winn

12 **Privacy Actors, Performances and the Future of Privacy Protection** ... 207
Charles Raab and Bert-Jaap Koops

Part IV Specific Issues

13 **First Pillar and Third Pillar: Need for a Common Approach on Data Protection?** ... 225
Diana Alonso Blas

14 **Who is Profiling Who? Invisible Visibility** ... 239
Mireille Hildebrandt

15 **Challenges in Privacy Advocacy** ... 253
Gus Hosein

16 **Developing an Adequate Legal Framework for International Data Transfers** ... 263
Christopher Kuner

17 **Towards a Common European Approach to Data Protection: A Critical Analysis of Data Protection Perspectives of the Council of Europe and the European Union** ... 275
Sjaak Nouwt

18 **Freedom of Information Versus Privacy: Friends or Foes?** ... 293
Ivan Szekely

19 Privacy Protection on the Internet: Risk Management and Networked Normativity 317
Pierre Trudel

Towards a New Generation of Data Protection Legislation 335
Herbert Burkert

Contributors

Jan M. Berkvens is senior counsel at the legal and tax department of Rabobank Nederland and professor of law and informatics at Radboud University Nijmegen. His research focuses on legal aspects of information technology such as e-commerce and payment systems. He is an expert in data protection issues.

Diana Alonso Blas is the Data Protection Officer of Eurojust, the European Union's Judicial Cooperation Unit, since November 2003. She studied law at the universities of San Sebastián (Spain), Pau et les Pays de l'Adour (France) and Leuven (Belgium). Subsequently she followed a LL.M. European law postgraduate program at the University of Leuven where she graduated magna cum laude in 1993. From 1994 to 1998 she worked as research fellow for the Interdisciplinary Centre for Law and Information Technology (ICRI) of the Catholic University of Leuven (K.U.L.). In this same period, she spent one year acting as privacy expert for the Belgian Data Protection Authority in Brussels. In April 1998, she joined the Dutch Data Protection Authority where she was a Senior International Officer working under the direct supervision of Peter Hustinx until the end of January 2002. During this period, she represented The Netherlands in several international working groups, such as the article 29 Working Party and the Consultative Committee on Convention 108 at the Council of Europe. From February 2002 to November 2003, she worked at the Data Protection Unit of Directorate General Internal Market of the European Commission, in Brussels. She is author of numerous articles and reports dealing with data protection at European level in the first and third pillar and is often invited as speaker at European and international data protection conferences. She has also performed as guest lecturer at the universities of Tilburg (Netherlands) and Edinburgh (UK). She is a Spanish national and speaks five languages.

Roger Brownsword is a graduate of the London School of Economics. Since September 2003, he has been professor of law at King's College London and honorary professor of law at the University of Sheffield. He is director of a newly formed research centre (TELOS), based on the School of Law at KCL that focuses on regulation, ethics and technology.

Professor Brownsword acted as a specialist adviser to the House of Lords' Select Committee on Stems Cells and, more recently, to the House of Commons'

Science and Technology Committee for its report on hybrids and chimeras. Since Autumn 2004, he has been a member of the Nuffield Council on Bioethics; he was a member of the Nuffield Working Party on Public Health; and he was a member of the Academy of Medical Sciences' committee on Brain Science, Addiction and Drugs that reported in Summer 2008.

He has published some 200 papers; his latest books are *Rights, Regulation and the Technological Revolution* (OUP, 2008) and a co-edited collection, *Regulating Technologies* (Hart, 2008); and he is the general editor of a newly launched journal, *Law, Innovation and Technology*.

Herbert Burkert is professor of public law, information and communication law and president of the Research Centre for Information Law at the University of St. Gallen, Switzerland, and a senior researcher at the Fraunhofer Institute for Intelligent Analysis and Information Systems in Germany (currently on leave of absence).

Lee A. Bygrave (<http://folk.uio.no/lee>) is associate professor at the Law Faculty of the University of Oslo. He is also research associate (formerly co-director) of the Cyberspace Law and Policy Centre at the University of New South Wales, Sydney. His teaching appointments range across numerous institutions, including the universities of Vienna, Stockholm, Tilburg, New South Wales and Oslo. He has published extensively within the field of privacy/data protection law. He is the author of an international standard work in the field, *Data Protection Law: Approaching Its Rationale, Logic and Limits* (The Hague: Kluwer Law International, 2002). Bygrave has advised on privacy and information security issues for a broad range of organizations, including the European Commission, Nordic Council of Ministers, Norwegian Government, U.S. National Academies, U.K. House of Lords Select Committee on the Constitution, and Telenor. In 2007, he was appointed by the Norwegian Government to serve on a Privacy Commission that was tasked to assess the state of privacy protection in Norway and to propose measures for bolstering such protection. The Commission submitted its final report to the Government in January 2009. Much of Bygrave's current academic research focuses on Internet regulation. He has recently produced an anthology titled *Internet Governance: Infrastructure and Institutions*, which was published in early 2009.

Karel De Gucht is Deputy Prime Minister and Minister of Foreign Affairs of Belgium. He is also a professor of European law at the Vrije Universiteit Brussel.

Paul De Hert is professor of law at the Faculty of Law and Criminology of Vrije Universiteit Brussel. He is the director of the research group on Fundamental Rights and Constitutionalism (FRC) and senior member of the research group on Law, Science, Technology & Society (LSTS). He is also associate professor of law and technology at the Tilburg Institute for Law, Technology, and Society (TILT)

Cécile de Terwangne has a MD in law (University of Louvain), a PhD in law (University of Namur) and a LLM in European and international law (European

University Institute of Florence). She is professor at the Law Faculty of the University of Namur (Belgium). She teaches civil liberties, computer and human rights, and data protection. She is director of the post-graduate Program in Law of Information and Communication Technologies at the University of Namur. She is research director in the Freedoms in the Information Society Unit of the Research Centre for Computer and Law (CRID – University of Namur). She has taken part to numerous European and national research projects in the fields of data protection, privacy and ICT, freedom of information, e-Government, re-use of Public sector information, etc. She is director of the «Revue du droit des technologies de l'information» (R.D.T.I.).

Jean-Marc Dinant obtained a Master degree in computer science in 1985, after two years of economics. After various research projects in the field of expert systems, adults training and telecommunication networks, he has joined the Belgian Data Protection Authority in 1993. Since then he has worked in strong collaboration with lawyers in the data protection area. He has left the Belgian DPA in 1998 while remaining a technical expert inside the art 29 working party until 2001. Since 1994, he is working as a researcher in the Research Centre on IT and Law (CRID) of the University of Namur where he tries to be a full duplex gateway between lawyers and technician in the context of privacy and data protection. Within the CRID, he is currently head of the Technology and Security Unit and coordinates various research projects dealing with technology, security and privacy. Since 2001, Jean-Marc Dinant has been a technical data protection expert for many institutions including the Council of Europe and the European Commission. He is also a Member of the Belgian Association of Expert witnesses since 2003. He is currently senior lecturer at the University of Namur where he is teaching cyber security and ending his PhD in Computer Science about Privacy Enhancing Technologies.

Serge Gutwirth is a professor of human rights, legal theory, comparative law and legal research at the Faculty of Law and Criminology of the Vrije Universiteit Brussel (VUB), where he studied law, criminology and also obtained a post-graduate degree in technology and science studies. He also holds a part-time position of lecturer at the Faculty of law of the Erasmus University Rotterdam where he teaches philosophy of law, since October 2003. He is holder of a 10-year research fellowship in the framework of the VUB-Research contingent for his project 'Sciences and the democratic constitutional state: a mutual transformation process'.

Gutwirth founded and still chairs the VUB-research group Law Science Technology & Society (http://www.vub.ac.be/LSTS). He publishes widely in Dutch, French and English. Currently, Serge Gutwirth is particularly interested both in technical legal issues raised by technology (particularly in the field of data protection and privacy) and in more generic issues related to the articulation of law, sciences, technologies and societies.

Mireille Hildebrandt is an associate professor of jurisprudence at Erasmus School of Law and Dean of education of the Research School of Safety and

Security in the Netherlands. She has written her PhD thesis on the principle of 'no punishment without trial', from the perspective of legal philosophy, anthropology and legal history. Since 2002 she has been seconded to the centre of Law Science Technology and Society (LSTS) at Vrije Universiteit Brussel, as a senior researcher and has been coordinator of profiling in the EU research consortium on the Future of Identity in Information Society (FIDIS). From 2007 to 2012 she works on a research project on 'Law and Autonomic Computing: Mutual Transformations', investigating the legal implications of ubiquitous and autonomic computing. Her research interests concern the impact of emerging and future ICT infrastructures on issues of privacy, autonomy, causality, agency, legal personhood and due process. She is an associate editor of Criminal Law and Philosophy and of Identity in Information Society (IDIS) and publishes widely on the nexus of philosophy of law and of technology, with special regard for criminal law. She co-edited (with Serge Gutwirth) and co-authored 'Profiling the European Citizen. Cross-Disciplinary Perspectives' (2008).

Gus Hosein is an academic, an advocate, and a consultant. He is a visiting senior fellow at the London School of Economics and Political Science where he lectures and researches on technology policy. He is a senior fellow with Privacy International in London where he co-ordinates international research and campaigns on civil liberties. He is also a visiting scholar at the American Civil Liberties Union, advising on international technology and liberty issues. Finally, he is a consultant to international, governmental, non-governmental, and private sector organizations on data governance, civil liberties, and privacy. He has a B.Math from the University of Waterloo and a PhD from the University of London. He is also a fellow of the British Computer Society (FBCS CITP) and a fellow of the Royal Society for the encouragement of Arts, Manufactures and Commerce (FRSA). For more information please see http://personal.lse.ac.uk/hosein.

Peter J. Hustinx has been European Data Protection Supervisor since January 2004. He has been closely involved in the development of data protection legislation from the start, both at the national and at the international level. Before entering his office, he was president of the Dutch Data Protection Authority since 1991. From 1996 until 2000 he was chairman of the Article 29 Working Party. He received law degrees in Nijmegen, the Netherlands, and in Ann Arbor, USA. Since 1986 he has been deputy judge in the Court of Appeal in Amsterdam.

Bert-Jaap Koops is a professor of regulation & technology at the Tilburg Institute for Law, Technology, and Society (TILT), the Netherlands. He is also a senior researcher at Intervict, the Tilburg institute for victimology and human security, and a member of *De Jonge Akademie*, a branch of the Royal Netherlands Academy of Arts and Sciences with 80 young academics.

His main research interests are law & technology, in particular criminal-law issues in investigation powers and privacy, computer crime, DNA forensics, and cryptography. He is also interested in other topics of technology regulation, such as information security, identity, digital constitutional rights, 'code as law', human enhancement, and regulation of bio- and nanotechnologies. Since 2004, he co-ordinates a research program on law, technology, and shifting power relations.

Koops studied mathematics and general and comparative literature at Groningen University, the Netherlands. He did a PhD in law at Tilburg University and Eindhoven University of Technology with a dissertation on cryptography regulation in 1999. He has co-edited five books in English on ICT regulation and published many articles and books in English and Dutch on a wide variety of topics. Koops' WWW Crypto Law Survey is a standard publication on crypto regulation of worldwide renown. He gave invited lectures in the U.S. at the University of Dayton, Ohio, and George Washington University, Washington, D.C., and in the U.K. at King's College London.

Christopher Kuner is partner and head of the International Privacy and Information Management Practice at Hunton & Williams in Brussels. In 2007 and 2008, he was voted the 'go-to person for EU privacy' in a survey of leading privacy lawyers conducted by Computerworld magazine. Mr. Kuner is a member of the Data Protection Experts Group (GEX-PD) of the European Commission, and is author of the book *European Data Protection Law: Corporate Compliance and Regulation* (Oxford University Press, 2nd edition 2007), which has also been published in Chinese by Law Press China. He is Chairman of the International Chamber of Commerce (ICC) Data Protection Task Force and the European Privacy Officers Forum (EPOF), and guest lecturer in data protection and IT law at Vienna University of Economics and Business Administration.

Ronald Leenes is an associate professor in law and (new) technology and academic director of TILT, the Tilburg Institute for Law, Technology, and Society. Ronald has a background in public administration and public policy (University of Twente) and has extensive research experience in the fields of artificial intelligence and Law, E-Government and since he joined TILT, technology (primarily ICTs) and law. His primary research interests are regulation of and by technology, specifically related to privacy and identity management. He leads research teams in the field of privacy-enhancing identity management and Online Dispute Resolution. He is also involved in research in ID fraud, biometrics and e-government. He was/is work package leader in the EU FP6 PRIME project and the EU FP7 project PrimeLife. He has contributed to and edited various deliverables for the EU FP6 Network of Excellence 'Future of IDentity in the Information Society' (FIDIS), and he participated in the Network of Excellence 'Legal Framework for the Information Society' (LEFIS). Ronald is a productive researcher with a large number of international publications in books and (refereed) journals and refereed conference volumes.

Sjaak Nouwt is working as a policy officer in health law at the Royal Dutch Medical Association (KNMG: www.knmg.nl) in Utrecht (Netherlands) on topics related to privacy and ICT. From 1985 to February 2009, he was an assistant professor at the Tilburg Institute for Law, Technology, and Society (TILT) of Tilburg University, Faculty of Law. At TILT, he taught master courses in *Privacy* *and Data Protection*, *Public Information Law*, and *Health Law*. In 1997, Nouwt published his doctoral thesis on the use of information technology in health care and the protection of medical data. He published several articles and (chapters in) books on privacy and data protection issues. He is editor-in-chief of a Dutch journal on Privacy and Information (*Privacy & Informatie*) and also of a Dutch journal on Data Protection in Health Care (*Journaal Privacy Gezondheidszorg*). Furthermore, he is a member of the editorial staff of several text-books, and loose-leaf publications on privacy and data protection. He is also a privacy consultant.

Isabelle Oomen joined the Tilburg Institute for Law, Technology, and Society (TILT) at the University of Tilburg as a junior researcher, after graduating from her sociology studies. She has conducted quantitative and qualitative research, as well as literature research, on privacy, identity, identity management, profiling, and e-government. Recently, Isabelle started her PhD research on privacy in online social networks. Her study is part of the project 'The Social Dimensions of Privacy' which is carried out by TILT and the University of Amsterdam.

Yves Poullet Ph.D. in law and graduated in philosophy, is full professor at the Faculty of Law at the University of Namur (FUNDP) and Liège (Ulg), Belgium. He teaches different topics like: 'Sources and principles of the law', 'Internet regulations', 'International commercial law', 'Human rights in the information society'. Yves Poullet heads the CRID, since its creation in 1979. He conducts various research projects in the field of new technologies with a special emphasis on privacy issues, individual and public freedom in the Information Society and Internet Governance. He is legal experts near the UNESCO and the Council of Europe. During 12 years (1992–2004) he has been a member of the Belgian data Protection Authority. In addition, he was since its origin, member of Legal Advisory Board of European Commission and the president of the Task Force 'Electronic Democracy and Access to public records'. He has received the Franqui Chair in 2004.

He also chaired the Belgian Computer Association Association Belge de Droit de l'Informatique (ABDI). He is an active member of the editorial board of various famous law reviews. He is a founder of the European Telecommunication Forum, ECLIP and FIRILITE.

Charles Raab is a professor emeritus and honorary professorial fellow in the School of Social and Political Science at the University of Edinburgh, where he was a professor of government and is associated with the Institute for the Study of Science, Technology and Innovation (ISSTI). He has conducted research and published books and articles extensively in the field of information policy and regulation, with particular emphasis upon privacy and data protection, surveillance, the use and sharing of personal data in government, personal identity, and freedom of information. He has held visiting positions at Tilburg University (TILT), Queen's University, Kingston, Ontario, the Oxford Internet Institute, and the Hanse-Wissenschaftskolleg at Delmenhorst, Germany. He serves on the editorial or advisory boards of many academic journals, and on the advisory boards of several research projects. He is a member of the Surveillance Studies Network, and participates in the Canadian-funded project on 'The New Transparency: Surveillance and Social Sorting' and in the European Union's COST Action on 'Living in Surveillance Societies' (LiSS). His consultancy work has included the European Commission, the United Kingdom Government, and the Scottish Government. He was the Specialist Adviser to the House of Lords Select Committee on the Constitution for their inquiry, *Surveillance: Citizens and the State*, 2nd Report, Session 2008–2009, HL 18.

Stefano Rodotà Professor of law, University of Roma 'La Sapienza'. Chair of the scientific Committee of the Agency for Fundamental Rights, European Union. Chair, Internet Governance Forum Italy. Former President of the Italian Data Protection Commission and of the European Group on Data Protection. Member of the Convention for the Charter of Fundamental Rights of the European Union. Visiting Fellow, All Souls College, Oxford. Visiting Professor, Stanford School of Law. Professeur à la Faculté de Droit, Paris 1, Panthéon-Sorbonne. Laurea honoris causa Université «Michel de Montaigne», Bordeaux. Former Member of the Italian and European Parliament, of the Parliamentary Assembly of the Council of Europe. Among his books: Tecnologie e diritti, Bologna, 1995; Tecnopolitica, Roma-Bari, 2004 (translated into French and Spanish); Intervista su privacy e libertà, Roma-Bari, 2005; La vita e le regole. Tra diritto e non diritto, Milano, 2006; Dal soggetto alla persona, Napoli, 2007.

Antoinette Rouvroy is FNRS (National Fund for Scientific Research) research associate and researcher at the Information Technology and Law Research Centre (CRID) of the University of Namur, Belgium. She is particularly interested in the mechanisms of mutual production between sciences and technologies and cultural, political, economic and legal frameworks. Her doctoral research at the European University Institute of Florence (Human Genes and Neoliberal Governance: A Foucauldian Critique. Abingdon and New-York, Routledge-Cavendish, 2008), looked at the knowledge–power relations in the post-genomic era. Her current interdisciplinary research interests revolve around the ethical, legal and political challenges raised by the new information, communication and surveillance technologies (biometrics, RFIDs, ubiquitous computing, ambient intelligence, persuasive technologies . . .) and their convergence.

Dag Wiese Schartum is a professor of law and chair of the Norwegian Research Center for Computers and Law (NRCCL) at the University of Oslo. Schartum's research interests comprise data protection, automated decision-making in government sector, access to government-held information and regulatory management. Dag Wiese Schartum has been member of several governmental expert committees and was, e.g., member of the committee drafting the Data Protection Act. In 2006 and 2008 the Ministry of Justice and Police engaged him and Lee A. Bygrave to evaluate and propose how the Norwegian Data Protection Act could be amended. List of books and articles by Schartum are available from http://www.schartum.no (cf. "bøker" and "artikler").

Ivan Szekely is an internationally known expert in the multidisciplinary fields of data protection and freedom of information. A long-time independent researcher, consultant and university lecturer, former chief counselor of the Hungarian Parliamentary Commissioner for Data Protection and Freedom of Information, he is at present Counselor of the Open Society Archives at Central European University and associate professor at the Budapest University of Technology and Economics. He has conducted research in the areas of data protection, information privacy, access to public information and archivistics. He participated in founding several national and international organizations in the area of data protection and FOI, shaping their strategies and activities. As member of experts' teams, he contributed to the framing and drafting of legislation regarding openness and secrecy in several new European democracies. A university professor, regular conference lecturer and author of notable publications, Szekely is member of several international research groups, among others, the 'Broadening the Range Of Awareness in Data protection' (BROAD), the 'Ethical Issues of Emerging ICT Applications' (ETICA) projects and the 'Living in Surveillance Societies' (LiSS) COST Action of the European Union.

Pierre Trudel is a full professor at the Public Law Research Center of the Faculty of Law of the Université de Montréal. He holds the L.R. Wilson Chair on information technology law and electronic commerce. His research and teaching focus on civil law, legal theory, legal epistemology, civil rights, fundamental information rights, intellectual property and information, media and communication law. He is a co-author with France Abran and Lucie Guibault, of Droit de la radio et de la télévision (Radio and Television Law), 1991, and recipient of the Québec Bar Foundation Award in 1993 and the Walter Owen Award in 1994. He also published *La carte à mémoire: ses aspects juridiques et technologiques* (Smart Card, Legal and Technological Aspects, 1992) and *La preuve et la signature dans l'échange de documents informatisés* (Evidence and Signature in EDI, 1993), (The Electronic Superhighway—The Shape of Technology and Law to Come, 1995, *L'intérêt public en droit de la communication* (1996), *Droit du cyberespace* (Cyberspace law), (1997), Cyberspace and Electronic Commerce law: general principles and legal issues (June 1999) and "The Development of Canadian Law with Respect to E-Government" in J.E.J. Prins, Designing e-Government, Kluwer Law International, 2007. He is currently involved in research and teaching on legal aspects of cyberspace regulation and Media law.

Jane K. Winn is the Charles I. Stone Professor as well as a faculty director of the Law, Technology and Arts program at the University of Washington School of Law. She is a graduate of the University of London and Harvard University. She also serves on the faculty of the University of Melbourne Law School where she has taught post-graduate courses in law and technology since 2001. In 2008, she was a Fulbright Scholar in China where she studied the impact of globalization and innovation on law. She is a leading international authority on electronic commerce law and technological and governance issues surrounding information security, and has widely published in law journals in the United States and Europe. Her current research interests include electronic commerce law developments in the United States, the European Union, and China. She is coauthor of *Law of Electronic Commerce* and the casebook *Electronic Commerce*.

Part I
Fundamental Concepts

Chapter 1
Data Protection in the Case Law of Strasbourg and Luxemburg: Constitutionalisation in Action

P. De Hert and S. Gutwirth

Although the 'formal' protection of the right to respect for private life, at least in areas covered by the first pillar, is in essence relatively satisfactory, there are concerns surrounding the weakening of the 'substantial' protection of that right.[1]

1.1 Formal or Political Constitutionalisation

1.1.1 The Underlying Interests of Data Protection

It is impossible to summarise data protection in two or three lines. Data protection is a catch-all term for a series of ideas with regard to the processing of personal data (see below). By applying these ideas, governments try to reconcile fundamental but conflicting values such as privacy, free flow of information, the need for government surveillance, applying taxes, etc. In general, data protection does not have a prohibitive nature like criminal law. Data subjects do not own their data. In many cases, they cannot prevent the processing of their data. Under the current state of affairs, data controllers (actors who process personal data) have the right to process data pertaining to others. Hence, data protection is pragmatic; it assumes that private and public actors need to be able to use personal information because this is often necessary for societal reasons. Data protection regulation does not protect us from data processing but from unlawful and/or disproportionate data processing.

P. De Hert (✉)
Law, Science, Technology & Society (LSTS) at the Vrije Universiteit Brussel, *Tilburg Institute of Law and Technology* (TILT) at Tilburg University
e-mail: paul.de.hert@vub.ac.be

S. Gutwirth
Vrije Universiteit Brussel (VUB) and Erasmus Universiteit Rotterdam

[1] Report on the First Report on the Implementation of the Data Protection Directive 95/46/EC, Committee on the Citizens' Rights and Freedoms, Justice and Home Affairs, European Parliament, Session Document, 24 February 2004 (Final A5-0104/2004), p. 13 http://ec.europa.eu/justice_home/fsj/privacy/docs/lawreport/ep_report_cappato_04_en.pdf

S. Gutwirth et al. (eds.), *Reinventing Data Protection?*
DOI 10.1007/978-1-4020-9498-9_1, © Springer Science+Business Media B.V. 2009

Data protection regulation's real objective is to protect individual citizens against unjustified collection, storage, use and dissemination of their personal details.[2] This objective seems to be indebted to the central objective of the right of privacy, to protect against unjustified interferences in personal life. Many scholars therefore hold data protection and privacy to be interchangeable. Data protection is perceived as a late privacy spin-off. We will come back to the relationship between privacy and data protection below. What we would like to underline here is that data protection regulation does a lot more than echoing a privacy right with regard to personal data. It formulates the conditions under which processing is legitimate. This entails, among other things that data must be processed fairly, for specified purposes and, on the basis of the consent of the person concerned or some other legitimate basis laid down by law. Data protection also prohibits certain processing of personal data, for instance 'sensitive data'.[3] A key principle to determining what is legitimate and what is prohibited is the purpose specification principle: data may only be processed when it is collected for specified, explicit and legitimate purposes and not further processed in a way incompatible with those purposes. Next to these guidelines on legitimate and unlawful processing, few specific subjective rights are granted to the data subject. These are *inter alia* the right to be properly informed, the right to have access to one's own personal data, the right to have data rectified the right to be protected against the use of automated profiling, the right to swift procedures in court, the right to assistance by Data Protection Authorities (DPAs) which are competent for a variety of tasks and enjoy broad discretionary powers (reporting, monitoring, complaints handling, rule development, enforcement), a right upon security measures to be implemented by 'controllers' and 'processors' and the right that only relevant data will be gathered and that they will not be disclosed except with consent of data subject or by authority of law.

We see data protection as a growing body of rules and principles that need to be taken into account by the legislator in drafting laws and by 'controllers' and 'processors of personal data'. This process is never over. New rules and principles are called for every time new challenges arise due to new (technological) developments. It is therefore not easy to define the underlying interest of data protection. Just as there are many visions of privacy in literature from narrow visions (*protection of the intimate sphere* proposed by inter alia Wacks, Inness),[4] older visions (*the*

---

[2] P.J. Hustinx, 'Data protection in the European Union', *Privacy & Informatie*, 2005, No. 2, (pp. 62–65), p. 62.

[3] Data protection law includes extra safeguards with regard to the processing of sensitive data or 'special categories of data', such as data on ethnicity, gender, sexual life, political opinions or the religion of the person. The special responsibility of the data processor towards sensitive data can be explained by the fact that the information at stake, for example medical data, belongs to the core of a person's private life. It is exactly this kind of information that individuals generally do not wish to disclose to others.

[4] Raymond Wacks, 'The Poverty of Privacy', *Law Quarterly Review*, 1980, vol. 96, p. 73 ff.; Julie C. Inness, *Privacy, Intimacy, and Isolation*, Oxford. University Press, 1992.

right to be let alone proposed by Warren & Brandeis or the dignity approach),[5] newer visions ('identity' as proposed by Hildebrandt)[6] over to broader visions (*privacy as freedom and informational self-determination* proposed by inter alia Westin and Gutwirth),[7] there are many possible 'readings' regarding the interests underlying data protection and their priority, ranging from autonomy, informational self-determination, balance of powers, informational division of powers, over integrity and dignity, to democracy and pluralism.[8]

1.1.2 Formal Constitutionalism and the History of Data Protection

The history of European data protection is a well-known example of legal creativity and perseverance of some of the visionary in the policy making world, realizing that the right to privacy in Article 8 of the European Convention for the protection of human rights and fundamental freedoms (ECHR), adopted in 1950, needed to be complemented to meet some of the challenges created by emerging technologies in the 1970s.[9] In the early 1970s the Council of Europe concluded that Article 8 ECHR suffered from number of limitations in the light of new developments, particularly in the area of information technology: the uncertain scope of private life, the emphasis on protection against interference by public authorities, and the insufficient response to the growing need for a positive and proactive approach, also in relation to other relevant organisations and interests.[10] As a consequence,

---

[5] Samuel D. Warren & Louis D. Brandeis, 'The Right to Privacy', *Harvard L. Rev.* 1890, pp. 195–215; Edward J. Bloustein, Privacy as an Aspect of Human Dignity: An Answer to Dean Prosser' *N.Y.U. L. REV.*, 1964, Vol. 39, p. 962 ff.

[6] M. Hildebrandt, 'Privacy and Identity', in Claes, E., Duff, E., Gutwirth, S. (eds.), *Privacy and the Criminal Law*, Antwerp- Oxford: Intersentia 2006, pp. 43–58.

[7] F. Westin, *Privacy and Freedom*, Bodley Head, London, 1967; S. Gutwirth, *Privacy and the information age*, Lanham/Boulder/New York/Oxford, Rowman & Littlefield Publ., 2002, 146p.

[8] E. Brouwer, *Digital Borders and Real Rights.* Nijmegen, Wolf Legal Publishers, 2007, (501p.), p. 170–175; P. De Hert & S. Gutwirth, 'Privacy, data protection and law enforcement. Opacity of the individual and transparency of power' in E. Claes, A. Duff & S. Gutwirth (eds.), *Privacy and the criminal law*, Antwerp/Oxford, Intersentia, 2006, p. 61–104; L. Bygrave, *Data Protection Law: Approaching Its Rationale, Logic and Limits*, Deventer, Kluwer Law International, 2002, 448p.; L. Bygrave, 'Regulatory logic of data protection laws', February 2007, (2p.), p. 1 (via http://www.uio.no/studier/emner/jus/jus/JUR5630/v07/undervisningsmateriale/lecture5v07.doc). Cf. the contribution of Poullet and Rouvroy in this book.

[9] See in more detail: P. De Hert & S. Gutwirth, 'Making sense of privacy and data protection. A prospective overview in the light of the future of identity, location based services and the virtual residence' in Institute for Prospective Technological Studies-Joint Research Centre, *Security and Privacy for the Citizen in the Post-September 11 Digital Age. A prospective overview*, Report to the European Parliament Committee on Citizens' Freedoms and Rights, Justice and Home Affairs (LIBE), July 2003, IPTS-Technical Report Series, EUR 20823 EN, p. 125–127. See also Birte Siemen, *Datenschutz als europäisches Grundrecht.* Berlin: Duncker & Humblot, 2006. 351 p. See on this excellent study the book review by Cornelia Riehle, *CML Rev. 2007*, pp. 1192–1193.

[10] P.J. Hustinx, *l.c.*, p. 62.

in 1981 the Council of Europe adopted a separate Convention on Data Protection (ETS No. 108)[11] dealing with data protection as protection of the fundamental rights and freedoms of individuals, in particular their right to privacy, with regard to the processing of personal data relating to them. These wordings demonstrate that data protection is both wider and more specific than the protection of privacy. It is wider since it also relates to other fundamental rights and freedoms of individuals, such as equality and due process. It is at the same time more specific, since it only deals with the processing of *personal data*. However, it is broader because it protects all personal data. We will see below that both the Strasbourg Court of Human Rights and the Luxembourg Court of Justice refuse to consider privacy protection to be applicable to all personal data.[12]

The Council of Europe Convention was followed by several EU regulatory initiatives[13]: the EU Directive 95/46/EC on the protection of individuals with regard to the processing of personal data and on the free movement of such data[14] Directive 97/66/EC of the European Parliament and of the Council of 15 December 1997 concerning the processing of personal data and the protection of privacy in the telecommunications sector,[15] replaced by Directive 2002/58/EC on privacy and electronic communications of 12 July 2002[16], and Regulation (EC) No. 45/2001 of the European Parliament and of the Council of 18 December 2000 on the protection of individuals with regard to the processing of personal data by the Community institutions and bodies and on the free movement of such data.[17] For our purposes, the constitutional recognition of data protection in the EU 2000 Charter of Fundamental Rights of the European Union is important.[18] In this non-legally binding Charter, a separate right to data protection is recognized next to the right to a private life for the individual. Whereas Article 7 of the Charter faithfully reproduces the wordings

[11] Council of Europe, Convention for the Protection of Individuals with regard to automatic processing of personal data, 28 January 1981, *ETS* No. 108. Available at: http://conventions.coe.int/Treaty/en/Treaties/Html/108.htm.

[12] Whereas data protection covers all personal data, privacy protection understood by the Court of Luxembourg only grants privacy protection to certain (uses of) data. Compare ECJ, *Rechnungshof (C-465/00) v Österreichischer Rundfunk and Others and Christa Neukomm (C-138/01) and Joseph Lauermann (C-139/01) v Österreichischer Rundfunk*, Judgement of 20 May 2003, joined cases C-465/00, C-138/01 and C-139/01, *European Court reports*, 2003, p. I-04989; §§ 74–75: while the mere recording by an employer of data by name relating to the remuneration paid to his employees cannot as such constitute an interference with private life, the communication of that data to third parties, in the present case a public authority, infringes the right of the persons concerned to respect for private life, whatever the subsequent use of the information thus communicated and constitutes an interference within the meaning of Article 8 of the European Convention on Human Rights.

[13] See for the rationale of these EU initiatives: P.J. Hustinx, *l.c.*, p. 63.

[14] *O.J.*, No. L 281, 23 November 1995, pp. 31–50.

[15] *O.J.*, No L 24, 30 January 1998, pp. 1–8.

[16] *O.J.*, No L 201, 31 July 2002, pp. 37–47.

[17] *O.J.*, 12 January 2001, L8, pp. 1–22.

[18] Charter of Fundamental Rights of the European Union of the European Parliament, December 7, 2000, *O.J.*, No. C 364, 2000, p. 1 et seq.

of the right to privacy as we know it from the 1950 Human Rights Convention,[19] Article 8 of the Charter focuses on the protection of personal data:

> Everyone has the right to the protection of their personal data. Such data must be processed fairly for specified purposes and on the basis of the consent of the person concerned or some other legitimate basis laid down by law. Everyone has the right of access to their data, and the right to have it rectified. Compliance with these rules shall be subject to control by an independent authority (Article 8 EU Charter).

In the ECHR there is no article that comes close to this provision. Apparently, something new is happening at constitutional level.[20] The Council of Europe's Convention on Data Protection (ETS No. 108) and the European Community's Data Protection Directive 95/46 only regard data protection as a facet of the existing fundamental rights such as the right to privacy. Here the constitutional lawmaker goes one step further and provides for an independent fundamental right.

The 2000 Charter was inserted (slightly modified) in the Treaty Establishing a Constitution for Europe signed on October 29, 2004.[21] This constitutional text encountered ratification problems in some Member States and was not formally carried through. Instead, its main provisions were copied in a Reform Treaty for the European Union which amend the framework proceded in the existing Treaties.[22] The final text of the treaty, drawn up during an Inter-Governmental Conference (IGC), was approved at the informal European Council in Lisbon on 18 and 19 October 2007. This 'Treaty of Lisbon' was signed by the Member States on 13 December 2007[23] and the feeling is that this time it will meet successful ratification.[24] Not all of the Constitution's innovations were taken up in the Reform Treaty but much of its substance has been maintained, including its provisions regarding human rights. The Treaty opens the way for the Union to seek accession to the European Convention for the Protection of Human Rights and Fundamental Freedoms (the aim of accession is envisaged in the revised Article 6.2 TEU) and it

---

[19] *'Everyone has the right to respect for his or her private and family life, home and communications'* (Article 7 EU Charter).

[20] O. De Schutter, 'Article II-68 – Protection des données à caractère personnel', in L. Burgorgue-Larsen, A. Levade and F. Picod (eds.), *Traité établissant une Constitution pour l'Europe: Commentaire article par article*, Brussels, Bruylant, 2005, pp. 122–152.

[21] Treaty Establishing a Constitution for Europe, *O.J.*, No. C 310, 16 December 2004, p. 1–474.

[22] The new 'Reform Treaty' was not meant to be a 'Constitution' and would *not* replace the existing treaties, namely the Treaty on European Union (TEU) and the Treaty of the European Community (TEC). It would be just an 'amending treaty' consisting in two substantive clauses modifying, respectively, the TEU (which would keep its name) and the TEC, which would instead be called 'Treaty on the Functioning of the Union' and the EU would acquire a single legal personality (as foreseen by the Constitutional Treaty).

[23] Treaty of Lisbon amending the Treaty on European Union and the Treaty establishing the European Community, signed at Lisbon, 13 December 2007, *O.J.*, No. C 306, 17 December 2007, pp. 1–271.

[24] It is up to each country to choose the procedure for ratification, in line with its own national constitution. The target date for ratification set by member governments is 1 January 2009. The pace will have to slow down following the outcome of the Irish referendum.

guarantees the enforcement of the Charter of Fundamental Rights of 7 December 2000, as adapted at Strasbourg, on 12 December 2007, 'which shall have the same legal value as the Treaties' (revised Article 6.1 TEU).[25] Hence, although the text of the Charter is not incorporated into the EU Treaty, it has been given a legally binding value for EU institutions and bodies as well as for the Member States as regards the implementation of Union law.[26] In addition, the Lisbon Treaty provisions provide for data protection in areas such as judicial cooperation in criminal matters and police cooperation[27] and for data protection in the area of common foreign and security policy.[28]

1.1.3 Rationale

The recognition of data protection as a fundamental right in the EU legal order has been welcomed for many reasons. First, there were considerations with regard to the legitimacy of the EU data protection framework. From the start, the 1995 Data Protection Directive was based on a double logic: the achievement of an Internal Market (in this case the free movement of personal information) and the protection of fundamental rights and freedoms of individuals. The Commission itself conceded that although both objectives are said to be equally important, in legal terms the economic perspective and internal market arguments prevailed.[29] Legislation at EU level was justified because of differences in the way that Member States approached this issue, which impeded the free flow of personal data between the

---

[25] An adapted version of the Charter was proclaimed on December 12, 2007 in Strasbourg, ahead of the signing of the Treaty of Lisbon containing a slightly modified version of the 2000 EU Charter, to make it resemble the text that was part of the rejected European Constitution.

[26] For the exceptions on this made for two Member States, see the Protocol on the application of the Charter of Fundamental Rights of the European Union to Poland and to the United Kingdom, *O.J.*, No. C 306, 17 December 2007, p. 156–157.

[27] See the new Article 16 B, replacing Article 286: '1. Everyone has the right to the protection of personal data concerning them. 2. The European Parliament and the Council, acting in accordance with the ordinary legislative procedure, shall lay down the rules relating to the protection of individuals with regard to the processing of personal data by Union institutions, bodies, offices and agencies and by the Member States when carrying out activities which fall within the scope of Union law and the rules relating to the free movement of such data. Compliance with these rules shall be subject to the control of independent authorities.

The rules adopted on the basis of this Article shall be without prejudice to the specific rules laid down in Article 25a of the Treaty on European Union'.

[28] *See Article 25a of the new TEU:* 'In accordance with Article 16 B of the Treaty on the Functioning of the European Union and by way of derogation from paragraph 2 thereof, the Council shall adopt a decision laying down the rules relating to the protection of individuals with regard to the processing of personal data by the Member States when carrying out activities which fall within the scope of this Chapter and the rules relating to the free movement of such data. Compliance with these rules shall be subject to the control of independent authorities'.

[29] Commission of the European Communities, *First Report on the implementation of the Data Protection Directive (95/46/EC)*, (COM (2003) 265), Brussels, 15 May 2003, 27p. (via http://eur-lex.europa.eu/LexUriServ/site/en/com/2003/com2003_0265en01.pdf), 3.

Member States.[30] Second, the rights-objective was less clear, especially since the Directive contained several business-friendly provisions that were far from being inspired by human rights arguments.[31] The recognition of a right to data protection in the Charter can be seen as a way to remedy this by adding emphasis to the fundamental rights dimension of the Directive.[32]

There are other, more convincing reasons to welcome the new right to data protection. Data protection and privacy are not interchangeable. There are important differences between the two in terms of scope, goals and content. As mentioned above, data protection explicitly protects values that are not at the core of privacy, such as the requirement of fair processing, consent, legitimacy and non-discrimination.[33] The explicit recognition in the new provision of a 'right of access to data that has been collected concerning him or her and the right to have it rectified' solves legal problems which were left unanswered by the case law of the European Court of Human Rights. Equally, in this case law there are no grounds for a right to have (all) data protection rules controlled and monitored by an independent authority, as it is foreseen by the last paragraph of the new provision.[34] Furthermore, the

---

[30] See also Commission Communication on the Protection of Individuals in Relation to the Processing of Personal Data in the Community and Information Security. COM (90) 314 final, 13 September 1990, (via http://aei.pitt.edu/3768/01/000273_1.pdf) (135p.), page 4: '*The diversity of national approaches and the lack of a system of protection at Community level are an obstacle to completion of the internal market. If the fundamental rights of data subjects, in particular their right to privacy, are not safeguarded at Community level, the cross-border flow of data might be impeded...*'. As a consequence the legal base of the Directive was Article 100a (now Article 95) of the Treaty.

[31] S. Gutwirth, *Privacy and the information age*, *o.c.*, pp. 91–95.

[32] Commission of the European Communities, '*First report*', *o.c.*, p. 3.

[33] Take for instance the right not to be discriminated against protected by Article 15 of the Data Protection Directive. According to this article every person has the right 'not to be subject to a decision which produces legal effects concerning him or significantly affects him and which is based solely on automated processing of data.' The article refers to automated processing of data 'intended to evaluate certain personal aspects relating to him, such as his performance at work, creditworthiness, reliability, conduct, etc.' The goal is to guarantee everyone's participation in important personal decisions. A dismissal based purely on the data from the company time clock is, as a result, unacceptable. It applies also to the rejection of a jobseeker based on the results of a computerized psycho-technical assessment test or to a computerized job application package. Those decisions have to take professional experience or the result of a job interview into account. The automated test is insufficient and it applies to sectors such as banking and insurance. EU Member States have to enact provisions that allow for the legal challenge of computerized decisions and that guarantee an individual's input in decision-making procedures. However, Member States are allowed to grant exemptions on the ban on computerized individual decisions if such a decision (a) is taken in the course of the entering into or performance of a contract, provided the request for the entering into or the performance of the contract, lodged by the data subject, has been satisfied or that there are suitable measures to safeguard his legitimate interests, such as arrangements allowing him to express his point of view; or (b) is authorized by a law that also lays down measures to safeguard the data subject's legitimate interests.

[34] Article 13 ECHR (right to an effective legal remedy) is not an independent right. The European Court refuses to consider issues under this provision, when there is no violation of another right of the ECHR.

Charter extends the protection of personal data to private relations and to the private sector.[35]

The non-interchangeability of privacy and data protection is not merely positivist, it has deeper character. While privacy obviously occupies a central place in data protection law, the characterisation of data protection law as solely or even essentially concerned with safeguarding privacy is misleading.[36] Data protection laws serve a multiplicity of interests, which in some cases extend well beyond traditional conceptualisations of privacy.[37] Few direct manifestations of intimacy-oriented conceptions of privacy can be found in the provisions of data protection laws and, conversely, broader privacy concepts are not of a nature to explain data protection principles such as purpose limitation, data quality or security.[38] Finally, we believe that the recognition of a separate right to data protection, next to privacy, to be more respectful to the European constitutional history. Just as there are different constitutional footings for privacy protection in the United States, the EU and Canada,[39] there exist distinctive constitutional traditions within the European Union which influence the way privacy and data protection are interpreted. Contrary to countries like Belgium and the Netherlands that have linked data protection from the start to privacy, countries like France and Germany, lacking an explicit right to privacy in their constitution, have searched and found other legal anchors for the recognition of data protection rights. French data protection is based on the right to liberty, whereas German data protection is based on the right to the recognition of human dignity. All these approaches, which are different from the US tradition that seems to build its data protection principles on public law principles such as fair information practices,[40] cannot be considered to be identical and might explain differences in data protection between EU Member States.

---

[35] Cf. Y. Poullet, 'Pour une justification des articles 25 et 26 en matière de flux tranfrontières et de protection des données' in M. Cools, C. Eliaerts, S. Gutwirth, T. Joris & B. Spruyt (reds), *Ceci n'est pas un juriste ... mais un ami. Liber Amicorum Bart De Schutter*, Brussels, VUBPress, 2003, p. 278.

[36] L. Bygrave, 'The Place Of Privacy In Data Protection Law', *University of NSW Law Journal*, 2001, (6p.), sub § 18 (via http://www.austlii.edu.au/au/journals/UNSWLJ/2001/6.html).

[37] Ibid.

[38] Ibid. § 15; E. Brouwer, *o.c.*, p. 205; P. De Hert & S. Gutwirth, 'Making sense of privacy and data protection', *l.c.*, p. 111 ff.

[39] See Avner Levin and Mary Jo Nicholson, 'Privacy Law in the United States, the EU and Canada: The Allure of the Middle Ground', *University of Ottawa Law & Technology Journal*, Vol. 2, No. 2, pp. 357–395, 2005 (also available at SSRN: http://ssrn.com/abstract=894079). The EU and Canada centrally supervise the private sector's use of personal data, whereas the US regulation of the private sector is minimal. Avner Levin and Mary Jo Nicholson look behind these and other differences in regulation to be found in the European Union (EU), the United Sates (US) and Canada and hold that they emanate from distinct conceptual bases for privacy in each jurisdiction: in the US, privacy protection is essentially liberty protection, i.e., protection from government. For Europeans, privacy protects dignity or their public image. In Canada, privacy protection is focused on individual autonomy through personal control of information.

[40] P. Blok, Botsende rechtsculturen bij transatlantisch gegevensverkeer, *Nederlands Juristenblad (NJB)*, 2001, pp. 1607–1612.

1.1.4 Life is Easier with Transformative Constitutions

How innovative was the Charter? At national level, the right to data protection was only directly or indirectly protected by the constitution in a few countries.[41] The 1976 Portuguese Constitution foresaw a right of knowledge regarding the automated processing of personal data and a ban on the use of personal ID numbers. Since its revision in 1983, the Dutch Constitution provides the legislator with the task of regulating the use of information technology and the protection of personal life.[42] Section 18.4 of the Spanish 1978 Constitution gives a similar mandate but only in so far as that data is linked to the exercise of the right to honour and privacy.[43] Most European constitutions do not speak about protecting personal data.

Therefore it is very interesting to note how few arguments were advanced to incorporate a separate right to data protection in the Charter. In the Explanatory report to the Charter no reasons are given, there is only a reference to the 1995 Directive and the 108 Council of Europe Convention.[44] According to the Commission the incorporation of the right to data protection gives added emphasis to the fundamental right dimension of EC Directive 95/46 on data protection.[45] Indeed the writing process of the Charter was unusual, since the draft was prepared by an ad-hoc Convention body comprising representatives from the European Parliament, national parliaments, the European Commission, governments and some observers.[46] During the preparation of the Draft the parties did not experience many difficulties. Part of the preparatory work was done by expert committees.

---

[41] E. Brouwer, *o.c.*, p. 167.

[42] Article 10 of the Dutch Constitution: '(1) Everyone shall have the right to respect for his privacy, without prejudice to restrictions laid down by or pursuant to Act of Parliament. (2) Rules to protect privacy shall be laid down by Act of Parliament in connection with the recording and dissemination of personal data. (3) Rules concerning the rights of persons to be informed of data recorded concerning them and of the use that is made thereof, and to have such data corrected shall be laid down by Act of Parliament' (http://www.servat.unibe.ch/law/icl/nl00000_.html).

[43] Section 18: '1. The right to honour, to personal and family privacy and to the own image is guaranteed. 2. The home is inviolable. No entry or search may be made without the consent of the householder or a legal warrant, except in cases of a flagrant delict. 3. Secrecy of communications is guaranteed, particularly regarding postal, telegraphic and telephonic communications, except in the event of a court order. 4. The law shall restrict the use of data processing in order to guarantee the honour and personal and family privacy of citizens and the full exercise of their rights' (Source: http://en.wikisource.org/wiki/Spanish_Constitution_of_1978/Part_I). See however the decision of November 30, 2000 in which the Spanish Constitutional Court recognised a fundamental right to data protection that differs from the right to privacy set out under Article 18 of the Constitution. See 'Spain. Constitutional Challenge to Data Protection Law', *World Data Protection Report,* 2001, p. 7.

[44] Council of the European Union, *Charter of Fundamental Rights of the European Union. Explanations relating to the complete text of the Charter. December 2000*, Luxembourg: Office for Official Publications of the European Communities, 2001, (77p.), p. 26.

[45] European Commission, *First Report on the implementation of the Data Protection Directive*, 15 May 2003. *o.c.*

[46] The Cologne European Council (3/4 June 1999) entrusted the task of drafting the Charter to a Convention. The Convention held its constituent meeting in December 1999 and adopted the draft

An explanation for the success of the Convention could be that incorporating the existing rights into one document without having to invent new rights was seen as merely a technical exercise. Working Party 29 used a very technical approach in its 1999 initiative to include data protection in the fundamental rights of Europe. This 'would make such protection a legal requirement throughout the Union and reflect its increasing importance in the information society'.[47] There would be no further detailed analysis of the existing constitutions of the Member States, no reference to the case law of the Strasbourg Court of Human Rights. Nevertheless, because of its recognition in the Charter one can claim that data protection became part of Western *constitutionalism*. One even could defend the view that data protection today is part of the European *Constitution*[48] regardless of the name we give to primary EU treaty law, and that it has achieved an independent fundamental status next to the right to privacy.[49]

In *Code and other laws of cyberspace* Lawrence Lessig distinguishes between two types of constitutions, one he calls codifying and the other transformative. Codifying constitutions preserve essential tenets of the constitutional or legal culture in which they are enacted and aim at protecting them against changes in the future, whereas transformative constitutions or transformative amendments to existing constitutions aim at changing essential aspects of the constitutional or legal culture in which they are enacted.[50] For Lessig, the US Constitution of 1789 qualifies as a transformative constitution, since it initiated a new form of government and gave birth to a nation, whereas the US Constitution of 1791 – the Bill of Rights – qualifies as a codifying constitution, entrenching certain values against future change. The Civil War amendments were transformative, since they aimed to break the American tradition of inequality and replace it with a tradition and practice of equality.[51]

There may be no doubt about the codifying character of the EU Charter, preserving a European human rights heritage and being the result of a merely 'technical' exercise. However, the transformative side of the Charter is less well-known. This

---

on 2 October 2000. Its composition was established at the European Council meeting in Tampere in October 1999. See on the composition: http://www.europarl.europa.eu/charter/composition_en.htm

[47] Working Party on the Protection of Individuals with Regard to the Processing of Personal Data Recommendation 4/99 on the inclusion of the fundamental right to data protection in the European catalogue of fundamental rights, September 1999, 5143 /99/ENWP 26, 3p (available via http://ec.europa.eu/justice_home/fsj/privacy/docs/wpdocs/1999/wp26en.pdf).

[48] When does a treaty become a constitution? 'A treaty as an interstate act may give rise to rights to individuals but this is a by-product of the settlement of relations between states. A constitution is the embodiment of the compromise of rights and duties between the people ant those exercising authority. Giving precision to rights of individuals is central to constitution making' (Elspeth Guild, 'Citizens, Immigrants, Terrorists and Others', in A Ward and S Peers (eds) *The EU Charter of Fundamental Rights: Politics, Law and Policy* Hart, Oxford, 2004, (pp. 321–246), p. 322).

[49] See B. Siemen, *o.c.*, par. 3.D.; H.K. Kranenborg, *Toegang tot documenten en bescherming van persoonsgegevens in de Europese Unie*, Deventer, Kluwer, 2007, (351p.), pp. 172–173.

[50] L. Lessig, *Code and Other Laws of Cyberspace*, New York, Basic Books, 1999, p. 213.

[51] L. Lessig, *o.c.*, p. 214.

is a side that is not only illustrated by the right to data protection but by many more examples[52] and indeed the codification of human dignity taken from the German Constitution as the mother right of the EU Charter, proudly occupying the royal throne of the Charter in its first article but absent as a concept in almost all Member State constitutions, except for the German one.[53] Lessig observes that of the two constitutional options, the transformative constitution is clearly the most difficult to realise. A codifying regime at least has inertia on its side; a transformative regime must fight.[54] Of course this implies not much more than the old wisdom about the difficulty to enforce rights and duties not being properly internalised by the legal subjects. The failure of some recent Canadian copyright initiatives with regard to the Internet should be understood in this perspective: attempts to use copyright as a tool to prohibit certain use of information failed for two reasons: it deviates from the original intent of copyright (the regulation of the interaction between professional actors responsible for the creation, publication, production and dissemination of works of the mind) and it is not rooted in a moral imperative but clashes with strong social norms that have developed specifically because of the informal, intuitive and global nature of the Internet.[55] End-users do not consider themselves as pirates and do not act with the intent of commercial gain. It is therefore no surprise, one author notes, to observe that the Canadian Supreme Court did not uphold the new copyright regulation.[56]

Hence, new legal and constitutional values are put to test and if the courts do not feel certain about them, they might resort to more familiar old values. Lessig sees

---

[52] The EU Charter incorporates most of the content of the ECHR but purposely proclaims additional rights not contained in the European Human Rights Convention of which data protection is only one example. Other examples are bioethics, the right to good administration, a general prohibition to outlaw discrimination on the grounds of gender, race and colour and certain social rights.

[53] The right to dignity is also mentioned in Section 10.1 of the Spanish 1978 Constitution but it is only one source of constitutionalism amongst others. Article 23 of the 1994 Belgian Constitution equally protects human dignity but this is tied to certain economic, social and cultural rights. See http://en.wikisource.org/wiki/Constitution_of_Belgium

[54] 'The codifying regime has a moment of self-affirmation; the transformative regime is haunted with self-doubt and vulnerable to undermining by targeted opposition. Constitutional moments die and when they do, the institutions charged with enforcing their commands, such as courts, face increasing political resistance. Flashes of enlightenment notwithstanding, the people retain or go back to their old ways and courts find it hard to resist' (L. Lessig, *o.c.*, 214).

[55] Daniel J. Gervais, 'The Purpose of Copyright Law in Canada', *University of Ottawa Law & Technology Journal*, 2005, Vol. 2, pp. 315–358. 'While Internet users apparently do not agree that their file-sharing behaviour is morally wrong, a view supported historically in many cultures where stealing a work of the mind meant plagiarizing or using without proper attribution, their cyberspace behaviour has shaped a new social norm of creating multiple links, by email, in chat groups, blogs or other Internet tools, with people with whom they share certain interests. This is reinforced by hyperlinks that allow users to 'intuitively' follow their train of thought. That requires access, not roadblocks. In a world where millions of Internet users are paying for high-speed to avoid having to wait to access material, a refusal to grant access because of a prohibition-based copyright is unlikely to be well received and accepted' (Daniel J. Gervais, *l.c.*, 335).

[56] Ibid.

this as a general problem in Cyberworld, where judges have to make judgments that do not seem to flow plainly or obviously from a legal text.[57] This brings us to our central question. How is data protection as a newly recognised constitutional value received in the field, i.e., by the courts? Subsequently, we will deal with the following lines of analysis: the reception of data protection by the European Court on Human Rights in Strasbourg (ECtHR) and the reception of data protection by the European Court of Justice in Luxembourg (ECJ). The reception of data protection by national courts also requires our attention but we will deal with this issue elsewhere.

1.2 The Material Constitutionalisation of Data Protection

1.2.1 Data Protection Tested in Strasbourg

1.2.1.1 A Right to Autonomy Under the Scope of Article 8 ECHR?

The 1950 European Convention is a very straightforward human rights declaration that, carefully avoids metaphysical references. In the Convention there is, for instance, no general recognition of the right to liberty, neither of the right to the protection of human dignity, nor of the right to autonomy or the right to self-determination. Avoiding these weighty references is not unwise from a comparative constitutional perspective. We briefly mentioned above that privacy and data protection in the European Member States are differently rooted. Hence, for instance, German case law developed a right of informational self-determination (meaning the capacity of the individual to determine in principle the disclosure and use of his/her personal data) on the basis of the concepts of dignity and self-determination in the German Constitution.[58] In the French Constitution, where these concepts are absent, data protection was based on a broader notion of liberty,[59] whereas the Dutch and Belgian Constitutions refer to privacy as the source of data protection.

For the richness of European diversity it is a good thing that the ECHR avoids any choice or prioritising of these higher values. It can however be questioned whether human rights application and interpretation is always feasible without referring to these core ethical values. We doubt it. As a result it did not come as a surprise to us that the right to autonomy appeared in the Convention language of Article 8, notably in *Pretty v. United Kingdom* (2002). The question put before the Court was whether the right to private life encapsulated a right to die with assistance, for persons paralysed and suffering from a degenerative and incurable illness. Pretty

[57] L. Lessig, *o.c.*, 215.

[58] Judgment of 15 December 1983, 1 BvR 209/83, BVerfGE 65.

[59] As a consequence Article 1 of the 1978 French Data Protection law states that information technology should not infringe upon human rights, including the right to privacy *and* individual or public liberties.

alleged that the refusal of the Director of Public Prosecutions to grant an immunity from prosecution to her husband if he assisted her in committing suicide and the prohibition in domestic law on assisting suicide infringed her rights under Articles 2, 3, 8, 9 and 14 of the Convention. The claim was not recognized but paragraph 61 of the Judgement contains a very relevant and broad recognition of the principle of personal autonomy:

> As the Court has had previous occasion to remark, the concept of 'private life' is a broad term not susceptible to exhaustive definition. It covers the physical and psychological integrity of a person (X. and Y. v. the Netherlands judgment of 26 March 1985, *Series A* No. 91, p. 11, § 22). It can sometimes embrace aspects of an individual's physical and social identity (Mikulic v. Croatia, No. 53176/99 [Section 1], judgment of 7 February 2002, § 53). Elements such as, for example, gender identification, name and sexual orientation and sexual life fall within the personal sphere protected by Article 8 (see e.g., the B. v. France judgment of 25 March 1992, *Series A* No. 232-C, § 63; the Burghartz v. Switzerland judgment of 22 February 1994, *Series A* No. 280-B, § 24; the Dudgeon v. the United Kingdom judgment of 22 October 1991, *Series A* No. 45, § 41, and the Laskey, Jaggard and Brown v. the United Kingdom judgment of 19 February 1997, Reports 1997-1, § 36). Article 8 also protects a right to personal development, and the right to establish and develop relationships with other human beings and the outside world (see, for example, Burghartz v. Switzerland, Commission's report, op. cit., § 47; Friedl v. Austria, *Series A* No. 305-B, Commission's report, § 45). Though no previous case has established as such any right to self-determination as being contained in Article 8 of the Convention, the Court considers that the notion of personal autonomy is an important principle underlying the interpretation of its guarantees.

We do not think that conceptually all is clear[60] but the ruling of the Court shows that the principle of personal autonomy has gained considerable importance within the right of privacy. Whether Article 8 ECHR also entails a right of determination, including informational self-determination, remains unanswered at this point. In *Pretty* the Court leaves this question deliberately open but we will see that the latest judgments of the Court reveal a tendency in this direction.[61]

1.2.1.2 The Broad Scope of Article 8 ECHR

The role of the European Court on Human Rights (and of the former European Commission for Human Rights) can be described as twofold, being both a self-contained system of human rights protection and the provider for guidelines for

---

60 In *Pretty* autonomy is considered a 'principle' and physical and social identity are issues of which 'aspects' are sometimes protected by the right to private life. In their joint dissenting opinion to Odièvre v. France judges Wildhaber, Bratza, Bonello, Loucaides, Cabral Barreto, Tulkens and Pellonpää consider autonomy and identity to be 'rights': 'We are firmly of the opinion that the right to an identity, which is an essential condition of the right to autonomy (see ECtHR, *Pretty v. the United Kingdom*, Application No. 2346/02, Judgment of 29 April 2002 § 61, *ECHR* 2002-III) and development (see ECtHR, *Bensaid v. the United Kingdom*, Application No. 44599/98, Judgement of 6 February 2001, § 47, *ECHR* 2001-I), is within the inner core of the right to respect for one's private life' (par. 11 of the Opinion).

61 Compare B. Siemen, *o.c.*, pp. 76–78.

the ECJ for concretising the fundamental rights of the European Community.[62] The case law of the European Court is traditionally hailed as a powerful demonstration of the strength of the 1950 Convention on Human Rights.[63] Although the Convention does not evoke modern means of communication, the Court, applying a 'dynamic and broad' interpretation of the Convention, has successively brought telephone conversations,[64] telephone numbers,[65] computers,[66] video-surveillance,[67] voice-recording[68] and Internet and e-mail[69] under the scope of Article 8.[70] The ease of this 'method' or approach is remarkable. Often no more than one paragraph is needed, for instance in *Copland* where the Court ruled that according to its Court's case law, 'telephone calls from business premises are prima facie covered by the notions of 'private life' and 'correspondence' for the purposes of Article 8 § 1. It follows *logically* that e-mails sent from work should be similarly protected under Article 8, as should information derived from the monitoring of personal Internet usage'.[71]

---

[62] C. Riehle, 'Book review' of B. Siemen, *C.M.L.J.*, 2007, p. 1193–1195.

[63] Case law of Strasbourg is available http://www.echr.coe.int/echr and can easily be consulted using the 'Application Number'. When the Application Number is not mentioned on that site a 'paper' source is given.

[64] ECtHR, *Klass v. Germany*, Application No. 5029/71, Judgement of 6 September 1978, § 41; ECtHR; *Amann v. Switzerland* [GC], Application No. 27798/95, Judgement of 16 February 2000, § 44; ECtHR, *Halford v. United Kingdom*, judgment of 25 June 1997, *Reports*, 1997-III, p. 1016, § 44.

[65] ECtHR, *Malone v. United Kingdom*, Application No. 8691/79, Judgement of 2 August 1984, § 84; ECtHR, *P.G. and J.H. v. the United Kingdom*, Application No. 44787/98, Judgement of 25 September 2001, § 42; ECtHR, *Copland v. the United Kingdom*, No. 62617/00, Judgement of 3 April 2007, § 43.

[66] ECtHR, *Leander v. Sweden*, Application No. 9248/81, Judgement of 26 March 1987, § 48; ECtHR; *Amann v. Switzerland*, § 65; ECtHR, *Rotaru v. Romania*, Application No. 28341/95 judgement of 4 May 2000, § 42–43.

[67] ECtHR, *Peck v. the United Kingdom*, Application No. 44647/98, Judgement of 28 January 2003, §§ 57–63; ECtHR, *Perry v. the United Kingdom*, Application No. 63737/00, Judgement of 17 July 2003, § 40.

[68] ECtHR, *P.G. and J.H. v. the United Kingdom*, §§ 59–60.

[69] ECtHR, *Copland v. the United Kingdom*, § 41.

[70] Article 8.1. ECHR states that: 'Everyone has the right to respect for his private and family life, his home and his correspondence'. For a detailed analysis of the Article 8 ECHR case law, see P. De Hert, *Artikel 8 EVRM en het Belgisch recht. De bescherming van privacy, gezin, woonst en communicatie* [Article 8 ECHR and the Law in Belgium. Protection of Privacy, House, Family and Correspondence], Gent, Mys en Breesch Uitgeverij, 1998, 367p. P. De Hert, 'Artikel 8 EVRM. Recht op privacy' [Article 8 of the Convention on Human Rights. The Right to Privacy] in Vande Lanotte, J. & Haeck, Y. (eds.), *Handboek EVRM. Deel 2 Artikelsgewijze Commentaar*, Antwerp-Oxford, Intersentia, 2004, 705–788; P. De Hert & A. Hoefmans, 'Het arrest *Copland* in het kader van de verdieping van de Europese rechtspraak op het gebied van privacybescherming', *European Human Rights Cases (EHRC)*, 13 June 2007, Vol. 8, No. 6, pp. 664–674.

[71] ECtHR, *Copland v. the United Kingdom*, § 41, with ref. to ECtHR, *Halford v. United Kingdom*, § 44 and ECtHR; *Amann v. Switzerland*, § 43 (italics added).

In many of these expansive judgements, the Court applies a broad definition of the notion of private life in Article 8 ECHR, extending it far beyond the walls of the private house and the intimate sphere. In this view 'private life' embraces development of interpersonal relationships[72] and protects not only the domestic sphere but also (data relating to) certain facts occurred in the public sphere.[73] The Court has even gone so far as to recognise privacy protection to firms and business activities,[74] which is a non-mandatory feature of data protection regulation (which optionally allows Members States to recognise data protection rights not only to natural persons but also to legal persons).

With respect to Article 8 and other rights enshrined in the Convention, the Court recognises positive state duties (making certain rights possible) next to negative state duties (not to infringe certain rights). The existence of these positive duties has allowed the Court to construct certain data protection rights, such as the right to access to data, compulsory in most cases under Article 8 ECHR (see below). Based on these notions of positive state duties, states can be held responsible for privacy infringements caused by private actors, such as firms and newspapers or by public authorities acting in roles that can also be assumed by private actors, for instance the role of employer or the press.[75] Although these private actors cannot be sued directly before the Strasbourg Court, this case law of the Court can be invoked by interested parties in a national court.[76]

---

[72] ECtHR, *Niemietz v. Germany*, Application No. 13710/88, Judgement of 16 December 1992, § 29: 'The Court does not consider it possible or necessary to attempt an exhaustive definition of the notion of 'private life'. However, it would be too restrictive to limit the notion to an 'inner circle' in which the individual may live his own personal life as he chooses and to exclude there from entirely the outside world not encompassed within that circle. Respect for private life must also comprise to a certain degree the right to establish and develop relationships with other human beings. There appears, furthermore, to be no reason of principle why this understanding of the notion of 'private life' should be taken to exclude activities of a professional or business nature since it is, after all, in the course of their working lives that the majority of people have a significant, if not the greatest, opportunity of developing relationships with the outside world. This view is supported by the fact that, as was rightly pointed out by the Commission, it is not always possible to distinguish clearly which of an individual's activities form part of his professional or business life and which do not. Thus, especially in the case of a person exercising a liberal profession, his work in that context may form part and parcel of his life to such a degree that it becomes impossible to know in what capacity he is acting at a given moment of time'.

[73] ECtHR, *Peck v. the United Kingdom*, §§ 57–63.

[74] ECtHR, *Société Colas Est and others v. France*, Application No. 37971/97, Judgement of 16 April 2002, § 40: 'Building on its dynamic interpretation of the Convention, the Court considers that the time has come to hold that in certain circumstances the rights guaranteed by Article 8 of the Convention may be construed as including the right to respect for a company's registered office, branches or other business premises (see, *mutatis mutandis*, *Niemietz*, cited above, p. 34, § 30)'.

[75] See on the role of the press and the conflict with the right to privacy, ECtHR, *Von Hannover v Germany*, Application No. 59320/00, Judgement of 24 June 2004 and 28 July 2005.

[76] See for a discussion of the applicability of Article 8 ECHR: B. Siemen, *o.c.*, pp. 177–204 (direct third-party applicability is not afforded by Article 8 ECHR; indirect third-party applicability against interferences by private persons is set through the laws).

1.2.1.3 Several Aspects of Data Protection Under the Scope of Article 8 ECHR

The Strasbourg organs have also brought several issues under the scope of Article 8 ECHR that are more specifically related to or characteristic data protection.[77] In order to bring new technologies under the Convention (supra), the Court has made skilful use of the co-presence in Article 8 ECHR of both the right to protection of private life *and* correspondence, often leaving open which one of the two needs to be regarded as the primary right.[78] Increasingly, the Court uses insights and principles taken from data protection regulation to consider issues raised by modern technologies.[79] Already in the 1980s it was recalled on several occasions that data protection is an issue that falls within the scope of Article 8.[80] But particularly

---

[77] For a detailed discussion: E. Brouwer, *o.c.*, 133–144; P. De Hert, 'Mensenrechten en bescherming van persoonsgegevens. Overzicht en synthese van de Europese rechtspraak 1955–1997' [Human Rights and Data Protection. European Case law 1995–1997], in *Jaarboek ICM 1997*, Antwerp, Maklu, 1998, p. 40–96; O. De Schutter, 'Vie privée et protection de l'individu vis-à-vis des traitements de données à caractère personnel', obs. sous Cour eur. D.H., arrêt Rotaru c. Roumanie du 4 mai 2000, *Revue trimestrielle des droits de l'homme*, No. 45, 2001, pp. 137–183.

[78] See on the protection of telephone numbers in *Malone*: 'As the Government rightly suggested, a meter check printer registers information that a supplier of a telephone service may in principle legitimately obtain, notably in order to ensure that the subscriber is correctly charged or to investigate complaints or possible abuses of the service. By its very nature, metering is therefore to be distinguished from interception of communications, which is undesirable and illegitimate in a democratic society unless justified. The Court does not accept, however, that the use of data obtained from metering, whatever the circumstances and purposes, cannot give rise to an issue under Article 8 (Art. 8). The records of metering contain information, in particular the numbers dialled, which is an integral element in the communications made by telephone. Consequently, release of that information to the police without the consent of the subscriber also amounts, in the opinion of the Court, to an interference with a right guaranteed by Article 8 (Art. 8)' (§ 84).

[79] See for instance ECtHR, *Copland v. the United Kingdom*, § 43: 'The Court recalls that the use of information relating to the date and length of telephone conversations and in particular the numbers dialled can give rise to an issue under Article 8 as such information constitutes an 'integral element of the communications made by telephone' (see Malone v. the United Kingdom, judgement of 2 August 1984, Series A No. 82, § 84). The mere fact that these data may have been legitimately obtained by the College, in the form of telephone bills, is no bar to finding an interference with rights guaranteed under Article 8 (ibid). *Moreover, storing of personal data relating to the private life of an individual also falls within the application of Article 8 § 1* (...). Thus, it is irrelevant that the data held by the college were not disclosed or used against the applicant in disciplinary or other proceedings' (italics added). See also ECtHR; *Amann v. Switzerland*, § 65 and ECtHR, *Rotaru v. Romania*, § 42–43 where the *Leander* acquis about storing personal data as falling under the scope of Article 8 ECHR is complemented with a brief discussion of the Council of Europe's Data Protection Convention of 28 January 1981 to support the argument that even stored data on business contacts should be considered under the light of Article 8 ECHR. See finally the reference to the 1981 Data Protection Convention in ECtHR, *P.G. and J.H. v. the United Kingdom*, § 57 to strengthen the argument that collection of public data by secret services is also a reason of concern from a human rights perspective.

[80] For instance: ECommissionHR, *Lundvall v. Sweden*, 11 December 1985, case 10473/83, *D.R.*, Vol. 45, 130. See also: ECtHR; *Amann v. Switzerland*, § 65; ECtHR, *Rotaru v. Romania*, Application No. 28341/95 judgement of 4 May 2000, §§ 42–43; ECtHR, *P.G. and J.H. v. the United Kingdom*, § 57.

since the mid-1980s reference to the data protection framework and the acknowledgment in one way or another of its principles has been more explicit. The Court has associated its broad interpretation of the term 'private life' in Article 8 ECHR with the equally broad notion of 'personal data' in data protection regulation.[81] In several cases the Court added that information (about persons) belonging in the public domain may fall within the scope of Article 8, once it is systematically stored.[82]

Also the Court recognised the right of individuals to have control, to a certain extent, of the use and registration of their personal information (informational self-determination). In this respect the Court has considered and recognised access claims to personal files,[83] claims regarding deletion of personal data from public files[84] and claims from transsexuals for the right to have their 'official sexual data' corrected.[85] Moreover, the Court has insisted on the need for an independent supervisory authority as a mechanism for the protection of the rule of law and to prevent the abuse of power, especially in the case of secret surveillance systems.[86] In other cases the Court demanded access to an independent mechanism, where specific sensitive data were at stake or where the case concerned a claim to access to such data.[87] In *Peck*, in *Perry* and in *P.G. and J.H.* the Court acknowledged the basic idea behind the fundamental principle of purpose limitation in data protection, viz that personal data cannot be used beyond normally foreseeable use.[88] In *Amann* and

---

[81] ECtHR, *Rotaru v. Romania*, § 43: 'The Court has already emphasised the correspondence of this broad interpretation with that of the Council of Europe's Convention of 28 January 1981 for the Protection of Individuals with regard to Automatic Processing of Personal Data, which came into force on 1 October 1985 and whose purpose is 'to secure ... for every individual ... respect for his rights and fundamental freedoms, and in particular his right to privacy with regard to automatic processing of personal data relating to him' (Article 1), such personal data being defined in Article 2 as 'any information relating to an identified or identifiable individual'.

[82] ECtHR; *Amann v. Switzerland*, § 65 ; ECtHR, *Rotaru v. Romania*, §§ 43–44; ECtHR, *P.G. and J.H. v. the United Kingdom*, § 57–58; ECtHR, *Segerstedt-Wiberg and others v. Sweden*, Application No. 62332/00, Judgement of 6 June 2006, § 72. See E. Brouwer, *o.c.*, 133 & 137.

[83] ECtHR, *Gaskin v. the United Kingdom*, Application No. 10454/83, Judgement of 7 July 1989; ECtHR, *Antony and Margaret McMichael v. United Kingdom*, Application No. 16424/90, judgement of 24 February 1995. ECtHR, *Guerra v Italy*, Judgement of 19 February 1998, *Reports*, 1998-I; ECtHR, *McGinley & Egan v. United Kingdom*, Applications nos. 21825/93 and 23414/94, Judgement of 28 January 2000.

[84] ECtHR, *Leander v. Sweden*, Application No. 9248/81, Judgement of 26 March 1987; ECtHR, *Segerstedt-Wiberg and others v. Sweden*, Application No. 62332/00, Judgement of 6 June 2006.

[85] ECtHR, *Rees v UK*, Judgement of 25 October 1986 *Series A*, No. 106; ECtHR, *Cossey v UK*, Judgement of 27 September 1990, *Series A*, No. 184; ECtHR, *B v France*, Judgement of 25 March 1992 *Series A*, No. 232-C; ECtHR, *Christine Goodwin v. the United Kingdom*, Application No. 28957/95, Judgement of 11 July 2002.

[86] ECtHR, *Klass v. Germany*, § 55; ECtHR, *Leander v. Sweden*, §§ 65–67; ECtHR, *Rotaru v. Romania*, §§ 59–60. See in detail: E. Brouwer, *o.c.*, 143–144.

[87] ECtHR, *Gaskin v. the United Kingdom*, Application No. 10454/83, Judgement of 7 July 1989; ECtHR, *Z. v Finland*, Application No. 22009/93, Judgement of 25 February 1997.

[88] ECtHR, *Peck v. the United Kingdom*, § 62; ECtHR, *Perry v. the United Kingdom*, § 40; ECtHR, *P.G. and J.H. v. the United Kingdom*, § 59. More in detail: E. Brouwer, *o.c.*, 138–139.

Segerstedt-Wiberg the Court demanded that governmental authorities only collect data that is relevant and based on concrete suspicions.[89] Finally, in the *Rotaru v. Romania* judgement of 4 May 2000 the Court acknowledged the right to individuals to financial redress for damages based on a breach of Article 8 caused by the data processing activities of public authorities.[90]

1.2.1.4 Strasbourg Criteria for Excessive, Unnecessary or Unjustified Collection of Processing of Data

What the Court does in its case law is to establish criteria that allow for an assessment of data protection under the ECHR. In terms of data protection regulation, these criteria are not new but it is useful to see the Court embracing them at the fundamental rights level of the ECHR. These criteria are so we contend, of the uttermost importance also for data protection when they regard the interpretation of broad but essential notions such as 'excessive', 'unnecessary' or 'unjustified' collection of processing of data.[91] These notions reappear in Article 6(1)(c) and Article 7(c) or (e) of the EU Data Protection Directive 95/46.

The question whether a certain practice is 'necessary in a democratic society' is however seldom answered by the Court, which usually first addresses the question 'is there a legal basis in law for the privacy infringing action?'. When it finds a breach of this legality requirement, it does not verify the other requirements.[92] This

[89] This requirement is part of the notion of 'foreseeable', one of the conditions that the Court attaches to the phrase 'in accordance with the law' contained in Article 8.2. See ECtHR; *Amann v. Switzerland*, § 61 and § 75 ff.; ECtHR, *Segerstedt-Wiberg v. Sweden*, § 79. More in detail: E. Brouwer, *o.c.*, 136–137.

[90] ECtHR, *Rotaru v. Romania*, § 83.

[91] We borrow from P. De Hert, 'Strafrecht en privacy. Op zoek naar een tweede adem' [Criminal Law and Privacy. Searching for a New Breath], *Rechtshulp. Maandblad voor de sociale praktijk*, 2003/10, 41–54. We recall that Article 8 ECHR does not formulate privacy as an absolute right. Exceptions are made possible in the second paragraph of the provision but the drafters of the Convention took care to provide safeguards against possible abuse of the right to formulate exceptions. Therefore, if any exception to the protection of data privacy is adopted respect has to be given to the conditions laid down in Article 8.2 ECHR, which is, any invasion of privacy for a legitimate reason (for purposes of criminal investigation, usually the prevention of crime) must be adopted 'in accordance with the law' and when 'necessary in a democratic society'. Those requisites are cumulative. Article 8.2. ECHR states that: 'There shall be no interference by a public authority with the exercise of this right except such as is in accordance with the law and is necessary in a democratic society in the interests of national security, public safety or the economic well-being of the country, for the prevention of disorder or crime, for the protection of health or morals, or for the protection of the rights and freedoms of others.'

[92] The Convention organs treat the requirements of Article 8.2 ECHR as successive hurdles. This means that where they find that a measure complained of is not 'in accordance with the law', then they do not proceed to examine whether the measure satisfies the requirement of 'necessity in a democratic society'. See for instance ECtHR, *P.G. and J.H.*, § 38. 'As there was no domestic law regulating the use of covert listening devices at the relevant time (. . .), the interference in this case was not 'in accordance with the law' as required by Article 8 § 2 of the Convention, and there has therefore been a violation of Article 8 in this regard. In the light of this conclusion, the Court is not

explains why in practice we find only a few rulings on the necessity requirement compared to the amount of rulings on the legality requirement. But there is more. We see not only a tendency to limit the analysis to the legality requirement but also a tendency to expand the analysis of the legality requirement by taking into account more and more human rights issues ('foreseeability', 'accessibility', 'protection against abuse', etc.).

Whatever the wisdom might be of this approach,[93] we need to realise that checking on the legality requirement is a fundamentally different matter from checking on the requirement 'necessary in a democratic society'.[94] Only the latter requirement deals with the political question whether (processing) power should be limited, stopped or prohibited or, in other words, whether 'opacity' of the individual must be protected.[95] Even if a restriction of privacy is foreseen by law and serves one of the legitimate objectives summed up in Article 8 § 2 ECHR, this restriction must still be 'necessary in a democratic society' and should not reach further than that. This condition inevitably implies an ultimate balancing of interests, a value judgement and/or a substantial choice, which cannot be found in an exegetic reading of the text, or in a strict application of logical rules.[96] Such a balancing of interests, which takes the weight of fundamental rights and freedoms duly into account, is essential.[97] It allows for the exercise of the political function of human rights. Behind the requirement 'necessary in a democratic society' lies the true constitutional question with regard to law enforcement and privacy: is there a justifiable necessity for (processing) actors to infringe the privacy right and to process data?

Even in cases when the necessity requirement is met, one cannot but feel some discontent. To believe most authors, the Court, when checking on the requirement of necessity, common to Article 8, 9, 10 and 11 ECHR, applies two criteria, namely the 'pressing social need' and the question if the interference can be considered 'proportionate to the legitimate aim pursued'. It would be a good thing for human

---

required to determine whether the interference was, at the same time, 'necessary in a democratic society' for one of the aims enumerated in paragraph 2 of Article 8'.'

[93] Our argument needs to take into account the small implications that judges make. Implying something without really saying it. Judges refrain from politically tainted arguments and prefer to play safe. In *Perry* the judges found a breach of the requirement 'in accordance with the law' and an analysis of the necessity requirement is therefore not made (§ 47–49) but one can sense throughout the first analysis the message of the Court that would it have done the second analysis, it would have applied a strict proportionality test (§ 41).

[94] About this condition see K. Rimanque, 'Noodzakelijkheid in een democratische samenleving -een begrenzing van beperkingen aan grondrechten', in *Liber Amicorum Frédéric Dumon*, Antwerp, Kluwer Rechtswetenschappen, 1983, deel II, 1220.

[95] See on the notion of opacity: P. De Hert & S. Gutwirth, 'Privacy, data protection and law enforcement. Opacity of the individual and transparency of power' in E. Claes, A. Duff & S. Gutwirth (eds.), *Privacy and the criminal law*, Antwerp/Oxford, Intersentia, 2006, p. 61–104.

[96] K. Rimanque, *l.c.*, 1229.

[97] Cf. S. Gutwirth, 'De toepassing van het finaliteitbeginsel van de Privacywet van 8 december 1992 tot bescherming van de persoonlijke levenssfeer ten opzichte van de verwerking van persoonsgegevens' [The application of the purpose specification principle in the Belgian data protection act of 8 December 1992], *Tijdschrift voor Privaatrecht*, 4/1993, 1409–1477.

freedom if the Court would really just do that, since these criteria, especially the criteria of 'pressing social need', put a heavy burden on state actions that are infringing on the rights contained in Article 8, 9, 10 and 11 ECHR.[98] However a closer look at the case law reveals that these criteria are only applied in specific cases, often with regard to Article 10 ECHR but seldom in cases with regard to Article 8 ECHR where the Court, as a rule, seems less inclined to put a heavy burden on the acting state.[99] Very seldom the two criteria appear in Article 8 ECHR cases and often the 'pressing social need' criteria is omitted in the reasoning of the Court.[100] Often the requirement of 'necessity' is brought back to the question of proportionality, in some cases supplemented by the requirement that the reasons for the interference are relevant and sufficient.[101] What is 'proportionate' will depend on the circumstances. According to M. Delmas-Marty, in determining proportionality the Court particularly takes into account the nature of the measure taken (its reach, whether it is general of absolute, its adverse consequences, the scope for abuse of the measure), whether the state concerned could have taken other measures or implemented them in a less drastic way, the status of the persons involved whose rights can legitimately be subject to greater limitation (e.g., prisoners) and finally, whether there are any safeguards that can compensate for the infringement of rights that a measure can

[98] In the context of Article 10 ECHR (freedom of expression) the Court has observed that 'necessary ... is not synonymous with *indispensable*, neither has it the flexibility of such expressions as *admissible*, *ordinary*, *useful*, *reasonable* or *desirable*, but that it implies a *pressing social need*' (ECtHR, *Handyside v. United Kingdom*, Judgement of 7 December 1976, *Series A*, No. 24, § 48).

[99] P. De Hert & S. Gutwirth, 'Grondrechten: vrijplaatsen voor het strafrecht? Dworkins Amerikaanse trumpmetafoor getoetst aan de hedendaagse Europese mensenrechten' (Human Rights as Asylums for Criminal Law. An assessment of Dworkin's Theory on Human Rights) in R.H. Haveman & H.C. Wiersinga (eds.), *Langs de randen van het strafrecht*, Nijmegen, Wolf Legal Publishers, 2005, p. 141–176; P. De Hert, 'Balancing security and liberty within the European human rights framework. A critical reading of the Court's case law in the light of surveillance and criminal law enforcement strategies after 9/11', *Utrecht Law Review*, 2005, Vol. 1, No. 1, 68–96. See: http://www.utrechtlawreview.org/

[100] Only in rare cases such as in *Peck* one finds some word games referring to the semantic exercise in the context of Article 10 discussed above. See the use of the term 'pressing social need' in the following quote: 'In such circumstances, the Court considered it clear that, even assuming that the essential complaints of *Smith and Grady* before this Court were before and considered by the domestic courts, the threshold at which those domestic courts could find the impugned policy to be irrational had been placed so high that it effectively excluded any consideration by the domestic courts of the question of whether the interference with the applicants' rights answered a pressing social need or was proportionate to the national security and public order aims pursued, principles which lay at the heart of the Court's analysis of complaints under Article 8 of the Convention.' (ECtHR, *Peck v. United Kingdom*, § 100).

[101] P. De Hert, *Artikel 8 EVRM en het Belgisch recht*, *o.c.*, 40–60. Compare *Peck*: 'In determining whether the disclosure was 'necessary in a democratic society', the Court will consider whether, in the light of the case as a whole, the reasons adduced to justify the disclosure were 'relevant and sufficient' and whether the measures were proportionate to the legitimate aims pursued' (ECtHR, *Peck v. United Kingdom*, § 76).

create.[102] Applied to data protection issues this means that the Court's proportionality assessment varies according to the gravity of the interference; the sensitivity of the information; the use made of the data and the safeguards implemented.[103] A strict proportionality test, coming close to the common standard with regard to Article 10 ECHR, will be applied in the case of secret surveillance,[104] interceptions of letters to legal advisors,[105] use of (data gathered by) telephone tapping and very sensitive data that can easily be used in a discriminatory way.[106]

Our discontent partly results from observations that we have already made. First, there are comparatively few Strasbourg judgements that offer criteria for excessive, unnecessary or unjustified collection of processing of data. One of the factors accounting for this is the overstretched focus of the Court on the legality requirement. Of course no one can object to the Court's ruling that a legal basis in law has to exist but also has to fulfil quality requirements such as 'foreseeability' and 'accessibility' but the assessment of these supplementary requirements often necessitates an analysis of issues that are more concerned with the rule of law guarantees foreseen in Article 6 ECHR (fair trial) and Article 13 ECHR (effective remedy). What is the added value of considering these issues under Article 8 ECHR? Secondly, based on our experience with this case law we believe that many Court judgements allow processing authorities much leeway. Only flagrant abuse or risky use of data that can easily be used in a discriminatory way is very closely scrutinised, whereas other kinds of processing of data are left untouched 'as long that there is no blood'. Attempts to challenge data protection unfriendly choices with regard to, e.g., Eurodac or passenger data, based on the 'necessity' requirement, are very likely to be unsuccessful. Debates about these data protection issues do not seem to be a major concern in Strasbourg.

---

102 M. Delmas-Marty, *The European Convention for the Protection of Human Rights*, Dordrecht, 1992, 71 quoted by I. Cameron., *o.c.*, 26. About proportionality see also: S. Van Drooghenbroeck, *La proportionnalité dans le droit de la convention européenne des droits de l'homme. Prendre l'idée simple au sérieux*, Bruxelles, Bruylant/Publications des FUSL, 2002, 790 p.; W. Van Gerven, 'Principe de proportionnalité, abus de droit et droits fondamentaux', *Journal des Tribunaux*, 1992, 305–309.

103 Compare L. Bygrave, 'Data protection law in context, particularly its interrelationship with human rights', February 2007, (4p.), p. 3 (via://www.uio.no/studier/emner/jus/jus/JUR5630/v07/undervisningsmateriale/lecture207.doc).

104 'Powers of secret surveillance of citizens, characterising as they do the police state, are tolerable under the Convention only insofar as *strictly* necessary for safeguarding the democratic institutions' (ECtHR, *Klass v. Germany*, § 42).

105 ECtHR, *Campbell v. United Kingdom*, Application No. 13590/88, Judgement of 25 March 1992, § 45.

106 'In view of the highly intimate and sensitive nature of information concerning a person's HIV status, any State measures compelling communication or disclosure of such information without the consent of the patient call for the *most careful scrutiny* on the part of the Court, as do the safeguards designed to secure an effective protection' (ECtHR, *Z v. Finland*, § 96).

1.2.1.5 Only Partial Recognition of Data Protection Under the Scope of Article 8 ECHR

The attitudes of judges can change and the foregoing analysis is therefore far from final or decisive. Let us be cautious. The very basis of data protection recognition in Strasbourg is not as solid as it looks. Although the concept of autonomy and a large notion of personal data are brought under Article 8 ECHR and although cases such as *Klass*, *Leander*, *Amann*, *P.G. and J.H.* and *Perry* show the Court's willingness to go beyond the traditional restricted concept of privacy defined as intimacy, it is important to see that basic data protection assumptions are not incorporated in the Strasbourg protection. Both the former Commission and the Court have held that not all aspects of the processing of personal data are protected by the ECHR. In the *Leander* case the Court stated that the refusal to give Leander access to his personal data falls within the scope of Article 8 ECHR.[107] A claim for access therefore can be based upon the same article.[108] But the Court also stipulated rather bluntly that this did not mean that Article 8 ECHR gives a general right to access to personal data.[109] By contrast, in data protection, a general right to access is explicitly recognised, with a special arrangement for personal data kept by police and security services.[110]

Also, the Court made a distinction between personal data that fall within the scope of Article 8 ECHR and personal data that do not. In the eyes of the Court there is processing of personal data that affects private life and processing of personal data that does not affect the private life of individuals.[111] Data protection regulation, on

[107] ECtHR, *Leander v. Sweden*, § 48.

[108] ECtHR, *Antony and Margaret McMichael v. United Kingdom*, § 91.

[109] ECtHR, *Gaskin v. United Kingdom*, § 37. In the case of McMichael the right to access is again recognised. Cf. ECtHR, *Antony and Margaret McMichael*, § 9. But, just as in the *Leander* case, a general right of access to personal data is not granted. In this case the Court does not explicitly deny such a right but it 'simply' does not mention the issue.

[110] See Article 8 and 9 of the 1981 Convention and Article 12 and 13 of the 1995 Directive.

[111] A good example is the 1998-case *Pierre Herbecq and the Association Ligue des droits de l 'homme v Belgium*. Cf. ECommHR, *Pierre Herbecq and the Association Ligue des droits de l 'homme v Belgium*, Decision of 14 January 1998 on the applicability of the Applications No. 32200/96 and 32201/96 (joined), Decisions and Reports, 1999, 92–98; *Algemeen Juridisch Tijdschrift*, 1997–1998, Vol. 4, 504–508. In these two joint Belgian cases the applicants complain about the absence of legislation on filming for surveillance purposes where the data obtained is not recorded in Belgium. The application was held inadmissible on the following grounds: 'In order to delimit the scope of the protection afforded by Article 8 against interference by public authorities in other similar cases, the Commission has examined whether the use of photographic equipment which does not record the visual data thus obtained amounts to an intrusion into the individual's privacy (for instance, when this occurs in his home), whether the visual data relates to private matters or public incidents and whether it was envisaged for a limited use or was likely to be made available to the general public. In the present case, the Commission notes that the photographic systems of which the applicant complains are likely to be used in public places or in premises lawfully occupied by the users of such systems in order to monitor those premises for security purposes. Given that nothing is recorded, it is difficult to see how the visual data obtained could be made available to the general public or used for purposes other than to keep a watch on places. The Commission also notes that the data available to a person looking at monitors is identical to that which he or she could have obtained by being on the spot in person. Therefore, all that can be

the contrary, does not distinguish different sorts of personal data on the basis of such a thing as 'intrinsic privacy-relevance'. The central notion of data protection is 'personal data', meaning any information relating to an identified or identifiable individual.[112] Data protection, although it recognises the existence of a special category of sensitive data,[113] is built up upon the idea that *all* personal data can be abused, including the more ordinary ones, such as names and addresses: the basic idea of data protection is to offer protection to all personal data (and a stronger protection to some types of sensitive data). This idea is without doubt based on common sense, since there can be a debate about the extent to which ordinary data should be protected but there can be little or no debate about the idea that some protection must be granted to such data. As an example consider the following: while prohibiting the processing of sensitive data about, for instance, Jewish people, is positive, it would be unwise not to observe that a simple list of names (ordinary data) can also convey the information required to target them and ought to be protected as well. Often, technical people favour an Internet without law and especially without data protection law considering this to be too bureaucratic or formal. It is amusing to note that those most familiar with the possibilities of ICT themselves oppose the idea that it can make sense to protect data such as names or data regarding consumer behaviour (e.g., clients of a Kosher e-market).

In cases such as *Amann, Rotaru* and *P.G. and J.H.*, the European Court seems to cover all these differences between its case law and the principles of data protection by applying a very broad privacy definition, an uncritical reference to the *Leander* case, a generous reference to the 1981 Council of Europe Convention and a very loose scrutiny of the requirements of the first paragraph of Article 8 ECHR.[114]

---

observed is essentially public behaviour. The applicants have also failed to demonstrate plausibly that private actions occurring in public could have been monitored in any way. Applying the above criteria, the Commission has reached the conclusion that there is, in the present case, no appearance of an interference with the first applicant's private life. It follows that this part of the application is manifestly ill-founded within the meaning of Article 27, § 2 of the Convention'.

[112] See Article 2(a) of the 1981 Convention and Article 2(a) of the 1995 Directive.

[113] See on 'sensitive data', viz personal data revealing racial origin, political opinions or religious or other beliefs, as well as personal data concerning health, sexual life of data relating to criminal convictions, Article 6 of the 1981 Convention and Article 8 of the 1995 Directive.

[114] For instance in ECtHR, *Amann v. Switzerland*, § 65–57: 'The Court reiterates that the storing of data relating to the 'private life' of an individual falls within the application of Article 8 § 1 (see the Leander v. Sweden judgement of 26 March 1987, *Series A*, No. 116, 22, § 48). It points out in this connection that the term 'private life' must not be interpreted restrictively. In particular, respect for private life comprises the right to establish and develop relationships with other human beings; there appears, furthermore, to be no reason in principle why this understanding of the notion of 'private life' should be taken to exclude activities of a professional or business nature (see the *Niemietz*, § 29 and *Halford v. United Kingdom*, judgement of 25 June 1997, § 42). That broad interpretation tallies with that of the Council of Europe's Convention of 28 January 1981 for the protection of individuals with regard to automatic processing of personal data, which came into force on 1 October 1985, whose purpose is 'to secure in the territory of each Party for every individual ... respect for his rights and fundamental freedoms, and in particular his right to privacy, with regard to automatic processing of personal data relating to him' (Article 1), such personal data being defined as 'any information relating to an identified or identifiable individual' (Article 2). In

However, these cases should be carefully interpreted. The reference to existing data protection treaties is formulated in a way that leaves room for discretion.[115] A closer reading shows that the old distinction between 'data that merits protection' and 'data that does not' is still at work and that processing of data is excluded from the privacy scope when (1) the data as such are not considered as private, (2) when there are no systematically stored images or sound recordings, or other data, (3) when the data are not systematically stored with the focus on the data subject and (4) when the data subject could reasonably expect the processing.[116] This explains the hesitation of the Court in *P.G. and J.H.* to put police use of listening devices in a police station (par. 52 et seq.) on the same level of protection as police use of a covert listening device in a suspect's flat (par 35 et seq.). Considering the latter under the scope of Article 8 ECHR is less troublesome for the Court, whereas from a data protection perspective there is no difference when applying its principles. The same can be said of the Court's hesitation to consider ordinary camera surveillance in the streets[117] and commercial metering of telecommunication data for billing purposes[118] as falling under the scope of Article 8.1 ECHR, whereas there is no doubt about the applicability of data protection principles to these 'legitimate' processing applications of data.

1.2.1.6 A Constructive Look at the Strasbourg Data Protection Acquis

There are many reasons to focus on the added value that Strasbourg can and does offer to data protection regulation. Without having at its disposal an explicit data

---

the present case the Court notes that a card on the applicant was filled in that stated that he was a 'contact with the Russian embassy' and did 'business of various kinds with the company [A.]'. See paragraphs 15 and 18 above. The Court finds that those details undeniably amounted to data relating to the applicant's 'private life' and that, accordingly, Article 8 is also applicable to this complaint'.

[115] Even when these cases show a willingness to protect aspects of 'public privacy' and the day may come that the Court will grant Article 8 ECHR-protection to all personal data; there remain other questions to be answered, such as, just to mention one, the question whether a right to access and correction can be considered as an integral part of rights contained in Article 8 ECHR. As long as these questions are not answered, there remains undeniably a proper role to play for data protection.

[116] H.R. Kranenborg, *o.c.*, pp. 311–312.

[117] ECtHR, *Perry v. the United Kingdom*, § 40: 'As stated above, the normal use of security cameras per se whether in the public street or on premises, such as shopping centres or police stations where they serve a legitimate and foreseeable purpose, do not raise issues under Article 8 § 1 of the Convention'.

[118] ECtHR, *P.G. and J.H. v. the United Kingdom*, § 42: 'It is not in dispute that the obtaining by the police of information relating to the numbers called on the telephone in B's flat interfered with the private lives or correspondence (in the sense of telephone communications) of the applicants who made use of the telephone in the flat or were telephoned from the flat. The Court notes, however, that metering, which does not per se offend against Article 8 if, for example, done by the telephone company for billing purposes, is by its very nature to be distinguished from the interception of communications which may be undesirable and illegitimate in a democratic society unless justified (see *Malone*, cited above, pp. 37–38, §§ 83–84)'.

protection right, the Court has brought many data protection aspects under the scope of Article 8 of the Convention. With more authority than any other possible existing institution, the Strasbourg Court has expressed the view that the protection of personal data is fundamentally important to a person's enjoyment of his or her right to respect for private life. Through its references to the 1981 Data Protection Convention, the Strasbourg Court has endorsed and spread the idea that data protection is more than just technical regulation. Hustinx rightly states that in the Court's view, Article 8 ECHR *probably* includes the obligation to give effect to the basic principles laid down in Convention 108, *in any case with respect to sensitive data.*[119] In doing so the Court has put some additional constitutional pressure on the implementation of this Convention.[120]

We could endlessly expand on the benefits of the Strasbourg case law for data protection[121] but in the foregoing we have also critically underlined some of the shortcomings of the Strasbourg reception of data protection: not all data are protected; the recognition of the rights to information and access is far from straightforward and, there is a shortage of information on the necessity requirement and the relevance of other Convention rights such as those contained in Article 6 and 13 ECHR, due to the Courts preference to include the idea behind the rights in its analysis of the legality requirement under Article 8 ECHR.

Still, it is better to explore what more Strasbourg can do, rather than to focus upon what it does not do for the protection of those whose data are engaged. It is not unreasonable to assume that some further input can be expected from the right to equality and non-discrimination, especially since the right enshrined in Article 14 ECHR is now complemented with a more autonomous right to equality and non-discrimination contained in Article 1 of the 12th Protocol to the ECHR that came into force on the 1st of April 2005. In *Segerstedt-Wiberg and Others v. Sweden*, a claim concerning unsuccessful requests to view records held by the Swedish Security Police was refused on the grounds that making them available might threaten national security or hinder police activities. The Court not only found certain violations of Article 8 ECHR[122] but also of Articles 10 ECHR (freedom of expression)

[119] P.J. Hustinx, *l.c.*, p. 62 (italics added).

[120] E. Brouwer, *o.c.*, pp. 131–151.

[121] In data protection all data is in principle treated alike, whether it is written, visual or other information. Rightfully the Court stresses the particular dangers of visual data as opposed to other data in ECtHR, *Von Hannover v Germany*, Judgement of 24 June 2004, § 59: 'Although freedom of expression also extends to the publication of photos, this is an area in which the protection of the rights and reputation of others takes on particular importance. The present case does not concern the dissemination of 'ideas', but of images containing very personal or even intimate 'information' about an individual. Furthermore, photos appearing in the tabloid press are often taken in a climate of continual harassment which induces in the person concerned a very strong sense of intrusion into their private life or even of persecution'.

[122] With regard to alleged violation of Article 8 and the storage of applicants' information, the Court held that the storage of the information had a legal basis under the 1998 Police Data Act. In addition, the scope of the discretion conferred on the competent authorities and the manner of its exercise was indicated with sufficient clarity. The Court also accepted that the storage of the

and 11 ECHR (freedom of association). The Court considered that the storage of personal data related to political opinion, affiliations and activities that had been deemed unjustified for the purposes of Article 8, constituted an unjustified interference with the rights protected by Articles 10 and 11 concerning all the applicants, except Segerstedt-Wiberg.[123]

Recently Birte Siemen has been examining the data protection rights guaranteed by the procedural rights under Articles 5, 6 and 13 ECHR. Articles 5 and 6 are only applicable in the context of a court procedure or imprisonment. In these procedures they guarantee full access rights. However, beyond these procedures, they only offer a limited added value with regard to the data subject's right of access. Siemen rightly highlights the impact of Article 6 and especially Article 13 on the right of remedy. Both supplement Article 8 ECHR in a useful way and expand significantly the legal protection of the data subject.[124] This point is well illustrated by *Segerstedt-Wiberg and Others v. Sweden*. In this case the applicants, confronted with a refusal to view records held by the Swedish Security Police, raised among others a violation of Article 13 ECHR (right to an effective remedy). The Court observed that the Swedish Parliamentary Ombudsman and Chancellor of Justice could receive individual complaints and had a duty to investigate them to ensure that the relevant laws had been properly applied. However, they lacked the power to render a legally-binding decision. Therefore, the Court found neither remedy to be effective within the meaning of Article 13 for all of the applicants. In identical terms the Court regarded as unsatisfactory the powers of the Records Board (empowered to monitor on a day-to-day basis the Secret Police's entry and storage of information and compliance with the Police Data Act). The Court noted that the Records Board had no competence to order the destruction of files or the erasure or rectification of information kept in the files. Even more significant is a similar ruling on the competences of the Swedish Data Inspection Board. This authority has wider powers than the Records Board. It has the power to examine individual complaints and to order the processor, on payment of a fine, to stop unlawful processing of information other than for storage. The Board was not itself empowered to order the erasure of unlawfully stored information but could make an application for such a measure to the County Administrative Court. However, the European Court had received no information indicating the effectiveness of the Data Inspection Board in practice. It had therefore not been shown that this remedy was effective.[125] In the view of the Court, those shortcomings were not consistent with the requirements of effectiveness in Article 13 and were not offset by any possibilities for the applicants

information in question pursued legitimate aims, namely the prevention of disorder or crime, in the case of Segerstedt-Wiberg and the protection of national security, for the other applicants. The Court concluded that the continued storage of the information that had been released was necessary concerning Segerstedt-Wiberg but not for any of the remaining applicants. In terms of the refusal to grant full access to the information, the Court held that Sweden was entitled to consider national security interests and the fight against terrorism over the interests of the applicants.

[123] ECtHR, *Segerstedt-Wiberg and others v. Sweden*, § 107.

[124] B. Siemen, *o.c.*, p. 204–211. See also P. De Hert, [Human Rights and Data Protection. European Case law 1995–1997], *l.c.*, p. 75–90; E. Brouwer, *o.c.*, 147 ff.

[125] ECtHR, *Segerstedt-Wiberg and others v. Sweden*, § 120.

to seek compensation.[126] The Court found that the applicable remedies, whether considered on their own or together, could not satisfy the requirements of Article 13 and that there had therefore been a violation of Article 13. Brouwer rightfully devotes a lot of attention to this case showing that data protection justice must not only be seen to be done, but also be done.[127] The added value of data protection authorities is assessed in practice, not in theory. When there are no positive performance indicators, then the European Court on Human Rights will not give its blessing.

1.2.2 Data Protection Tested in Luxembourg

Let us now turn to the reception of data protection by the Luxembourg Court of Justice.

1.2.2.1 *Österreichischer Rundfunk* and *Lindqvist*

Several judgements have been pronounced by the European Court of Justice (ECJ) on matters regarding the scope of application of the Directive 95/46/EC. Two of them should be mentioned here: *Österreichischer Rundfunk* and *Lindqvist.*[128] These cases demonstrate that judicial authority also plays a full role in the process of harmonisation, since the judges of the European Court of Justice are clearly asserting the full application of the Directive.

The first decision, *Österreichischer Rundfunk*, addressed the question whether it was legally tenable to convey information regarding the income of civil servants to both the Austrian public and to the Austrian Rechnungshof (Court of Auditors) according to a national Austrian Act that pursued objectives in the public interest in the field of public accounts budget control and transparency.[129] Several organisations resisted the law and argued that it violated Directive 95/46/EC. The question

---

[126] ECtHR, *Segerstedt-Wiberg and others v. Sweden*, § 121.

[127] E. Brouwer, *o.c.*, 147.

[128] ECJ, *Rechnungshof (C-465/00) v Österreichischer Rundfunk and Others and Christa Neukomm (C-138/01) and Joseph Lauermann (C-139/01) v Österreichischer Rundfunk*, Judgement of 20 May 2003, joined cases C-465/00, C-138/01 and C-139/01, *European Court reports*, 2003, p. I-04989; ECJ, 6 November 2003, Case C-101/01, *(Lindqvist), European Court reports*, 2003, p. I-12971.

[129] On this case: H. Kahlert, 'Einheitliches Schutznimeau für personenbezogene Daten in der Gemeinschaft', *European Law Reporter*, 2003 p.286–287; C. Haguenau-Moizard & N. Moizard, 'Informations concernant les salariés et protection des bases de données', *Revue de jurisprudence sociale*, 2003, p.945–949; J.-M. Belorgey, St. Gervasoni, & Ch. Lambert, 'Jusqu'où peut aller la transparence dans la rémunération des dirigeants du secteur public?', *L'actualité juridique; droit administratif*, 2003, p.2149–2150 ; P. Miguel Asensio, 'Avances en la interpretación de la normativa comunitaria sobre protección de datos personales', *Diario La ley*, 2004 No. 5964 p.1–8; P. Blok, 'Inkomens, Internet en informationele privacy', *Nederlands tijdschrift voor Europees recht*, 2004 p. 30–36; B. Siemen, 'Grundrechtsschutz durch Richtlinien / Die Fälle Österreichischer Rundfunk u.a. und Lindqvist', *Europarecht*, 2004 p. 306–321 ; M. Ruffert, 'Die künftige Rolle des EuGH im europäischen Grundrechtsschutzsystem', *Europäische Grundrechte-Zeitschrift*, 2004

whether Directive 95/46/EC applied to these matters was put before the ECJ by the *Rechnungshof* (Court of Audit) and by Ms Neukomm and Mr Lauermann and their employer Österreichischer Rundfunk (ÖRF). The *Rechnungshof* and the Austrian Government held that Directive 95/46 was not applicable, since the control activity in the contested Austrian Act did not fall within the scope of Community law and showed no link with Internal Market issues. The Luxembourg Court was therefore asked to judge whether the Data Protection Directive, focusing on internal market issues, was also applicable in the case of processing undertaken by a public authority in the context of its public mission. In the second decision, *Lindqvist*, a woman working voluntarily for her local church, had published information concerning an illness suffered by another voluntary worker on the parochial website.[130] Before the ECJ Ms. Lindqvist challenged the applicability of the Data Protection Directive to information published on a non-structured website.

In both cases, the Court asserted the applicability of the Directive: it ruled that the Directive was to be applied as a general rule and that its non-application should represent an exception to be considered narrowly.[131] In *Österreichischer Rundfunk* the Court recalls its former case law that internal market inspired Community Law

---

p. 466–471; L. Mormile, 'Trattamento dei dati personali per finalità pubbliche: il giudice del rinvio arbitro di un difficile bilanciamento', *Europa e diritto private*, 2004 p. 691–708.

[130] See on the Lindqvist judgement: H. Kahlert, 'Personenbezogene Daten im Internet', *European Law Reporter*, 2003, p.435–437; A. Roßnagel, 'EuGH: Personenbezogene Daten im Internet', *Multimedia und Recht*, 2004, p.99–100; P. Miguel Asensio, 'Avances en la interpretación de la normativa comunitaria sobre protección de datos personales', *Diario La ley*, 2004, No. 5964 p.1–8; R. Winkelhorst & T. Van der Linden-Smith, 'Persoonsgegevens op Internet', *Nederlands juristenblad*, 2004, p.627–631; Kl. Taraschka, 'Auslandsübermittlung' personenbezogener Daten im Internet', *Computer und Recht*, 2004, p.280–286; L. Burgorgue-Larsen, 'Publication de données à caractère personnel sur Internet, liberté d'expression et protection de la vie privée', *Recueil Le Dalloz*, 2004, Jur., p.1062–1063; B. Siemen, 'Grundrechtsschutz durch Richtlinien / Die Fälle Österreichischer Rundfunk u.a. und Lindqvist', *Europarecht*, 2004, p.306–321; M. Siano, 'La pagina Internet non 'esporta' dati all'estero: la Corte di giustizia definisce l'ambito di applicazione della direttiva sulla tutela dei dati personali e sulla loro libera circolazione', *Diritto pubblico comparato ed europeo*, 2004, p.461–469; Fl. Mariatte, 'Protection des données personnelles', *Europe*, 2004, Janvier Comm. n° 18 p.19–21; F. Hörlsberger, 'Veröffentlichung personenbezogener Daten im Internet', *Österreichische Juristenzeitung*, 2004, p.741–746; R. Panetta, 'Trasferimento all'estero di dati personali e Internet: storia breve di una difficile coabitazione', *Europa e diritto private*, 2004, p.1002–1017; G., Cassano, 'Cimino, Iacopo Pietro: Qui, là, in nessun luogo...Come le frontiere dell'Europa si aprirono ad Internet: cronistoria di una crisi annunciata per le regole giuridiche fondate sul principio di territorialità', *Giurisprudenza italiana*, 2004, p.1805–1809; P. De Hert & W. Schreurs, 'De bescherming van persoonsgegevens op het Internet: nuttige verduidelijking door de rechtspraak', noot bij HvJ, 6 november 2003 (Bodil Lindqvist t. Zweden), *Auteur & Media*, 2004/2, p. 127–138; K. Rosier, 'ECJ decides on protection of personal data on the Internet', *Stibbe ICTlaw Newsletter*, 2004, No. 13, pp. 2–3.

[131] In the opinion of the Court, one such exception was laid down in Article (2) in relation to both common foreign and security policy and police and judicial co-operation. The Court rejected the argument for so-called 'minimal harmonisation' which, in the Court's opinion, contradicted the 'total harmonisation' goal of the Directive. The Member States should cease departing from the commonly agreed framework achieved by the Directive. See Yves Poullet, 'EU data protection policy, The Directive 95/46/EC: Ten years after', *Computer law & security report*, 2006, 206–217.

does not presuppose the existence of an actual link with free movement between Member States in every situation referred to by the measure founded on that basis. In *Lindqvist* the ECJ found that the main principles of Directive 95/46/EC apply to using personal data on websites. The act of referring, on an Internet page, to various persons and identifying them by name or by other means, for instance by giving their telephone number or information regarding their working conditions and hobbies, constitutes 'the processing of personal data wholly or partly by automatic means' within the meaning of Article 3(1) of Directive 95/46. Although the EJC accepted that Ms. Lindqvist's processing activities were not economic but had charitable and religious aims, it held that such processing of personal data was not covered by any of the exceptions listed in Article 3, paragraph 2 of the Directive, including the second exception, provided for by the second indent of paragraph 2 'activities which are carried out in the course of private or family life of individuals'. This exception could not be invoked when the processing of personal data consist in publication on the Internet so that those data are made accessible to an indefinite number of people (see paragraphs 27, 38, 43–48).[132]

Both decisions make it clear that the EU 1995 Directive has a wide scope and that it is the standard reference point within the European Information Society context, although some of its provisions, particularly those on international data transfer, 'do not fit well to the new realities of the Internet'.[133]

Österreichischer Rundfunk was the Court of Justice's first decision on Directive 95/46/EC and it is particularly interesting for our constitutional inquiry. The ECJ recalls the essential 'internal market' rationale of the 1995 EU Directive[134] but at the same time, it also strongly emphasises the human rights rationale of the

---

[132] A second question submitted to the Court was whether or not the fact of loading personal data on an Internet site, thereby making those data accessible to anyone who connects to the Internet, including people in a third (non EU) country was to be considered as a 'transfer [of data] to a third country' within the meaning of Directive 95/46 intended to allow the Member States to monitor transfers of personal data to third countries and to prohibit such transfer where they do not offer an adequate level of protection. The Court ruled that such processing is not a transfer to third countries within the meaning of Article 25 of Directive 95/46. Another interpretation would result in an impossible situation where Member States would have to be obliged to prevent any personal data being posted on Internet sites as soon as one of the countries from where the web pages were accessible could be considered as not ensuring an adequate level of protection required by the Directive. Hence one cannot presume that Article 25 applies to the loading, by an individual in Mrs Lindqvist's position, of data onto an Internet page, even if those data are thereby made accessible to persons in third countries with the technical means to access them (see §§ 63–64, 68, 71).

[133] P.J. Hustinx, *l.c.*, p. 62.

[134] ECJ, *Österreichischer Rundfunk*, §. 42: 'In those circumstances, the applicability of Directive 95/46 cannot depend on whether the specific situations at issue in the main proceedings have a sufficient link with the exercise of the fundamental freedoms guaranteed by the Treaty, in particular, in those cases, the freedom of movement of workers. A contrary interpretation could make the limits of the field of application of the directive particularly unsure and uncertain, which would be contrary to its essential objective of approximating the laws, regulations and administrative provisions of the Member States in order to eliminate obstacles to the functioning of the internal market deriving precisely from disparities between national legislations'.

Directive. Indeed it considered that the provisions of the Directive, in so far as they govern the processing of personal data liable to infringe fundamental freedoms (in particular the right to privacy), *must necessarily be interpreted in the light of fundamental rights*, which form an integral part of the general principles of law whose observance the ECJ ensures.[135] Crucial principles and references in the Directive regarding lawful processing (as for example in Article 6 and 7 of the Directive) must be ascertained on the basis of criteria drawn from Article 8 ECHR, viz legality, legitimacy and necessity.[136]

Of course this emphasis should be welcomed from a constitutional perspective but there nevertheless remains some reason for constitutional concern. Although at the time of the Judgement, the EU Charter was known and referred to by the Advocates Generals and the Court of First Instance, the ECJ makes not a single reference to the constitutional status of data protection in Article 8 of the Charter.[137] On the contrary, there is an almost absolute focus on the right to privacy enshrined in Article 8 ECHR as the main source of interpreting the Directive. The EC Directive 95/46 *must* be interpreted in accordance with the right to private life as protected in Article 8 ECHR.[138] A breach of the right to privacy implies an unlawful processing in the sense of the Directive[139]; no breach of privacy implies no breach of the Directive.

---

[135] ECJ, *Österreichischer Rundfunk*, §. 68: 'It should also be noted that the provisions of Directive 95/46, in so far as they govern the processing of personal data liable to infringe fundamental freedoms, in particular the right to privacy, must necessarily be interpreted in the light of fundamental rights, which, according to settled case law, form an integral part of the general principles of law whose observance the Court ensures (see, inter alia, Case C-274/99 P Connolly v Commission [2001] ECR I-1611, paragraph 37)'.

[136] ECJ, *Österreichischer Rundfunk*, § 66–72.

[137] By the end of April 2003, the Advocates General had referred to the Charter in 34 cases they handled concerning human rights since the Charter's proclamation in December 2000. The Court of First Instance made its first reference to the Charter of Fundamental Rights in a case involving max. mobil, an Austrian mobile phone operator and the European Commission (Court of First Instance, *max.mobil Telekommunikation Service GmbH v Commission* Case T-54/99, Judgement of 30 January 2001). Notwithstanding the pressure by the AG's, the EJC did not follow the example and did not refer to the Charter. See for a detailed discussion of the recognition of the Charter in the case law: http://www.jeanmonnetprogram.org/conference_lapietra/ecfr.html. A (negative) reference to the Charter is made by the United Kingdom in ECJ, 20 May 2003, (*Österreichischer Rundfunk*), §. 56: 'The United Kingdom Government submits that (...) the provisions of the Charter of Fundamental Rights of the European Union, proclaimed in Nice on 18 December 2000 (*O.J.*, No. C 364, 2000 p. 1), to which the Verfassungsgericht briefly refers, are of no relevance'.

[138] ECJ, *Österreichischer Rundfunk*, §. 68.

[139] See ECJ, *Österreichischer Rundfunk*, §. 91 where the ECJ rules that when national courts conclude that national legislation is incompatible with Article 8 ECHR, that legislation is also incapable of satisfying the requirement of proportionality in Articles 6(1)(c) and 7(c) or (e) of Directive 95/46 and where the ECJ also rules that each of the exceptions included in Article 13 of that Directive must comply with the requirement of proportionality with respect to the public interest objective being pursued. In the words of the ECJ: 'that provision cannot be interpreted as conferring legitimacy on an interference with the right to respect for private life contrary to Article 8 of the Convention.'

Data protection as privacy, no more no less.[140] This narrow perspective on data protection explains why the Court finds no (privacy) problem in the communication of data to third parties.[141]

The foregoing shows that the ECJ uses a number of criteria drawn from Article 8 ECHR to evaluate the lawfulness of disputed processing.[142] Paragraph 83 of *Österreichischer Rundfunk* even suggests a strict proportionality test when assessing the necessity requirement.[143] Hence there should be no reason for concern when the European Parliament challenged the necessity of a deal concluded by the European Commission before the ECJ allowing the transfer of 34 categories of passenger data to the United States. However, the ECJ equally underlines that, according to the European Court of Human Rights (ECHR), the scope of the national authorities' margin of appreciation on the proportionality of measures can vary depending on the nature of the legitimate aim pursued and on the particular nature of the interference involved,[144] implying that the national authorities' margin of appreciation is especially wide in relation with measures approved for security and anti-terrorism purposes.

1.2.2.2 The PNR Case

Since January 2003, European airlines flying to the United States have been obliged by the US to provide the US customs authorities with electronic access to the data contained in their automated reservation and departure control systems, referred to as 'Passenger Name Records' (hereinafter 'PNR data'). Based on US laws adopted following the terrorist attacks of 9/11, airline companies are obliged to submit the data before or immediately after the airplane takes off and, if they fail to do so, they can be fined a maximum of $5,000 for each passenger whose data have not been appropriately transmitted. The PNR data comprise 34 fields of data, including

---

[140] According to the ECJ, if national courts were to conclude that the national legislation with regard to the processing of personal data is incompatible with Article 8 of the Convention, that legislation would also be 'incapable of satisfying the requirement of proportionality in Articles 6(1)(c) and 7(c) or (e) of Directive 95/46' (ECJ, *Österreichischer Rundfunk*, §. 91).

[141] ECJ, *Österreichischer Rundfunk*, § 74: 'It necessarily follows that, while the mere recording by an employer of data by name relating to the remuneration paid to his employees cannot as such constitute an interference with private life, the communication of that data to third parties, in the present case a public authority, infringes the right of the persons concerned to respect for private life, whatever the subsequent use of the information thus communicated, and constitutes an interference within the meaning of Article 8 of the Convention'.

[142] P.J. Hustinx, *l.c.*, 63.

[143] ECJ, *Österreichischer Rundfunk*, §. 83: 'According to the European Court of Human Rights, the adjective 'necessary' in Article 8(2) of the Convention implies that a 'pressing social need' is involved and that the measure employed is 'proportionate to the legitimate aim pursued' (see, inter alia , the Gillow v. the United Kingdom judgment of 24 November 1986, *Series A*, No. 109, § 55). The national authorities also enjoy a margin of appreciation, 'the scope of which will depend not only on the nature of the legitimate aim pursued but also on the particular nature of the interference involved' (see the Leander v. Sweden judgment of 26 March 1987, *Series A*, No. 116, § 59)'.

[144] ECJ, *Österreichischer Rundfunk*, §. 83 (see the foregoing footnote).

not only name and address but also contact details, such as telephone numbers, e-mail addresses, information on bank numbers and credits cards and also on the meals ordered for the flight. The US demand for data held by European firms for billing purposes without the consent of the passengers to the transfer or a proper legal basis clearly violated several European data protection regulations. The European Commission tried to solve the problem by negotiating with the US officials a series of requirements and subsequently adopting a Decision 2004/535/EC on adequacy based on Article 25 EC Directive on Data Protection[145], whose adoption meant that the Commission was convinced that the US would ensure an adequate level of data protection for the transfers. This decision enabled the Council to adopt the Agreement of 17 May 2004 between the European Community and the United States of America to officially allow the transfers. This Agreement was incorporated in Decision 2004/496.[146] When negotiating these instruments, the Commission, followed by the Council, assumed that it was competent to do so on the basis of the provisions in Community law regarding transportation and data protection.

Before the EJC the European Parliament raised several pleas for annulment of both the decision on adequacy and the Council 2004/496, concerning an incorrect application of the Directive, the incorrect choice of Article 95 EC as legal basis for Decision 2004/496 and breach of, respectively, the second subparagraph of Article 300(3) EC, Article 8 of the ECHR, the principle of proportionality, the requirement to state reasons and the principle of cooperation in good faith. With regard to the first two pleas (incorrect reading of the Directive and incorrect choice of Article 95 EC as legal basis for Decision 2004/496), the Parliament submitted that:

– the adoption of the Commission decision on adequacy infringed Article 3(2) of the Directive, relating to the exclusion of activities that fall outside the scope of Community law.[147]

---

[145] Commission Decision 2004/535/EC of 14 May 2004 on the adequate protection of personal data contained in the Passenger Name Record of air passengers transferred to the United States' Bureau of Customs and Border Protection (notified under doc no C (2004) 1914), *O.J.*, No. L 235, 6 July 2004, p. 11–22.

[146] Council Decision 2004/496/EC on the conclusion of an agreement between the European Community and the US on the processing and transfer of PNR ('Passenger Name Records') data, *O.J.*, No. L 183, 20 May 2004, p. 83–85.

[147] Article 3.2 of the Directive is worded as follows: 'This Directive shall not apply to the processing of personal data: – in the course of an activity which falls outside the scope of Community law, such as those provided for by Titles V and VI of the Treaty on European Union and in any case to processing operations concerning public security, defence, State security (including the economic well-being of the State when the processing operation relates to State security matters) and the activities of the State in areas of criminal law'.

– that Article 95 EC did not constitute an appropriate legal basis for Decision 2004/496.[148] The decision did not have as its objective and subject-matter the establishment and functioning of the internal market by contributing to the removal of obstacles to the freedom to provide services and it did not contain provisions designed to achieve such an objective. Its purpose is to make lawful the processing of personal data that is required by United States legislation. Nor could Article 95 EC justify Community competence to conclude the Agreement, because the Agreement relates to data processing operations that are excluded from the scope of the Directive.

On 30 May 2006, the ECJ annulled Council Decision 2004/496/EC and Commission Decision 2004/535/EC, arguing that they could not have their legal basis in EU transport policy (a first pillar provision).[149] A careful reading of the preamble to

[148] The second sentence of Article 95(1) EC is worded as follows: 'The Council shall, acting in accordance with the procedure referred to in Article 251 and after consulting the Economic and Social Committee, adopt the measures for the approximation of the provisions laid down by law, regulation or administrative action in Member States which have as their object the establishment and functioning of the internal market.'

[149] ECJ, *European Parliament v Council of the European Union* and *European Parliament v Commission of the European Communities*, Joined Cases C-317/04 and C-318/04, Judgement of 30 May 2006, *O.J.*, No. C 178/2. See Sp. Simitis, 'Übermittlung der Daten von Flugpassagieren in die USA: Dispens vom Datenschutz?', *Neue juristische Wochenschrift*, 2006, p.2011–2014; D. Westphal, 'Übermittlung europäischer Fluggastdaten', *Europäische Zeitschrift für Wirtschaftsrecht*, 2006, p.406–408; P. Schaar, 'EuGH-Entscheidung zur Fluggastdatenübermittlung – Grund zur Begeisterung?', *Multimedia und Recht*, 2006, p.425–426; H. Kahlert, 'Europäische Flugpassagierdaten in amerikanischen Händen – (k)ein rein kompetenzrechtliches Problem', *European Law Reporter*, 2006, p.242–245; P. Szczekalla, 'Übermittlung von Fluggastdaten an die USA', *Deutsches Verwaltungsblatt* 2006 p.896–899; E. Pahlawan-Sentilhes, 'Coup d'arrêt aux transferts de données sur les passagers en partance pour les Etats-Unis', *Recueil Le Dalloz* 2006 IR. p.1560–1561; V. Michel, 'La dimension externe de la protection des données à caractère personnel: acquiescement, perplexité et frustration', *Revue trimestrielle de droit européen*, 2006 p. 549–559; D. Gabel & Ch. Arhold, 'Fluggastdaten (PNR): Der Beschluss des Rates über den Abschluss des Abkommens zwischen der EG und den USA über die Verarbeitung und Übermittlung personenbezogener Daten im Luftverkehr sowie die Angemessenheitsentscheidung der Kommission sind nichtig', *Europäisches Wirtschafts- & Steuerrecht – EWS*, 2006, p.363–364; E. Pedilarco, 'Protezione dei dati personali: la Corte di giustizia annulla l'accordo Unione europea-Stati Uniti sul trasferimento dei dati dei passeggeri aerei', *Diritto pubblico comparato ed europeo*, 2006, p.1225–1231; Fl. Mariatte,'La sécurité intérieure des États-Unis ... ne relève pas des compétences externes des Communautés', *Europe*, 2006 Juillet Etude No. 8 p.4–8; A. Mantelero, 'Note minime in margine alla pronuncia della Corte di giustizia delle Comunità europee sul trasferimento dei dati personali dei passeggeri dei vettori aerei verso gli Stati Uniti, Contratto e impresa', *Europa*, 2006, p.1075–1081; G. Tiberi, 'L'accordo tra la Comunità europea e gli Stati Uniti sulla schedatura elettronica dei passeggeri aerei al vaglio della Corte di giustizia', *Quaderni costituzionali*, 2006 p.824–829; V. Sotiropoulos, 'I 'tetarti' apofasi tou DEK schetika me tin prostasia prosopikon dedomenon – I ypothesi PNR/USA', *To Syntagma*, 2006, p.938–952; V. Sotiropoulos, 'I diavivasi prosopikon dedomenon epivaton ptiseon apo tin EE stis IPA gia skopous katapolemisis tis tromokratias – i ypothesi 'PNR/USA' sto DEK', *Efimerida Dioikitikou Dikaiou*, 2006 p.358–363; E. Dirrig, 'La jurisprudence de la Cour de justice et du Tribunal de première instance.

the EU-US agreement led the EJC to find that its purposes were: to enhance security, to fight against terrorism, to prevent and combat terrorism, related crimes and other serious crimes, including organised crime; and to prevent flight from warrants or custody for those crimes.[150] Thus, the ECJ held that the data transfers concerned fell within a framework established by the public authorities related to public security.[151]

Chronique des arrêts. Arrêt *Passenger Name Records*', *Revue du droit de l'Union européenne*, 2006, No. 3 p.698–702; M. Mendez, 'Passenger Name Record Agreement', *European Constitutional Law Review*, 2007 Vol.3 p.127–147; M. Banu, 'Protecţia persoanelor fizice în privinţa tratamentului de date cu caracter personal. Transport aerian. Decizia 2004/496/CE. Acord între Comunitatea Europeană Şi Statele Unite ale Americii. Dosare ale pasagerilor aerieni transferate către Biroul vamal Şi de protecţie a frontierelor al SUA. Directiva 95/46/CE. Articolul 25. State terţe. Decizia 2004/553/CE. Nivel adecvat de protecţie', *Revista română de drept comunitar*, 2007 No. 2 p.131–134; P. De Hert & G.-J. Zwenne, 'Over passagiersgegevens en preventieve misdaadbestrijding binnen de Europese Unie', *Nederlands juristenblad*, 2007, p.1662–1670: G.-J. Zwenne & P. De Hert,'Sur les données des dossiers passagers, la directive 'vie privée' 95/46/CE et la non-adéquation de la législation européenne', *Revue européenne de droit de la consommation*, 2007, p.223–242; P. De Hert & G. González Fuster, 'Written evidence on the PNR Agreement', Evidence submitted to House of Lords Sub-Committee F, E/06–07/F49 PNR, 5p. submitted February 2007 via http://www.parliament.uk/parliamentary_committees/lords_s_comm_f/eufwrevid.cfm.

150 ECJ, *European Parliament v Council of the European Union* and *European Parliament v Commission of the European Communities*, § 56–59: 'It follows that the transfer of PNR data to CBP constitutes processing operations concerning public security and the activities of the State in areas of criminal law. While the view may rightly be taken that PNR data are initially collected by airlines in the course of an activity which falls within the scope of Community law, namely sale of an aeroplane ticket which provides entitlement to a supply of services, the data processing which is taken into account in the decision on adequacy is, however, quite different in nature. As pointed out in paragraph 55 of the present judgment, that decision concerns not data processing necessary for a supply of services, but data processing regarded as necessary for safeguarding public security and for law-enforcement purposes. The Court held in paragraph 43 of Lindqvist, which was relied upon by the Commission in its defence, that the activities mentioned by way of example in the first indent of Article 3(2) of the Directive are, in any event, activities of the State or of State authorities and unrelated to the fields of activity of individuals. However, this does not mean that, because the PNR data have been collected by private operators for commercial purposes and it is they who arrange for their transfer to a third country, the transfer in question is not covered by that provision. The transfer falls within a framework established by the public authorities that relates to public security. It follows from the foregoing considerations that the decision on adequacy concerns processing of personal data as referred to in the first indent of Article 3(2) of the Directive. That decision therefore does not fall within the scope of the Directive'.

151 L Creyf and P Van de Velde, 'PNR (Passenger Name Records): EU and US reach interim agreement', *Bird & Bird Privacy & Data Protection Update*, October 2006, No. 11, 2p. (http://www.twobirds.com/english/publications/newsletters/). On 3 July 2006, the Council and the Commission notified termination of the agreement with effect from 30 September 2006. On 7 September 2006, the European Parliament adopted a report in which it asked the Council to negotiate – under the Parliament's oversight – an interim agreement, whereby the Parliament wanted to ensure that the US offers adequate protection of the passenger data collected and which should provide for a change to the 'push' system (under which US authorities must request specific data, which will then be selected and transferred) instead of the present 'pull' system (whereby access is granted to the full database and airline passengers data are directly accessed online by the authorities concerned). In its report, the Parliament further requested joint decision-making rights over the negotiation of the final agreement with the US. On 6 October 2006, shortly after the Court-set deadline of 30 September, EU negotiators reached an interim agreement with their US

Hence, not the Commission within the first pillar but the Council within the third pillar should have acted and negotiated with the United States.

In his initial reaction to the PNR judgment, the European Data Protection Supervisor[152] declared that the ruling of the ECJ had created a loophole in the protection for citizens, since it suggested that the transmission of information to third countries or organisations from European databases such as the Visa Information System or the Schengen Information System would escape the applicable rules of the 1995 Data Protection Directive, as long as the transmission is intended for police or public security use. The Court judgment has been seen as a failure for the European Parliament, as it had launched the procedures but mainly on different grounds, namely, that Commission Decision 2004/535/EC and Council Decision 2004/496/EC accepted a disproportionate transfer of data to the United States without proper data protection guarantees. The Parliament held that the agreement and its accompanying 'adequacy' decision violated the principle of proportionality, particularly in reference to the quantity of data collected and the retention period foreseen.

The ECJ did not have the opportunity to address the argument in its judgement for the PNR case, as it annulled both the Council Decision 2004/496/EC on the conclusion of the agreement, on the one hand and the Commission Decision 2004/535/EC holding that the US Bureau of Customs and Border Protection (CBP) offered a sufficient level of protection for personal data transferred from the EU, on the other hand, on formal grounds related to their legal basis (see above). On the contrary, Advocate General Léger did examine the proportionality argument in his Opinion in Cases C-317/04 and C-318/04[153] and he did it in an extremely interesting, albeit potentially dangerous, manner, which deserves special attention. Indeed, before expressing his views of the validity of the proportionality argument, Advocate General Léger manifested a series of highly interesting remarks on the scope of the control to be exercised by the ECJ concerning proportionality. He first

counterparts. The conflict of laws situation that has existed since 1 October 2006 thereby appears to be, at least temporarily, solved. The interim agreement would ensure a similar level of protection of the PNR data as before and it would also comply with the US request that the PNR data can be more easily distributed between different US agencies. A move from the 'pull' system to the 'push' system should be undertaken at a later date. The nature of PNR data available to US agencies remains unchanged. The interim agreement will apply from its date of signature, which is due to be completed by 18 October and will expire no later than 31 July 2007. By this date a new (superseding) agreement should be reached between the parties who meet again in November 2006 to begin discussions on that point.

[152] Regulation 45/2001 of 18 December 2000 provides for supervision by a special supranational authority: the European Data Protection Supervisor, or EDPS. In 2002, the Council adopted a decision on the regulations and general conditions governing the performance of the European Data Protection Supervisor's duties (Decision No. 1247/2002 of 1 July 2002, *O.J.*, No. L 183, 12 July 2002.). The creation of the EDPS is based on Decision 1247/2002 of 1 July 2002 on the regulations and general conditions governing the performance of this organisation's duties (*O.J.*, No. L 183, 12 July 2002).

[153] Léger, Philippe (2005), *Conclusions de l'Avocat Général M. Philippe Léger présentées le 22 novembre 2005*, [Opinion of the Advocate General in Cases C-317/04 and C-318/04] Luxembourg.

made reference to the ECtHR case law to declare that according to such case law interferences with private life might require a strict judicial control (§ 229). Second, he underlined that, also according to ECtHR case law, when the interferences are established with the purpose of national security or to fight against terrorism, public authorities enjoy wider discretionary powers (§ 230). Finally, he concluded that, in the PNR case, the latter notion shall predominate and, therefore, judicial control could not be strict: recognising to public authorities wide discretionary powers to determine which measures are to be considered proportionate, the judicial control should limit itself to the appreciation of any possible manifest error in such assessment (§ 231). This limitation of the scope of the judicial control marked the Advocate General's analysis of the proportionality of the measures foreseen in the first PNR agreement, which he concluded to be proportionate taking into account the wide discretionary powers that, in his view, should be recognised to the EC and the Council (§ 246).[154]

Advocate General Léger's opinion can be perceived as a worrying sign, supporting the view that citizens cannot rely on the judiciary to protect them against any intrusive security measures that public authorities might declare proportionate. Elsewhere we have highlighted that this alarming progressive self-effacement of the judiciary in its role to assess the proportionality of intrusive measures is not yet widely recognised and therefore certain public authorities might still chose to indulge in increasingly intrusive measures in the belief that, if citizens were to judge them disproportionate, they could always refer to the courts – a conclusion which no longer seems valid.[155] Rather than a limited formal compliance check from our judges, we expect a strict review of all the different alternatives encountered and their different impact on privacy and individual rights. Does the US need 34 categories of data? Why are the EU PNR agreements concluded with Australia and Canada less infringing on human rights? Are Australian and Canadian security forces wrongly less demanding or do they combine security and privacy better?[156]

Advocate Léger's Opinion is also dramatically unsatisfactory from a data protection perspective. Here we see a case that is wholly data protection relevant next to the proportionality issue of the measure ('is sending passenger data to the US necessary?'). The case is loaded with pure data protection aspects. Why does the US government need these data for such a long period? Are the European passengers informed about the transfer? Is there effective supervision in the US for complaints

---

[154] « *L'ensemble de ces garanties nous conduisent à considérer que,* eu égard à la grande marge d'appréciation qui doit, selon nous, être reconnue en l'espèce au Conseil et à la Commission, *l'ingérence dans la vie privée des passagers aériens est proportionnée au but légitime poursuivi par le régime PNR* » (underlined by the authors) (Léger, 2005:I-64).

[155] G. González Fuster & P. De Hert, 'PNR and compensation: how to bring back the proportionality criterion', *BNA's World Data Protection Report*, 2007, Vol. 7, August, No. 8, pp. 4–10.

[156] Sophie In't Veld and others, Joint motion for a resolution on the PNR agreement with the United States, European Parliament, 10 July 2007 (via http://www.quintessenz.org/doqs/000100003894/2007_07_11_EU-parl_PNR_joint%20resolution.pdf).

from Europe? Who has access to the data in the US? Will it be used for specific goals? All these issues are disregarded by Léger and replaced by a very formal and simple general proportionality check that we know from the privacy case law. The old Constitution (with its leeway for governments in the area of security) is apparently still very active and there are few indications that an independent status for data protection is a separate constitutional concern.

1.2.2.3 Future Testing in Luxembourg: Public Access and Data Protection

The right of access to documents and the right of individuals with regard to protection of their personal data are both rooted in the EC Treaty (Articles 255 and 286 respectively). They have been implemented through two Regulations: (EC) No. 45/2001 on data protection (see *above*) and (EC) No. 1049/2001 on public access to documents[157] and have been codified in the Charter of Fundamental Rights.[158] The two rights can be contrastive when access is specifically requested to information relating to an individual. The European Data Protection Supervisor has addressed this issue in a background paper, providing useful practical guidance for handling such requests.[159]

In *The Bavarian Lager Company Ltd. v Commission* (Case T-194/04) a judgement was delivered by the Court of First Instance on 8 November 2007.[160] The case concerned the disclosure of the names of certain people in their official public capacity (no private data was requested), the names were contained in the minutes of the meeting (no images or sound recording and no systematic and data subject focused storage occurred) and the participants could reasonably expect disclosure since they were acting in their public capacity and participating in a meeting of the European

---

[157] Regulation No. 1049/2001 of the European Parliament and of the Council of 30 May 2001 regarding public access to European Parliament, Council and Commission documents, *O.J.*, No. L 145, 31 May 2001, pp. 43–48.

[158] See Article 42 of the Charter (Right of access to documents): 'Any citizen of the Union and any natural or legal person residing or having its registered office in a Member State, has a right of access to European Parliament, Council and Commission documents'. See also Article 41 (Right to good administration): '1. Every person has the right to have his or her affairs handled impartially, fairly and within a reasonable time by the institutions and bodies of the Union. 2. This right includes:

- the right of every person to be heard, before any individual measure which would affect him or her adversely is taken;
- the right of every person to have access to his or her file, while respecting the legitimate interests of confidentiality and of professional and business secrecy; (...)'

[159] 'Public Access to Documents and Data Protection', Background Paper Series, July 2005, No. 1.

[160] ECtF Instance, *The Bavarian Lager Co. Ltd v Commission of the European Communities*, Cases C-194/04, Judgement of 8 November 2007, *European Court reports*, 2007 (http://eur-lex.europa.eu/LexUriServ/LexUriServ.do?uri=CELEX:62004A0194:EN:NOT).

Commission.[161] The Court held that access to documents containing personal data falls under Regulation No. 1049/2001 and not under Regulation No. 45/2001. The Court recalled that Recital 15 of Regulation No. 45/2001 states that access to documents, including conditions for access to documents containing personal data, is governed by the rules adopted on the basis of Article 255 EC, concerning the right of access to documents. Article 4(1)(b) of Regulation No. 1049/2001 on the public access to documents indicates that EU institutions shall refuse access to a document where disclosure would undermine the protection of 'privacy and integrity of the individual, in particular in accordance with Community legislation regarding the protection of personal data'. Community legislation includes, inter alia, Regulation No. 45/2001, which establishes the conditions for certain lawful processing of personal data not requiring the consent of the data subject. Processing under the scope of Regulation No. 1049/2001 is an example of such lawful processing. Considering this and the need to construe and apply restrictively exceptions to rights, the Court concluded that for the exception of Article 4(1)(b), to apply the disclosure of data should undermine the privacy and the integrity of the individual in the sense of Article 8 ECHR, in accordance with Article 6(2) EU and that it was not the case. Additionally, the Court stated that the Commission erred in law by holding that the applicant had to establish an express and legitimate purpose or need to obtain the disclosure of the names to which it had been refused access. Finally, the Court established that the exception to access based on arguments related to the protection of the purpose of inspections, investigations and audits [Article 4(2) of Regulation No. 1049/2001] did not apply.

Of course our attention is drawn to the way the Court conceives of the relation between privacy and data protection. In the judgement, the Court emphasized that the concept of 'private life' is broad and may include the protection of personal data but not all personal data necessarily fall within the concept of 'private life'

---

161 On 11 October 1996, a meeting took place attended by representatives of the Commission's Directorate-General for the Internal Market and Financial Services, the United Kingdom Department of Trade and Industry and representatives of the Confederation des Brasseurs du Marche Commun. Bavarian Lager had asked to participate at that meeting but the Commission had refused. Following a number of requests by Bavarian Lager based on Community legislation concerning public access to documents, the Commission disclosed to it, *inter alia*, the minutes of the meeting of 11 October 1996, stating that the names of five persons who had attended that meeting had been blanked out, two of them having expressly objected to disclosure of their identity and the Commission having been unable to contact the three others. Bavarian Lager made a confirmatory request for the full minutes, containing the names of all the participants, which the Commission rejected by a decision of 18 March 2004. The Commission took the view that Bavarian Lager had not established either an express and legitimate purpose or any need for such disclosure, as was required (so it argued) by the regulation on the protection of personal data and that, therefore, the exception concerning the protection of private life, laid down by the regulation on public access to documents, applied. It further took the view that disclosure would compromise its ability to carry out investigations. Bavarian Lager applied to the Court of First Instance for the annulment of that decision.

and, a fortiori, not all personal data should be considered by their nature capable of undermining the private life of the individual.[162] Regulation No. 1049/2001 contains an exception to public access related to the privacy and the integrity of the individual, in which, according to the Court's interpretation, the main interest protected is 'private life', not 'personal data': access to documents shall be refused on the basis of such exception where disclosure would undermine the protection of privacy and integrity of the individual. The Court recalled that professional activities are not, in principle, excluded from the concept of 'private life' within the meaning of Article 8 of the ECHR but they are not always included in it either. In this case the right to privacy does not apply. The mere presence of the name of a person in a list of participants at a meeting, acting on behalf of the body they represent, does not compromise the protection of the privacy and integrity of the person.[163]

The strategy consisting in using the differences between privacy and data protection as part of the solution to solve the collision between the right to access and the right to data protection, has been proposed in literature before.[164] However, the ease with which the Court of First Instance uses the old constitution distinguishing two kinds of personal data does not sit comfortably with the formal constitutional codification of data protection within EU law. In vain the Commission argued that both data protection and access are rights of the same nature, importance and degree and have to be applied together. Where a request is made for access to a public document containing personal data, a balance must be sought on a case-by-case basis.[165] The reasoning of the Court is simple: since there is no privacy, data protection does not apply. However, according to Article 4 of Regulation No. 1049/2001, concerning exceptions to the right of access: '1. The institutions shall refuse access to a document where disclosure would undermine the protection of: (...) (b) privacy and the integrity of the individual, *in particular in accordance with Community legislation regarding the protection of personal data*' (italics added). Hence, the obligation for the Court to take data protection seriously and to apply legislation as much as possible when balancing it with other constitutional values. More specific

[162] ECtFInstance, *The Bavarian Lager Co. Ltd v Commission of the European Communities*, §§ 114–115.

[163] ECtFInstance, *The Bavarian Lager Co. Ltd v Commission of the European Communities*, §§ 121–126.

[164] H.R. Kranenborg, *Access to documents and data protection in the European Union. On the public nature of personal data*, Deventer, Kluwer, 2007, 351p.; P. De Hert, 'Les données à caractère personnel et la publicité des documents administratifs', Titre XI in P. De Hert (ed.), *Manuel sur la vie privée et la protection des données*, Bruxelles, Ed. Politéia, feuillets mobiles, mise à jour No. 6 (2001), 94p.; De Hert, P., 'De grondrechten en wetten m.b.t. openbaarheid van bestuursdocumenten en bescherming van de persoonlijke levenssfeer. Analyse van de onderlinge relatie en commentaar bij het arrest Dewinter van de Raad van State' [Comparing fundamental rights and bills with regard to privacy and freedom of information], *Publiekrechtelijke Kronieken-Chronique de Droit Public (C.D.P.K.)*, 2001, No. 4, pp. 374–425.

[165] ECtFInstance, *The Bavarian Lager Co. Ltd v Commission of the European Communities*, § 77.

this implies a duty for the Commission and *Bavarian Lager Company* to respect data protection principles such as non-disclosure and purpose specification. There is a whole world of options between the right not to grant access because of data protection and the right not to grant data protection because of access. The Court should have thus taken this into consideration to achieve a better balance between the two rights.

1.3 Conclusions

The right to privacy is without doubt part of primary EC legislation because of its adoption in Article 8 ECHR. Although codified in the EU Charter, it is not as easy to establish whether the right to data protection as such (in a broader scope) has the same status.[166] The incorporation of data protection in Constitutions is probably a good political statement but it is far too early to evaluate its legal effects. Our analysis of the case law in Luxembourg and Strasbourg reveals that the right to data protection has not yet achieved its full status.

Previously, we quoted Lessig's observation of the need for transformative constitutions to fight harder than just codifying constitutions.[167] This analysis is followed by some compelling paragraphs on the vulnerable role of the courts in making the Constitution materialise. For Courts to impose transformative values after the approval of a constitution is a very critical step, since they operate within a political context and are the weakest branch of resistance within that political context. Lessig notes that even a strong statement of principle enacted within a Constitution's text allows a court only so much freedom to resist. Although the same can be said about codifying constitutions, the problem increases with regard to transformative parts of the Constitution regarding Cyberworld. When judges have to make judgments that do not seem to flow plainly or obviously from a legal text, their judgment will appear to have been politically influenced. Whenever it seems as though a Court is doing no more than simply confirming founding commitments, it creates the idea that this Court is simply acting to ratify its own views of a proper constitutional regime rather than enforcing judgments that have been constitutionalised by others. In other words, it appears to be making 'political moves.'

Our analysis needs to be enriched with an analysis of further developments, a broader analysis of human rights case law and an analysis of data protection case

---

[166] H.R. Kranenborg, *o.c.*, p. 313.
[167] L. Lessig, *o.c.*, p. 214.

law in the Member States. With regard to Strasbourg case law, we need to consider judgements such as *Schenk*[168] and *Khan*[169] in which the Court refuses to recognise the exclusionary rule. As regards case law, in Member States a discussion is needed regarding the English *Durant case*[170] and the Belgian *Court of Cassation*

---

[168] In *Schenk* a person is charged who was criminally convicted in his own country, partly on the grounds of the recording of a telephone call made by him (ECtHR, *Schenk v. Switzerland*, Judgement of 12 July 1988, *NJCM*, 1988, 570–575; *N.J.*, 1988, No. 851). The recording was made, in secret, by the person he was phoning and was offered to the government. Schenk pleaded on the grounds of the illegality of the evidence used. The Swiss Supreme Court did not preclude that the recording fell under the applicable Swiss criminal regulations on the interception of telecommunication but was of the opinion, after considering the interests at stake, that the recording could to be used as evidence material. Schenk went to Strasbourg and stated before the Commission that the evidence material used gave his trial an unfair character in the sense of Article 6 subsections 1 and 2 of the ECHR. In its report of 14 May 1987, the Commission was of the opinion that Article 6 subsection 1 had not been violated. Schenk's reference to Article 6 subsection 2 of the ECHR was rejected as an erroneous interpretation of this regulation. Before the Court a representative of the Commission additionally asserted that the person concerned was actually considered innocent by the Swiss judges until his guilt had been proven in accordance with the law, the view on the judgement of the Swiss courts was that the trial as a whole was 'perfectly' lawful, in spite of non-observance of a criminal regulation (*Schenk*, § 50). This rather peculiar additional argument ('no treaty violation because the Swiss judges state that everything is all right') shows that for Strasbourg the admissibility of evidence is in principle a matter for national law. This opinion is confirmed, in so many words, by the Court with the analysis of Article 6, subsection 1 of the ECHR. 'While Article 6 of the Convention guarantees the right to a fair trial, it does not lay down any rules on the admissibility of evidence as such, which is therefore primarily a matter for regulation under national law. The Court therefore cannot exclude as a matter of principle and in the abstract that unlawfully obtained evidence of the present kind may be admissible. It was only to ascertain whether Mr. Schenk's trial as a whole was fair' (*Schenk*, § 46). See in the same sense: ECtHR, *Lüdi v. Switzerland*, Judgement of 15 June 1992, § 43; ECtHR, *Vidal v. Belgium*, Judgement of 22 April 1992, § 33; ECtHR, *Dombo Beheer v. The Netherlands*, Judgement of 27 October 1993, 274, § 31; ECtHR, *Schuler-Zgraggen v. Switzerland*, Judgement of 24 June 1993, § 66. In Schenk's case Article 6, subsection 2, ECHR has not been violated. There is no evidence in the trial records that show that he was considered guilty by the Swiss judges during the trial. Any prejudice, on the part of the judges, cannot not be derived from the addition of the recording to the evidence (*Schenk*, § 51). With regard to Article 6 subsection 1 of the ECHR the Court judged earlier in the trial that this regulation was not violated: on the whole the prosecutor had a fair trial, because during the trial the person had the opportunity to dispute the facts and because the recorded material was not the only piece of evidence (ECtHR, *Schenk*, resp. § 47 and 48).

[169] ECtHR, *Khan* v. *United Kingdom,* judgement of 12 May 2000. The *Khan* judgement accepted that the admission of evidence obtained in breach of the privacy right against an accused person is not necessarily a breach of the required fairness under Article 6 (the right to a fair trial). Evidence was secured by the police in a manner incompatible with the requirements of Article 8 of the Convention and yet, it was admitted in evidence against the accused and let to his conviction, since the process taken as a whole was fair in the sense of Article 6 ECHR. Compare 'applicants had ample opportunity to challenge both the authenticity and the use of the recordings'; (ECtHR *P.G. and J.H. v. the United Kingdom*, judgement 25 September 2001, § 79).

[170] Court of Appeal (civil division) 8 December 2003, *Michael John Durant t. Financial Services Authority,* [2003] EWCA Civ 1746. See Edwards, Lilian, 'Taking the 'Personal' Out of Personal Data: Duran v. FSA and its Impact on Legal Regulation of CCTV', *SCRIPT-ed*, Vol. 1, Issue 2, June 2004, pp. 341–349.

judgment of 27 February 2001,[171] both demonstrating a clear willingness of the local judges to reject data protection regulation implications by applying a very narrow interpretation of *personal data*. Some years ago, Bygrave observed that the role of judiciary and quasi-judicial bodies was relatively marginal.[172] Today there is case law but it is questionable whether the new constitutional framework provides enough personal data protection. Both Brouwer and Bygrave have warned against reducing data protection to privacy to prevent data protection issues from being too easily brushed aside as either minor or relatively insignificant matters.[173] So far Strasbourg and Luxembourg have only produced a few cases on the relationship between data protection and privacy but the result is far from promising for data protection principles. Rulings such as in *Bavarian*, hesitations such as in *P.G. and J.H.* and reasoning such as in Advocate General Léger's Opinion cast doubts on the constitutional status of data protection and create the risk that data protection principles will continue to be considered 'soft law' instead of becoming 'hard law' based on a constitution.[174]

Data protection principles might seem less substantive and more procedural compared to other rights norms but they are in reality closely tied to substantial values and protect a broad scale of fundamental values other than privacy.[175] Because of its reputation of only focusing on the benefits for individuals, putting data protection in the privacy frame hampers the realisation of the societal benefits of data protection rights and therefore puts these rights essentially in conflict with the needs of society.[176]

---

[171] Cass. 27 February 2001, *Computer.* 2001, p. 202, annotated by J. Dumortier., *Vigiles*, 2001, vol. 6, No. 4, pp. 153–157, annotated by P. De Hert; *R.W.*, 2001–2002, annotated by P. Humblet. The judgement that was disputed before the Court of Cassation was delivered by the Court of Appeal from Ghent, 2 February 1999, published in *RPO-T*, 2001, vol. 1, No. 2, pp. 30–33, annotated by P. De Hert. See also: P. De Hert, 'Caméras cachées dans des magasins, la controverse suite à un arrêt de cassation', *Sécurité privée*, 2001, No. 11, 27–30; P. De Hert & S. Gutwirth, 'Cassatie en geheime camera's: meer gaten dan kaas' [The *Cour de cassation* and secret camera's: more holes than cheese], *Panopticon*, 2001, pp. 309–318; P. De Hert, 'De waarde van de wet van 8 december 1992 bij de bewijsbeoordeling in strafzaken', *Tijdschrift voor Strafrecht*, 2002, Vol. 3/6, pp. 310–317.

[172] L. Bygrave, 'Where have all the judges gone? Reflections on judicial involvement in developing data protection law', in P. Wahlgren (ed.), *IT och juristutbildning. Nordisk årsbok i rättsinformatik 2000*, Stockholm, Jure AB, 2001, pp. 113–125).

[173] E. Brouwer, *o.c.*, p. 206; L. Bygrave, 'The Place of Privacy in Data Protection Law', § 20.

[174] Compare E. Brouwer, *o.c.*, p. 206.

[175] E. Brouwer, *o.c.*, p. 206.

[176] L. Bygrave, 'The Place of Privacy in Data Protection Law', § 20.

Chapter 2
The Right to Informational Self-Determination and the Value of Self-Development: Reassessing the Importance of Privacy for Democracy

Antoinette Rouvroy and Yves Poullet

2.1 Introduction

In December of 1983, the German Federal Constitutional Court[1] declared unconstitutional certain provisions of the revised Census Act (Volkszählungsurteil) that had been adopted unanimously by the German Federal Parliament but were nevertheless challenged by diverse associations before the Constitutional Court. That now classical *avant-garde* decision ruled, based on Articles 1 (human dignity) and 2 (personality right) of the Constitution, that the

> basic right warrants (...) the capacity of the individual to determine in principle the disclosure and use of his/her personal data.

This was one of the first and most famous articulation of a 'right to informational self-determination', understood by the Court as

> the authority of the individual to decide himself, on the basis of the idea of self-determination, when and within what limits information about his private life should be communicated to others.

As we experience a new phase in the development of the information society with, in the technological domain, the advent ubiquitous computing and ambient intelligence and, in the socio-political sphere, the materialization of the shift from a 'control society' to a 'surveillance society'[2], the purpose of the present paper,

A. Rouvroy (✉)
Research associate at the National Fund for Scientific Research (FNRS) and at the IT and Law Research Centre (CRID), University of Namur

[1] BVerfGE 65, 1 – Volkszählung Urteil des Ersten Senats vom 15. Dezember 1983 auf die mündliche Verhandlung vom 18. und 19. Oktober 1983 – 1 BvR 209, 269, 362, 420, 440, 484/83 in den Verfahren über die Verfassungsbeschwerden.

[2] As Gilles Deleuze powerfully explained (Gilles Deleuze, 'Post-scriptum sur les sociétés de contrôle', *L'autre Journal*, n.1, 1990), the proper of modern norms – and that is what characterizes the gradual shift from the disciplinary society described by Michel Foucault and that presupposed the existence of a multiplicity of 'detention' facilities (psychiatric hospitals, factories, schools, prisons,...) to the control society that can increasingly do without physical constraint and direct surveillance, is that it is individuals themselves who have to impose themselves not only to respect

S. Gutwirth et al. (eds.), *Reinventing Data Protection?*

DOI 10.1007/978-1-4020-9498-9_2, © Springer Science+Business Media B.V. 2009

twenty-four years after that German *avant-garde* decision, is to elucidate the conceptual relationships existing between the *rights* to privacy and data protection on the one hand, and on the other hand, the fundamental *values* those rights are assumed to protect and which were identified by the German Constitutional Court as human dignity and self-development.[3]

In the present contribution, we argue that privacy, as a legal right, should be conceived essentially as an *instrument* for fostering the specific yet changing *autonomic capabilities* of individuals that are, in a given society at a given time, necessary for sustaining a vivid democracy.[4] What those needed capabilities are is obviously contingent both on the characteristics of the constituency considered[5] and on the state of the technological, economic and social forces that must be weighed against each other through the operation of legislative balancing.[6] Capacity for both reflexive autonomy allowing to resist social pressures to conform with dominant views[7] and for deliberative abilities allowing participation in deliberative processes are arguably among the skills that a vivid democracy needs citizens to have in the circumstances of our times.

Those capabilities are threatened in unprecedented manners by the intensification of observation and monitoring technologies such as CCTV, data mining and profiling, RFID and the 'internet of things', ubiquitous computing and 'ambient intelligence'.[8] The news that Microsoft was filing a patent claim for a spyware

---

but also to adhere to the norms, who have to integrate those norms in their biography, through their own actions and reiterations. Power takes, in modern society, the form of offers of services or of inciting actions much more than of of constraints.

[3] The choice made by the German Constitutional Court to rely on these values instead of others may well be contingent to the German constitutional history and culture. The link established between self-determination and dignity does have normative consequences though, to the extent that the notion of dignity suggests incommensurability and inalienability.

[4] See in the same sense Cass R. Sunstein, *Why Societies Need Dissent*, Harvard University Press, 2003, pp. 157–158: 'The Right to privacy (...) can be illuminated if we see it as an effort to allow people to escape reputation pressures. Suppose, for example, that people are allowed to read whatever they like in the privacy of their own homes, or that actions which are forbidden in public, either by law or by norms, are legally protected if done in private. Or suppose that law creates safeguards against public observation of what is done in certain sanctuaries. If this is so, the privacy right will operate to reduce or to eliminate the pressure imposed by the actual or perceived views of others (...) privacy rights helps to insulate people from conformity.'

[5] Important elements of cultural and epochal incommensurability make the development of a universal theory of privacy most implausible.

[6] The German decision explicitly acknowledges that 'The general personality law (...) gains in importance if one bears in mind modern developments with attendant dangers to the human personality.'

[7] See Cass R. Sunstein, *Why Societies Need Dissent*, Harvard University Press, 2003: 'Well-functioning societies take steps to discourage conformity and to promote dissent. They do this partly to protect the rights of dissenters, but mostly to protect interests of their own.'

[8] For further reflections on how the Internet revolution and more recently the Ambient Intelligence technologies are metamorphosing the risks incurred by the individuals and their basic rights and call for new legislative actions reinforcing the different identified facets of the right to privacy, see Antoinette Rouvroy, 'Privacy, Data Protection, and the Unprecedented Challenges of Ambient Intelligence', *Studies in Ethics, Law, and Technology* 2008, vol. 2, Issue 1. Available at: http://works.bepress.com/antoinete_rouvroy/2

system linking employees to their computers with wireless sensors and enabling employers to monitor their employees' blood pressure, body temperature, heart rate and facial expression throughout the day, exemplifies the phenomenon: under constant, yet most of the time remote, surveillance and subjected to automatic or semi-automatic decisions taken by the 'system' on the basis of constant observation of their choices, behaviours and emotions, individuals may be said increasingly under the influence of those 'normative technologies' and, therefore, decreasingly capable of living by their fully autonomous choices and behaviours.

The German Court acknowledged that self-imposed restrictions on deviant behaviours, or on participation in assembly or civil society initiative by fear that these behaviours and participations be disclosed to others with adverse consequences ensuing

> would not only impair his chances of development but would also impair the common good ("Gemeinwohl"), because self-determination is an elementary functional condition of a free democratic community based on citizens' capacity to act and cooperate.

The importance of privacy and data protection regimes today, it will be argued, derives from the support they provide for individuals to keep or develop those autonomic capacities to act and cooperate.

Our contribution will consist in four parts. In the first section, we wish to reassess the need for the type normative inquiry we are engaged in. In the second section, we wish to dispel some misleading interpretations that could be made of the trope 'informational self-determination'. Then, in the third section, the German Federal Constitutional Courts's decision will be commented, as to enlighten the present relevance of its rationales. A fourth section will allow us to clarify certain issues regarding the 'values' or 'basic rights' of dignity and self-determination or autonomy. Finally, we explore various 'facets' of the generic right to privacy and finding how those facets might be articulated around the principle of self-determination.

2.2 Why Re-Anchoring the Rights to Privacy and Data Protection in the Fundamental Ethical and Political Values?

Re-anchoring the rights to privacy and data protection in the fundamental ethical and political values from which they derive their normative force and that they are meant to advance has become crucial.

In the United States, the Supreme Court has repeatedly conditioned acknowledgement of the existence of a right of privacy in any given area of human life to the pre-existence of 'reasonable expectations of privacy' of those areas. Scholars have widely criticized the insufficiency of that non-normative assessment in technology-intensive societies. Nicole E. Jacoby, for example, comparing how judges in the US and in Germany identify when and in which circumstances an individual's right to privacy has been violated, showed that, in dealing with new technical surveillance measures the 'expectations of privacy' standard in use in the United States was much less protective of the individual confronted with surveillance than the

German Court's reliance on the principle, anchored in the value of human dignity, that individuals have an inviolable domain in which they may freely develop their personality.[9] Indeed, the obvious disadvantage of the volatile standard of 'expectations of privacy' is that expectations are not, as a matter of fact, independent of the level of surveillance and scrutiny in place. It means that in societies with intense surveillance systems, individuals indeed do not expect to have much privacy left. The scope of privacy, in such a conceptualization, may not extend much beyond the very narrow areas of life that surveillance technologies are not yet able to capture and is inherently dependent on the actual stage of technological development.

A theory of privacy relying on 'expectations of privacy' can not be justified either by saying that what privacy is about is the right individuals have not to be 'surprised' by surveillance devices did not expect to be there. Even where people know they are observed and thus have no expectation of privacy because they have been informed that surveillance devices are in use, surveillance, even overt and not hidden, may cause people harm that they would probably call invasions of their privacy. The most unsophisticated example of this would be an instance where video cameras would have been placed in public toilets. More subtle instances would be, for example, instances where employees would know they are being monitored by their employer and their productivity evaluated in real time. Although they do not have *expectations* of privacy in that case, they still have lost something that very much resembles 'their privacy'.

It is not useless to recall though that although 'expectations of privacy' do not play such an important role for the definition of the scope of privacy in Europe, the decrease of expectations of privacy will necessarily negatively impact on the probability that people will indeed claim respect of their right to privacy in those new areas where they are 'observed', or refuse their consent to being 'observed'. Preserving awareness about issues of privacy might happen to be both of paramount importance and enormously challenging the more we progress in the surveillance society.

Another method, more usual in Europe, for balancing competing interests and establishing whether or not, in each situation, there is a right to privacy or not, and whether or not legitimate and sufficiently compelling reasons exist for allowing interferences with that right, is normative inquiry required by Article 8§2 of the European Convention on Human Rights, among other texts:

> There shall be no interference by a public authority with the exercise of this right except such as is in accordance with the law and is necessary in a democratic society in the interests of national security, public safety or the economic well-being of the country, for the prevention of disorder or crime, for the protection of health or morals, or for the protection of the rights and freedoms of others.

[9] Nicole E. Jacoby, 'Redefining the Right to Be Let Alone. Privacy Rights and the Constitutionality of Technological Surveillance Measures in Germany and the United States', *Bepress Working Papers Series*, 2006, No. 1515.

One of the most paradigmatic examples of normative inquiry has been exhibited in the already mentioned German Constitutional Court's (Bundesverfassungsgerichtshof) decision of December 15, 1983[10], about the constitutional limits to governmental collection of personal data for statistical purposes. The German Constitutional Court traced the foundations of a general 'right to informational self-determination' ('Informationelles selbstbestimmung') and thus of legal data protection regimes and, more broadly, of the right to privacy, to the fundamental right to the 'free development of one's personality'[11] protected by Article 2.1. of the German Constitution:

> The value and dignity of the person based on free self-determination as a member of a free society is the focal point of the order established by the Basic Law. The general personality right as laid down in Arts 2 (1) i.c.w 1(1) GG serves to protect these values (...)

The German Constitutional Court's 1983 'census decision' might be an invaluable source of inspiration to address the unprecedented challenges of the advanced information society, where the combined socio-political and technological challenges of the time have made privacy (as well as expectations of privacy) and data protection claims appear relatively weak compared to the systematic normative privileging of transparency ensuing from the absolute logics of security and economic efficiency on the one hand[12] and, on the other hand, the development and dissemination of increasingly sophisticated and ubiquitous surveillance and tracking systems collecting and processing even the most trivial information about individuals.

It appears a reasonable assumption to have that in order to both re-situate the pervasive absolute logics in their relative frame and adapt our legal framework to the nature of the threats exactly are the values we consider threatened in the advanced information society presupposes one knows. Referring the right to privacy to the

---

[10] Constitutional Court, Dec. 15, 1983, *EuGRZ*, 1983, p; 171 and ff. On this decision, read E.H. Riedl, 'New bearings in German Data Protection', *Human Rights Law Journal*, 1984, Vol. 5, No. 1, pp. 67 and ff.; H. Burkert, 'Le jugement du Tribunal Constitutionnel fédéral allemand sur le recensement démographique et ses consequences', *Dr. Inf.*, 1985, pp. 8 and ff. See also E. Brouwer (2007), *Digital Borders and Real Rights*, Nijmegen, Wolf Legal Pub, 501 p.

[11] Although the Court acknowledges that the scope and content of that 'personality right' had not been conclusively settled by case law, it nevertheless indicates that that right 'comprises the authority of the individual to decide for himself based on the idea of self-determination – when and within what limits facts about one's personal life shall be disclosed.' Yet, far from the interpretation of privacy as 'property' advanced by law and economics scholars, one understands from reading the decision through that this 'authority' of the individual is not an end in itself: it prevents situations where inhibition of the individual's 'freedom to plan or to decide freely and without being subject to any pressure/influence (i.e., self-determined). The right to self-determination in relation to information precludes a social order and a legal order enabling it, in which the citizens no longer can know who knows what, when, and on what occasion about them.'

[12] Where by individual transparency is systematically encouraged and reluctance to disclose personal information is often interpreted as meaning that the individual indeed has something (wrong) to hide. On the contrary, businesses are discouraged from being 'transparent' where the market negatively sanctions disclosure of trade secrets.

values in which it finds its roots provides contemporary scholars confronted with the unprecedented and unpredictable developments of information and communication technologies with solid objectives against which to assess the adequacy of current legislation and propose reasoned improvements.

We should note, however, that the recent enactment of Article 8 of the Charter of the European Union and the quasi-constitutional status thereby acknowledged to the right to data protection, instead of clarifying the issue, might, on certain points, further complicate the normative assessment. Indeed, the provision could well be interpreted as ascribing data protection a final, intrinsic value, thereby obscuring what seems to us an important aspect: the rather 'intermediate' or 'instrumental' value of data protection as a 'tool' for the preservation and promotion of more fundamental and basic values (namely the value of autonomic self-development and political participation). Moreover, among the disadvantages of granting a *final* rather than merely an *intermediate* value to the rights to data protection and privacy is the risk of increased rigidity and lack of plasticity of the relevant laws and their ensuing inability to meet the evolving challenges of the contemporary and future information society. In a sense, we wish to explain how privacy and data protection interact to form the immune system of the psychic space and, as any immune system, must evolve to fit the evolutions of the 'informational and societal ecosystem'.

The traditionally individualist conception of human rights may, moreover, inspire misleading interpretations of the recent constitutionalisation of the right to data protection. Especially in an era of possessive individualism such as ours, data protection – or the empowerment of individuals with regard to their personal data – risks being interpreted as making the satisfaction individuals' immediate preferences with regard to their personal data, their choices to keep undisclosed or to commodify personal information a *final value*. It is well-known that those preferences would lead a large part of the population to waive any protection of their personal data provided they receive immediate gratifications or commercial advantages. What would be lost in such an interpretation is the *intermediate value* of data protection as an instrument aimed at fostering the autonomic capabilities of individuals and therefore not something they may dispose of or trade on the market of personal information. Possessive individualism combined with the perception of personal information as a commodity freely exchangeable on the market risks, moreover, to result in a situation where disclosure by some of 'their' personal data unavoidably disadvantages those who would prefer not to disclose 'their' personal information.[13]Reassessing the normative grounds of privacy and data protection are thus, in this regard as well, necessary.

[13] When allowed (by law and/or technology) the transparency of *individuals* is usually rewarded on the short- term, whereas their opacity owes them sanctions. When *enterprises* are considered, the opposite is true: transparency puts them at commercial or industrial disadvantage whereas opacity is more profitable.

2.3 The Right to 'Informational Self-Determination': The Subject as Object?

Before turning to the reminder of the German decision which, as will be explained, is highly relevant to discuss the issues just mentioned, we would like to clarify an important conceptual point. The conception of privacy viewed as 'informational self determination' (where data protection issues are – misleadingly – conceived as exhausting what is at stake when one speaks of privacy) is now often taken to be the fundamental justification ground for data protection regimes, not only in Germany but also in the rest of Europe. Yet, that concept of 'informational self determination' is often misunderstood.

Our impression is that the right to informational self-determination should not be interpreted as suggesting that controlling and manipulating information and data about oneself is an exercise of 'self-determination'. Information and data are not the pre-existing 'elements' or 'building blocks' of an individual's personality or 'self'. Such a conception would be misleading and unduly reductionistic: the 'self' is not merely irreducible but also essentially different from 'data' and 'information' *produced about it.* What the expression 'informational self-determination' means is rather that an individual's control over the data and information produced about him is a (necessary but insufficient) precondition for him to live an existence that may be said 'self-determined'. This is an important thing to recall today, as personal data (genetic and/or digital) have become *proxies* for persons with the intensification of governmental 'identity projects'. The recent debates in France about the 'offer' to make DNA testing available to immigration applicants to give evidence of family links with persons legally living in France epitomize a current western governmental tendency to make personal and even more so genetic, information a salient feature of individuals' identities and citizenships and to privilege profiles constructed about people in application of non-transparent algorithms over the applicants' biographical narratives.

Such a misunderstanding has had a very ambivalent impact for the protection of privacy. 'Informational self-determination', in a context of pervasive possessive individualism and at a time where private property and the laws of the market are perceived as the most efficient ways to allocate rights, the right to 'informational self-determination' has increasingly been understood as implying a sort of alienable property right of the individual over his personal data and information, perceived as his property (even in cases where personal information relates to that person's identity, the notion of 'identity theft' attests to the transformation of personal information into the status of 'thing' detached from the data subject). Yet 'information' does not pre-exist to its 'expression' or disclosure (information is always somewhat constructed) – no 'natural', originary rights could thus logically be held by an individual over information and data relating to him. These considerations have consequences with regard to the current debates about commodification *vs.* inalienability of personal information and individual privacy, as will be suggested later on.

The originality of the German Court's holdings in this regard is that, relating informational self-determination to the notion of dignity, it suggests a default regime of market inalienability of personal information. Still, one has to acknowledge that the position of the German Court contrasts with other often competing ways of defining and valuing informational self-determination. To say things caricaturally, the libertarian approach for example, would probably consider the right to data protection an alienable, commodifiable right, whereas egalitarian scholars would rather consider inalienability rules to be essential to protect individuals against discrimination and stigma, especially in the socio-economic sphere. For the purpose of the present contribution, we assume we are in a society placing human dignity and personal autonomy high in the hierarchy of fundamental values, as did the German Federal Constitutional Court of 1983.

2.4 The German Federal Constitutional Court's 'Census' Decision of 1983

The German Court came to acknowledge the protection of personal data not as an end in itself or a final or primary value but 'merely' as a tool (though an essential one), making possible the *exercise* of the fundamental and basic individual 'right' to self-development, while being itself distinct from autonomy, self-determination or self-development (depending how one calls the primary values sustaining privacy). The clarification of this 'intermediate' value of privacy is important if only because it avoids the common conflation of the legal concept of privacy with the broad philosophical, political and psychological concepts of autonomy, self-determination or self-development[14] and the ensuing difficulty to figure out how, exactly, the law should intervene to protect those impalpable values. Most interesting to us, in this German decision, is the argumentation of the Court. Those rationales, we wish to show, may be immensely useful to help clarifying conceptual intricacies characterising privacy and data protection in view of the emerging challenges raised by the exponential development of information and communication technologies on the threshold of an 'ambient intelligence era'.

The following excerpt of the decision deserves quotation. Its wording might be considered not only to describe the situation existing in 1983 but to anticipate the more recent developments of the technologies, as we will show later:

> This authority (the possibility of the individual to decide for himself) particularly needs protection under present and future conditions of autonomic data processing. It is particularly endangered because in reaching decisions one no longer has to rely on manually collected registries and files, but today the technical means of storing individual statements about personal or factual situations of a certain or verifiable people with the aid

[14] The popular theories of privacy as the 'right to be let alone' (Westin and Brandeis), or, as the 'right of the individual . . .to be free from unwarranted government intrusion' (according the Judge Brennan's conception in *Eisenstadt v. Baird* (1972)) lead to confusions between privacy and liberty.

of automatic processing are practically unlimited and can be retrieved in a matter of seconds irrespective of distance. Furthermore, they can be pieced together with other data collection – particularly when integrated information systems are built up – to add up to a partial or virtually complete personality profile, the persons controlled having no sufficient means of controlling its truth and application. The possibility of inspection and of gaining influence have increased to a degree hitherto unknown, and may influence the individuals' behaviour by the psychological pressure exerted by public interests. Even under certain conditions of modern information processing technology, individual self-determination presupposes that the individuals left with the freedom of decision about actions to be taken or to be omitted, including the possibility to follow that decision in practice. If someone cannot predict with sufficient certainty which information about himself in certain areas is known to his social milieu and cannot estimate sufficiently the knowledge of parties to whom communication may be possibly be made, he is crucially inhibited in his freedom to plan or to decide freely and without being subject to any pressure influence. If someone is uncertain whether deviant behaviour is noted down and stored permanent as information, or is applied or passed, he will try not to attract attention by such behaviour. If he reckons that participation in an assembly or a citizens' initiative will be registered officially and that personal risks might result from it, he may possibly renounce the exercise of his respective rights. This would not only impact his chances of development but would also impact the common good ("*Gemeinwohl*"), because self-determination is an elementary functional condition of a free democratic society based on its citizen's capacity to act and to cooperate.

2.4.1 Data Protection Laws Grounded Directly on Fundamental Constitutional Rights

First, there is the acknowledgement that privacy, or data protection, has an 'intermediate' rather than a 'final' value: they are 'tools' through which more fundamental values, or more 'basic' rights – namely human dignity and individual personality right – are pursued. Earlier in the decision, the German Court held that:

> The standard to be applied is the general right to the free development of one's personality. The value and dignity of the person based on free self-determination as a member of the society is the focal point of the order established by the Basic Law (Grundgesetz). The general personality right as laid down in Article 2 (1) and Article 1 (2) GG serves to protect these values – apart from other more specific guarantees of freedom – and gains in importance if one bears in mind modern developments with attendant dangers to the Human personality.

By this assertion, the Court establishes a clear and direct link between the Data Protection regime and two basic values enshrined in the Constitution, interpreting legal data protection regimes as mere *implementations* of those fundamental constitutional rights. The first of those fundamental constitutional rights is the right to respect and protection of one's 'dignity' guaranteed by Article 1 of the Constitution[15] and the second one is the right to 'self-development', enacted by Article 2

[15] Article 1 GG: *'The dignity of man shall be inviolable. To respect and protect it shall be the duty of all states and authorities'.*

of the Constitution.[16] The fact that the Court will refer directly to these principles without mentioning the already existing Data Protection Law is noticeable. In its view, the major data protection principles derive *directly* from these two Constitutional provisions that consecrate the value of autonomy (self-determination) and the incommensurability (dignity) of each person in the society. To be more precise, the Data Protection regime is a tool for ensuring those fundamental values and must be interpreted *in light of those values*, a consideration that would logically have important consequences not only, as already mentioned, in the debates relating to the (in)alienability the rights to privacy and data protection but also for the legislative balancing (proportionality test) in the implementation of data protection principles. Additionally, the Court suggests that these two provisions are not on the same level as the other constitutional provisions guaranteeing more specific freedoms like freedom of association, religion, and expression, all presupposing previous acknowledgement and respect of dignity and of the right to self-development.

2.4.2 Fundamental Values Protected by Evolving Laws in a Contingent World

Second, there is the acknowledgement that technological evolution may require legal protections of privacy to evolve, simply because those technological evolutions threaten, in new ways, the fundamental value of personal autonomy: according to the court, the emergence of legal data protections attests and responds to such a need for legal evolution. Self-determination, according to the Court, 'is endangered primarily by the fact that, contrary to former practice, there is no necessity for reaching back to manually compiled cardboard-files and documents, since data concerning the personal or material relations of a specific individual {personal data [cf. Federal Data Protection Act Article 2 Para. 1]} can be stored without any technical restraint with thanks to automatic data processing and can be retrieved any time within seconds, regardless of the distance. Furthermore, in case of information systems integrated with other databases, data can be integrated into a partial or complete picture of an individual, without the informed consent of the subject concerned, regarding the correctness and use of data.' What 'self-determination' presupposes and what it allows in a given society is unavoidably contingent on many evolving factors. Besides the state of technological development – suggested by L. Lessig as the central, if not exclusive, reason to adapt our normative instruments – taking the nature of prevailing institutional arrangements and socio-political structures into

[16] Article 2 GG: '*Everybody shall have the right to the free development of his personality insofar he does not violate the rights of others or offend against the constitutional order or the moral order.*'

account is critical in explaining the chronological development of the various and interdependent facets of the right to privacy.

It also means that the laws guaranteeing privacy and enforcing data protection must evolve as to fit the technological and socio-political evolutions generating new threats for the individuals' capacity for 'self-development' of their personality. According to the Constitutional Court's opinion the development of the data processing technologies obliged the State to revise and adapt the guarantees it provides to individuals in order to protect and foster the capabilities needed to implement their right to freely self-determine their personality. In the circumstances of the day, the legal protections offered to the individuals' capabilities for self-development would probably need to address the specific threats accompanying the development of ubiquitous computing and ambient intelligence, as will be further explored in Section 3.

The 'evolutionist' approach of law attested by the Constitutional Court ought to be underlined. In such a perspective, the importance of protecting the individual aptitude to self-determination is not only grounded on the interests of the concerned individuals but also and fundamentally so, in the collective or societal interest in preserving a free and democratic society: individual autonomy and deliberative democracy presuppose a series of rights and liberties allowing individuals to live a life characterized as (partly at least) self-determined, self-authored or self-created, following plans and ideals – a conception of the good – that they have chosen for themselves.[17] In that sense, the right to privacy is not something citizens are entitled to barter. Privacy is rather a social structural imperative in a democracy, since a precondition to democratic deliberation is that individuals feel free and are free to express themselves without fear of being judged out of context or by public and/or private bureaucracies interpreting their expressed thoughts and behaviours from a distance, on the basis of information collected and processed by them. Maintaining and fostering private *and public* expression of individuals' thoughts, preferences, opinions and behaviours is among the obligations of the State in democratic societies.[18] The German Constitutional Court therefore explicitly acknowledged that

[17] See Onora O'Neill, *Autonomy and Trust in Bioethics (Gifford Lectures, 2001)*, Cambridge University Press, 2002, recalling the wide variety of notions that have been associated to the concept of autonomy by scholars such as Gerald DWORKIN, *The Theory and Practice of Autonomy*, Cambridge University Press, 1988, listing liberty (positive or negative), dignity, integrity, individuality, independence, responsibility and self-knowledge, self-assertion, critical reflection, freedom from obligation, absence of external causation and knowledge of one's own interest as concepts that have been equated to the concept of autonomy, or as Ruth Faiden and Thomas Beauchamps, *A History and Theory of Informed Consent*, Oxford University Press, 1986, according to whom autonomy may also be defined as privacy, voluntariness, self-mastery, choosing freely, choosing one's own moral position and accepting responsibility for one's choices.

[18] 'From it follows that it is a prerequisite of free development of the personality under modern conditions of data processing; the individual needs protection against unlimited collection, storage and transmission of his personal data.'

> it is a prerequisite of free development of the personality under modern conditions of data processing; the individual needs protection against unlimited collection, storage and transmission of his personal data.

The basic right to informational self-determination (based on the fundamental principles of dignity and self-development) provides individuals the power to decide themselves about issues of collection, disclosure and use of their personal data.

The right to informational self-determination is not absolute though, as the Court explicitly acknowledges that

> The individual does not possess a right in a sense of an absolute, unlimitable mastery of "his" data; rather he is a personality dependant on communication developing within the social community. Information, even if personality based, is a reflection of social reality and cannot be associated purely with the individual concerned. The Basic Law has decided the tension between the individual and society in favour of the individual being community related and community bound.

As already mentioned above, due to this conception of the individual who needs interactions with others, the (individual, private businesses, governmental) stakeholders' respective interests must be balanced against each other.[19] Therefore, the Court recalls the importance of the 'proportionality principle' as a constitutional principle that 'follows from the essence of basic rights, as an expression of the citizens' claim to freedom (. . .). Considering the dangers of utilizing automatic data processing outlined above, the legislator more than previously is under the duty to institute organisational and procedural safeguards which counteract the dangers of infringements of the personality rights.'

Interferences with the right to informational self-determination are allowed only when 'predominant public (or private) interests' outweigh the individual interest founding the right to self-development and that no alternative solutions less intrusive might be found to achieve these interests. Clarity and transparency of legal rules and principles ('Normenklarheit') following the more general principle of the rule of law ('Rechtstaat') must also be respected according to the Court decision.

---

[19] According to P.De Hert and S.Gutwirth ('Privacy, Data Protection and law enforcement. Opacity of the individuals and transparency of the power', in *Privacy and the Criminal Law*, E. Claes et alii (ed.), Interscientia, Antwerpen-Oxford, 2006, p.74): 'Never does an individual have an absolute control over an aspect of his or her privacy. If individuals do have freedom to organise life as they please, this will only remain self-evident up to the point that it causes social or inter-subjective friction. At that stage, the rights, freedoms and interests of others, as well as the prerogatives of the authorities come into play. The friction, tension areas and conflicts create the need for a careful balancing of the rights and interests that give privacy its meaning and relevance. This shows clearly that, although quintessential for a democratic constitutional state, because it refers to liberty, privacy is a relational, contextual and per se social notion which only requires substance when it clashes with other private or public interests.'

2.4.3 *Privacy as a Social-Structural Tool for Preserving a Free and Democratic Society: The Co-Originality of Private and Public Autonomy*

Third, there is the acknowledgement that privacy and data protection are social-structural tools for preserving a free and democratic society. The right to self-development attaches to the members of a free society. In other words, privacy and data protection regimes are not there merely to protect the best right holders interests of the (and, indeed, as has been widely discussed in debates about the commodification of personal information, those best interests many sometimes be better promoted by disclosing personal information than by maintening 'secrecy') but are necessary, in a democratic society, to sustain a vivid democracy. There, the German decision is crystal clear in its consideration that 'if one cannot with sufficient surety be aware of who knows what about them. Those who are unsure if differing attitudes and actions are ubiquitously noted and permanently stored, processed or distributed will try not to stand out with their behaviour. Those who count with the possibility that their presence at a meeting or participation in a civil initiation be registered by the authority, will be incited to abandon practising their basic rights (Basic Law, Article 8 §. 9).'

As a matter of fact, the 1983 German Constitutional Court decision considers individual autonomy not as a radical seclusion and independence of the person vis-à-vis his social environment but as the autonomy of a person radically inserted in society and living and communicating with others. On that point, the decision reiterates the point of view already expressed in 1954[20] by the same Supreme Court:

> L'image de l'Homme qui sous-tend la Loi fondamentale n'est pas celle d'un individu solitaire et souverain. Dans la tension existent entre l'individu et la collectivité, la Loi fondamentale a au contraire voulu privilégier les liens de relation et solidarité entre la personne et la Communauté.[21]

The liberty protected by the Constitution is in no way comparable with 'Robinson Crusoë's liberty, German scholars acknowledged.[22] The right to self-development is not conceived as a liberty held in isolation by an individual living secluded from the rest of society but, on the contrary, as a right enjoyed as member of a free society. The Constitutional Court refers to the Kantian concept of freedom that presupposes individuals to have the possibility to develop their personalities through interactions and conversations they have with others and which, thus, is circumscribed by the

[20] BVerfG July 20, 1954, *BVerfGE*, 4, 7, 15–16.

[21] Translation suggested by M.T. Meulders-klein, 'L'irrésistible ascension de la 'vie privée' au sein des droits de l'homme', in F. Sudre (ed.), *Le droit au respect de la vie privée au sens de la Convention européenne des droits de l'homme*, Collection Droit et Justice 63, Bruxelles, Nemesis, Bruylant, 2005.

[22] Besides the authors already mentioned, one may also refer to Mainz, Dürig, Herzog, *Grunggesetz Kommentar*, München, C.H.Beck, under Article 2.

legitimate demands of society.[23] This justifies the fact that, because individuals need interactions and cooperation with others and with the State in order to self-develop, data protection organises a system of *disclosure* of personal data respectful of the individual's right to self-determination, as both opacity and transparency therefore contribute to sustaining the individual's self-development.

Self-determination, it may even be argued, is not an independent value but a tool for guaranteeing the democratic functioning of society.

> Human rights and liberties not only restrict the power of the State but also empower citizens to participate in the political system. These rights and liberties enable citizens to develop and exercise their moral powers informing revising and in rationally pursuing their conceptions of the good.[24]

Inspiration for thinking about the mutual reinforcement of private and public autonomy (the idea that they are 'co-originated') can be found in Habermas's discourse theory of law according to which 'Just those action norms are valid to which all possibly affected persons could agree as participants in rational discourses'. In such a perspective, the right to self-development constitutes a precondition to real democratic discussion. This idea of the 'co-originality' of private and public autonomy also transpires, implicitly, in most defences of privacy based on its structural value for society by authors like Schwartz and Treanor, Flemming and others.[25]

2.5 'Dignity' and 'Autonomy': A Few Words of Conceptual Clarification

The Karlsruhe judges anchored their approach of the right to privacy in two distinct constitutional provisions reflecting the primacy, in the German constitutional order, of two fundamental values: human dignity on the one hand and individual

---

[23] Let us note here that theoretically, on Kantian grounds, on the condition that the State is legitimate, there are no reasons to think of the individual's and the State's interests as conflicting with each other (see the Kantian ideal of universalisable reason according to which an autonomous individual cannot reasonably wish something that is not, at the same time, something that all his community, thus the State, would wish. In this regard, Rawls's conception that the State's unique justification is the guarantee of the maximum liberty for each individual is somewhat radically alien to Kant's lessons, as taken over by Habermas among others).

[24] P. De Hert and S. Gutwirth already quoted, p. 64. These authors are referring to Rawls', Dworkin's and Habermas's conceptions of Human Rights.

[25] Jürgen Habermas, *Between Facts and Norms*, MIT Press, 1996; P.M. Schwartz, and W.M. Treanor, 'The New Privacy', Michigan Law Review, 101, 2003, p.216; James E. Flemming, 'Securing Deliberative Autonomy', *Stanford Law Review*, Vol. 48, No. 1, 1995, pp. 1–71, arguing that the bedrock structure of deliberative autonomy secures basic liberties that are significant preconditions for persons' ability to deliberate about and make certain fundamental decisions affecting their destiny, identity, or way of life. On deliberative democracy, see James E. Flemming, 'Securing Deliberative Democracy', *Fordham Law Review*, Vol. 72, p. 1435, 2004. On the concept of co-originality, see Rainer Nickel, 'Jürgen Habermas' concept of co-originality in times of globalisation and the militant security state', IUE Working Paper Law, 2006/27.

self-development in a free society on the other hand. The combination of those values inspired the Court's acknowledgement that a 'generic right to personhood' ('An Allgemeines Persönlichkeitsrecht'), existed as the hardest core of the legal constitutional order of the German Republic. That right, transposed in the technological context of 1983, was to be understood as a right to informational self-determination that justified the adoption of the Data Protection Act. Reference to its constitutional inspiration guides the interpretation to be given of that Data Protection Act.

Reference to the value of human dignity places the legal regime of data protection in a human-centred perspective and in a vision of society requiring technological developments to be developed at the service of the development of human personality, which is, 'the attributes of an individual which are irreducible in his selfhood.'[26] According to the German Constitutional Court, 'the right to privacy protects the individual's interest in becoming, being and remaining a person.'[27] Dignity, unlike autonomy, is unconditionally 'attached' to each human being. A person who, as a matter of fact, is not 'autonomous' has, nevertheless, 'dignity'. In a Kantian sense, human dignity is a condition of human beings that they are acknowledged because of their theoretical or generic capacity to exhibit autonomy, without regard to whether they actually develop that capacity for autonomy or not.

Privacy is thus a legal concept, or an 'intermediate value' for the fostering of the socio-political ideals (or 'final values') of liberty, autonomy and self-determination. Autonomy and self-determination (exhibited for example when individuals hold ideas or have lifestyles that might be politically and socially unpopular) cannot be characterized as legal 'rights', they are not something that the State can 'provide' the individuals with and the mere abstention by the State to intrude or interfere with 'private' or 'intimate' affairs is obviously not enough to 'make' individuals autonomous.[28] Like happiness, autonomy or self-determination, is a matter of degree. The conditions for individual autonomy are so diverse, so subjective in a sense, that no law could really ensure the genuine effectuation of a 'right to autonomy'.[29]

They are capabilities that not all individuals wish and/or have the aptitude to develop. Individual autonomy, not more than musical talent, artistic gifts of happiness, is something that the State, through the law, could never 'provide' to

---

[26] P. Freund, quoted by D. Solove, 'Conceptualizing Privacy', 90 *Cal. Law Rev.*, 2002, 1090.

[27] J.H. Reiman, 'Privacy, Intimacy, and personhood', in *Philosophical dimensions of Privacy*, F.D. Schoeman (ed.), p. 314. See also, J. Rubenfeld, 'The Right of Privacy', 102 *Harv. Law Rev.*, 1989, pp. 737–807.

[28] Sustaining that mere immunity from intrusion or interference from state or from others with my 'personal' affairs makes me an autonomous person amounts to confusion between the concepts of autonomy and of *negative liberty*. To give a paradigmatic example: a left alone child under the age of five is indeed enjoying the *negative liberty* that non interference in one's private affairs provides but he is certainly not enjoying *autonomy* and may moreover be assumed to be deprived from *real liberty*, subjected as he will probably be to hunger and all other threats that children left alone endure.

[29] Considering the 'right to autonomy' as a fundamental human right would require justification for any restriction on that 'right' imposed by the parents to their child.

individuals. A 'right to be autonomous' would not make more sense for the law than a 'right to be happy'. What does exist is a right to the pursuit of happiness (e.g., the American Declaration of Independence of 1776 proclamation: 'We hold these truths to be self-evident, that all men are created equal, that they are endowed by their Creator with certain unalienable Rights, that among these are Life, Liberty and the pursuit of Happiness') and, arguably, a right to the pursuit of autonomy.

However, despite the law's inability to 'create' or 'guarantee' individual autonomy, showing *respect* for individual autonomy[30] and, as far as possible, providing some of the conditions necessary for individuals to develop their capacity for individual deliberative autonomy (the individual process of self-governance) and for collective deliberative democracy (the group-oriented process for critical discourse indispensable to a vivid democracy) have become the most fundamental and basic ethical and legal imperatives in contemporary western societies, where respecting those imperatives is perceived as a precondition to the legality and legitimacy of the law. Individual autonomy and deliberative democracy presuppose a series of rights and liberties allowing individuals to spend a life characterized as (in part at least) self-determined, self-authored or self-created, following plans and ideals – a conception of the good – that they have chosen for themselves.

An important lesson derived from the German Constitutional Court's approach, is, as previously said, the fact that privacy is not considered merely as an individualistic value. As P. Regan[31] expressed it, 'Privacy has value beyond its usefulness in helping the individual to maintain his or her dignity or develop personal relationships. Most privacy scholars emphasize the individual is better off if privacy exists. I maintain that the society is better off as well when privacy exists. I maintain that privacy serves not just individual interests but also common, public and collective purposes.'

---

[30] Respect for individual autonomy of persons and thus for the choices they make, is contingent, in law, to the consideration that the subject is *indeed* autonomous in the choices he makes. That condition of autonomy implies the absence of either physical, mental or economic coercion. Legal interference with lawful, fully conscious and unforced choices of capable individuals is considered unacceptable, even if interference arises for the sake of the subject's own good, in which case one speaks of unacceptable legal paternalism.

[31] P. M. Regan, *Legislating Privacy, Technology, Social Values and Public Policy*, New York, 1995, pp. 321. See also D. Solove '*The Digital person, Technology and privacy in an Information Age*', New York University Press, 2004, pp. 57 and ff. and Schwartz, 'Beyond Code for Internet Privacy: Cyberspace Filters, Privacy control, and Fair Information Practice', *Wisconsin Law Rev.*, 2000, p.787.): 'In place of Lessig's idea that privacy protects a right of individual control, this Article has developed a concept of constitutive privacy. Information Privacy is a constitutive value that safeguards participation and association in a free society. Rather than simply seeking to allow more and more individual control of personal data, we should view the normative function of information privacy as inhering in its relation to participatory democracy and individual self determination. Information Privacy rules should carry out a constitutive function by normally defining multi-dimensional information territories that insulate personal data from the observation of different parties.'

As expressed by Burkert[32], privacy may be considered a '*fundamentally fundamental right'*. Privacy is not a freedom on the same rank than the others: essential to human dignity and individual autonomy and translating these moral principles in the legal sphere, privacy is a necessary precondition to the enjoyment of most other fundamental rights and freedoms.

However, one may but acknowledge the quintessential indeterminacy of privacy. Awkward as it may appear, this indeterminacy is unavoidable, as what one understands as being in the scope of privacy is 'fundamentally' contingent on the societal context in which our autonomic capabilities as individuals have to be protected. In that sense, one may only agree with Burkert's view that privacy is also a 'fundamentally relative right.'[33] What is meant by privacy and how it is protected must evolve to face the changing threats to human dignity and individual autonomy and must be found taking fully into account the context in which our liberties have to express themselves, as Solove argued.[34] The enactment of data protection legislations should be seen in that light as an attempt, certainly not the last one, to face the unprecedented challenges of the already elapsed time when those data protection regimes were set.

2.6 The 'Facets' of Privacy and How They Can Be Articulated to Protect and Promote Autonomous Self-Development

Exploring what 'self-development' would mean in a society such as ours and identifying the legal instruments susceptible to contribute to the protection of such a capability in the circumstances of our times, will amount to analyse the different aspects or conceptions of the generic right to 'privacy', in the chronological order of their surfacing in jurisprudence and scholarship.

Privacy has first been conceptualized as 'seclusion' (opacity, or privacy as solitude)[35], before being understood as also encompassing a dimension of

---

[32] H.Burkert, 'Dualities of Privacy – An Introduction to 'Personal Data Protection and Fundamental Rights'', *in Privacy- New visions*, M.V. Perez, A. Palazzi, Y. Poullet (eds.), Cahier du Crid, to be published in 2008.

[33] 'This is not an attempt to reconstruct a ranking of fundamental rights, an exercise that would only undermine the legitimacy of all fundamental rights including those, which might end up on a 'higher' rank. The term 'fundamentally fundamental' is only meant as a pointer to the functional importance of 'privacy' as a fundamental right. This importance, however, seems to clash with what we have already observed before when speculating on this fundamentalism and what I would call here the factual unimportance of 'privacy' due to its relativity: 'Privacy' is being regarded as a 'relatively fundamental' right which has to – it seems – reconstitute itself anew in a balancing of interests in each and every new informational conflict.'

[34] D.J. Solove, '*Conceptualizing Privacy'*, 90 *California Law Review*, 2002, 1085 et s. ; P.Blok, *Het recht op privacy*, Boom Juridische uitgevers, 2003.

[35] See Ruth Gavison, 'Privacy and the Limits of the Law', 89 *Yale Law Journal*, 1980, pp. 421–471. See also Judith W. Decew, *In Pursuit of Privacy: Law, Ethics and the Rise of Technology*, Cornell University Press, 1997.

'non-interference' (decisional privacy, or privacy as liberty)[36] and, finally, of individual informational control or empowerment ('the ability of an individual to control the terms under which their personal information is acquired and used'[37], formalised through fair information practices).[38]

Those 'facets' of privacy have emerged from competing theoretical constructions that have long struggled against each other to gain the monopoly in defining what privacy is about. Our aim here will be to attempt reconciling those 'visions' or 'theories' of privacy, insisting on their common roots and their complementariness. Of particular interest to us will be the question how the 'data protection branch' of privacy would benefit from reassessing its connectedness with the other traditional branch of privacy sometimes simply defined as 'the right to be let alone' but implying both a notion of seclusion and a notion of decisional autonomy, as attested by the evolution in this regard of both the Strasbourg Human Rights jurisprudence giving effect to Article 8 of the European Convention of Human Rights and the US Supreme Court decisions relating to privacy.

2.6.1 The Right to Privacy as 'Seclusion', 'Opacity' or 'Solitude'

The scholarly genesis of the right to 'informational privacy' may be traced back to Warren and Brandeis' classical 1890 Harvard Law Review article of 1890. Already then, privacy was presented as an adaptation of, or as an adjunction to, pre-existing legal rights, that technological and social evolution had rendered necessary: 'Political, social, and economic changes entail the recognition of new rights, and the common law, in its eternal youth, grows to meet the new demands of society.' And already then, it was acknowledged that '[T]he principle which protects personal writings and all other personal productions, not against theft and physical appropriation, but against publication in any form, is in reality not the principle of private property, but that of an inviolate personality' that Warren and Brandeis equated with the 'right to be left alone' when writing that '(...) the protection afforded to thoughts, sentiments, and emotions, expressed through the medium of writing or of the arts, so far as it consists in preventing publication, is merely an instance of the enforcement of the more general right of the individual to be let alone'. That 'principle' was conceived to protect 'the privacy of the individual from invasion

[36] See *Griswold v. Connecticut*, 281 US 479 (1965), a case taken to be the first judicial acknowledgement of the right of privacy by the US Supreme Court, in which it invalidated a law forbidding married people from using contraceptives.

[37] M.J. Culnan, 'Protecting Privacy online: Is self-regulation working?', 19 *Journal of Public Policy Market*, 2000, 1, pp. 20 and ff.

[38] See for instance Charles Fried, 'Privacy: A Rational Context.', in. M. David Ermann, Mary B. Williams and Claudio Guitierrez, *Computers, Ethics, and Society*, Oxford University Press, 1990; Arthur Miller, *The Assault on Privacy*, Harvard University Press, 1971.

either by the too enterprising press, the photographer, or the possessor of any other modern device for rewording or reproducing scenes or sounds.'[39]

In Europe, the right to privacy is explicitly acknowledged by Article 8 of the European Convention of Human Rights. The initial interpretation of that right resembled the American 'right to be left alone', in the intimacy of one's private and family life, home and correspondence, but – and this is quite paradoxical in view of the subsequent evolutions in this regard – contrary to the American doctrine of privacy, the European right was not primarily directed against interferences by other individuals (journalists) but against intrusions by the State in the sanctity of home and of correspondence. The early version of the right to privacy was, in the context of traditional society, not merely seen as ensuing from the principle of human dignity but also as a precondition to the free development of personality. It means that each individual must have a physical place where to express him or herself and the possibility to exchange views or to reveal his intimate convictions to others through private communications means without being observed from outside or by third parties.[40]

As a matter of fact, total transparency would impair the possibility for individuals to freely develop their personality. They need some 'secrecy, anonymity and solitude', 'withdrawal and concealment'[41] in order to reflect on their own preferences and attitudes, or, in other words, to reflexively make and revise choices in life, as well as to develop meaningful relationships with others. Friendship and love do not easily develop in a crowd; they necessitate selective retreat and seclusion. Even in the traditional villages, the role played by the walls of the private home included the protection of a sphere of intimacy where individuals felt allowed to give up, for the time of the private encounter, the role he or she endorses in public. In that sense, the 'right to opacity' is a precondition to the very existence of the 'authenticity' of the self and to the implementation of the ability we have, as human beings, to develop our personal identity. Our 'inviolate personality' may only grow in the shadow of partial opacity.[42] The 'right to opacity' protects the individual from others watching, scrutinizing or spying on his or her private realm. It protects against public and

---

[39] S. Warren and L. Brandeis, 'The Right to Privacy', *Harvard Law Review*, 4(5), 1890. See also D. Solove, 'Conceptualizing Privacy', 90 *California Law Rev.*, 2001, pp. 1041–1043.

[40] About the history of the privacy concept, read notably D.J. Solove, *'Conceptualizing Privacy'*, 90 *California Law Review*, 2002, 1085 et s. ; P.BLOK, *Het recht op privacy*, Boom Juridische uitgevers, 2003.

[41] R.Gavison, 'Privacy and the limits of Law', 89 *Yale Law Journal*, 1980, pp. 433 and ff.

[42] See on that issue, the reflections proposed by J. Rayman ('Driving to the Panopticon: A Philosophical Exploration of the Risks to Privacy Posed by the Highway of the Future', 11 *Santa Clara Computer & Techn. Law Journal*, 1995, pp. 22 and ff.), J. Cohen (' Examined Lives: Informational Privacy and the Subject as Object', 52 *Stanford Law Rev.*, 2000, pp. 1373 and ff.) and H.Nissenbaum ('Privacy as contextual Integrity', 79 *George.Washington Law Rev.*, 2004, pp. 150 and ff., who asserts that '*the freedom from scrutiny and zones of 'relative insularity' are necessary conditions for formulating goals, values, conceptions of self and principles of action because they provide venues in which people are free to experiment, act and decide without giving account to others or being fearful of retribution*'.

private global surveillance. As will be suggested later on, this 'right to seclusion' might well be even more vital today in our modern society than ever before, justifying the new legal tools put into place in order to protect 'opacity' against the new technological and socio-political challenges of the day. What characterizes the present Internet world is precisely the unprecedented possibility that surveillance be exercised over each of us through the multiple traces we leave in cyberspace and through the gradual invasion of our private sphere by terminals of multiple and ubiquitous nature (from personal computers, GPS, mobile phones, RFID, etc.), dissolving the traditional separation between public and private spaces.

Privacy as 'seclusion' or as the 'right to be left alone' suggested a geographical scope of application: the 'private sphere' to which the right to privacy applied was bordered by the house's walls or by the private letter's material envelope. As such, the right to privacy as 'seclusion' has attracted much criticism from feminist scholars like Catherine MacKinnon who demonstrated that because privacy prevented the State to interfere in the protected area of family life, it allowed domestic violence to occur and left its victims helpless.[43] The feminist critique of privacy makes it clear that the right to privacy, originally, was not a protection for the individual subject as much as a protection of the familial structure, understood as the basic institution in society.

2.6.2 Privacy as 'Decisional Autonomy'

In Griswold v. Connecticut[44], a case usually taken to be the starting point of the jurisprudential trajectory of the American constitutional right to privacy as 'decisional autonomy', the Supreme Court voided a State criminal law prohibiting the use or distribution of any contraception drug or instrument to married persons on the ground that a protection from State intrusion into marital privacy was a constitutional right, one that was a 'penumbra' emanating from the specific guarantees of the constitution. The nature and scope of this 'penumbral' right to privacy remained uncertain though. Judge Douglas, who spoke for the Court, appeared concerned not only by the intrusion by the police into the private marital bedroom necessary to investigate breaches of the prohibition but also by the special relationship that constitutes marriage and which should not be intruded or controlled by the State. As a result from this dual justification, conservative interpreters of Griswold perceive the decision as protective of the institution of marriage, while other commentators consider that concerns with policy access to the marital bedroom are peripheral to the Court's central concern to provide autonomy with respect to intimate decisions. These alternative rationales make it unclear whether the Court's intention was to protect the institution of marriage per se or whether it intended to protect marriage

---

[43] C. MacKinnon, *Towards a Feminist Theory of the* State, Cambridge: Harvard University Press, 1989.

[44] Griswold v. Connecticut, 381 US 479, 493 (1965).

not for its own sake but because this special relationship provides individuals with a context that fosters autonomous choices on fundamental and existential issues of life such as the choice whether to conceive a child or not. Despite the uncertainties of interpretations, this 'penumbral' right of privacy has been one of the main foundations of the later Supreme Court decision in Roe v. Wade[45] to overturn State abortion statutes. From there on, privacy acquired its truly individual character as a right protecting freedom of choice in intimate issues such as the decision, for a woman, whether to bear or beget a child. 'Decisional privacy', encompasses 'the rights of individuals to make certain kinds of fundamental choices with respect to their personal and reproductive autonomy'.[46] In *Planed Parenthood v. Casey* Case[47], the Supreme Court expressed the consideration that

> At the heart of liberty is the right to define one's own concept of existence, of meaning, of the universe, and of the mystery of human life. Beliefs about these matters could not define the attributes of personhood were they formed under compulsion of the State.[48]

Notwithstanding the different legal strategies to cope with it, autonomy as self-determination or as autonomous construction of one's personality is, in US[49] like in Europe, the crucial value behind privacy.

In Europe, the explicit acknowledgement of privacy in the European Convention on Human Rights made its individualistic orientation indisputable from the start. Moreover, from an initially 'negative' undertone suggesting that the right to privacy merely implied the obligation for the State to abstain from interfering in the private matters of the individuals, the European Court of Human Rights soon interpreted the obligations held by the State quite extensively. Although, according to Konvitz, the essence of privacy is merely 'the claim that there is a sphere of space that has not been dedicated to public use of control'[50], the notions of 'private and family life' has been interpreted extensively by the ECHR, to the effect that the right to privacy protects individuals against invasions of privacy by public authorities or, through the Convention's *horizontal effect*, by other individuals.[51] According to the

---

[45] Roe v. Wade, 410 US 113 (1973).

[46] N.M. Richards, 'The Information Privacy Law Project', *Georgetown Law Journal*, 2006, p.

[47] 505 US 833 (1992).

[48] On the American conception of Privacy and its link with the 'Autonomy' concept, read A.J. Rappaport, 'Beyond Personhood and Autonomy: Theory and Premises of Privacy', *Utah Law Review*, 2001, pp.442 and ff.

[49] On that point particularly, J.S. Mill, *On Liberty*, G.Himmelfarb (ed.), 1984.

[50] Konvitz, 'Privacy and the Law: A Philosophical Prelude', *Law and Contemporary Problems*, 1966, 31, 272, 279–280.

[51] Since the 1981 judgement in *Young, James and Webster v. United Kingdom* (Eur.Ct.H.R., 13 August 1981, Series A No.44) the European Court on Human Rights acknowledges an *horizontal effect* to the Convention, extending the scope of protections to relations between private parties: §49: 'Although the proximate cause of the events giving rise to this case was [an agreement between an employer and trade unions], it was the domestic law in force at the relevant time that made lawful the treatment of which the applicants complained. The responsibility of the respondent State for any resultant breach of the Convention is thus engaged on this basis.' Through this horizontal effect of the Convention, the fundamental rights seem to gain positive effectiveness. The matter is highly

Strasbourg jurisprudence the State is not merely under the obligation to abstain from interfering with individuals' privacy but also to provide individuals with the material conditions needed to allow them to effectively implement their right to private and family life.[52] In other words, according to the theories of the 'positive duties' of the State combined with that of the 'horizontal effect' of the ECHR broadly applied by the European Court of Human rights, States are under the obligation to take all appropriate measures in order to protect fundamental rights of the individuals including against infringements by other non-state parties.

As to the 'scope' of privacy, it has been interpreted by the European Court of Human Rights as encompassing all the domains in which individuals are confronted with the need to make fundamental choices in their life, including their sexual life and sexual preferences[53], their personal and social life[54], their relationships with other human beings[55], the choice of their residence in full knowledge of the environment etc.[56]

Interestingly, the inclusion, in the scope of the right to privacy, of the choice of one's residence in full knowledge of the environment attests to the fact that access to essential information is indeed a precondition to the free development of one's personality. This has justified a number of legislative initiatives in our countries to

---

controversial, however, just as controversial as the question of the conception of privacy either as a mere *privilege* or as a (subjective) *right*. See also *X and Y v. Netherlands*, 8978/80 (1985) ECHR 4 (26 March 1985), Series A, Vol. 91: 'although the object of Article 8 (Art. 8) is essentially that of protecting the individual against arbitrary interference by the public authorities, it does not merely compel the State to abstain from such interference: in addition to this primarily negative undertaking, there may be positive obligations inherent in an effective respect for private or family life (see the Airey judgment of 9 October 1979, Series A No. 32, p. 17, para. 32). These obligations may involve the adoption of measures designed to secure respect for private life even in the sphere of the relations of individuals between themselves.'

[52] The positive duty of the State to provide the means necessary in order to allow effective enjoyment of rights is not as such recognised in the United States, neither by the law, nor by the jurisprudence. This might be only superficially coherent with classical liberalism. Mill's assertion that 'The only freedom which deserves that name is that of pursuing our own good is our own way. . .each is the proper guardian of his own health, whether bodily or mental and spiritual. Mankind are greater gainers by suffering each other to live as seems good to themselves than by compelling each to live as seems good to rest.' (J.S. MILL, op.cit, p. 72, does not necessarily imply that the State should not provide the individuals with the resources they need to pursue their own good.

[53] X and Y v. Netherlands, 8978/80 (1985) ECHR 4 (26 March 1985), Series A, Vol. 91.

[54] Beldjoudi v. France, 12084/86 (1992) ECHR 42 (29 March 1992).

[55] Niemietz v. Germany, 13710/88 ECHR 80 (18 December 1992) Series 1, Vol. 251 B.: 'The Court does not consider it possible or necessary to attempt an exhaustive definition of the notion of 'private life'. However, it would be too restrictive to limit the notion to an 'inner circle' in which the individual may live his own personal life as he chooses and to exclude entirely the outside world not encompassed within that circle. Respect for private life must also comprise to a certain degree the right to establish and develop relationships with other human beings.'

[56] On all these issues, read the different articles published in F.SUDRE (ed.), *Le droit au respect de la vie privée au sens de la Convention européenne des droits de l'homme*, Collection Droit et Justice 63, Bruxelles, Nemesis, Bruylant, 2005.

develop what has been called Universal access to the Information infrastructure and guaranteed access to public informational resources, etc.[57] The Guerra case judged by EHRC[58] is in that perspective and illustrates this movement. In that decision, on the basis of the Article 8 of the EHRC, the Strasbourg judges have asserted the governmental obligation to deliver information about environmental risks to Italian families, which had planned to install their home close to a polluting industrial complex. The Court held that the choice of residence, which is essential to family life, implies, in our Information Society, that the information required for exercising that choice be available to the families.[59]

Besides the development of a right to autonomous and informed decision making in existential matters, the Strasbourg jurisprudence also understood the right to privacy as encompassing informational issues, understanding Article 8 of the European Convention on Human Rights as guaranteeing the individual right to control personal information, including in the workplace[60] (the scope of the right to privacy and of the right to data protection may intersect with regards to 'informational privacy'), the right to access one's personal records.[61]

---

[57] This idea of a 'Public Domain Content' has been clearly promoted by the UNESCO. See, Point 15 of the 'Recommendation concerning the Promotion and Use of Multilingualism and Universal Access to Cyberspace', adopted by the UNESCO General Conference at its 32nd session (Oct. 2003): 'Member States should recognize and enact the right of universal online access to public and government-held records including information relevant for citizens in a modern democratic society, giving due account to confidentiality, privacy and national security concerns, as well as to intellectual property rights to the extent that they apply to the use of such information. International organizations should recognize and promulgate the right for each State to have access to essential data relating to its social or economic situation.'

[58] Guerra v. Italy Case, February 19, 1998.

[59] About this question of the link between Privacy and the different facets of a new Right of access to Public Information resources, read C. de Terwangne, *Société de l'information et mission publique d'information*, Doctoral thesis, Namur, 2000, available at http://www.crid.be/pdf/public/These_cdeterwangne.pdf.

[60] See the recent decision by the European Court on Human Rights, in *Copland v. United Kingdom*, 62617/00 [2007] ECHR 253 (3 April 2007), in which the Court held that monitoring of an employee's emails, Internet usage and telephone calls had breached the employee's right to privacy. The Court held that even monitoring the date and length of telephone conversations and the number dialled could give rise to a breach of privacy. The arguments of the court included the fact that the employee had not been informed that her telephone calls might be subject to monitoring and that, at the time, no law exited in the UK that allowed employers to monitor their employees communications. Indeed, the Regulation of Investigatory Power Act of 2000 was not yet in force at that time. The Court does not investigate whether that Act might be inconsistent with the Human Rights Act however.

[61] Gaskin v. United Kingdom, 10454/83 (1989 ECHR 13 (7 July 1989), Series A No. 160. See also Odièvre v. France, 42326/98 (2003) ECHR 86 (13 February 2003), where the ECHR acknowledged that the right to privacy (Article 8 of the European Convention on Human Rights) protects, among other interests, the right to personal development and acknowledged that matters relevant to personal development included details of a person's identity as a human being and the vital interest in obtaining information necessary to discover the truth concerning important aspects of one's personal identity.

2.6.3 Privacy as 'Informational Self-Determination': Reinventing Data Protection?

2.6.3.1 The Rationales of Data Protection

The fundamental principles of data protection (fair processing, performed for specific purpose, on the basis of the subject's consent or of other legitimate basis laid down by law, subjective rights of the data subject to access and rectify collected data) had been formalized in the Convention for the Protection of Individuals with regards to Automatic Processing of Personal Data of the Council of Europe[62] and reiterated in the fair information principles formalised in the European directive on the protection of individuals with regard to the automatic processing of personal data[63] and in the European directive concerning the processing of personal data and the protection of privacy in the electronic communication sector.[64] 'The ability of an individual to control the terms under which their personal information is acquired and used'[65] is often presented as the hallmark of data protection.

The rationale behind the data protection regimes relates to the risks to individual self-determination carried by the early development of the Information technologies infrastructures. The use of Information Technologies has been considered, from the beginning, as worsening power asymmetries between data subjects (the individuals whose data are processed) and the data controllers (in charge of the collection, storage, processing, use and dissemination of data). Technological developments gradually brought about a situation where '(a) there is virtually no limit to the amount of Information that can be recorded, (b) there is virtually no limit to the scope of analysis that can be done – bounded only by human ingenuity and (c) the information may be stored virtually forever.'[66]

These developments had of course direct impact on the autonomy of the data subjects: vast collections and intensive processing of data enable data controllers such as governmental authorities or private companies to take decisions about individual subjects on the basis of these collected and processed personal information without allowing for any possibility for the data subjects to know exactly which data would be used, for which purposes, for which duration and overall without control of the necessity of these processings in consideration of the purposes pursued by the

[62] Convention for the Protection of Individuals with regards to Automatic Processing of Personal Data of the Council of Europe, ETS No. 108, Strasbourg, 28 January 1981.

[63] Directive 95/46/EC of the European Parliament and of the Council of 24 October 1995 on the protection of individuals with regard to the processing of personal data and on the free movement of such data, *Official Journal* L 281, 23 November 1995.

[64] European Directive 2002/58/EC EC of the European Parliament and of the Council of 17 July 2002 concerning the processing of personal data and the protection of privacy in the electronic communication sector.

[65] M.J. Culnan, 'Protecting Privacy online: Is self-regulation working?', 19 *Journal of Public Policy Market*, 2000, 1, pp. 20 and ff.

[66] H. Nissenbaum, 'Protecting Privacy in a Information Age: the Problem of Privacy in Public.', 17 *Law and Phil.*, 1998, pp. 576.

public or private bureaucracies. Data Protection regimes were thus designed (and, in some countries, translated into self-regulatory measures) in order to better balance 'informational power'. This resulted in a widening of the protection previously limited and centred on intimate and sensitive data, which now included all personal data defined as 'information about identified or identifiable individuals' and in the attribution of new rights to the data subjects, including an 'access right' allowing a better control over the uses and dissemination of personal data and, finally, the imposition of limitations to the permissible processing by data controllers, especially through the requirements that data processing will be fair, legitimate (another word for proportionate both as regards the existence of the processing and its content) and secure.[67]

These main principles might be viewed as a development of the self-determination principle in the area of the personal data flows. 'Informational privacy' had been defined traditionally by the U.S scholars following the A.Westin wording[68], as the 'claim of individuals, groups or institutions to determine for themselves when, how, and to what extent information about them is communicated through others'. That American definition inspires some scholars to use the argument that there was a sort of 'intangible property right' held by each individual over his or her personal data[69] and that individuals could legally 'sell' their personal information on the market and, in that way, 'choose their optimal mix of privacy without parental intervention from the State'. We will come back on this issue later in the discussion of the recent EU Constitutional or quasi constitutional acknowledgement of the right to Data Protection.

2.6.3.2 'Classical Privacy' and Data Protection: Complementarities and Interactions

The legal protections offered by Article 8 of the European Convention of Human Rights (and taken over in Article 7 of the Charter of Fundamental Rights of the European Union) and by the right to data protection now acknowledged by Article 8 of the Charter of Fundamental Rights of the European Union and implemented by the two data protection directives, interact in a variety of ways. The European Court of Human Rights has acknowledged that 'informational privacy' is among what Article 8 of the ECHR protects. In this regard, data protection directives are

---

[67] Security is envisaged in its broadest sense, meaning both integrity, confidentiality, accountability and availability.

[68] A.Westin, *Privacy and Freedom*, New York, Ateneum, 1967, p. 7. For other similar definitions, read D. Solove, 'Conceptualizing Privacy', article already quoted, pp. 1110 and ff.

[69] The theoretical approach of the Privacy viewed as a 'property right' has been developed particularly by the author defending the economic analysis of the Law. See on this approach, among numerous authors, R.A. Possner, *Economic Analysis of the Law, New York*, 1998, pp. 46 and ff (considering Data Privacy law functionally as *'a branch of property Law');* E.J. Jagger, 'Privacy, Property, Intangible Costs and the Commons', 54 *Hastings Law Rev.*, 2003, pp. 899; J. Rule and L. Hunter, 'Towards a property right in personal Data,' in *Visions of Privacy, Policy Choices for the Digital Age*, C.J. Bennett and R. Grant (ed.), 1999, p. 168.

among the *tools* through which the individual exercises his right to privacy. More generally, having the guarantee that personal information (personal data) will not be collected and used in manners that totally escape from the individual's control is indeed a precondition for the individual to feel genuinely free from unreasonable constraints on the construction of his identity.

Yet, data protection is also a tool for protecting other rights than the right to privacy: preventing the processing of information relating to the individual's racial or ethnic origin, political opinions, religious or philosophical beliefs, trade-union membership and concerning the individual's health or sexual life, the data protection directives prevent potential discriminations on those grounds. On the other side, the right to privacy is irreducible to the right to data protection: it guarantees the inviolability of the home (spatial privacy), has to do with the inviolability of the human body and protects the individual's emotions and relationships with others. What privacy protects is irreducible to personal information. Privacy and data protection intersect but are also different tools for enabling individual reflexive autonomy and, as a consequence, also collective deliberative democracy. These tools are not to be put on the same footing though. Whereas the concept of privacy refers to the double aspects of the guarantees the State has to provide to the citizens in order to ensure their capabilities of self-development; the concept of data protection appears in a second step, taking fully into account the new risks threatening the two 'aspects' of privacy (the right to seclusion and the right of decisional autonomy), ensuing from the development of the information and communication technologies. It thus appears obvious from there that data protection regimes are intended both, with regard to the 'seclusion' aspect of privacy, to protect our 'private sphere'(for instance by forbidding the processing of certain sensitive data or by enlarging the secrecy of the correspondence to electronic mails) on the one hand and, on the other hand, with regard to the 'decisional autonomy' aspect of privacy, to increase the transparency of information flows and to limit them in order to prevent disproportionate informational power relationships to be developed or perpetuated between public and private data controllers and citizens.

2.6.3.3 Data Protection and Its 'Constitutionalization': Opportunities and Ambiguities

The role played by the European Union, particularly through Directive 95/46/EC of the European Parliament and of the Council of 24 October 1995 on the protection of individuals with regard to the processing of personal data and on the free movement of such data[70] and Directive 2002/58/EC EC of the European Parliament and of the Council of 17 July 2002 concerning the processing of personal data and the protection of privacy in the electronic communication sector[71], could make believe

---

[70] *Official Journal* L 281, 23 November 1995.

[71] *Official Journal* L 201, 31 July 2002. See also the Directive 2006/24/EC of the European Parliament and of the Council of 15 March 2006 on the retention of data generated or processed in connection with the provision of publicly available electronic communication services or of public

that the 'right to data protection' is above all the result of the need, for the European single market, to harmonize data protection regimes as to ease the free circulation of goods and services. But the European Data Protection regime has its roots in the European human rights regime and more particularly, in Article 8 of the European Convention on Human Rights and in the Convention No. 108 for the Protection of Individuals with regard to the Automatic Processing of Personal Data enacted in 1981 (before that, data protection had already been enacted in the Swedish Law of 1973). The Charter of Fundamental Rights of the European Union[72], in its Article 7, §1 reasserts the existence of the right to private and family life, home and communication, whereas Article 8 of the same Charter acknowledges, as already noted, that the right to data protection has the status of a fundamental right:

1. Everyone has the right to the protection of personal data concerning him or herself.
2. Such data must be processed fairly for specified purposes and on the basis of the consent of the person concerned or some other legitimate basis laid down by law. Everyone has the right of access to data that has been collected concerning him or herself and the right to have it rectified.
3. Compliance with these rules shall be subject to control by an independent authority.

This acknowledgement of the right to Data Protection as a fundamental right, distinct from the traditional fundamental right to privacy, enacted in Article 7 of the Charter is questionable and invites some comments. This 'constitutionalization' of data protection might be considered 'an added' to the extent that it enlarges the application of the main principles of the Directive to all processing of personal data, including those that are not covered by the Directives but processed in the context of EU second and third pillars. The constitutional status given to Data Protection provides data protection regime with a sort of constitutional privilege over competing legislative texts and allows for Constitutional control of its implementation respect by the Constitutional Courts. To this well intentioned acknowledgement of the fundamental importance of the right to data protection, two critiques may be raised: the first one relates to the wording of the second paragraph, which seems to suggest that consent would provide *per se* a legitimate ground for any processing. The second critique is more fundamental: by placing the right to data protection' at the same level as privacy, the European text carries the risk that the fundamental anchoring of data protection regimes in the fundamental values of dignity and autonomy will soon be forgotten by lawyers and that legislators will soon forget to refer to these fundamental values in order to continuously assess data protection legislations, taking into account the evolution of the Information Society.

---

communications networks and amending the Directive 2002/58/EC, *Official Journal*, L 105, 14 April 2006 P. 0054–0063.

[72] 2000/C 364/01.

The Limited Value of the Consent as Legitimate Ground for Data Processing

One may but regret some of the dangers raised by the wording of Article 8. In situations other than those where the legitimacy of processing is grounded in a legislative text, Article 8 explicitly acknowledges consent by the data subject as a necessary and sufficient condition legitimizing data processing, whereas consent is often derived from the simple interaction in the networks. Growing conflation of consent and interaction makes the condition of consent less and less demanding. Most websites include, as part of the transactional process with their customers, specific steps aimed at collecting consents to various processing they find profitable, including the possibility to share any obtained data with third parties, to create users' profiles and to use those profiles for individualized marketing (operated by themselves or by others) purposes. In some cases, consumers are driven to consent through financial incentives (fees or price reductions; gratuitous participation in a lottery, etc.). The use of some services may be dependent on such express consent to processing of the data obtained through the operation of those services.[73]

This approach is advocated using the argument that the 'right to data protection' is the right for the individual to decide about the dissemination of his or her own information. And as nobody is better placed to judge if he or she wants to disseminate data about his or her self, individual consent is necessarily a legitimate ground for the processing of personal data. The argument, making of personal data the alienable property or commodity of the data subject, is disputable[74]: medical data, for example, may arguably be said to belong to the medical practitioner in charge of the patient and who 'produced' the information contained in the medical file, as much as to the patient himself.[75] In the 'property approach', personal data

[73] Margaret Jane Radin, 'Justice and the Market Domain', *in* John Chapman, J. Roland Pennock, *Markets and Justice*, New York University Press, 1989, p. 168: 'the domino theory asserts that market evaluations of objects and activities are imperialistic, diving out other and better ways of perceiving and evaluating objects and activities. Once some individuals attach a price at a given object, relation or activity, they and others tend to lose their capacity to perceive or evaluate that object, relation or activity as anything but a commodity with a specific market price. Moreover, the theory asserts, once certain objects or activities are commodified, there is a tendency for other objects or activities of the same sort or even of other sorts also to be seen and evaluated merely in terms of their actual or potential market value.'

[74] The context of the Internet creates new possibilities for Internet users to express his or her consent. In a first version of P 3 P (Platform for Privacy Preferences), the Internet's user had the possibility to negotiate his or her privacy preferences against financial advantages. This possibility has been discussed extensively in the American literature, see P.M. Schwartz, 'Beyond Lessig's Code for Internet Privacy: Cyberspace, Filters, Privacy control and Fair Information Practices', *Wisconsin Law Review*, 2000, p. 749 et s. ; M. Rotenberg, 'What Larry doesn't Get the Truth', *Stan. Techn. L. Rev.*, 2001,1, disponible sur le site: http://www.sth.Stanford .edu/STLR/Articles/01_STLR_1.

[75] As Kang & Butner observed: *'But Economist, merely creating property rights in personal data says nothing about to whom property is initially assigned, correct? So let's say a citizen bought prodigious amounts of St John's herb from a vendor last Friday. Which of them owns the 'property', that is the knowledge of the citizen's purchase? And what precisely would such ownership entail'* (J.Kang & B. Buchner, 'Privacy in Atlantis', 18 *Harv. Journal Law &*

is considered a valuable commodity that may be the object of bargains and transactions with other people through licenses.[76] Closely connected with the property approach, the contract approach puts party agreement at the heart of personal data processing. Regardless of whether personal data are viewed entirely as property, the contractual approach allows parties to make promises regarding personal data and their processing'.[77] As observed by Schoeman[78], 'One difficulty with regarding Privacy as a claim or entitlement to determine what information about one self is to be available to others is that it begs the question about the moral status of privacy. It presumes privacy is something to be protected at the discretion of the individual to whom the information relates.'

Much more objections than one could report in the present contribution exist against considering consent as a sufficient condition of legitimacy of the processing of personal data. For our purpose here, it suffices to recall that under the EU Directive, consent, as defined by Article 2.h) of the Directive[79] is not presented as a completely sufficient basis for legitimating processing. In any case – even in case of unambiguous consent – it may be possible to declare the processing illegitimate if that processing is disproportionate. The control of proportionality clearly suggests the need for societal control or monitoring of the legitimacy of the processing.

Other, more classical, arguments might be advanced for justifying the insufficiency of the consent.[80] The information asymmetry and power inequality, disadvantageous to the data subject or, as argued by D. Solove[81] among others, the fact that a large portion of 'personal data' may in fact be relevant not only to the individual but also to others with whom the individual entertains or has entertained relationships. Another line of argument refers to the difficulty, for the consenting

---

Techn., 2004, p.9. This article is written in the form of a Socratic discussion between protagonists of different thesis and representatives of different functions in a Society in order to build up a consensus about the main principles of a future Privacy legislation). This assignation might be justified following a market-based approach by the greater efficiency of this solution.

[76] As regards the similarities between this kind of contract and the Licensing contracts about works protected by the Intellectual Property, read P. Samuelson, 'Privacy as Intellectual Property', 52 *Stanford Law Rev.*, 2000, pp. 1125 and ff.; J. Litman, 'Information Privacy/Information Property', 52 *Stanford Law Rev.*, 2000, pp. 1250; K. BASHO, 'The Licensing of the personal information. Is that a solution to Internet Privacy?', 88 *California Law Rev.*, 2000, pp. 1507.

[77] J.Kang & B. Buchner, 'Privacy in Atlantis', 18 *Harv. Journal Law &Techn.*, 2004, p.4.

[78] F. Schoeman, 'Privacy Philosophical Dimensions of the Literature', in *Philosophical Dimensions of the Privacy*, F.D. Schoeman (ed.), 1984, p. 3.

[79] Article 2 h defines the data subject's consent as 'any freely, given specific and informed indication of his or her wishes by which the data subject signifies his agreement to personal data relating to him being processed.' This consent implies that the data controllers have given the relevant information about the mode and the extent of the data processing for which consent is given.

[80] See particularly, M.A. Froomkin, 'Regulation and Computing and Information Technology'. Flood control on the Information Ocean: Living with Anonymity, Digital Cash and distributed Databases, 15, *Jour Law & Com.*, 1996, pp.395 and ff. (this author speaks about a 'myopic, imperfectly informed consumer'.); J.Cohen, 'Examined Lives: Informational Privacy and the subject as object', 52 *Stanford Law Journ.*, 2000, pp. 1373 and ff.

[81] D.J. Solove, 'Conceptualizing Privacy', 90 *Calif. Law Rev.*, 2002, p. 1113.

data subject, to keep track of personal data in secondary transfers and to verify in what measure these secondary transfers are respecting the conditions of the initial license given by the data subject.[82]

Some of those 'weaknesses of consent' could be remedied, as has been done in the context of the consumer protection, by reinforcing the right to be informed and affording new rights to the consumer including class action, when appropriate, in order to decrease power and information inequalities and asymmetries in the Information market (information technology[83] may be of great help in this regard, allowing for example the digital 'marking' of each bit thereby empowering the data subjects with regard to the control and limitation of their transfers. Others – especially those ensuing from socio-economic and other structural inequalities among stakeholders may be more challenging.

The Anchorage of Data Protection Legislation in the Protection of Fundamental Human Values

Another inconvenience of making the 'right to data protection' a distinct fundamental right is that it risks obscuring the essential relation existing between privacy and data protection and further estrange data protection from the fundamental values of human dignity and individual autonomy, foundational to the concept of privacy and in which data protection regimes have their roots, as has already been argued. Keeping in mind those fundamental values and the 'instrumental' value of data protection in this regard is crucial if one is to adapt the legal regime to the changing technological circumstances of the time. Moreover, acknowledging the fundamental values behind the right to data protection makes it clear that, contrary to certain interpretations of that right, it is not amenable to a kind of individual alienable property right over personal data. Finally, taking the fundamental roots of data protection seriously justifies that one should not content ourselves with the current tendency to consider individual consent as sufficient criterion for establishing the legitimacy of whatever processing is considered useful by public or private bureaucracies.

This 'return to the basics' approach provides powerful arguments to refuse the 'information market' approach advocated by some. It goes without saying that those basic values will be immensely useful in showing the direction for the revisions of our data protection regimes[84], arguably necessary due to the unprecedented

---

[82] Already in 1989, P. Samuelson, 'Information as Property: Do Ruckelshause and Carpenter Signal a changing Direction in Intellectual Property Law?', 18 *Cath. U.L. Rev.*, 1989, pp. 365 and ff.

[83] DRM technologies developed for protecting works covered or not by intellectual Property Rights might be also used here. On that issue, J.Zitrain, 'When the publisher can teach the Patient: Intellectual Property and Privacy in an era of Trusted Protection', 52 *Stanford Law Rev.*, 2000, p.1201 insisting about the fact that in both cases, it is about protecting the data, whether it is a brilliant article protected by Intellectual Property Rights or my shopping habits considered as personal data.

[84] About the need to have a third generation of Data Protection legislation in order to face the new challenges of ICT recent developments and about new principles to enact in that context,

challenges raised by the recent and future developments of the global Information Society on the threshold of the 'ambient intelligence era'.[85]

2.7 Conclusion: Privacy as a Bidirectional Principle Fostering the Autonomic Capabilities of Individuals

Agre, reflecting on privacy, commented that

> ... control over personal information is control over an aspect of the identity one projects to the world, and ... the freedom from unreasonable constraints on the construction of one's own identity.[86]

The two aspects – freedom from unreasonable constraints (from the State or from others) in the construction of one's identity and control over (some) aspects of the identity one projects to the world – are at the heart of what the various 'facets' of privacy are all about. Yet, more fundamentally and against the common view that the 'freedom in the construction of one's personality' and 'control over information about oneself one projects on the world' pursue different, though complementary, normative goals, we would like to argue that their common normative justification and objective, or, to say it more plainly, the final value they are meant to advance, is the capacity of the human subject to keep and develop his personality in a manner that allows him to fully participate in society without however being induced to conform his thoughts, beliefs, behaviours and preferences to those thoughts, beliefs, behaviours and preferences held by the majority. Privacy and data protection regimes should thus be understood as 'mere' tools (evolving

---

Y.Poullet, 'Pour une troisième génération de législations de protection des données', *JusLetter*, No. 3, October 2005), we tried to show the extent to which directive 2002/58 when it regulates the traffic and location data generated by the use of communication services pays little attention to the fact that these data are data of a personal nature. *'The very definition of the **'data'**, whose protection is at the very heart of the recent directive does not follow that of 1995 exactly. The definitions of 'traffic in data' and 'localization' listed in article 2 carefully avoid expressions like 'data of a personal nature' which, however, circumscribe the field of application of the directive 95/46/EC, of which the 2002 directive would be just one application. Both articles 2 c) and preamble 14 of the Directive define localization data via simple reference to the user's terminal equipment. When it is a question of commenting on the concept of traffic in data, preamble 15 talks 'about information consisting of a denomination, a number or an address, provided by he who sends an electronic message or he who uses a connection to send an electronic message.What are we to say? These data may not be data of a personal nature, in other words the search for a link with an identified or identifiable person is no longer necessary'.*

[85] Antoinette Rouvroy, 'Privacy, Data Protection, and the Unprecedented Challenges of Ambient Intelligence', *Studies in Ethics, Law, and Technology* 2008, vol. 2, Issue 1, Available at: http://works.bepress.com/antoinete_rouvroy/2 (forthcoming, 2008). See, also about the new techniques of RFID body implants, the Opinion of the European Group on the Ethics of the Sciences and New Technologies of the European Commission, '*Aspects éthiques des implants TIC dans le corps humain*', March 16th, 2005.

[86] Philip E. Agre, Marc Rotenberg (eds.), *Technology and Privacy. The New Landscape*, MIT Press, 1998, p. 3.

when required by the new threats that socio-economic, cultural and technological changes impose on individual and democratic self-determination), meant to pursue that one single common goal: sustaining the uniquely human capacity for individual reflexive self-determination and for collective deliberative decision making regarding the rules of social cooperation. We consider this as one unique, rather than two separate, goal given the mutual 'production' or reinforcement of public and private autonomy.[87] Privacy, as a principle catalyzing the tension inherent in individual existence between the need for retreat from others and the need for participation and interaction with others, is, depending on the context and circumstances, constantly requiring the adaptation of the legal instruments that find, in that principle, both their roots and horizon. It is not, as has been suggested by other scholars, that the 'classical' privacy regime is there to protect the facets of human life that need 'opacity' to best develop and that data protection regimes are there to organize the partial disclosures that social life and interactions require. Rather, both facets – 'seclusion' and 'inclusion and participation', are, depending on the circumstances, best preserved by a combination of legal tools protecting against undue interference in existential matters, or protecting personal data against a series of illegitimate collections and misuses.

Thus, 'classical' privacy regimes and data protection should be conceived together as forming the evolving bundle of legal protections of the fundamental individual and social structural value of the autonomic capabilities of individuals in a free and democratic society. Guaranteeing the generic right to privacy (or the principle of privacy, should we maybe say), given the crucial role it plays in enabling the autonomic capabilities of the individual legal subject, is a precondition to any meaningful exercise of all other rights and freedoms acknowledged by the Council of Europe. This is particularly explicit in the case of freedom of expression but is also true regarding all other fundamental rights and freedoms, including, crucially, those social and economic rights[88] that guarantee the full participation of the individual in the social and political fabric of society.

[87] See above, notes 24 and 25, and accompanying text.

[88] As Burkert (quoted supra footnote 33) asserts it: 'Even in their passive state fundamental rights need economic and social framework conditions which make the use of such rights meaningful. This observation is reflected in the (still heavily contested) extension of fundamental rights into the area of economic and social rights. Some of the discussions at the World Summit of the Information Society, already mentioned above, might well be seen as a tentative connection of 'privacy' to such social and economic rights in the information society'.

Chapter 3
Data Protection as a Fundamental Right

Stefano Rodotà

We live at a time when the issues related to the protection of personal data feature a markedly contradictory approach – indeed, a veritable social, political and institutional schizophrenia. There is increased awareness of the importance of data protection as regards not only the protection of the private lives of individuals but their very freedom. This approach is reflected by many national and international documents, lastly the Charter of Fundamental Rights of the European Union, where data protection is recognised as a fundamental, autonomous right. Still, it is increasingly difficult to respect this general assumption, because internal and international security requirements, market interests and the re-organisation of the public administration are heading towards the diminution of relevant safeguards, or pushing essential guarantees towards disappearance.

What should we expect from the future? Will the trend that surfaced up over the past few years continue, or will one get back, albeit with difficulty, to the concept underlying the origins of personal data protection, which opened up a new age for the protection of freedoms with a really forward-looking approach?

If one looks at reality with detachment, there are reasons for pessimism. Even before 9/11, in particular because of market requirements and the trend towards setting up ever larger databases on consumers and their behaviours, there were talks of the "end of privacy". However, if one nowadays looks at the way the world is changing, there surfaces a more radical question to answer. The end of privacy is increasingly talked about. Some years ago, Scott McNally, CEO of Sun Mycrosystems, said brutally: "You have zero privacy anyway. Get over it". In a movie of 1998 by Tony Scott, "Enemy of the State", one of the main characters said: "The only privacy you have is in your head. Maybe not even there". This doubt is turning into a disturbing reality. Research is in progress on *cerebral fingerprints*, the individual memory is being probed in search of traces that can point to the memory of past events and, therefore, be taken as evidence of participation in such events. A century ago, in stressing the role played by the subconscious, Freud noted that the Self was no longer in control. Nowadays one can safely maintain that the mental privacy, the

S. Rodotà (✉)
Professor of law at the University of Rome "La Sapienza".
e-mail: s.rodota@tiscali.it

S. Gutwirth et al. (eds.), *Reinventing Data Protection?*

DOI 10.1007/978-1-4020-9498-9_3,

most intimate sphere, is being threatened, violating person's most secluded dimension. After 9/11, "privacy in the age of terror" would appear to be doomed. Not only is privacy no longer regarded as a fundamental right; in fact, it is too often considered a hindrance to security and overridden by emergency legislation.

Reality is becoming increasingly estranged from the fundamental rights' framework, for three basic reasons. Firstly, after 9/11 many reference criteria changed and the guarantees were reduced everywhere in the world, as shown, in particular, by the Patriot Act in the USA and the European decisions on transfer of airline passenger data to the US as well as on the retention of electronic communications data. Secondly, this trend towards downsizing safeguards was extended to sectors that are trying to benefit from the change in the general scenario – such as those related to business. Thirdly, the new technological opportunities make continuously available new tools for classification, selection, social sorting and control of individuals, which are resulting in a veritable technological drift that national and international authorities are not always capable to adequately counter.

In this manner, some of the principles underlying the system of personal data protection are being slowly eroded; this applies, first and foremost, to the purpose specification principle and the principle concerning separation between the data processed by public bodies and those processed by private entities. The multifunctionality criterion is increasingly applied, at times under the pressure exerted by institutional agencies. Data collected for a given purpose are made available for different purposes, which are considered to be as important as those for which the collection had been undertaken. Data processed by a given agency are made available to different agencies. It means that individuals are more and more transparent and that public bodies are more and more out of any political and legal control. It implies a new distribution of political and social powers.

However, the strong protection of personal data continues to be a "necessary utopia" (S. Simitis) if one wishes to safeguard the democratic nature of our political systems. If you consider what happened in the past century, you can descry a process of unrelenting reinvention of privacy, grounded precisely on the implementation of democratic values, which can be easily appreciated by briefly considering the different definitions of privacy over time.

After the landmark definition by Warren and Brandeis – "the right to be left alone" – other definitions have been developed to mirror different requirements. In a world where our data move about ceaselessly, "the right to control the way others use the information concerning us" (A. Westin) becomes equally important. Indeed, the collection of sensitive data and social and individual profiling may give rise to discrimination; privacy is therefore to be also regarded as "the protection of life choices against any form of public control and social stigma" (L. M. Friedman), as "vindication of the boundaries protecting each person's right not to be simplified, objectified, and evaluated out of context" (J. Rosen). Since the information flows do not simply contain "outbound" data – to be kept off others' hands – but also "inbound" information – on which one might wish to exercise a "right not to know" – privacy is also to be considered as "the right to keep control over one's own information and determine the manner of building up one's own private sphere" (S. Rodotà). Vindicating the individual's autonomy in the information society, a landmark decision of the Bundesverfassungsgericht, in 1983, recognised the "informational self-determination".

These definitions are not mutually exclusive, mark a progressive inclusion of new aspects of freedom in a widening concept of privacy. The most recent definitions do not supersede past ones, exactly because they are grounded on different requirements and operate at different levels. Even prior to the marked acceleration brought about by technological and scientific innovation, the manner in which the conventional definition of privacy was applied had already evolved. The right to be left alone was not construed merely as an expression of the golden age of the bourgeoisie, which had protected its immaterial sphere by means of the same prohibition against trespass that had long been a feature of landed property. Under the impulse given by Louis Brandeis, a view had emerged whereby privacy was also regarded as a tool to protect minorities, dissenting opinions – therefore free speech and the right to freely develop one's personality. This is where a (seeming) paradox comes up: the strong protection of the private sphere ultimately does not safeguard privacy or keeps the unwanted gaze at bay; in fact, it allows individual beliefs and opinions to be freely made public. This opened up the path leading to the ever closer association between privacy and freedom.

This evolution went hand in hand with the development – starting from the early '70s – of several national and international instruments. Alongside the first generation of domestic laws on privacy, other initiatives should be recalled. The OECD in 1980 and the Council of Europe in 1981 had adopted two instruments in this area – namely, the Guiding Principles and Convention 108, respectively. In 1995, with European Directive 95/46, it was explicitly affirmed that the approximation of laws "must not result in any lessening of the protection they afford but must, on the contrary, seek to ensure a high level of protection". In 2000, the Charter of Fundamental Rights of the EU recognised data protection as an autonomous right. This can be considered the final point of a long evolution, separating privacy and data protection.

The evolution is clearly visible by comparing the EU Charter with the provisions made in the 1950 Convention of the Council of Europe. Under Article 8 of the Convention, "everyone has the right to respect for his private and family life, his home and his correspondence". Conversely, the Charter draws a distinction between the conventional "right to respect for his or her private and family life" (Article 7), which is modelled after the Convention and "the right to the protection of personal data" (Article 8), which becomes thereby a new, autonomous fundamental right. Moreover, Article 8 lays down data processing criteria, expressly envisages access rights and provides that "compliance with these rules shall be subject to control by an independent authority".

The distinction between the right to respect for one's private and family life and the right to the protection of personal data is more than an empty box. The right to respect one's private and family life mirrors, first and foremost, an individualistic component: this power basically consists in preventing others from interfering with one's private and family life. In other words, it is a static, negative kind of protection. Conversely, data protection sets out rules on the mechanisms to process data and empowers one to take steps – i.e., it is a dynamic kind of protection, which follows a data in all its movements. Additionally, oversight and other powers are not only conferred on the persons concerned (the data subjects), as they are also committed to an independent authority (Article 8.3). Protection is no longer left to data subjects, given that there is a public body that is permanently responsible for it. Thus, it is a redistribution of social and legal powers that is taking shape. It is actually the endpoint of a long evolutionary process experienced by the privacy concept – from its original definition as the right to be left alone, up to the right to keep control over one's information and determine how one's private sphere is to be built up.

Furthermore, Article 8 should be put in the broader context of the Charter, which refers to the new rights arising out of scientific and technological innovation. Article 3 deals with the "right to the integrity of the person", i.e., the protection of the *physical* body; Article 8 deals with data protection, i.e., the *electronic* body. These provisions are directly related to human dignity, which Article 1 of the Charter declares to be inviolable, as well as to the statement made in the Preamble to the Charter – whereby the Union "places the person at the heart of its activities". Thus, data protection contributes to the "constitutionalisation of the person" – which can be regarded as one of the most significant achievements not only of the Charter. We are faced with the true reinvention of data protection – not only because it is expressly considered an autonomous, fundamental right but also because it has turned into an essential tool to freely develop one's personality. Data protection can be seen to sum up a bundle of rights that make up citizenship in the new millennium.

Still, as I have already pointed out, this is taking place in a scenario markedly fraught with conflicts. The fundamental right to data protection is continuously eroded or downright overridden by alleging the prevailing interests of security and market logic. To counter this *regressive* reinvention, we need political and legal strategies to not only defend what has been formally recognised but to also develop its inherent potential. This is nowadays a daunting task. Data protection is under attack every day. Is there room for an *affirmative* reinvention, or is a defensive approach the only practicable option? The two objectives may not be kept separate – which is why a strategy should be developed, as summarised in the ten-point analysis I am going to briefly describe.

1. Not all legal systems confer the status of a fundamental right on data protection. This entails special responsibilities on the part of those countries and world regions, such as the EU, where the threshold for safeguards is set especially high – even though it was just the European Union that failed to stick to its principles when negotiating with the United States in issues like transfer of passengers' data, data retention, Swift, etc.
2. Being aimed at affording a strong protection to individuals, the right to data protection may not be considered as subordinate or subject to other rights. It means that we must go beyond the simple balancing test technique, because the very nature of data protection as "fundamental right" (Y. Poullet).
3. Accordingly, restrictions or limitations are only admissible if certain specific conditions are fulfilled, rather than merely on the basis of the balancing of interests. Article 8 of the Convention for the protection of human rights provides

that "there shall be no interference by a public authority with the exercise of these rights except such as is in accordance with the law and is necessary in a *democratic* society". Article 51 of the Charter of the European Union states that "any limitation on the exercise of the rights and freedoms recognised by this Charter must be provided for by law and must respect the *essence* of those rights and freedoms". This means that limitations are only admissible for specific purposes; that they should never impinge on the essence of the rights in question; and that they must in any case pass a democracy test, i.e., even where they do not impact on the essence of the rights. Additionally, Article 26 of the Convention on human rights and biomedicine of the Council of Europe rules out that limitations may be provided for "in the interest of national security... economic well-being...protection of morals" – whilst all these limitations are envisaged in the Convention for the protection of human rights. This means that more stringent safeguards are always required in respect of especially sensitive data.

4. Safeguards should not be grounded on principles whereby the individual is regarded only or mainly as the owner of the data concerning him or her. The right to data protection has to do with protecting one's personality – not one's property. This means that certain data categories, in particular medical and genetic data, may not be used for business-related purposes.
5. Data protection is an expression of personal freedom and dignity; as such, it is not to be tolerated that data is used in such a manner as to turn an individual into an object under continuous surveillance. We are confronted with changes of the uses and perception of the human body that have to do with the anthropological features of persons. We are confronted with a stepwise progression: from being "scrutinised" by means of video surveillance and biometric technologies, individuals can be "modified" via the insertion of chips or "smart" tags readable by Rfid in a context that is increasingly turning us into "networked persons" – persons who are permanently on the net, configured little by little in order to transmit and receive signals that allow tracking and profiling movements, habits, contacts and thereby modify the meaning and contents of individuals' autonomy. That is incompatible with the very nature of data protection as a fundamental right.
6. The fundamental right to personal data protection should be considered a promise just like the one made by the king to his knights in 1215, in the Magna Charta, that they would not be imprisoned or tortured illegally – "nor will go upon him nor send upon him." This promise, the *habeas corpus*, should be renewed and shifted from the physical body to the electronic body. The inviolability of the person must be reconfirmed and reinforced in the electronic dimension, according to the new attention paid to the respect for the human body. All forms of reductionism must be rejected.
7. As well as the principles of purpose specification, relevance and proportionality, special importance should be attached to data minimization; this means that no personal data should be collected if the specific purpose can be achieved without processing personal data. Above all, this could prevent the management of major societal issues from being delegated by politics to technology.

8. This entails the need for introducing "privacy impact assessment" procedures similar to those that are already in place to assess environmental impact. The pollution of civil liberties is no less important than environmental pollution.
9. Ad-hoc initiatives are required to more adequately regulate the various types of data retention; prevent the downsizing and/or elimination of informed consent; and enhance independent controls. Generally speaking, all new opportunities offered by biometrics, genetics, nanotechnology, Rfid, location techniques and human body implants must be scrutinised, making close reference to the data protection as an expression of human dignity.
10. The fundamental right to data protection should be considered an essential component of the Internet Bill of Rights to be discussed by the UN Internet Governance Forum in Rio de Janeiro of November 2007. The electronic space requires a new, multilevel constitutionalism, where global data protection can play an essential role for starting with a more comprehensive dimension of human rights, so forging a new citizenship (an extension of guarantees to the Second Life has been proposed through an Avatar's Bill of Rights). This consciousness is reflected by the new activism of the business community. The first into the field was Microsoft, which proposed a Charter for the digital identity. This was followed by a joint initiative by Microsoft, Google, Yahoo! and Vodafone who announced the publishing – by the end of the year – of a Charter for the protection of free speech on the Internet. In July, Microsoft presented its "Privacy Principles" and more recently, Google, having rejected a European Union proposal to block "dangerous" search terms ("bomb", "terrorism", "genocide" and the like), proposed the adoption of a global standard for privacy that would be supervised by a "Global Privacy Counsel" attached to the United Nations. It is apparent and widely recognized that there is an emergent need to protect fundamental rights, especially those concerning the freedom of expression and the protection of personal data. Safeguarding these rights cannot be left to private parties, since they will tend to offer guarantees that suit their interests.

In this perspective, reinventing data protection is an unrelenting process that is indispensable not only to afford adequate protection to a fundamental right but also to prevent our societies from turning into societies of control, surveillance and social selection.

At the beginning I made reference to a necessary utopia. A utopia that does not direct our gaze towards the remote future but rather obliges us to consider the reality surrounding us. Data protection is not only a fundamental right among others but the most expressive of the contemporary human condition. Recalling this at all times is not vaniloquy, because any changes affecting data protection impact on the degree of democracy we all can experience.

Chapter 4
Consent in Data Protection Law: Privacy, Fair Processing and Confidentiality

Roger Brownsword

4.1 Introduction

In the context of a rapidly developing Information Society, the Data Protection Directive[1] seems both well-intentioned and timely: it reflects a rights-based approach to privacy and to the fair, accurate, transparent and proportionate processing of personal data.[2] Yet, in England, as in the United States, EU data protection law has few friends[3], – for example, in the Naomi Campbell case, one of the first opportunities for the English appeal courts to comment on the local implementing legislation, Lord Phillips MR described the Data Protection Act, 1998, as 'cumbersome and inelegant'.[4] If the Act were thought to be making a positive contribution to the social and economic well-being of the nation, then the lawyers might have to bear this particular cross. After all, there is plenty of legislation that fits Lord Phillips'

R. Brownsword (✉)
King's College London, London, UK
e-mail: roger.brownsward@kcl.ac.uk

Director of TELOS and Honorary Professor in Law at the University of Sheffield. An earlier version of this paper (under the title 'Consent in Data Protection Law: A Vote of 'No Confidence'?') was presented at a conference on 'Reinventing Data Protection?', held in Brussels on October 12–13, 2007. I am grateful for comments made by delegates as well as for helpful conversations with Deryck Beyleveld, Bert-Jaap Koops, Joel Reidenberg and Marc Rotenberg. Needless to say, the usual disclaimers apply.

[1] Directive 95/46/EC. Also, see the Council of Europe's Convention for the Protection of Individuals with Regard to the Automatic Processing of Personal Data, 1981.

[2] Compare Serge Gutwirth and Paul De Hert, 'Privacy, Data Protection and Law Enforcement. Opacity of the Individual and Transparency of Power' in Erik Claes, Antony Duff and Serge Gutwirth (eds.), *Privacy and the Criminal Law* (Antwerp and Oxford: Intersentia, 2006) p. 61.

[3] For an (unenthusiastic) American appraisal, see Peter P. Swire and Robert E. Litan, *None of Your Business: World Data Flows, Electronic Commerce and the European Privacy Directive* (Washington DC: Brookings Institution Press, 1998).

[4] *Naomi Campbell v Mirror Group Newspapers* [2002] EWCA Civ 1373 at para 72; similarly, at the trial, Morland J had already likened the Act to a 'thicket': see [2002] EWHC 499 (QB) (at para 72). On final appeal to the House of Lords, there was no further consideration of the Act, it being agreed between the parties that the DPA claim stood or fell with the main claim for breach of confidence: see [2004] UKHL 22, para 32 (Lord Nicholls).

S. Gutwirth et al. (eds.), *Reinventing Data Protection?*
DOI 10.1007/978-1-4020-9498-9_4,

description. However, the lawyers are not on their own. The fact of the matter is that data protection law has been subjected to a sustained chorus of criticism, especially from the public health and medical professionals who contend, at their most extreme, that compliance with the Act is 'killing patients'.[5]

Most recently, the legislation has been subjected to a heavy round of criticism at the hands of Neil Manson and Onora O'Neill.[6] At almost every turn, Manson and O'Neill find the Act to be problematic – fundamentally, because it presupposes a flawed (container and conduit) model for the communication of information as well as assuming that certain types of information, so-called 'personal data', need to be protected against processing irrespective of the purposes of the data processor.[7] Central to their criticisms is the relationship between data protection regimes and the consent of data subjects. As Manson and O'Neill rightly state, the Act 'assigns individual consent a large, indeed pivotal, role in controlling the lawful acquisition, possession and use of "personal" information.'[8] Accordingly, if European data protection law is deeply flawed, it is reasonable to assume that the root of the problem is to be located in and around the concept of consent. Perhaps, as some of the critics contend, we should weaken the requirements for 'unambiguous' or 'explicit' consent[9] or, even better, dispense altogether with the requirement of individual consent.

Against this tide of criticism, my purpose in this paper is not to defend the drafting of either the Data Protection Directive itself or the implementing legislation in the United Kingdom. In both cases, the law is unacceptably opaque – and, indeed, in the case of the Directive, I believe that regulators set off on the wrong foot by highlighting the value of privacy. Nevertheless, in general, I do want to defend the rights basis of European data protection law and, in particular, I want to defend the central role accorded to the consent of data subjects within such a regime. In order to mount such a defence, it is necessary to respond to criticisms that are being directed at the legislation from two quite different wings – first, the criticisms made by utilitarians (who complain that, in practice, the law obstructs the pursuit of welfare-maximising projects) and, secondly, the arguments presented by those such as Manson and O'Neill who operate with a duty-based (Kantian) ethic.

On the one wing, we have the utilitarians. Of course, critics of this stripe are famously liable to find problems with regulatory regimes that put a premium on respect for individuals by demanding that we take rights seriously.[10] This attitude

---

[5] For guidance, see Parliamentary Office of Science and Technology, 'Data Protection and Medical Research' (Postnote Number 235, January 2005). For relevant references and a sober assessment, see Deryck Beyleveld, 'Medical Research and the Public Good' (2007) 18 KLJ 275, at 286–287. For the official response, see P. Boyd, 'The Requirements of the Data Protection Act 1998 for the Processing of Medical Data' (2003) 29 *J. Med. Ethics* 34; and http://www.dataprotection.gov.uk/dpr/dpdoc.nsf.

[6] Neil C. Manson and Onora O'Neill, *Rethinking Informed Consent in Bioethics* (Cambridge: Cambridge University Press, 2007) Ch. 5.

[7] Ibid., Ch. 5.

[8] At 112.

[9] Directive 95/46/EC, Articles 7(a) and 8.2(a).

[10] Compare, e.g., Ronald M. Dworkin, *Taking Rights Seriously* (London: Duckworth, 1978).

is reflected in the utilitarian view that consent requirements are simply a tax on transactions. To such critics, I could give a very short response. I could simply say that, in Europe, there is a politico-legal commitment to respect for human rights; that is, I could say that Europe has chosen rights rather than utility as the governing ethic. However, this is not the response that I want to make. Rather, my point against the utilitarian critique is that it is a serious mistake to think that data protection law gives data subjects a right to consent (or, more pointedly, a right to refuse to consent) as such. Data subjects have informational rights and it is because they have such rights (and only because they have such rights) that their consent (or refusal) is material; but it bears repetition that, whatever the rights held by data subjects, they do not include a sovereign right to veto any act concerning their personal data. Indeed, if we proceed on the assumption that, irrespective of the rights held by data subjects, we can never make use of personal data without the data subject's consent, we commit the Fallacy of Necessity.

Stated shortly, the fallacy is to assume that, where an individual has a negative attitude towards some act x (such as processing some data), then it cannot possibly be legitimate to do x without having that individual's consent. To the contrary, though, if the individual in question does not have a relevant covering right in relation to act x, the lack of consent is immaterial. When a rights ethic governs, consent is not free-standing; it is always anchored to a covering right. It is extremely important, therefore, to be clear about whatever rights data subjects have (so that we know precisely when and why the consent of a data subject becomes an issue). Even if this mistake is avoided, there is a second opportunity for misdirection. Let us suppose that the individual in question does have a relevant covering right. While, given this supposition, it is quite correct to insist that the individual's consent is material, it is a fallacy to think that we can never justify the doing of x without that individual's consent. For, in exceptional cases, it might be legitimate to do x if this is a necessary and proportionate response to a more compelling rights claim (whether a competing or a conflicting rights claim). To avoid the Fallacy of Necessity, therefore, it is important to be clear about both the data subject's rights and the possible application of overriding rights.

Hence, against the utilitarian critics, my point is that, so long as we persist with and propogate such fallacies, we will see the data protection regime in an altogether false light and the law becomes far too easy a target for its critics. This is not to say that, once the fallacy is avoided, utilitarians will find no criticism of data protection law. Rather, it is to say that, so long as the fallacy is in play, the strength of any utilitarian critique cannot be properly evaluated – and nor can we properly evaluate the qualities of a rights-based data protection regime.

On the other wing, we have critics such as Manson and O'Neill. They argue that privacy interests should be given regulatory protection through various informational obligations and, more particularly, that 'a focus on norms of *confidentiality* may have a number of advantages over appeals to *data protection* requirements.'[11]

[11] Manson and O'Neill, op cit, note 6 above, at 99.

To the extent that Manson and O'Neill suppose that we get a clearer fix on consent once we separate background informational obligations from the foreground requirement that consent should be 'informed', I entirely agree. However, for two reasons, I believe that the argument that we should rest data protection on an obligation of confidentiality is diversionary. The first reason is that, even though Manson and O'Neill's approach is duty-based rather than rights-based, consent continues to be an important dynamic in the scheme that they advocate. In other words, if we believe that Manson and O'Neill's critique will take consent out of data protection law, then we are mistaken. The second reason is far more important: it is that I doubt that traditional information protective regimes – whether anchored to privacy rights or confidentiality obligations – offer the best approach to modern data protection demands. To be sure, these traditional regimes do stretch across to modern Information Society environments but this is not the regulatory target at which they were directed. By contrast, this is precisely the target at which data protection regimes need to be primarily aimed, especially so as the Information Society evolves into an IT-enabled profiling community.[12] If the Directive's target was the relatively out-of-the-ordinary processing of personal data by highly visible computers and data controllers, we now need to regulate (with an emphasis on public rather than private monitoring and enforcement) for processing and profiling carried out on a daily basis by much less visible operators.[13] In the Information Society – in our 'digitally disciplined democracies', as Herbert Burkert[14] has evocatively put it – we 'do much less face' and much more Facebook; and regulation needs to recognise the radical change in the way that we interact with one another, whether in the marketplace, at work, in the health and education systems, or in our capacity as citizens.[15] The duty of confidentiality is simply not up to such a task.

There is one other introductory point to be made. Consent is not only under attack from those who judge that it obstructs legitimate public interest initiatives such as medical research; it is also under fire from those who think that the token consent of data subjects gives data processors far too easy an exit from their data

---

[12] Compare Mireille Hildebrandt, 'A Vision of Ambient Law' in Roger Brownsword and Karen Yeung (eds.), *Regulating Technologies* (Oxford: Hart, 2008); and Roger Brownsword, 'Knowing Me, Knowing You—Profiling, Privacy and the Public Interest' in Mireille Hildebrandt and Serge Gutwirth (eds.), *Profiling the European Citizen* (2007) 362.

[13] As already recognised by Directive 2002/58/EC (the Directive on privacy and electronic communications). But, even then, the world of technology does not stand still. See, e.g., the discussion in Daniel B. Garrie and Rebecca Wong, 'Regulating Voice Over Internet Protocol: An EU/US Comparative Approach' (2007) 22 *American University International Law Review* 549, at 580, where it is concluded that 'as technology is evolving with respect to VoIP and oral Internet communications [the regulatory position] is becoming progressively greyer....' Generally, see Roger Brownsword, *Rights, Regulation and the Technological Revolution* (Oxford: Oxford University Press, 2008) Ch. 6.

[14] Herbert Burkert, in his concluding comments at the conference on 'Reinventing Data Protection?', held in Brussels on October 12–13, 2007.

[15] Compare the timely discussion in Peter Bradwell and Niamh Gallagher, *FYI: the New Politics of Personal Information* (London: DEMOS, 2007).

protection responsibilities.[16] Whereas the former believe that it is too *difficult* to obtain consent, the premise of the latter critique is that it is far too *easy* to meet the consent requirement. Let me make it clear, therefore, that when I defend consent against the former, I am defending a principle that demands that we take consent seriously. If, in practice, the obtaining of consent is perfunctory and routine, then that is not at all in line with the requirements of principle. It is no part of my intention to defend a practice that falls short of our principles; what I want to defend is a principle that makes individual rights and consent focal; and what I want to see in practice is respect for data subjects that lives up to our declared principles.

In these introductory remarks, it remains only to say that the paper is in two principal parts. In Part II, I address the question of whether, as a matter of principle, consent has a legitimate role in a data protection regime. Are the critics right to accuse consent of being an indefensible obstacle to the achievement of valuable goods such as health and well-being? In Part III, I address the question of whether, in practice, a data protection regime would serve us better if it rested on a duty of confidentiality.[17]

4.2 The Centrality of Consent

Where a data protection regime is underwritten by an ethic of rights and where (as I take it) the ethic is based on a choice (or will) theory of rights, there is no escaping the fact that consent must be central to that regime.[18] This is because, quite simply, consent is an integral dynamic within such a rights-based approach. In other ethical approaches, utilitarian or dignitarian, consent is either viewed contingently or as of little importance.[19] However, for such a rights ethic, consent is fundamental. Our first task, therefore, is to be clear about how consent works in an ethic that is rights-based. Once this has been clarified, we can respond directly to the utilitarian critique that consent is getting in the way of welfare-maximising public interest projects.

---

[16] Quite possibly, this is more of an American than a European concern. At any rate, it was a discussion with Marc Rotenberg and Joel Reidenberg that brought this point to my attention.

[17] For the purposes of this paper, I will treat Europe as a 'community of rights' in the sense that there is a commitment to protect and promote the fundamental rights of its members. The data protection regime, as an articulation of rights is fully in line with this commitment. To this extent, the justificatory burden lies with the critics. Generally, on a 'community of rights', see Roger Brownsword, *Rights, Regulation, and the Technological Revolution* (Oxford: Oxford University Press, 2008) Ch. 1.

[18] For the opposition between choice (or will) and interest theories of rights, see HLA Hart, 'Bentham on Legal Rights', in AWB Simpson (ed.), *Oxford Essays in Jurisprudence* (Second Series) (Oxford: Clarendon Press, 1973) 171; and D.N. MacCormick, 'Rights in Legislation' in P.M.S. Hacker and J. Raz (eds.), *Law, Morality, and Society* (Oxford: Clarendon Press, 1977) 189.

[19] Compare Roger Brownsword, note 17 above, Ch. 3.

4.2.1 Consent as a Procedural Justification

In a community of rights, the principal (but not exclusive) function of consent is to authorise an act that would otherwise constitute a violation of a right. Here, the consenting agent, A, is precluded from raising a complaint about the conduct of the recipient agent B (B's 'wrongdoing' as it otherwise would be). For example, in the first clause of Recital 33 of the Directive, we read:

> Whereas data which are capable by their nature of infringing fundamental freedoms or privacy should not be processed unless the data subject gives his explicit consent.

This principle is cashed out in Articles 7 and 8 of the Directive. So, to take the clearer exemplification, Article 8.1, which deals with the processing of what it calls 'special categories of data' requires Member States to prohibit 'the processing of personal data revealing racial or ethnic origin, political opinions, religious or philosophical beliefs, trade-union membership, [or]...concerning health or sex life.' However, where 'the data subject has given his explicit consent to the processing of those data', then Article 8.2 lifts the prohibition. To express this more straightforwardly in rights terms: agents have a right that covers the processing of certain special categories of data[20]; but, where an agent consents to the processing of such data, then that agent is precluded from asserting a wrongdoing (at any rate, so long as the processing is within the scope of the consent).

It is in this way that, in a rights-based regime, consent functions as a justifying reason. However, precisely because B relies on A's authorisation for the doing of x rather than on the rightness of the doing of x itself, it becomes clear that consent operates as a distinctive form of justification. In particular, we should note the following three distinguishing features of 'consent as a justification'. First, consent functions as a 'procedural' rather than as a 'substantive' (or, 'on the merits') form of justification. Secondly, as a procedural justification, consent amounts to a limited 'in personam' (or 'agent relative') response. Consent does not comprehensively justify the action as such; rather, the consenting agent is precluded from asserting that he or she has been wronged. Thirdly, where consent is relied on as a shield, it justifies by way of negating a wrong rather than by way of overriding a right. Each of these features merits a word or two of explanation.

First, whereas a substantive (or, 'on the merits') form of justification refers to some set of background standards characterising (in the justificatory argument) particular acts as permitted (including required), a procedural justification refers to an authorising act or decision. For example, if agent B (let us say, an epidemiologist) contends that it is permissible to consult patients' medical records in a certain mining area because the information will contribute to our understanding of a particular dust disease, he relies on a substantive justification (resting on the permissibility of actions that are calculated to improve public health or develop therapies for a particular condition). By contrast, if agent B claims to be so entitled by reference to the

[20] This looks very much like a 'privacy' right; but, for the purposes of the point that I am making in the text, nothing hinges on whether we so characterise it.

consent of the patients or certain doctors or health officials, or his research sponsor, then the justification does not rest on background standards, contested or otherwise; rather the claimed justification is procedural in the sense that B relies on some authorising act or decision, not background standards, to assert the permissibility of the particular actions in question.

Secondly, where consent is relied on, it justifies 'in personam' (that is, only in an 'agent-relative' way). The consenting agent but only the consenting agent, is precluded from asserting that he or she has been wronged. In other words, although agent A, who has consented to the doing of x by agent B, is precluded from asserting that the doing of x violates A's rights, this does not make the doing of x right *tout court* (i.e., right as against all comers). So, if the complaint about B's accessing the medical records comes from those who have so consented, then B may respond that such complaints by such parties are precluded by their consent. However, none of this justifies the carrying out of the research as such. Other agents might have grounds for complaint to which it is no answer for B to rely on A's consent. In other words, even if A's consent gives B a complete answer to A, it might give B no answer at all to C (for example, to a patient who has not consented).

Thirdly, where B relies on A's consent as a justification, B does so in order to negate what would otherwise be a wrong in relation to A. To put this another way, given that A's consent *authorises* the action in question, it must follow that B, by doing the authorised act x, does no wrong to A. A's consent to B doing x entails that, as between A and B, the doing of x by B is permissible. This is to be distinguished from treating the doing of x by B as justified by reference to overriding rights, or all things considered as the lesser of two wrongs. In such a case, where A has not consented to the doing of x by B and where the doing of x violates A's rights, then the doing of x, even if justified all things considered, involves a wrong to A.[21] Reflecting this pattern of reasoning, Articles 7 and 8 of the Directive, in line with Recitals 33 and 34, identify a considerable number of reasons that will suffice to justify the processing of data without the data subject's consent. For example, if B processes data without A's (the data subject's) consent but this is necessary in order to save A's life or to save C's life, then B's act will be justified.[22]

Putting these three distinguishing features together we have the following. In a community of rights, consent functions as a procedural justification, giving the recipient of the consent (B) a complete answer to the consenting agent (A); no wrong is done to the consenting (authorising) agent (A) by the recipient agent (B); but it does not follow that the recipient agent (B) does no wrong to third-party agents (such as C). In the absence of consent, a wrong will be done to agents whose rights are violated even if, all things considered, the wrongdoing can be substantively justified as the lesser of two evils.

---

[21] Mutatis mutandis, these comments apply to the case in which B relies on A's consent in order to hold A to the rules of the agreed set.

[22] Articles 7(d) and 8(c) (processing necessary in order to protect the vital interests of the data subject) and Article 8.3 (processing required for the purposes of preventive medicine, medical diagnosis, the provision of care or treatment and so on).

The attraction of consent as a justifying reason is not hard to understand. Quite simply, not only does consent provide the recipient, B, with a complete answer to the consenting agent, A but it does so without the former having to engage contestable substantive justifications – or, at any rate, such 'on the merits' justifications do not have to be offered to the consenting party (even if such substantive justifications cannot be altogether avoided in relation to third parties).

Nevertheless, the life-line offered by consent as a justification should not be abused. If we are to take consent seriously, at a practical level, we must guard against the 'routinisation' of consent; it will not do simply to direct a would-be consenting agent to 'sign here and here' or to 'just tick the box'. Nor, of course, will it do to treat the giving of notice (that data will be processed) and the absence of objection as if it were an informed consent that is properly signalled as such. Steps should be taken to ensure that the standards governing the adequacy of consent are fully articulated and stringently applied. The collection of consent, however commonplace, should not be approached in a mechanical or a perfunctory manner. Equally, we must discourage lazy or casual appeals to consent. Where substantive justification is called for, we should settle for nothing less; in particular, we should not be satisfied with artificial procedural justifications that are tendered in their place.[23] Conversely, where substantive arguments are called for to support condemnation of a particular act or practice, they should not be suppressed in favour of a more convenient procedural objection to the effect that no adequate covering consents are in place. In every way, procedural justification should respect the ideals of transparency.

In sum, we begin to understand consent once we appreciate that it has an important role to play in justificatory arguments; and we refine that understanding once we distinguish between appeals to procedural and substantive considerations. However, we should not make the mistake of thinking that consent as a procedural justification is the whole justificatory story.

4.2.2 The Fallacy of Necessity

If some communities under-value and fictionalise consent, then others can over-value it, becoming fixated with the twin ideas that consent is proof against any kind of wrong and that an absence of consent is a cause for complaint. It is important not to get carried away with consent to the point where simple fallacies become written into our practical reason. Two fallacies are pervasive. One, the fallacy of treating consent as a sufficient justifying reason (the Fallacy of Sufficiency)[24], is not material to the present discussion. However, the other fallacy, (the Fallacy of Necessity), is fundamental.

---

[23] For an egregious example, see *Strunk v Strunk* 445 S.W. 2d 145 (Ky. 1969); and, for general discussion, see Deryck Beyleveld and Roger Brownsword, *Consent in the Law* (Oxford: Hart, 2007) Ch. 4.

[24] See Roger Brownsword, 'The Cult of Consent: Fixation and Fallacy' (2004) 15 KCLJ 223.

The Fallacy of Necessity, the fallacy of thinking that it is necessary to have an agent's consent before an action that impacts on the agent's plans or preferences (or, in relation to which, the agent merely has a negative attitude) can be justified, encourages two mistakes. One mistake is to think that where there is no consent there must be a wrong (and, thus, there must be a remedy); and, the other is to think that consent offers the only justification in response to a prima facie wrong.

If we view consent from either a rights-based position or, as Manson and O'Neill do, through the lens of a duty-based theory, the fallacy can be expressed very simply: if an act is morally permissible, informed consent is simply not required.[25] If, for example, my quoting Manson and O'Neill is morally permissible, I do not need their consent to do so. If it is morally permissible for me to know that Manson and O'Neill's recent book was published by Cambridge University Press, I do not need either the authors' or the publisher's consent to hold this information. If my passing on this information to my students is morally permissible, I do not need the authors' or the publisher's consent. Crucially, what determines whether such acts are morally permissible is not the presence or absence of consent but the application of background duties (or rights).

Mutatis mutandis, the same holds with rights-based reasoning: if no right is violated, no wrong is done and there is no wrong for consent to cure. If, for example, Naomi Campbell's right under Article 8(1) of the ECHR was not engaged by the press coverage of her attendance at a Narcotics Anonymous meeting in London, her claim did not get off the ground; and the fact that she had not consented to the coverage was irrelevant. If, however, Campbell's right to privacy was engaged, then for the newspaper to proceed without her consent would involve the commission of a prima facie wrong. Within a rights-based framework, the burden would then be on the newspaper to show that its coverage was justifiable all things considered because it was a necessary and proportionate act designed to serve more compelling rights (such as the Article 10 right to freedom of expression). In other words, notwithstanding the lack of Campbell's consent to the coverage, the newspaper might have argued that its acts were legitimate either because they were morally permissible simpliciter (no rights were engaged) or because, all things considered, they amounted to the lesser of two evils. To assume that Campbell's lack of consent entails wrongdoing, without considering either the non-engagement of a right or the possibility of an overriding rights justification, is to commit the Fallacy of Necessity.

By way of further illustration, recall the alleged data misuse that was tested out in the *Source Informatics*[26] case. There, the question was whether the Department of Health had stated the legal position correctly in advising that there would be a breach of confidence if patients' prescription information, albeit in an anonymised form, was commercially exploited without their consent.[27] Simply pleading a lack of

---

[25] Op cit, note 6 above, at 110–111.

[26] *R v Department of Health ex parte Source Informatics Ltd* [1999] 4 All ER 185; [2001] QB 424 (CA).

[27] For criticism, see, e.g., Deryck Beyleveld and Elise Histed, 'Betrayal of Confidence in the Court of Appeal' (2000) 4 *Medical Law International* 277; Deryck Beyleveld, 'Conceptualising Privacy

consent would not suffice; the patients would be wronged only if one of their rights was violated. At first instance, Latham J (seemingly attributing a proprietary right to the patients) ruled that the Department's advice was correct. However, Latham J's decision was reversed by the Court of Appeal, where it was held that there would be a breach of confidence only if the prescription information was used unfairly against patients, which in turn hinged on whether the patients' privacy right was infringed; and, on this point, the Court, recognising only a narrowly conceived privacy right, held that the right would not be infringed provided that the information was anonymised. Had the information not been anonymised, the patients' lack of consent to the processing would have been decisive –not in a free-standing way but by virtue of there being no consent-based cover for the infringement of the privacy right. The patients' lack of consent would also have been decisive if the privacy right was understood more broadly, or if a rights-based approach to confidentiality had been taken, or indeed if (as Latham J thought) a proprietary interest was implicated. Moreover, on any such analysis, the act of anonymising the information would be an unauthorised act and a prima facie breach of the patients' rights.

To turn *Source Informatics* around, let us suppose that a claim were to be made by a patient who did not wish to be given information about his or her own genetic make-up. The claimant protests, 'I did not consent to this; I did not wish to know'. To get such a claim up and running, the claimant must focus, not on the absence of consent but on the underpinning 'right not to know'.[28] Whether or not such an underpinning right is, or should be, recognised is not the present issue. Rather, the point is that, before we criticise the law or a particular court decision as making too much or too little of consent, we should remind ourselves that if there is no right there is no claim – and, even if there is no consent, this makes not a scrap of difference; no right, with or without consent, adds up to no claim.[29]

4.2.3 Is It a Mistake to Assign Consent a Pivotal Role?

In the light of this clarification, should we think that all is well with data protection law? Let me concede at once that the regulatory architecture of data protection law in Europe is far from satisfactory. In the case of the Data Protection Directive, it is unclear precisely how the provisions in Articles 7 and 8 relate back to the provisions in Article 6, which require Member States to make provision for the fair and lawful processing of personal data as well as its collection 'for specified, explicit and legitimate purposes'. In this latter Article there is no express mention of the data

in Relation to Medical Research Values' in Sheila A.M. McLean (ed.), *First Do No Harm* (Aldershot: Ashgate, 2006) 151, 152–154; and Graeme Laurie, *Genetic Privacy* (Cambridge: Cambridge University Press, 2002).

[28] Background support for such a 'right not to know' is provided by Article 10(2) of the Convention on Human Rights and Biomedicine, 1996 and by Article 5(c) of the UNESCO Universal Declaration on the Human Genome and Human Rights, 1997.

[29] See, further, Gavin Phillipson, 'Transforming Breach of Confidence? Towards a Common Law Right of Privacy under the Human Rights Act' (2003) 66 MLR 726.

subject's consent; yet, if privacy or other data-related rights are in play, we might suppose that the requirement of fair and lawful processing implies either that the data subject has consented or that overriding rights are implicated. More seriously, the Directive threads together the strands of three overlapping information regimes (for privacy, for the processing of personal data and for confidentiality). This, to say the least, is far from ideal; and, if we are to be clear about whether a data subject has relevant rights, we need to disentangle these strands – strands which, as a set, are designed to protect a range of informational interests.

First, there is an interest in informational privacy, this relating to information that is classified as 'private' for the simple reason that it is no one's business other than mine (or the particular person in question). Arguably, the special categories of data picked out by Article 8.1 of the Directive appropriately constitute the classes of data that are covered by such a right. Would we not agree that the data so identified really is just my business? However, even if there are some paradigms of purely private information (such as a person's medical record), there is a serious lack of clarity about the point at which the informational privacy right is engaged. For example, in the important case of *R v Chief Constable of South Yorkshire, ex parte LS and Marper*,[30] one of the questions was whether Article 8(1) (the privacy right) of the European Convention on Human Rights was engaged by the police practice of retaining DNA samples and profiles. Because the samples, if sequenced, might reveal sensitive medical information about the person from whom the sample was taken, it was reasonably clear that privacy was engaged by the retention of the samples. However, the status of the profiles, which are based on non-coding regions of DNA, was much less clear. In general, the profiles, when matched to crime scene samples, would disclose only whether or not a particular person had been in a particular place at a particular time. Did information of this kind come within the class that is protected by the privacy right? The courts were unsure. So, for example, Lord Steyn, who gave the leading speech in the House of Lords, concluded that retention of the profiles either does not engage Article 8(1) at all or engages it only very modestly.[31]

To return to Article 8.1 of the Directive, we can concede that there is room for argument about whether the classes of data specified therein are correctly identified as falling under the protection of a privacy right. Nevertheless, by recognising that not all personal data simpliciter falls within the protection of the privacy right, we share the view expressed by Manson and O'Neill that 'private information is at most a subset of the information that is true of a person and not already public knowledge.'[32] Adopting this view, we should not treat all information that relates to me (all my personal data) as being covered by my privacy right. Like the business on a divided agenda, my life is neither fully public nor is it fully private.

---

[30] [2002] EWCA Civ 1275, [2004] UKHL 39.

[31] [2004] UKHL 39, at para 31. For a different view, and a successful appeal to the European Court of Human Rights, see the *Case of S and Marper v The United Kingdom* (Applications nos 30562/04 and 30566/04, 4 December, 2008).

[32] Op cit, note 6 above, at 103.

Where information is protected by a privacy right, the right-holder will have a claim right that others do not try to access that information – to use the term coined by Serge Gutwirth and Paul De Hert, the informational privacy right is an 'opacity' right.[33] However, what is the position where my personal details are not so protected? Ex hypothesi, I have no claim right that others do not try to access that information (provided, of course, that the inquiries that others make do not violate other rights that I have). However, it does not follow that I am required to disclose such information about myself (in some cases, at least, I might be permitted to keep my personal details to myself). For example, I might not be required to tell you that I work at King's College London; but, in less than a second, a Google search will reveal that very fact and I doubt that you are infringing my privacy rights or any other rights that I have by making the search. On the other hand, if you were to try, without my authorisation, to access the details of my contract of employment, that probably would violate my privacy right. So, whatever information it is that privacy rights protect and how they protect it, it does not follow that this is the same information that we are concerned with in the two other regimes and vice versa. It follows that one of the key tasks for any data protection regime is to make it absolutely clear what (special class of) data is covered by an informational privacy right.

Secondly, there is what we can call the interest in the 'fair processing and fair (and secure)[34] use of personal data' (which I will truncate as the interest in 'fair processing of personal data'), which translates into a bundle of rights that, in Gutwirth and De Hert's terms, are to a considerable extent concerned with 'transparency'.[35] In this light, consider again the growing practice of the taking and processing of DNA samples for forensic purposes. On the face of it, such taking and processing engages both the privacy and the fair processing of personal data rights; and, in the absence of the source's consent, the justification for such actions lies in their being, broadly speaking, for the purpose of preventing and detecting crime.[36] Recently, the Nuffield Council on Bioethics has expressed concern about the use of the National DNA Database as a research resource.[37] Insofar as this involves the use of the samples, this raises a question of privacy (plus a question about confidentiality where third-party

---

[33] Op cit, note 2 above.

[34] After the dramatic loss, in October 2007, by H.M. Revenue and Customs of two discs containing the personal records of some 25 million people, including dates of birth, addresses, bank account and national insurance numbers, we can take it that secure use is likely to be recognised as one of the more important aspects of this interest. See Esther Addley, 'Two Discs, 25m Names and a Lot of Questions' *The Guardian*, November 24, 2007 http://www.guardian.co.uk/uk_news/story/0,,2216251,00.html (last accessed December 8, 2007).

[35] Ibid. The importance of the data subject's interest in transparency is underlined by Articles 10 and 11 of the Directive; according to these provisions, the data subject has a right to be informed that his or her personal data are being processed as well as being told the purpose of such processing.

[36] See Article 13(1)(d) of the Data Protection Directive and Article 8(2) of the European Convention on Human Rights.

[37] Nuffield Council on Bioethics, *The Forensic Use of Bioinformation: Ethical Issues* (London, September 2007) Ch. 6.

access is allowed). Less obviously, perhaps, the use of the profiles might raise an issue about the right to fair processing of personal data, because it is extremely unlikely that when an arrestee supplies a sample he or she is informed (as required by Article 10 of the Directive) that the purpose of the processing might include certain kinds of research.

Once we have disentangled the right to fair processing of personal data from the privacy right, we can treat personal data as a broad class of information that relates to me (qua data subject). But, just how broad is this class of data? Can we be more precise about identifying data that 'relates to' me? In *Durant v Financial Services Authority*[38], the Court of Appeal ruled that '[m]ere mention of the data subject in a document [or file] held by a data controller does not necessarily amount to his personal data.'[39] In the leading judgment, Auld LJ suggested that data is more likely to be treated as personal where it is 'biographical in a significant sense' and where the information has the 'putative data subject as its focus'.[40] Summing up, Auld LJ said:

> In short, it is information that affects his *privacy*, whether in his personal or family life, business or professional capacity.[41]

However, on the analysis that I have been advancing in this paper, such a summation confuses privacy with personal data; and, if we base data protection on privacy, we will tend to treat the range of personal data too narrowly. On the facts of *Durant*, where the Court of Appeal plainly had little sympathy with the applicant's attempt to use the data protection legislation for collateral purposes, we might or might not think that the court got it wrong; but, in the larger picture, it is important that the relationship between privacy rights and personal data processing rights is kept clean and clear.

Having got the extent of personal data correctly in focus, it is very important to remember that this is *not* a right that applies to the processing of personal data regardless of the means or the medium. As Article 3.1 of the Directive makes clear:

> This Directive shall apply to the processing of personal data wholly or partly by automatic means, and to the processing otherwise than by automatic means of personal data which form part of a filing system or are intended to form part of a filing system.

In other words, this is a right that is largely geared for the processing of personal data by modern computing and information technology.[42] The extension for non-automatic processing that forms part of a filing system is designed to neutralise

---

[38] [2003] EWCA Civ 1746. Durant was refused leave to appeal to the House of Lords but an appeal is being made to the European Court of Human Rights. Compare *Dexia v Applicant* 12-07-05 (www.rechtspraak.nl No LJN AS2127) where a Dutch court faced rather similar issues.

[39] *Durant*, at para 28.

[40] Ibid.

[41] Ibid., emphasis added. See, too, Buxton LJ at para 79.

[42] Even in the otherwise excellent DEMOS discussion paper, note 15 above, we read (at 50): Data protection (DP) is an area of law that seeks to maintain an individual's limited right to privacy by regulating the collection, use and dissemination of personal information regarding the

rather obvious attempts to evade the regulatory controls.[43] But this is largely history and it is the automatic processing of personal data that is the future. Even medical files are being converted from paper to digital electronic files and, in the future, it is what happens to personal data in our digitally disciplined democracies that counts.[44] It follows that another key task for any data protection regime is to make it absolutely clear what general class of data counts as personal data and what rights are recognised in relation to the processing of that data.

Thirdly, there is an interest in the confidentiality of information. The confidentiality right covers the distribution and circulation of information that is given by one agent, A, to another, B. Where A's confidentiality right is engaged, B will violate that right by passing on the information to C or D. There is plenty to argue about in relation to the application of the key ideas of *relationships* of confidence or *information* which, in itself, is confidential; but we need not pursue these matters at this stage. In principle, the general focus of the right of confidentiality is reasonably clear; the specification of the circumstances in which the right is engaged might be unclear; but, we can live with it, and it is not presently under attack.[45]

Although these regimes intersect in a complicated way, the form and shape of each segment is the same. There are foundational individual rights. Acts outside the scope of the rights are (other things being equal) permissible; consent is irrelevant. Acts within the scope of the rights need to be authorised by the right-holder's consent. If acts within the scope of the rights are not authorised by the right-holder's consent, they can be justified only by reference to compelling overriding rights.

To argue that consent interferes with legitimate public interest purposes begs the question in favour of utilitarianism and misrepresents the place and significance of consent. In a rights framework, public interest will help to define the shape and scope

---

individual. It is about making sure that the whereabouts and security of, and access to, information is managed or regulated.

Getting tangled up with privacy is not the point; the point is that data protection law is not engaged unless personal information is being *IT processed*.

[43] See Recital 27 and Ian J. Lloyd, *Information Technology Law* 3rd ed (London: Butterworths, 2000) 67–68.

[44] According to Postnote 235, January 2005, note 5 above, 'By 2010 an NHS Care Record for every patient should be available to all doctors and nurses treating a patient in England and Wales. This single electronic record is envisaged to eventually contain an individual's health and care information from birth to death. The NHS proposes that anonymised data will be collected from records for secondary uses such as analysis, audit and research.'

[45] In *Naomi Campbell v Mirror Group Newspapers* [2004] UKHL 22, at para 15, Lord Nicholls summarised the English legal position thus:

[T]he law imposes a 'duty of confidence' whenever a person receives information he knows or ought to know is fairly and reasonably to be regarded as confidential. Even this formulation is awkward. The continuing use of the phrase 'duty of confidence' and the description of the information as 'confidential' is not altogether comfortable. Information about an individual's private life would not, in ordinary usage, be called confidential. The more natural description today is that such information is private. The essence of the tort is better encapsulated now as misuse of private information.

of individual rights.[46] The three root informational rights (privacy, fair processing of personal data and confidentiality) are poorly defined, seriously misunderstood and they urgently need to be reviewed. But, if none of the rights are engaged, consent is simply not an issue. If one of the rights is engaged, consent is an issue but, for the sake of the public interest (qua more compelling rights), action that goes ahead without consent might still be justified. We have already given the example of one of the informational rights being overridden by the conflicting right to life of an agent; but there might also be cases in which one informational right is overridden for the sake of another (more compelling) *informational* right.

Indeed, in *Durant*, we have just such an example of a conflict between the rights of those who supplied information in confidence to the FSA and the data protection rights of those data subjects (such as Durant) about whom information was supplied.[47] Formally, this is a case in which C supplies information (this information relating to A) to B in circumstances in which the information is covered by C's right of confidence. Prima facie, B will violate C's right if the information is transmitted to A without C's consent. B processes this information in a way that puts it into the category of personal data relating to A. A, arguing his right to fair processing of personal data, demands disclosure of the information held by B. Prima facie, B will violate A's right if he declines to disclose the information to A. Here, we have a dilemma. As Auld LJ puts it:

> In such a case both the data subject [A] and the source of the information [C] about him may have their own and contradictory interests to protect. The data subject may have a legitimate interest in learning what has been said about him and by whom in order to enable him to correct any inaccurate information given or opinions expressed. The other may have a justifiable interest in preserving the confidential basis upon which he supplied the information or expressed the opinion.

No matter what B does, there seems to be no clean solution. Section 7(4) of the Data Protection Act purports to resolve the problem by providing that B 'is not obliged to comply with [A's] request' unless: (a) C has consented to the disclosure (in which case, of course, there is no difficulty); or (b) notwithstanding that C has not consented, 'it is reasonable in all the circumstances to comply with [A's] request'; or (c) (stated simply) the information is in a health record or C is a relevant health care professional. The difficult case, then, is one in which C has not consented and where B must assess whether it is reasonable to prioritise A's right. According to Auld LJ, the legislative provisions 'appear to create a presumption or starting point that the information relating to that other, including his identity, should not be disclosed without his consent'; but this is a presumption that may be rebutted.[48] In determining whether it is reasonable to rebut the presumption and to give priority to A's interests, we read:

---

46 Compare Deryck Beyleveld, 'Conceptualising Privacy in Relation to Medical Research Values' in Sheila A.M. McLean (ed.), *First Do No Harm* (Aldershot: Ashgate, 2006) 151, 160–163; and op cit, note 5 above.

47 See [2003] EWCA Civ 1746, paras 52–67.

48 Ibid., at para 55.

> Much will depend, on the one hand, on the criticality of the third party information forming part of the data subject's personal data to the legitimate protection of his privacy and, on the other, to the existence or otherwise of any obligation of confidence to the third party or any other sensitivity of the third party disclosure sought. Where the third party is a recipient or one of a class of recipients who might act on the data to the data subject's disadvantage. . ., his right to protect his privacy may weigh heavily and obligations of confidence to the third party(ies) may be non-existent or of less weight. Equally, where the third party is the source of the information, the data subject may have a strong case for his identification if he needs to take action to correct some damaging inaccuracy, though here countervailing considerations of an obligation of confidentiality to the source or some other sensitivity may have to be weighed in the balance.[49]

Such remarks, however, raise more questions than they answer. First, the problem is expressed in terms of the importance of the personal data relative to the data subject's *privacy* interest. Quite apart from slipping from A's *right to fair processing of personal data* to A's informational *privacy* right, it matters a great deal whether C has obtained information relating to A in breach of A's privacy right – because, if that is so, A has a privacy-based claim against C as well as the fair processing of personal data claim against B that we took to be the premise of the puzzle. Secondly, if the problem concerns C, not as one who supplies information to B but as a potential recipient of information (relating to A) held by B, then we certainly need to inquire as to the circumstances in which B has obtained the information from A and, crucially, whether the information is covered by a duty of confidentiality. Whatever the circumstances, as Auld LJ says, 'obligations of confidence to the third party(ies) may be non-existent' – that is, B's obligation of confidence to C may be non-existent – because, quite simply, if B has an obligation of confidence it is to A (not to C). Thirdly, when we get back to what we took to be the puzzle in *Durant*, we are left unclear whether the particular right that A has and which is to be set against C's confidentiality right is one of privacy or of the fair and transparent processing of personal data, or both; and we are given no indication of how such rights might be ranked.[50]

Taking stock, if there is a major problem with the data protection legislation, I suggest that it lies in the lack of clarity concerning the scope and definition of the three informational rights that it brings together under the general rubric of data protection. We need to be quite clear about the scope of the informational privacy right, the right to fair and transparent processing of personal data and the confidential information right; we need to be clear about the relationship between these rights; and we need to have a sense of how they rank inter se and as against

---

49 Ibid., at para 66.

50 Compare A. Kent, 'Consent and Confidentiality in Genetics: Whose Information is it Anyway?' (2003) 29 *J. Med. Ethics*, 16 at 18 for the following hypothetical: assume two brothers, A and C who have the same doctor, B; C is diagnosed with a fatal, late onset, dominantly inherited genetic disorder; this means that A, as C's brother, is at 50% risk. Now, '[u]nder the terms of the Data Protection Act, data controllers are obliged to tell data subjects if they hold significant information about them. [A] is unaware of the risk. [C wishes his own] confidentiality to be respected.' How should B, as a data controller, act?

other non-informational rights. To be sure, this is asking for a high level of clarification.[51] However, in the absence of such clarity, those who take their legal obligations seriously can be left uncertain of their position and this can lead to a perverse over-application of the regime[52] – as, indeed, it can lead to the kind of under-application that we arguably see in *Durant*. The informational rights need to be respected; but we only need to exercise respect where the rights actually are engaged.

Given such uncertainty, we should focus on what needs to be put right in the rights-based architecture of informational protection. What we should categorically not do is yield to those utilitarians who would prefer to avoid the inconvenience of having to obtain consent. The debate that we should be having, in other words, is not whether consent is too strong a requirement; rather, we should be arguing about the scope of the rights accorded to data subjects and the scope and weight of the public interest reasons that permit data to be automatically processed lack of consent notwithstanding.

4.3 Would a Duty of Confidentiality Serve Us Better?

Even if it is conceded that there has been some misunderstanding about consent, that the utilitarian criticisms are opportunistic, it might still be contended that, in practice, a different ethical approach would serve us better. One persistent argument is that consent has become unworkable because we have no stable or sensible understanding of how much information we should be giving for consent to be adequately informed. With this I agree. However, the response, I suggest, is not to give up on consent but to distinguish between background informational responsibilities and the particular requirement of *informed* consent. This is where I begin in this part of the paper.

Having drawn this distinction, does it follow that we should accept Manson and O'Neill's invitation to base data protection, not on the rights of data subjects but on the informational obligation of confidentiality? For two reasons, I argue against acceptance: first, because it would probably come to much the same thing in practice, including much the same with regard to the role accorded to individual consent; and, secondly and much more importantly, because I believe that a dedicated rights-based protection of the interest in fair processing of personal data is vital in a world where personal information is automatically processed to an extent not dreamed of when the need for data protection law was first accepted.

---

[51] Arguably, the ECJ made a start on this task in *Lindqvist* (Approximation of laws) [2003] EUECJ C-101/01 (06 November 2003). There, the ECJ is clear about the broad scope of personal data (see paras 24–27) but the Court's comments about the relationship between data protection , privacy and freedom of expression are much less decisive (see paras 79–90).

[52] See the concerns expressed in Academy of Medical Sciences, 'Personal Data for Public Good: Using Health Information in Medical Research' (London, January 2006).

4.3.1 Informed Consent and Informational Obligations

In principle, the following two questions are quite distinct.[53] First, how much information does a person need to have before they are sufficiently informed for the purpose of giving an authorising consent? Secondly, what background informational rights and obligations do agents have to one another, irrespective of whether an agent is in a consent situation? For example, we might ask whether one agent has a duty to warn another about a hazard of some kind (a fire, an unsafe bridge, a hole in the ground, a raging bull on the loose, or whatever), not so that the latter can give an informed consent but simply to assist the other in avoiding the hazard.

There is much to be said about how we should respond to these two questions, about how we should articulate the informational conditions for a valid consent and what background informational rights and duties should be specified. However, having written about such matters elsewhere,[54] I will pass over the details on this occasion. For present purposes, the crucial point is to appreciate that, as a matter of principle, there are two distinct sets of questions and that *it is the second set that is prior*. In other words, in a community of rights, consent functions as a dynamic between agents but not in a way that is independent of the background scheme of rights and duties; the operation of consent is always relative to the established set of rights and obligations. In other words, until the background rights, including the background informational rights have been established, consent has no reference point.

Even if the distinction is clear enough in principle, in practice, we soon lose sight of it and nowhere more so than in clinical and research practice, where there is a tendency to run the two questions together under the general rubric of informed consent. Typically, we talk about informed consent in the context of claims made by patients who complain that their physicians did not properly inform them about the risks associated with their treatment and, as a result, they embarked on the treatment without having given an adequate consent. To counter this tendency, we should keep reminding ourselves about a reverse hypothetical in which a patient decides *against* medical treatment. Here, there is no consent; in this sense informed consent is not an issue. Nevertheless, the patient, subsequently learning that the medical options were not fully disclosed and that there were options that should have been identified for consideration, now complains that her right to be informed has been breached. This surely is a perfectly intelligible claim. Regardless of whether the complaint can be made out on the facts, in principle, the patient has reason to complain – not because she gave a consent that was not sufficiently informed but because she was not sufficiently informed to contemplate giving consent.[55]

---

[53] Compare Manson and O'Neill, note 6 above, where this distinction, if not absolutely explicitly drawn, is surely implicit.

[54] See, Roger Brownsword, op cit, note 17 above, Chapter Three.

[55] Compare the insightful analysis (and critique of English tort law) in Emily Jackson, "Informed Consent' to Medical Treatment and the Impotence of Tort' in Sheila A.M. McLean (ed.), *First Do No Harm* (Aldershot: Ashgate, 2006) 273.

Having separated out the informational requirements for consent from background informational responsibilities, this is by no means the end of our difficulties with informed consent. However, it suggests how we might address problems about informational overload and uncertainty with regard to the informed consent requirement.[56] Arguably, a consent is sufficiently informed if the right-holder understands that consent is an option (that there is no penalty for refusal) and that, if consent is given, then (within the scope of the consent) the recipient will be justified in acting in ways that would otherwise violate the consenting party's rights. Whether or not one agrees with this minimalist view, it would be absurd to condemn any regulatory regime that hinges on informed consent simply because we are unable to get our heads around the two distinct sets of informational requirements.

4.3.2 Should We Base Data Protection on a Duty of Confidence?

If we start with the idea of informational obligations, what might we prescribe? According to Manson and O'Neill[57]:

> Obligations to respect others' informational privacy are first order obligations not to act in certain ways. They include obligations to refrain from attempting to find out certain things; obligations not to disclose certain things; obligations not to communicate certain things to some, or to any, others.

Against this general background of informational obligations, obligations of confidentiality would be triggered whenever communications or relationships were of a confidential nature. In such cases, the confidants would have an obligation not to take unfair advantage of the information given to them. This proposal might draw some support from the Court of Appeal's approach in *Source Informatics*; but is it the way ahead? For the two reasons already mentioned, I suggest that it is not.

4.3.2.1 Would Consent Still Feature in Such a Regime?

Imagine two information-protecting regimes, one based on the privacy right, the other based on a duty of confidence. In each of the regimes, the respective cornerstone rights and duties support a number of rights and duties, pertaining to collection, use and transmission of information. Insofar as the rights and duties so specified vary from one regime to another, the regimes (depending upon their interpretation) might have a differential application in practice. However, this flows from the scope and specification of the background rights and duties; it is nothing to do with consent. Let us stipulate, therefore, that the substantive coverage of the respective rights and duties in the two regimes is identical. Now we can ask what this means for consent.

---

56 See, further, Roger Brownsword, 'Informed Consent: To Whom it May Concern' (2007) 15 *Jahrbuch für Recht und Ethik* 267.

57 Op cit, note 6 above, at 102.

In some modern duty-based ethics, particularly the dignitarian ethic that is so important in the context of modern biotechnology, consent is something of a sideshow.[58] Here, the fundamental axiom is that human dignity should not be compromised; and it follows that the duty to respect human dignity is not switched off by the consent of others any more than that it is switched on again by a withdrawal or a refusal of consent. If a regime of information protection that is based on a duty of confidence disables consent in this way, then its practical application would be significantly different to the application that flows from a regime based on the privacy right. However, for those (not, of course, including myself) who would like to see consent removed from the regulatory scene, the overall effect would not be to free up the processing of personal data but, to the contrary, to prohibit various information processing practices.

Although Manson and O'Neill recommend a duty-based approach, their ethic still accords consent a pivotal role. For, according to Manson and O'Neill: 'Confidentiality can be invoked for specific aspects of professional, commercial or other relationships, and can be waived by seeking consent from the confider.'[59] So, for example, if doctors receive information in confidence from their patients and where it becomes apparent that it is in the interests of a third party to be made aware of this information, Manson and O'Neill would leave room for the patients to waive the protection of confidentiality – which is precisely what, mutates mutandis, the position would be under a regime based on the privacy right. In other words, whether the regime is based on privacy (rights) or confidentiality (duties), best practice will advise seeking the patient's consent before transmitting the information; and, if the consent cannot be obtained, it is only in exceptional circumstances that the breach (of privacy or confidence) will be treated as justifiable.

The significance of this point is as follows. If we want to remove the requirement of consent from the data protection regime (which, to repeat, is not at all my position), then Manson and O'Neill's proposal is not going to have that effect. Following their proposal, consent would remain a pivotal feature of data protection law. However, it would be anchored to a duty of confidentiality rather than a right of privacy, or the like. The relevant question for present purposes, therefore, is whether a duty of confidentiality is the best anchoring point for data protection.

4.3.2.2 Would a Regime Based on an Obligation of Confidence Adequately Cover Fair and Transparent Processing of Personal Data?

It bears repetition that the context in which we ask the question of whether norms of confidentiality would serve us better is one of the Information Society. This is how

---

58 See Roger Brownsword, 'Bioethics Today, Bioethics Tomorrow: Stem Cell Research and the 'Dignitarian Alliance" (2003) 17 *University of Notre Dame Journal of Law, Ethics and Public Policy* 15, 'Three Bioethical Approaches: A Triangle to be Squared' (Tokyo, September 2004) (available at <www.ipgenethics.org/conference/transcript/session3.doc>), and 'Stem Cells and Cloning: Where the Regulatory Consensus Fails' (2005) 39 *New England Law Review* 535.

59 Note 6 above, at 126–127.

the context is set for the *APEC Privacy Framework*[60] (which, famously, can include Google amongst its admirers):

> Information and communications technologies, including mobile technologies, that link to the Internet and other information networks have made it possible to collect, store and access information from anywhere in the world. These technologies offer great potential for social and economic benefits for business, individuals and governments, including increased consumer choice, market expansion, productivity, education and product innovation. However, while these technologies make it easier and cheaper to collect, link and use large quantities of information, they also often make these activities undetectable to individuals. Consequently, it can be more difficult for individuals to retain a measure of control over their personal information. As a result, individuals have become concerned about the harmful consequences that may arise from the misuse of their information. Therefore, there is a need to promote and enforce ethical and trustworthy information practices in on- and off-line contexts to bolster the confidence of individuals and businesses.[61]

Within such a setting, it bears repetition that data protection, as currently constituted in Europe, brings together three distinct informational interests (and, concomitantly, rights) that, as a set, form an information-protecting regulatory tricolour. Privacy is focused narrowly on private information but it protects it in a broad fashion against initial collection and subsequent unauthorised use; fair data processing covers a broad class of personal data but it protects it in a very specific context; and confidentiality protects information that is communicated in a particular kind of relationship or that is marked up in a particular way, in both cases the protection being against onward transmission (or, in Manson and O'Neill's formulation, against unfair advantage-taking). It is not simply a matter, however, of understanding that each band of the tricolour makes a distinctive contribution; we also need to be aware of the particular strengths and weaknesses (especially the latter) of each band in today's Information Society.

First, the recent English experience with privacy and confidentiality is not a happy one. While these seem to be relatively strong remedies on paper, the reality is that they are largely employed by the rich and famous to negotiate the bounds of acceptable media coverage.[62] In this role, privacy and confidentiality have rather taken over from the law of defamation as the favoured form of claim but this is not a significant change – in relation to this kind of litigation, Britain is still a class-divided society. Moreover, whereas confidentiality was originally designed to protect commercial secrets, it has now been distorted out of all recognition in order to serve as the basis of free-standing privacy claims.[63] So, the situation is unsatisfactory whether we focus simply on the doctrinal landscape or look more broadly at access to justice. Of course, it might be said that these are no more than local difficulties. Even so, so far as England is concerned, the legal community

---

60 Asia-Pacific Economic Cooperation, *APEC Privacy Framework* (Singapore: APEC Secretariat, 2005).

61 Ibid., para 2.

62 See, e.g., *The Guardian*, September 17, 2007, supplement on Media Law.

63 See Rachael Mullheron, 'A Potential Framework for Privacy? A Reply to *Hello!*' (2006) 69 MLR 679; and compare note 45 above.

would surely doubt the wisdom of seeking to build a regulatory regime on the duty of confidence. By contrast, in line with Article 28 of the Directive, the rights of data subjects are overseen by the Information Commissioner. This does not preclude individuals taking private enforcement action; and nor, bearing in mind the Commissioner's limited resources, does it guarantee full protection. Nevertheless, it is a very different regulatory model to one that relies on happenstance litigation and development of the law through the cases.

Secondly, to the extent that actions for privacy (and, parasitically, confidentiality) hinge on whether there was a 'reasonable expectation' that the information would be respected as private – as Lord Nicholls put it in *Campbell*, '[e]ssentially the touchstone of private life is whether in respect of the disclosed facts the person in question had a reasonable expectation of privacy'[64] – the scope of the claim can be reduced as practice modifies what is *expected* and then what is *reasonably* expected.[65] In a society that is becoming ever more reliant on IT, a drift away from privacy can easily occur. This danger is well described by Bert-Jaap Koops and Ronald Leenes[66]:

> Technology affects the 'reasonable expectation of privacy'. . . .In the vast majority of technologies developed and used in real life, its influence is to the detriment of privacy. That is, technology often has the side-effect of making privacy violations easier. . . .
>
> . . . .Examples in law enforcement and e-government show technology offers increasing opportunities for large-scale monitoring – from intercepting all telecommunications. . .to monitoring the movements of people. In the private sector, technology enables more control of people, from workplace and transaction monitoring to personalization of consumer relationships, with new applications like facial recognition and RFID monitoring looming ahead.
>
> . . . .People gladly adopt the new possibilities. In fact, after a lapse of time, one gets so used to this new control mechanism that one may no longer perceive it as a side-effect but as an intrinsic – and perhaps intended – characteristic of the technology. This is when the 'reasonableness' of a privacy expectation shifts: once the new technology is accepted as being inherently control-friendly, there no longer is a reasonable expectation that this control is not exerted. . . .
>
> The eroding effect of technology on privacy is thus a slow, hardly perceptible process. There is no precise stage at which one can stab a finger at technology to accuse it of unreasonably tilting the balance of privacy. Exactly because of the flexible, fluid nature of privacy, society gradually adapts to new technologies and the privacy expectations that go with them.[67]

In a community where agents have become de-sensitised to the routine obtaining and use of what might once have been viewed as sensitive personal information, there will be little expectation of informational privacy and, when such an

[64] *Campbell v Mirror Group Newspapers Limited* [2004] UKHL 22, para 21.

[65] For a robust defence of British practice (as against the Continental European standards upheld in *Von Hannover v Germany* [2004] EMLR 21, see, *Murray v Express Newspapers plc* [2007] EWHC 1908 (Ch)).

[66] Bert-Jaap Koops and Ronald Leenes, ''Code' and the Slow Erosion of Privacy' (2005) 12 *Michigan Telecommunications and Technology Law Review* 115.

[67] Ibid at 176–177.

expectation is asserted, it will probably be rejected as unreasonable.[68] It is the very ordinariness of what was once extraordinary that we need to keep an eye on. To revert to an earlier illustration, imagine if I were to protest that you had no right to use Google to find out that I am a law professor at King's College London. Technology not only erodes privacy in practice, with the practice-based conception it also shifts the boundaries of reasonable expectation and erodes privacy in principle.

Thirdly, following on from the previous point, Article 6 of the Data Protection Directive requires that Member States should make provision for the fair and lawful processing of personal data. On the face of it, this is an important protection for the data subject, quite possibly encouraging the view that, in the absence of the data subject's consent to the processing, there will need to be overriding rights in play.[69] Yet, in practice, Article 6 has been interpreted much less protectively and, as the recent English High Court decision in *Murray v Express Newspapers plc*[70] all too clearly illustrates, the data protection right can be corroded by the practice-based weakness of the adjacent privacy (and confidentiality) rights. In *Murray*, an unauthorised photograph of the author, J.K. Rowling, her husband and their young son David was taken while they walked in an Edinburgh street. This occasioned no distress because the family had no knowledge that the photograph was being taken; and neither was the subject-matter of the photograph in any way embarrassing. It was simply a photograph of the Murray-Rowling family on the Edinburgh streets. The primary question was whether, when this photograph was taken with an intention that it should be used by a national newspaper, the privacy rights of the family, specifically of young David, were engaged. According to Patten J:

> [I]f the law is such as to give every adult or child a legitimate expectation of not being photographed without consent on any occasion on which they are not, so to speak, on public business then it will have created a right for most people to the protection of their image. If a simple walk down the street qualifies for protection then it is difficult to see what would not. For most people who are not public figures in the sense of being politicians or the like, there will be virtually no aspect of their life which cannot be characterized as private. Similarly, even celebrities would be able to confine unauthorized photography to the occasions on which they were at a concert, film premiere or some similar occasion.

---

[68] Compare Aimee Jodoi Lum, 'Don't Smile, Your Image has just been Recorded on a Camera-Phone: The Need for Privacy in the Public Sphere' (2005) 27 *University of Hawai'i Law Review* 377, at 386:

Many of the same social conditions exist today as they did in the 1990's, but the explosion of technological advances has made individuals far more susceptible to invasions of privacy than ever before. America's voyeuristic tendencies and obsession with reality TV further exacerbates the problem because behaviours that might otherwise be considered unacceptable become normalized.

[69] Compare the *APEC Privacy Framework*, note 60 above, para 18 of which provides that personal information 'should be obtained by lawful and fair means and where appropriate, with notice to, or consent of, the individual concerned.' Consent, we might say, is rather weakly implicated. By contrast, in para 19, it is the consent of the individual concerned that offers the first line of justification for secondary uses of personal information. Yet, why should we give more emphasis to consent in relation to further uses of the information and less in relation to the original collection of the data?

[70] [2007] EWHC 1908 (Ch). For a successful appeal against the High Court's decision to strike out the claim, see [2008] EWCA Civ 446.

> I start with a strong disposition to the view that routine acts such as the visit to the shop or the ride on the bus should not attract any reasonable expectation of privacy. . . .Even after *Von Hannover* [in the European Court of Human Rights] there remains, I believe, an area of routine activity which when conducted in a public place carries no guarantee of privacy.[71]

What we see in these remarks is a repetition of the conflation of privacy and personal data that we saw earlier in *Durant*. It is imperative that the interest in privacy is not confused with the interest in the fair processing of personal data, or vice versa. For, while it might be perfectly reasonable to reject the idea that a routine walk through the Edinburgh streets engages the privacy interest, it is not at all reasonable to dismiss the idea that routine activities do not engage the interest in fair processing of personal data. Yet, in *Murray*, having held that the privacy right was not engaged, Patten J thought it followed that (for data protection purposes) the photograph must have been obtained both lawfully and, in the absence of actual deception, fairly. But, we surely need to record the distinction between, on the one hand, the simple and unavoidable observation of the Murray family and, on the other, the acquisition of that data with a view to its automatic processing. In almost any kind of society, we will acquire some personal data about others; but the context of the dispute in *Murray* is not just any kind of society, it is an information society. It is one thing to set a fairly high (and, possibly, getting even higher) threshold for the engagement of the privacy (or confidentiality) right; it is quite another thing to replicate this threshold in relation to the right to fair processing of personal data. If we do this, as happened in *Murray*, the informational interests of data subjects are vulnerable to routine neglect; and, by the time that the consent of data subjects becomes an issue, a great deal of routine damage will have been done.[72]

Fourthly, when there is a growing concern about the development of surveillance societies in Europe, this is precisely the time when we should not abandon or weaken our data protection values.[73] For instance, according to John Gibb:

---

[71] [2007] EWHC 1908 (Ch), paras 65–66.

[72] Compare, Peter Bradwell and Niamh Gallagher, *FYI: the New Politics of Personal Information* (London: DEMOS, 2007) at 17.

There is a disconnect between people's standard concerns about privacy and Big Brother on the one hand and, on the other, their willingness to be part of a world to which surveillance of some form is fundamental.

As a result, few people connect those concerns to their everyday experiences. This is not surprising, given that personal information is often gathered as part of transactions, interactions or situations we enjoy or find beneficial.

It is this combination of the seemingly benign collection of personal information (for IT processing) with its everyday routineness that is so insidious.

[73] The fact that the Directive has limited scope, especially in the area of national security, does not mean that we should ignore this phenomenon. See, e.g., Joined Cases C-317/04 *Parliament v Council* (OJ C 228, 11 September 2004, p. 31) and C-318/04 *Parliament v Commission* (OJ C 228, 11 September 2004, p. 32) (concerning the legality of the agreement made by the European Commission and the USA with regard to disclosure of airline passenger name records). For commentary, see, Ioannis Ntouvas, 'Air Passenger Data Transfer to the USA: the Decision of the ECJ and Latest Developments' International Journal of Law and Information Technology (August 29, 2007) at http://ijlit.oxfordjournals.org/cgi/content/full/eam003v1 (accessed November 5, 2007).

> Once identity card information is pooled and cross-referenced with other personal data, including Inland Revenue and Customs and Excise records, Criminal Records, the new and fast-growing [national DNA database], the NHS database, the huge amount of knowledge gained and stored from smart cards and credit cards, immigration records, the Department for Education database, the Passport Office, driving licences, bank records, library records and the National Register of Births, Marriages and Deaths, everything about us will be known – and that's probably more than we know about ourselves.[74]

If we heed this message, we surely will think that what matters in the foreseeable future is not that a privileged few can follow Naomi Campbell into court to recover damages against the tabloid press for privacy violations, nor that the same few can obtain injunctions to prevent the publication of 'kiss and tell' stories that breach confidentiality; what matters is that there is some regulatory oversight in relation to the myriad personal data that, nowadays, is routinely collected and fed into a computing system (whether for commercial or non-commercial, governmental or non-governmental, purposes). Once so collected, that data is not only susceptible to deep mining and profiling, it is also liable to spread far and wide.[75] At present, data protection law recognises that each and everyone of us, not just the privileged few, has a legitimate interest in the data being used fairly and for a proper purpose, being maintained in an accurate and secure form and so on.[76] The suite of rights recognised by data protection regimes probably needs to be revisited and, to this extent, Manson and O'Neill are surely right in complaining that the current regime fails to draw sensible distinctions between the proper and improper purposes of personal data processors. Nevertheless, rethinking the regime is not the same as giving up on bespoke protection of what I am calling the right to fair processing of personal data.

Finally, to repeat my earlier point, once the law clearly distinguishes the three informational rights and specifies their individual scope, there needs to be some reflection on the importance of each right relative not only to one another but also to other rights that are recognised. If we measure the importance of a particular right relative to the needs of agents, then informational rights are not matters of life and death but they are still of considerable importance and they will not be lightly overridden by non-informational rights. As between the informational rights themselves, it is difficult to say where the first priority should be. In general, privacy seems to have a priority over confidentiality because the latter often will not be engaged unless the right holder has first authorised the release of information that is protected by the privacy right. As for the right to fair and transparent processing of personal data, this would be of little significance in a society where interactions and transactions are not yet IT enabled. But, where dealing is routinely conducted

---

[74] John Gibb, *Who's Watching You?* (London: Collins, 2005) 236.

[75] Compare Anton H. Vedder, 'KDD, Privacy, Individuality, and Fairness' in Richard A. Spinello and Herman T. Tavani (eds.), *Readings in Cyberethics* 2nd ed (Sudbury, Mass.: Jones and Bartlett, 2004) 462; and James H. Moor, 'Toward a Theory of Privacy for the Information Age', in Spinello and Tavani, op cit, 407.

[76] Directive 95/46/EC, Article 6.

in electronic environments, agents have an intense interest in what use is made of their personal data and this right assumes much greater significance. Arguably, then, the outcome of such reflection on the ranking of the informational rights would be to accord less weight to the confidentiality right than to either privacy or data processing rights.

4.4 Conclusion

According to the authors of a recent report for the Information Commissioner, the development of the surveillance society is not so much a conspiracy as 'a part of just being modern.'[77] Under such conditions of modernity[78], as the technologies of surveillance[79] become increasingly sophisticated, less obtrusive and embedded, citizens will not always be aware that they are being monitored and regulated. Thus:

> [The] continuous software-sorting of people and their life chances in cities is organised through myriad electronic and physical 'passage points' or 'choke points', negotiated through a widening number of code words, pass words, PIN numbers, user names, access controls, electronic cards or biometric scans. Some are highly visible and negotiated willingly (a PIN credit card purchase or an airport passport control). Others are more covert (the sorting of Internet or call centre traffic). On still other occasions, the passage point is clear (a CCTV camera on a street or a speed camera on a motorway) but it is impossible to know in practice if one's face or car number plate has actually been scanned.[80]

More generally, the 'combination of CCTV, biometrics, databases and tracking technologies can be seen as part of a much broader exploration. . .of the use of interconnected "smart" systems to track movements and behaviours of millions of people in both time and space.'[81]

In the context of these developments, we find proposals for a vote of no confidence in data protection law and a backlash against the need for individual consent. Against such a proposal, in this paper, I have argued on two fronts. First, I have argued that we should not let critics get away with the Fallacy of Necessity. If they get away with it, they will distort the consent requirements of data protection law and create a soft target. Secondly, I have argued that, as far as modern (and rapidly developing) ICT-enabled environments are concerned, data protection (qua the right to fair and transparent processing of personal data) is the key stripe in the regulatory tricolour and, if we are concerned about the integrity of information in

---

[77] Kirstie Ball, David Lyon, David Murakami Wood, Clive Norris and Charles Raab, *A Report on the Surveillance Society* (September 2006), para 1.6.

[78] Ball et al, op cit, note 77 above, identify the key characteristics of such a society as one in which 'we find purposeful, routine, systematic and focused attention paid to personal details, for the sake of control, entitlement, management, influence or protection' (para 3.1).

[79] For a review of the range of such technologies, see ibid at para 9.3 et seq.

[80] Ibid, para 9.10.2.

[81] Ibid, para 9.10.3.

an information age, it is the last piece of regulatory protection that we should be contemplating giving up.

Stated summarily, my principal conclusions are threefold. First, we need a regulatory regime that clearly identifies and distinguishes (i) an informational privacy right, (ii) a right of informational confidence and (iii) a bespoke set of rights covering the ICT-enabled processing of personal data.[82] Secondly, not least (but not exclusively for this reason) because of the European commitment to respect for human rights, such a regime should be rights-based. And, thirdly, and necessarily, the consent of rights-holders should continue to be treated as pivotal within such a regime. Accordingly, unless a rights-holder consents to what would otherwise be an infringement of one of the rights in the informational set, a wrong is done; and the only justification will be that the act was carried out for the sake of overriding rights.

References

Academy of Medical Sciences, *Personal Data for Public Good: Using Health Information in Medical Research*, London, January 2006.

Addley, E., 'Two Discs, 25 m Names and a Lot of Questions', *The Guardian*, November 24, 2007.

Asia-Pacific Economic Cooperation, *APEC Privacy Framework*, Singapore, APEC Secretariat, 2005.

Ball, K., Lyon, D., Murakami Wood, D., Norris, C., and Raab, C., *A Report on the Surveillance Society*, September 2006.

Beyleveld, D., 'Conceptualising Privacy in Relation to Medical Research Values' in Sheila A.M. McLean (ed.), *First Do No Harm* Aldershot, Ashgate, 2006, pp. 151–163.

Beyleveld, D., 'Medical Research and the Public Good', *King's Law Journal* Vol. 18, 2007, pp. 275–289.

Beyleveld, D. and Brownsword, R., *Consent in the Law*, Oxford, Hart, 2007.

Beyleveld, D. and Histed, E., 'Betrayal of Confidence in the Court of Appeal' *Medical Law International* Vol. 4, 2000, pp. 277–311.

Boyd, P., 'The Requirements of the Data Protection Act 1998 for the Processing of Medical Data' *Journal of Medical Ethics* Vol. 29, 2003, pp. 34–35.

Bradwell, P. and Gallagher, N., *FYI: the New Politics of Personal Information*, London, DEMOS, 2007.

Brownsword, R., 'Bioethics Today, Bioethics Tomorrow: Stem Cell Research and the "Dignitarian Alliance"' *University of Notre Dame Journal of Law, Ethics and Public Policy* Vol. 17, 2003, pp. 15–51.

Brownsword, R., 'Three Bioethical Approaches: A Triangle to be Squared' (Tokyo, September 2004) (available at <www.ipgenethics.org/conference/transcript/session3.doc>)

Brownsword, R., 'The Cult of Consent: Fixation and Fallacy', *King's College Law Journal*, Vol. 15, 2004, pp. 223–251.

Brownsword, R., 'Stem Cells and Cloning: Where the Regulatory Consensus Fails' *New England Law Review* Vol. 39, 2005, pp. 535–571.

Brownsword, R., 'Informed Consent: To Whom it May Concern' *Jahrbuch für Recht und Ethik*, Vol. 15, 2007, pp. 267–289.

Brownsword, R., 'Knowing Me, Knowing You – Profiling, Privacy and the Public Interest' in Mireille Hildebrandt and Serge Gutwirth (eds.), *Profiling the European Citizen*, Dordrecht, Springer, 2008, pp. 362–382

[82] For the beginning of such a separation, see Articles 7 (privacy) and 8 (data protection) of the Charter of Fundamental Rights of the European Union (2000/C 364/01).

Brownsword, R., *Rights, Regulation and the Technological Revolution*, Oxford, Oxford University Press, 2008.
Dworkin, R.M., *Taking Rights Seriously*, London, Duckworth, 1978.
Garrie, D.B. and Wong, R., 'Regulating Voice Over Internet Protocol: An EU/US Comparative Approach' *American University International Law Review* Vol. 22, 2007, pp. 549–581.
Gibb, J., *Who's Watching You?*, London, Collins and Brown, 2005.
Gutwirth, S. and De Hert, P., 'Privacy, Data Protection and Law Enforcement. Opacity of the Individual and Transparency of Power' in Claes, E., Duff, A., and Gutwirth, S. (eds.), *Privacy and the Criminal Law*, Antwerp and Oxford, Intersentia, 2006.
Hart, H.L.A., 'Bentham on Legal Rights', in Simpson, A.W.B. (ed.), *Oxford Essays in Jurisprudence* (Second Series) Oxford, Clarendon Press, 1973, p 171.
Hildebrandt, M., 'A Vision of Ambient Law' in Brownsword, R. and Yeung, K. (eds.), *Regulating Technologies*, Oxford, Hart, 2008.
Jackson, E., ' "Informed Consent" to Medical Treatment and the Impotence of Tort' in McLean, S.A.M. (ed.), *First Do No Harm*, Aldershot, Ashgate, 2006, pp. 273–286.
Kent, A., 'Consent and Confidentiality in Genetics: Whose Information is it Anyway?' *Journal of Medical Ethics*, Vol. 29, 2003, pp. 16–18.
Koops, B-J and Leenes, R., ' "Code" and the Slow Erosion of Privacy' *Michigan Telecommunications and Technology Law Review*, Vol. 12, 2005, pp. 115–188.
Laurie, G., *Genetic Privacy*, Cambridge, Cambridge University Press, 2002.
Lloyd, I.J., *Information Technology Law* 3rd ed., London, Butterworths, 2000.
Lum, A.J., 'Don't Smile, Your Image has just been Recorded on a Camera-Phone: The Need for Privacy in the Public Sphere' *University of Hawai'i Law Review*, Vol. 27, 2005, pp. 377–416.
MacCormick, D.N., 'Rights in Legislation' in Hacker, P.M.S. and Raz, J. (eds.), *Law, Morality, and Society*, Oxford, Clarendon Press, 1977, p. 189.
Manson, N.C. and O'Neill, O., *Rethinking Informed Consent in Bioethics*, Cambridge, Cambridge University Press, 2007.
Moor, J.H., 'Toward a Theory of Privacy for the Information Age', in Spinello, R.A. and Tavani, H.T. (eds.), *Readings in Cyberethics* 2nd ed., Sudbury, Mass., Jones and Bartlett, 2004, pp. 407–417.
Mullheron, R., 'A Potential Framework for Privacy? A Reply to *Hello!*' *Modern Law Review*, Vol. 69, 2006, pp. 679–713.
Ntouvas, I., 'Air Passenger Data Transfer to the USA: the Decision of the ECJ and Latest Developments' *International Journal of Law and Information Technology* (August 29, 2007) at http://ijlit.oxfordjournals.org/cgi/content/full/eam003v1.
Nuffield Council on Bioethics, *The Forensic Use of Bioinformation: Ethical Issues*, London, September 2007.
Parliamentary Office of Science and Technology, *Data Protection and Medical Research* (Postnote Number 235, January 2005).
Phillipson, G., 'Transforming Breach of Confidence? Towards a Common Law Right of Privacy under the Human Rights Act' *Modern Law Review*, Vol. 66, 2003, pp. 726–758.
Swire, P.P. and Litan, R.E., *None of Your Business: World Data Flows, Electronic Commerce and the European Privacy Directive*, Washington DC, Brookings Institution Press, 1998.
Vedder, A.H., 'KDD, Privacy, Individuality, and Fairness' in Spinello, R.A. and Tavani, H.T. (eds.), *Readings in Cyberethics* 2nd ed., Sudbury, Mass., Jones and Bartlett, 2004, pp. 462–470.

Chapter 5
The Concepts of Identity and Identifiablity: Legal and Technical Deadlocks for Protecting Human Beings in the Information Society?

Jean-Marc Dinant

5.1 The Protection of Data as Seen by Computer Science

Generally speaking, technology in itself does not deal with personal data and even not with privacy but rather, from the very beginning, with data security, wherever those data may concern a human being and wherever this human being is identified or identifiable. Originally and during many decades, the security conception in the field of the information technology has been based on three corner stones: integrity, availability and confidentiality of information systems.

Recently, the identification and authentication of users has appeared as a new requirement for security. Roughly speaking, this authentication does not claim to be, in se, a corner stone of ICT security but rather a means to achieve the integrity, the availability and the confidentiality of information systems. In fact, to permit an assessment of the security of an information system, it may be useful to log all the transactions that may compromise the availability, the integrity and the confidentiality of the information system. In an insecure virtual world, populated by bugs and hackers, such a systematic collection of the traffic can make sense. Behind the identification of users, the authentication becomes more and more crucial in a virtual world in which a continuously growing amount of transactions between bodies and relations between humans do not involve the simultaneous physical presence of the implied parties and where a wide majority of information systems can be reached through the Internet by everybody in the world in real time, without needing to enter in a geographically delimited area.

The general requirement for user's authentication and identification has lead to a new branch inside information security: the so called Identity Management Systems. In this context, the wording "identity" does not relate to a philosophical or legal notion but rather to a kind of management of rights granted to particular identified and authenticated users within an information system. The assessment of the security of an information system can not be achieved without an infrastructure of rights

J.-M. Dinant (✉)
Technology and Security Research Unit, Centre of Research in IT and Law, University of Namur, Namur, Belgium
e-mail: reinventingprivacy@dinant.org

S. Gutwirth et al. (eds.), *Reinventing Data Protection?*
DOI 10.1007/978-1-4020-9498-9_5, © Springer Science+Business Media B.V. 2009

management describing who can access to what (availability), who can not access to which kind of information (confidentiality) and who has the right to modify which kind of information and in which circumstances (integrity).

In this framework and since many years, log files have been structured, deployed and enabled by default in each kind of information server (HTTP, FTP, RAS, SMTP, POP, SQL, etc.). Those log files have been originally designed for debugging purposes and, in this context, every information related to the request and the requester – including but not limited to – date and time, IP address, identification of the user, his location, the device used, the operating system of the device, the brand and version of the client software, etc may be relevant and becomes thus collected and stored. This is to say that, on the Internet, every client device communicating with a server (this is done daily by reading a web page, placing a post on a blog, sending or receiving a mail, chatting, etc) by default and systematically leaves numerous traces at the server side. Those traces are stored in log files and those log files may, in their turn, be archived in data warehouses. The huge amount of traffic data stored in data warehouses is currently more and more exploited, for a new purpose having no link with security requirements or debugging purposes. After many months or years, those traffic data are, in their huge majority, electronic evidence of perfectly legal (trans)actions that do not bring any substantial added value to the preservation of the availability, the confidentiality or the integrity of modern information systems.

Nowadays, predictive analytic modelling rises up as a new discipline combining data mining and statistics to build behavioural modelling of users. Both due to the raising performance of processing (in terms of speed and algorithmic progresses) and the endless rising capacity of massive data storage, it becomes now possible to apply single pass algorithms to several millions of individual transactions to extract a typical behavioural model of users in a few hours or days. The techniques used for weather forecast on the basis of a thousand observations can now, technically speaking, be applied to millions of human transactions and are used to predict human behaviour rather than weather, with a reasonable range of error.

Three characteristics of such a massive human data analysis need to be underlined.

- First of all, the predictive modelling does not use human common sense. A predictive model while being applied to an individual, permit, on the basis of certain characteristics of his past history to predict characteristics of his behaviour in the future. This modelling is the result of computation and not of reasoning. The modelling can predict what will probably happen but is totally unable to explain why a given individual will have this or that kind of behaviour. There is no semantic in predictive modelling. Even if human reasoning may instinctively take place in the mind of a human being facing predictive modelling's results.
- One may be feared while remembering the fable of Jean de la Fontaine "the wolf and the lamb". This lamb was desperately arguing that he was not guilty. After having admitted that the lamb was not guilty, the wolf falsely asserts that

it was his brother's fault. While becoming aware that the lamp does not have any brother, the wolf concluded that it should have been the fault of someone of the lamb's family. Jean de la Fontaine thereby explains that the law of the strongest is always the best. And this law permits the wolf to eat the lamb without any further jury. Predictive modelling can produce an automated decision about an individual on the basis of what others have committed. Commercial decisions like contracting, revolving a contract or fixing a price do not need to be motivated.

- Predictive modelling, even if processed versus harmless data may lead to highly sensitive information, by side effect, just because there is no semantic control of the modelling. We have been told about a particular data mining result into bank transactions. From the data analysis of an important group of customers of a bank, rises up a profile of rich individuals starting to sell all their auctions without any link with their competitiveness. The analysis software has put the emphasis on the correlative link between this particular profile and the date of the death of those individuals. This strange behaviour was mainly originating from rich individuals in the few months before their death. The data mining process was in fact identifying and isolating the very typical profile of rich human beings who know that they have contracted a fatal disease and have urgently decided to distribute their economies to their family and friends. The bank has now a technical tool, seamlessly applicable to all their customers, that will permit to identify, with a minor range of error, the fact that particular customers know that they will die in the following months. This information may be considered as totally intrusive. It is not to say that this information is irrelevant, notably in the case in which the bank also deals with life insurance.

Industry and DPA does not agree on the point of knowing if anonymous traceability constitutes a personal data processing or not. Since many years, user's privacy has been a raising concern among telecommunication engineers but the actual widespread of security embedded in ICT remains symbolic.

The EC do not need new legal tools but may take immediate action, namely on the basis of Art 3 & 5.2 of EC Directive 99/5 and Art 15 of the EC Directive 2002/58. It is worrying to note that, in a recent communication of May 2007, the EC is looking for an intervention of the Parliament and the Council and is, for instance, still desperately emphasing P3P, a privacy inefficient protocol invented in 2002 and implemented since then by less then 5% of the web sites and unsupported by Firefox, Opera or Safari.

The technical knowledge of privacy advocates, consumer's organisations and even of the European Commission remain stable while the technology is becoming more and more subtle and seamlessly intrusive. As a concrete result, wide spreading of transclusive hyperlinks and continuous and individual monitoring of Internet users is nowadays the rule while non surveillance appears to be one exception. In the following sections, we will briefly analyse and remind actual problems and how they have not actually been resolved.

5.2 The Withdrawal of the PSN Number

Privacy advocates will never forget the PSN story in 1999. After having input an electronic serial number into their Pentium III processors and after many months of pressure originating from privacy advocates, Intel decided to withdraw this number. Since the very beginning of the hardware industry, the central processors units (CPU), the heart of each personal computer, have been identified by mean of a Serial Number written on the top cover of the chip. Intel announced on January 1999 that they were planning to include a unique Processor Serial Number (PSN) in every one of its new Pentium III chips (earlier implementations in PII for laptops have been reported). What was new with the Intel Processor Number is that the Serial Number is not only on the top cover of the chip but is part of the electronic circuit of the chip itself. It means that a dedicated processor instruction can obtain this unique ID. This instruction can be theoretically included in a script at the client side incorporated in a web page. The PSN can then be used as an identifier to trace a particular user, just like a cookie.

Due to public pressure and namely to a parodist web site called www.bigbrotherinside.com, Intel decided to withdraw this PSN from the central processor and the Pentium IV from Intel did not include this PSN any more.

Unfortunately, the vast majority of substantial parts of a computer, at the exception of the central processor, i.e., among others, all USB devices like mouse, keyboards, printers, modems, stick and RAM memories, memory cards, network cards, motherboards, hard disk and last but not least, RFID's and so on do include such an electronic identifying number.

Furthermore, a few months ago, Apple has included in all their new Intel based Macs a TPM chip that identifies and authenticates a single Apple computer through solid cryptographic means. This fact, even if published by the press, has not triggered any substantial reaction

5.3 Many Billions of Transclusive Hyperlinks Per Day by Google and Co are Widely Superceding the Echelon Monitoring Capacities

According to Wikipedia, transclusion is "*the inclusion of the content of a document into another document by reference*". The transclusion can be made at the server side or at the client side. In the first case, the server itself, before transmitting a web page, examines the HTML code and replaces in real time some markers by data, which can be, for instance, the result of a call to a SQL server. It is the way in which the well-known MySQL/PHP team works.

The transclusion can also be performed in real time by the browser itself. In this case, the browser will seamlessly issue an HTTP request to download content to a web site potentially external to the visited domain (i.e., not belonging to the same domain). By doing so, the browser, while opening an HTTP connection, *can* send or receive cookies but will *systematically* send the visited webpage URL through the referring page systematically sent in the header of the HTTP request. To be short, external web sites know, while being accessed by transclusive hyperlinks, the complete URL of the web page visited, the individual IP address, the browser brand and the version of the OS[1], etc. As we will detail below, transclusive hyperlink is the technique massively used by cyber marketing companies many billion of times a day since a decade now.

It means that, by default, a cyber marketing company knows in real time all the keywords typed by a particular netizen on a search engine on which he is advertising, the computer, operating system, browser brand of the netizen, the IP address he is using and the time and duration of the HTTP sessions. Those data are called the "clickstream": and permit to infer some supplementary data like[2]

1. The country where the netizen lives
2. The Internet domain to which he belongs
3. Sector of activity of the company employing the netizen
4. Turnover and size of the employing company
5. Function and position of the surfer within this company
6. Internet Access Provider
7. Typology of web sites currently visited.

The cookies issues have already been widely discussed. The cookie mechanism was introduced by Netscape in their well-known Navigator in 1996. The SET-COOKIE is invisibly taking place in the HTTP response header and may thus be sent through transclusive hyperlinks. The icing on the cake is called web redirection. Through transclusive hyperlinks, cyber marketing agencies are collecting, on an individual basis, the daily clickstream of the vast majority of netizens. If the cookie feature remains enabled (as it is by default in most widespread browsers like IE, Firefox, Safari and Opera), the traceability of hundreds of millions of users is activated and permit cyber marketing agencies (and to secret services?) to follow each person, notwithstanding changes of IP addresses, for many years.[3]

In Belgium, all the press on line, many social networks, many forums, auctions websites, etc are monitored by Google-Analytics. As a concrete result, the webmaster may benefit from beautiful pie-charts showing their audience. As a concrete result, just because the huge majority of web sites are using the same technology with real time transclusive hyperlinks to the Google website in US, Google can

---

[1] I did call that browser chattering as far as those data are not necessary to a correct data transmission. The original HTTP specification was foreseeing a field named "from" containing nothing else than the email address of the internet user.

[2] Serge Gauthronet, "On-line services and data protection and the protection of privacy" European Commission, 1998, p.31 and 92 available at http://europa.eu.int/comm/dg15/en/media/dataprot/studies/servint.htm

[3] In practice, the cookies are not linked to a particular computer but to a particular user of a computer. That is to say, two different users with their own session on the same computer will use different cookie files.

know, on the individual basis of the IP address, the individual clickstream of netizens among virtually all web sites within and outside Europe.

One may object that the dynamic IP addressing scheme is offering a protection and avoids cross profiling the same individual day after day. Technically speaking, this is not a valuable objection if we do take into account the fact that

- Doubleclick is systematically using a permanent unique identifying cookie
- Doubleclick is present among various web sites and it is almost impossible to surf ten minutes on popular web sites without opening transclusive hyperlinks to DoubleClick
- As a consequence, DoubleClick is able to identify all the dynamic IP addresses used by the same netizen, just because those IP addresses have been sent together with a single unique identifying cookie
- Google bought DoubleClick in May 2007.

5.4 The Ontological Approach

Since about five years, there has been much research funded by the EC related to the ontology of privacy and identity (Fidis, Rapid, Prime, Swami, etc). One tangible output of those researches is the classification built by Andreas Pfitzmann[4], which identifies different levels of privacy (unobservability, untraceability, pseudonymity and anonymity). These concepts may be used on the Internet to gauge the level of privacy of a netizen. From a technical point of view, whenever an intrusive popup window or a spam may be personal data processing or not, is irrelevant as far as intrusive popup windows or spam obviously compromise the availability, the integrity and the confidentiality of the netizen's information system.

European Data Protection legislation (General Data Protection Directive[5] and eDirective[6]) does not, in practice, fill two major gaps in the net of the protection of the privacy. Among the men in the street, there is currently confusion between privacy and data protection. In Europe, legal protection is mainly granted to so-called "personal data[7]", i.e., data related to an identified or identifiable person. This

[4] Andreas Pfitzmann, Marit Köhntopp: Anonymity, Unobservability, and Pseudonymity – A Proposal for Terminology; in: H. Federrath (Ed.): Designing Privacy Enhancing Technologies; Workshop on Design Issues in Anonymity and Unobservability, July 25–26, 2000, Intern. Computer Science Institute (ICSI), Berkeley, CA, LNCS 2009, Springer-Verlag, Heidelberg 2001, 1–9.

[5] Directive 95/46/EC of the European Parliament and of the Council of 24 October 1995 on the protection of individuals with regard to the processing of personal data and on the free movement of such data, OJ L 281, 23.11.1995, p. 31.

[6] Directive 2002/58/EC of the European Parliament and of the Council of 12 July 2002 concerning the processing of personal data and the protection of privacy in the electronic communications sector (Directive on privacy and electronic communications), OJ L 201, 31.07.2002, p. 37.

[7] Following Article 2 (a) of Directive 95/46: " 'personal data' shall mean any information relating to an identified or identifiable natural person ('data subject'); an identifiable person is one who

is to say that global surveillance of individual actions such as browsing, consumer's behaviours, receptivity to eMarketing and so on are not, as such, in the "ratio materiae" of European Directives, as long as data collected remain fully anonymous. The anonymous surveillance is not forbidden by the EU data protection legislation even if this kind of surveillance may be contrary to Article 8 of the European Convention of Human Rights.[8] This is not to say that anonymous observations are, legally speaking, systematically allowed. It will certainly not be the case when the surveillance is conducted by using intrusion techniques such as trojan horses, malware, spyware or viruses, or communication tapping in the framework of a "man-in-the-middle" attack. In brief, the right to data protection does not exhaust the right to privacy.

A second lack in the European data protection legislation with respect to the protection of privacy can be found in the notion of "data controller" as laid down by Art . 2 (d) of the general data protection directive. The controller is the natural or legal person, public authority, agency or any other body that alone or jointly with others determines the purposes and means of the processing of personal data.

Both the definition of personal data and the definition of the data controller create two holes in the net in European data protection legislation towards privacy protection. On the first hand, human data not related or linkable to individuals are not subject to the application of the directive. On the second hand, massive human data processing (e.g., invisible processing through implicit hyperlinks to third party (so called "web bugs") and third party identifying cookies) have no data controllers, as far as Bill Gates is not the "data controller" of invisible HTTP connections (involving the sending of cookies and referring pages) seamlessly processed by MSIE, even if, just as underlined by the Recommendation, "those who design technical specifications and those who actually build or implement applications or operating systems bear some responsibility for data protection from a societal and ethical point of view."

In May 2007, the EC Commission issued a communication on promoting Data Protection by Privacy Enhancing Technologies.[9]

After giving a general definition of what can be included in PETS: "appropriate technical measures ..." and underlining that PETS should be "an integral part in any efforts to achieve a sufficient level of privacy[10] protection", four examples of

can be identified, directly or indirectly, in particular by reference to an identification number or to one or more factors specific to his physical, physiological, mental, economic, cultural or social identity;"

[8] See in this direction the recent opinion 4/2007 of the Article 29 data protection working party on the concept of personal data, pp 24: "Where data protection rules does not apply, certain activities may still constitute an inference with Article 8 of the European Convention on Human Rights, which protect the right to private and family life... Other sets of rules, such as torts laws, criminal law or antidiscrimination law may also provide protection to individuals in those cases where data protection rules do not apply and various legitimate interests may be at stake."

[9] Communication from the Commission to the European Parliament and the Council on Promoting Data Protection by Privacy Enhancing Technologies (PETs) /* COM/2007/0228 final */, Brussels, 2.05.2007.

[10] Fortunately, the target is here to improve the privacy, not the personal data protection.

PETS are given. Those examples include the automatic anonymization, Encryption tools, Cookie-cutters and P3P.

Those examples are problematic because they are neglecting the current state of the art and the fundamental concern of data subjects, whatever the name put on it (privacy, security or data protection).

The encouragement to the anonymization of data may let believe that anonymous surveillance is fully compatible with privacy. The highest level of privacy remains non observation and involves that data related to human beings such as – but not limited to – localization, consumption habits, surfing behaviours, etc., are not recorded at all. This privacy level is detailed as being the first level of privacy and security in the ISO standard 15408. This issue is becoming more and more sensitive, notably due to the wide spreading of RFID's in all our surrounding objects. With regard to a general privacy requirement, routine observation of a growing number of slices of human lives seems not socially acceptable, even if those observations are anonymized as soon as possible.[11]

In the field of encryption, the communication focuses on the prevention against interception during the transmission of information (so-called "man-in-the-middle" attack). Encryption tools like PGP for the electronic mail, SSL for the surf and SSH for file transfer are nowadays widely available and deployed. Those tools are secure enough to resist a brute force attack.

The mention of cookies-cutters appears the most surprising example of some kind of innovative Privacy Enhancing Technologies. In practice, since many years, all modern browsers provide embedded and user-friendly cookie control features. Genuinely, out of the box browsers like MSIE, Firefox, Safari or Opera provide since many years cookie management tools that may inhibit or reduce the permanency of cookies, providing a relevant distinction between cookies sent by the current website and cookies sent by invisible third parties. At the light of those privacy enhancements embedded in the current technology, a cookie-cutter approach under the form of an external program or a plug-in seems today, with respect to the current state of the art, to be widely deprecated.

Perhaps the communication of the European Commission should have been more innovative and efficient by suggesting the total suppression of the cookie mechanism itself. This suppression is not unrealistic, because, from a functional view point, alternative solutions, less privacy killing, exist to fill actual and legitimate proposes of cookies.

Session cookies may very easily be put at the visible URL level (e.g., www.ebay.com?sessionID=ZE34TR) rather than in the invisible HTTP header. This system is widely used by many web servers working with PHP or ASP. For permanent

---

[11] See also the recent opinion 4/2007 of the Article 29 data protection working party on the concept of personal data P. 24: "Where data protection rules does not apply, certain activities may still constitute an inference with Article 8 of the European Convention on Human Rights, which protect the right to private and family life... Other sets of rules, such as torts laws, criminal law or antidiscrimination law may also provide protection to individuals in those cases where data protection rules do not apply and various legitimate interests may be at stake."

cookies, if they originate from third parties, they will allow following a single user seamlessly (cookies are linked to a user and not to a computer) on an individual basis during his whole click stream (pages of newspaper read, keywords typed on search engines, interventions in discussions forums, etc.) and are clearly putting the privacy of the surfer at risk (confidentiality breach). If the cookie originates from a web site voluntarily visited, it appears to be more efficient to implement a classic system of userID/password that will permit to the user, through a simple and positive action to be identified and profiled, or, on the opposite, to surf the web site anonymously. Here again, all modern browsers are proposing embedded password management systems that are more secured than cookies and that avoid repeated typing of an ID and password to the user (the browser seamlessly recognizes a recent authentication form and automatically proposes the last typed ID and password; at the opposite of the cookie mechanism, the user may not be identified nor tracked without his preliminary and ad hoc consent).

Cookie type	Privacy risk	PET solution
Direct session	None: Traceability risk not higher than that of a dynamic IP address	Put the cookie in the URL www.ebay.com?sessionID=ZE34TR rather than in the invisible HTTP header
Direct remanent	Important: Unfair and invisible identification and trackability	Use of ID/password Management systems already embedded in all modern browsers
Third party (session or remanent) = Transclusive hyperlink	Very High: Unfair, routine and invisible trackability by a foreign, invisible and untrusted third party	Must be forbidden

A browser without any cookie capability – this should have been a realistic and popular privacy enhanced requirement.

In the P3P field, following a survey performed by SecuritySpace[12], P3P policy deployment ratios have evolved between 1 and 5% of web sites ranked since the P3P's launching in 2002. It has to be noticed that Opera, Safari and Firefox does not support P3P, this means that Apple, Linux and Unix users are out of the game. The single reference implementation of P3P lies in MSIE on MS-Windows and permits, by default, to cyber marketing (like DoubleClick) and audience measurement companies to put an identifying permanent cookie on the workstations of millions of naïve netizens (for the purpose of tracking them through the referring page systematically sent by common browsers). In practice, it is sufficient for a marketing company to establish a compact privacy policy aiming that no personally identifiable information is collected or stored to pass through the P3P default settings of MSIE. P3P was deeply criticized many years ago both by the Article 29 working

[12] http://www.securityspace.com/s_survey/data/man.200706/p3p.html

party[13] and by the International Working Party on the Protection of Individuals[14] in these terms: "There is a risk that P3P, once implemented in the next generation of browsing software, could mislead EU-based operators into believing that they can be discharged of certain of their legal obligations (e.g., granting individual users a right of access to their data) if the individual user consents to this as part of the on-line negotiation". The Electronic Privacy Information Center speaks about a Pretty Poor Privacy.[15]

Data subjects may regret that, in this enumeration of examples, the issues of Global Unique Identifier (like the MAC address in Ipv6 addresses or serial number of RFID chips) or transclusive hyperlinks (web bugs) to untrusted third parties have not been considered.

5.5 When Non DP Laws Help to Fill the Gaps in Existing Data Protection Legislation to Enhance Privacy Protection

The objectives described in the Communication are (1) to support the development of PETs, (2) to support the use of PETs by data controllers and (3) to encourage consumer's to use PETs.

Within the first objective, the Communication proposes to identify the need and the technological requirements of PETs and plans to call national authorities and the private sector to invest in the development of PETs. It has to be underlined that the focus here is not the protection of personal data but to provide "the foundation for user-empowering privacy protection".

In the framework of the second objective, the Communication aims to promote the use of PETs by industry and to ensure the respect for appropriate standards in the protection of personal data through the standardisation and the coordination of national technical rules on security measures for data processing. Very surprisingly, the Recommendation does not mention ISO and notably the recent standard ISO 15408. Finally, the Communication wants to involves public authorities, promoting their use of PETs.

The last objective is to encourage consumers to use PETs by raising their awareness and develop an EU-wide system of privacy seals.

At the lecture of these objectives, I got the feeling that the Communication may perhaps be a mix between the objectives of PETs and the means to reach the objectives. Furthermore, the wide spreading of PETs is not an objective in itself but rather a means to enhance the privacy of human beings through Europe, without having to pay the price of negotiating the immutable value of privacy to obtain a user-friendly information society.

---

[13] http://ec.europa.eu/justice_home/fsj/privacy/docs/wpdocs/1998/wp12_en.pdf

[14] http://www.datenschutz-berlin.de/doc/eu/gruppe29/wp11_en.htm

[15] http://www.epic.org/reports/prettypoorprivacy.html

Before creating new Privacy Enhancing Technologies, it appears evident that it is more effective to routinely produce information technologies that are privacy keeping, by default.

In the field of the mobile phone, we have reached a very good balance between privacy and surveillance. The consumer can benefit from the Calling Identification Line Indication that permits to identify the number of the mobile calling; at the same time the same consumer can benefit from the Calling Line Identification Restriction that allows him to hide his own number when calling somebody. For security reasons, emergency services can know, whatever the CLIR status can be the calling number of the emergency service caller. Just because the calling number is technically transmitted by the telecom operator, the transmission of a false phone number is quite impossible. The communication is fully encrypted by a 40 bit key and a man-in-the-middle attack appears to be very difficult. Each phone has a unique identifier (IMEI) but this identifier is sent to the telecom operator who does not relay it to the called person's terminal. This high level of privacy has been reached also because there has been a long tradition of privacy in the telecommunication world. But to me, a relevant cause of this success story is the fact that a mandatory telecommunication agreement (including privacy consideration) was necessary before putting a mobile phone device on the market.

In the field of electronic mail, a netizen may very easily change his sender address (what spammers do a billion times a day) just because the email address is sent by the email program and not by the network operator. If a netizen is using Ipv6 configured by default in MS-Windows workstations, the recipient of an email may track the same netizen even if (s)he is using different legitimate "anonymous" email addresses just because the Ipv6 address incorporates by default the serial number of the network interface card of the PC ("Mac Address").

In the field of the Internet, it may be relevant to have a glance at recent history. The technological move originated in the very beginning from the Personal Computers appearing at the beginning of the eighties. Local Area Network (LAN) started to appear in the mid-eighties and the World Wide Web started in the early 90s. The cookies mechanism itself was specified by Netscape in 1996, without any reference to the newly born Directive 95/46.

Now the Internet is present everywhere, but telecommunication terminals[16] (not limited to hardware but including software and firmware) are not privacy compliant, more precisely, software like browsers are not "incorporating [sufficient] safeguards to ensure that the personal data and privacy of the user and the subscriber are

[16] In the wide meaning of Directive 99/5 of the European Parliament and of the Council of 9 March 1999 on radio equipment and telecommunications terminal equipment and the mutual recognition of their conformity in Article 2 (b): *(b)* "'telecommunications terminal equipment' means a product enabling communication or a relevant component thereof which is intended to be connected directly or indirectly by any means whatsoever to interfaces of public telecommunications networks (that is to say, telecommunications networks used wholly or partly for the provision of publicly available telecommunications services)."

protected" (one of the essential requirements foreseen in Article 3.3.c of Directive 99/5).

It has to be noticed that such privacy specifications have already existed for many years. For instance, the word "privacy" appears 28 times in the RFC defining the HTTP protocol. But, insofar as they appear in the form of recommendations ("should") the ITC industry did not implement them into software like browsers. Concerning the incorporation of the Mac Address in Ipv6 addresses, privacy compliant alternatives like the "Privacy Extensions for Stateless Address Autoconfiguration in Ipv6", a RFC issued by the well-known IETF.

Last but not least, it may appear very surprising that the Communication – issued by the Commission – does not take on board existing legal tools that permit the European Commission itself to enforce privacy regulation by the ICT industry. Notably Article 5.2 of Directive 99.5, which states "Where a Member State or the Commission considers that conformity with a harmonised standard does not ensure compliance with the essential requirements referred to in Article 3, which the said standard is intended to cover, the Commission or the Member State concerned shall bring the matter before the committee" or Article 15 of Directive 2002/58 that states "2. Where provisions of this Directive can be implemented only by requiring specific technical features in electronic communications networks, Member States shall inform the Commission . . .3. Where required, measures may be adopted to ensure that terminal equipment is constructed in a way that is compatible with the right of users to protect and control the use of their personal data, in accordance with Directive 1999/5/EC . . ."

Will Europe, finally, take the opportunity to put into the prestigious "CE" label stamped on telecommunication hardware and software some substantive, innovative and mandatory requirements for a European Privacy Compliant Technology?

Part II
The Actors

Chapter 6
Role of Trade Associations: Data Protection as a Negotiable Issue

Jan Berkvens

6.1 Economic Interests Versus Fundamental Rights

There are various kinds of trade association. Most trade associations represent a given industry or sector. They are organised both at national and at European level. The trade associations are in turn united in umbrella organisations at national and at European level. Some umbrella organisations have a worldwide scope. In the period when privacy legislation came into being, all these organisations played a relatively active role in attempting to influence the legislation. Economic considerations were an important factor in this connection. The interlocutors were mainly civil servants and members of parliament. Since the introduction of the legislation the role of the trade associations has remained limited. During the various evaluations at national and international level they have let their voice be heard to varying degrees.[1] One of the reasons of the limited role is that many regulatory duties have been transferred to the privacy regulators. However, these regulators are not true market regulators. They do not represent political or commercial interests but instead champion a single fundamental right. This means that there is little scope for traditional negotiations based on economic interests. Privacy cannot be bartered for economic interests.

6.2 Processing in the Context of Customer Relations

Privacy rules distinguish between the public and private sectors. As far as the public sector is concerned, the basic principle is that there should be a statutory basis for the collection and processing of personal data by government. There is not much room for further processing of data. Such processing is not compatible with the purpose for which they were collected.

J. Berkvens (✉)
Law and Informatics, Faculty of Law, Radboud University Nijmegen, Netherlands
e-mail: j.berkvens@jur.ru.nl

[1] E.g., various contributions of trade associations to the 2003 evaluation of Directive 95/46.

S. Gutwirth et al. (eds.), *Reinventing Data Protection?*

DOI 10.1007/978-1-4020-9498-9_6, © Springer Science+Business Media B.V. 2009

Much of the personal data processed in the private sector is data in the context of a customer relationship. I will disregard here the employer–employee relationship and the activities of charities. The expression *processing in the context of a customer relationship* must be broadly interpreted. It covers the use of consumer data for market research, for marketing purposes and in the course of concluding and performing contracts. The post-contract stage also involves processing operations. For example, the filing of papers or electronic documents to serve as proof in the event of disputes.

6.3 Chief Aim is Profit

Processing operations are carried out in companies not only in a commercial context but also as part of other processes. For example, data are processed to comply with statutory obligations. Data are also processed in order to avoid payment default. The aim of all processing operations is to make a profit. The processing of data is not an aim in itself. Neither carrying out market research nor engaging in marketing operations is an independent aim. Similarly, complying with statutory obligations and avoiding payment default are not entrepreneurial objectives. Nor do data processing operations in the primary commercial process constitute an aim in themselves. The aim of a company is to make a profit. It processes data in the course of achieving its profit objective. Data protection however does not serve commercial purposes. The processing operations can be broken down in keeping with the different activities that form the chief objective.

6.4 Supporting Sectors

Consumer-oriented processing operations are carried out not only in companies that deliver goods and/or services to consumers. They also take place in support organisations such as trade information agencies, debt collection agencies and marketing firms. These businesses are concerned with hived-off activities, which nonetheless form part of the consumer-oriented B2C commercial process in the ordinary way.

6.5 Consumer Protection

The relationship between enterprises and their customers is governed by the Civil Codes. The Civil Codes focus on relations between consumer and enterprise. The obligations of both parties are over centuries elaborated in Civil Codes. In recent years many new bodies of rules have been introduced in the field of consumer protection. The great majority come from European legislation. I am thinking of the Unfair Contract Terms Directive, which is designed to prevent unreasonable contract provisions.[2] I am also thinking of the rules on e-commerce[3] and distance

[2] Directive 1993/13/EC.
[3] Directive 2000/31/EC.

selling[4] as well as the rules on misleading advertising and the rules on consumer information.[5] Moreover, consumer authorities have been set up and easily accessible dispute resolution schemes created.[6] In the financial sector there is the Payment Services Directive[7] and the Distance Marketing of Financial Services Directive.[8] All these rules focus on the consumer-enterprise relationship and reflect the wish of consumers to get a good product at a fair price and on fair terms. They emphasise the need for sound information.

6.6 Standard Terms and Conditions

Trade associations potentially play a major role in the introduction of standard terms and conditions. They consult with representatives of consumer organisations about the conditions relevant to their sector. If there are structural deficiencies in the way in which an industry operates, consultations on this are held directly between those concerned: in other words, consumers and enterprises. These discussions can take place in ad hoc forums but may also be more institutionalised, for example the discussions in the Netherlands within the framework of the Social and Economic Council (SER). Under the direction of a neutral chairman those concerned negotiate on the issues under consideration.[9]

6.7 Balance of Interests

A characteristic of the consultation is that all problems are discussed in their mutual context. This, in any event, helps each party to understand the background to the wishes of the other party and enables them to reach a compromise through negotiation. If consumer protection lags behind in an important field, the legislator can itself take steps to introduce mandatory rules.

6.8 The Choices from the Past

If this argument were taken to its logical conclusion, consumer organisations would raise the subject of protection of personal data in their talks with trade associations. Strangely enough, this never happens. Where data protection conditions are

---

4 Directive 1997/7/EC.

5 Directive 2005/29/EC.

6 E.g., regulation EC 861/2007.

7 Adopted 24 April 2007, not yet published.

8 Directive 2002/65/EC.

9 The SER website contains a large list of negotiated terms and conditions: http://www.ser.nl/nl/taken/zelfregulering/consumentenvoorwaarden.aspx

discussed, this is in the context of privacy codes of conduct. It is noteworthy that the privacy codes of conduct are established in consultation between privacy regulators and trade associations without the involvement of consumers. Under the first Dutch Data Protection Act there was a statutory obligation for enterprises to consult with consumers.[10] However, the Dutch Consumers' Association did not attach much priority to the subject. Ultimately, it was represented in various consultations by an action group consisting in concerned citizens.[11] In keeping with Directive 95/46, the obligation to negotiate with consumers about privacy codes of conduct has been dropped in the new Data Protection Act.

This was perhaps understandable because the concept of the privacy code of conduct had originated in the Netherlands and it had been seen that the consultations with consumer organisations had not really been a success. Nevertheless, it is a pity. After all, in the new configuration under Directive 95/46, the emphasis is put on consultations between trade associations and privacy regulators. As a result, the discussion tends to focus exclusively on the privacy aspects of a normal commercial relationship between consumer and enterprise.[12] The fact that data processing relates to just one small part of a much larger collection of issues is overlooked. The consumer can no longer set priorities. He has been excluded from any discussion of privacy issues.

6.9 Standard Terms and Conditions as Medium?

Nonetheless, this need not be the case. Many trade associations make use of standard terms and conditions that regulate relations between their members and their members' customers. Such standard terms and conditions could be the medium through which consumers once again have a say on privacy issues. After all, standard terms and conditions are of a wide-ranging nature and regulate the specific characteristics of the transactions between the parties concerned. The matters dealt with in the standard terms and conditions include the formation of the contract, the logistical aspects of the performance to be provided, the consequences of imputable breaches of contract, the liability of the parties, any warranties that may apply and a few formal matters such as the applicable law. If provisions have a very one-sided nature, application can be made to have them treated as void or voidable under the Unfair Contract Terms Directive.[13] Consumer organisations can play a role in this connection by instituting class actions.

---

[10] Section 15 of the Wet persoonsregistraties 1989.

[11] Overkleeft-Verburg, *De Wet persoonsregistraties*, WEJ Tjeenk Willink, Zwolle, 1995, chapter 6. Also special edition on self-regulation of Privacy en Registratie, 1994/2–3.

[12] The impact of Article 27 of Directive 95/46 varies. Vide chapter 14 of *the Analysis and impact study on the implementation of Directive EC 95/46 in Member States.*

[13] Directive 1993/13/EC.

6.10 Standard Terms and Conditions as Information Instrument

Standard terms and conditions can also play a role in the context of providing information to consumers. For this purpose they can include provisions that do not in themselves change the nature of the relationship between the enterprise and consumer but instead inform the consumer, or even the supplier, about the qualities of products, services and processes.

In various sectors standard terms and conditions are already used to convey date protection-related information. Standard terms and conditions can be used to explain the policy of enterprises on the use of customers' personal data. They can focus on the exchange within corporate groups and conglomerates and the possibility of opting out. Other subjects are the use of data for combating fraud, the use of cookies and the use of RFID. International aspects can also be covered. First of all, the fact that data processing can be outsourced to parties outside the EU. Second, that data exchange takes place within corporate groups and sectors, for example in the context of anti-fraud measures.

Standard terms and conditions are close to the day-to-day reality and regulate specific situations. They can therefore easily be used to make arrangements about privacy aspects as part of the totality of the relationship between enterprises and their customers. They form a level below the level of the national and international privacy codes of conduct. In principle, they also bring the consumer organisations back into the picture. In the consultations between the trade association and the consumer organisations, it might be an interesting experiment to test the practical merits of the privacy aspects in the context of the overall relationship. Consumer organisations can express their view on what they consider to be relevant and reasonable in the relationship between enterprises and consumers. Dispute committees for particular industries or sectors could then give rulings on disputes concerning the privacy rules.

The agreements made in this way would have the character of a contract between parties, as a result of which the underlying processing of personal data meets the requirements of Articles 7 (b) and 26 (1) (b) or (c) of Directive 95/46.

6.11 Conclusion

Bring as many aspects as possible back within the scope of the negotiation between enterprises and consumers. Make data protection issues negotiable issues. In short, restart the dialogue between the entrepreneur and the consumer.

[The author is senior counsel at the legal and tax dept. of Rabobank Nederland and professor at Radboud University Nijmegen].

Chapter 7
The Role of Data Protection Authorities

Peter Hustinx

7.1 Introduction

I am delighted to deliver this contribution about the role of data protection authorities (DPAs) and let me be very clear at the outset about my main message.

The title of my speech in the initial draft programme was: 'Do we need data protection authorities?'. My answer to this more challenging question is not simply 'yes' but rather 'YES, BUT'. In other words, a positive answer with two important conditions:

1. within a legal framework that allows them to be effective,
2. with a strategic approach and the ability to make a difference.

I am here in good company: Article 8.3 of the EU Charter of Fundamental Rights, which has now become a binding element of the Reform Treaty, provides that 'compliance with data protection rules shall be subject to control by an independent authority'. Recently, the Declaration of Civil Society Organisations, adopted on 25 September 2007 in Montreal, stated that 'stronger, more aggressive action by privacy commissioners is required', finding them 'uniquely positioned to defend our society's core values and rights of privacy'.

The existence of DPAs has been a typical feature of European data protection law since its inception but the reasons for their establishment have not always been clearly articulated and it has also taken some time before this element developed into a constitutional principle.

Taking a closer look at the reasons underlying their establishment can help to better appreciate the role of these bodies and to understand why they are now widely considered as a key element of the privacy landscape. Such an analysis is also important to find ways that help them to develop their role and to enhance their effectiveness.

P. Hustinx (✉)
European Data Protection Supervisor (EDPS), Brussels, Belgium
e-mail: edps@edps.europa.eu

S. Gutwirth et al. (eds.), *Reinventing Data Protection?*
DOI 10.1007/978-1-4020-9498-9_7, © Springer Science+Business Media B.V. 2009

7.2 Historic Background

In retrospect, it is surprising to see that, in spite of experience developed in Germany, Sweden and France, the concept of a 'data protection authority' played only a very limited role in the Convention on Data Protection, also known as Convention 108 of the Council of Europe, when it was concluded in 1981.

The central obligation of each Party in Article 4 is to take 'the necessary measures in its domestic law to give effect to the basic principles for data protection' set out in the Convention. Article 10 provides that each Party must establish 'appropriate sanctions and remedies' for violations of these basic principles. The explanatory report clearly mentions the need to guarantee '*effective protection*' but leaves the way in which this should happen for each Party to decide. The existence of supervisory authorities is only mentioned as a feature of national laws. The original drafters of the Convention were obviously reluctant to impose this on all Parties as a basic legal requirement.

This situation changed with the adoption of the European Data Protection Directive 95/46, which took the Council of Europe Convention as a starting point but specified it and added to it in many ways. Article 28 of the Directive introduced an obligation for each Member State to have a supervisory authority responsible for ensuring compliance, and 'acting with complete independence'. Recital 62 of the preamble underlined that 'the establishment in Member States of supervisory authorities, exercising their functions with complete independence, is an essential component of the protection of individuals with regard to the processing of personal data'.

The words '*acting* with complete independence' were a compromise formula, chosen to ensure some flexibility but it is hard to see how 'complete independence' could exist without sufficient institutional safeguards in place. This issue is highly relevant in a case presently before the European Commission and involving Germany, which is likely to end up before the Court of Justice in the near future.

Article 28 of the Directive also provides that supervisory authorities should have certain powers, such as consultative powers, investigative powers, effective powers of intervention, the power to engage in legal proceedings or bring violations to the attention of judicial authorities, to deal with complaints, etc. This seems to assure them a central position. However, they never decide in last resort and their decisions may be appealed to the courts.

The adoption of the Directive has led to an Additional Protocol to Convention 108, which basically takes up all elements of Article 28 of the Directive. The preamble of this Additional Protocol clearly states that 'supervisory authorities, exercising their functions in complete independence, are an element of the effective protection of individuals with regard to the processing of personal data.' The explanatory report even concludes that data protection supervisory authorities 'have become an essential component of the data protection supervisory system in a democratic society.' This report also puts a lot of emphasis on the notion of 'effective protection' and the role of supervisory authorities in ensuring it.

This trend is finally also visible in Article 8 of the European Charter of Fundamental Rights, which has now been made binding in the Reform Treaty. Article 8 has recognized the protection of personal data as a separate fundamental right. Its third paragraph – as already mentioned – provides for control by an independent authority.

This all means that the principle of 'independent supervision' and the existence of 'independent supervisory authorities' have developed, at least at the European level, into a constitutional element of the right to data protection in a democratic society. This seems to be based on their primary mission to 'ensure compliance' and is closely linked to the notion of 'effective protection'. This also means that it is crucial for independent supervisory authorities to regularly think about their own effectiveness and to consider ways to measure and where necessary improve their performance.

7.3 Further Analysis

It is probably only fair to say that this approach was facilitated by the fact that all 'early starters' in Europe and subsequently all Council of Europe and EU Member States, were dealing with 'data protection' as *an issue of general and structural importance for a modern society* and therefore typically opted for a general legal framework with a wide scope, including both public and private sectors and hence virtually all relevant areas of society (often referred to as the 'omnibus approach').

Such frameworks usually consisted in a mix of substantive rules, individual rights and formal procedures, to allow a step-by-step – and where necessary differentiated – implementation in the various sectors of society, to respond to the characteristics and specific needs of those areas or their special fields of interest. Since no other public authority was in the position to follow this development and to ensure a consistent approach, this task was given to 'data protection authorities', which were established for this purpose. This decision should of course also be understood in the light of social and political preferences in Europe to see a *public authority* deal with this task.

It is tempting to also point at the fact that 'data protection' developed in Europe in the context of human rights was recognized as a *fundamental right* of its own. The truth is however that no other fundamental right – except the right to a fair trial – is structurally associated with the role of an independent body to ensure its respect and further development. This right is special in the sense that it is considered to be in need of '*structural support*' through the establishment of an independent authority with adequate powers and resources.

Certain other fundamental rights, such as the freedom of expression and the freedom of assembly and association, already have strong institutional stakeholders, such as the media, labour unions or political parties but that is not the case for data protection. Most of what is happening in this area is moreover invisible and often difficult to understand or deal with without technical expertise. That explains the general trend to charge an independent authority with the task to address these issues.

It is also useful to consider *what might have been alternative approaches*. The first and perhaps most obvious alternative would have been to limit data protection law to sets of rights and obligations and to leave conflict resolution to *existing mechanisms, such as the court system and civil procedure*. However, this would have had at least three negative consequences. Firstly, it would have put most 'right holders' in a very difficult position, left alone with the 'onus of initiative', without adequate expertise and with a very uneven distribution of interests, mostly limited at the individual side and typically rather large at the data user's end. Secondly, as a result, it would have taken a long time before the meaning of legal norms would have become sufficiently clear to have any preventive impact. Thirdly, the consistency of this impact in various sectors would have been dubious and unpredictable and the value of data protection as a fundamental right would have suffered considerably as a result.

The same would apply to most common procedures in *administrative law* and more so since these procedures typically deal with administrative 'decisions', directly affecting the individual, rather than with processing of personal data, which may or may not be at the basis of such a decision. An independent public authority was therefore in a much better position to protect the interests of individual right holders in a consistent way and to strike a fair balance with other private or public interests, where necessary.

Relying on the *criminal law* as yet another alternative, would have been hardly more attractive. Firstly, in short, the use of criminal law requires clear and precise legal norms but these are mostly not available in data protection, except in special fields. Secondly, violations of data protection provisions would have to compete in practice with other types of simple or complicated 'ordinary crime' and it would be unlikely that enforcement of data protection law would have a high priority on the list. The lack of expertise to deal with these matters in an integrated fashion would in any case have led to unsatisfactory results. As a result, criminal law has played only a limited role as 'back up' for enforcement in special cases.

It is therefore not surprising that national law mostly opted for an approach '*sui generis*' involving a data protection authority with a specific mandate and a special position, since it had to deal with other parts of government as well as with various private parties and interests. These authorities were given a wide responsibility to deal with all relevant issues in an integrated manner and thus also to 'generate' guidelines for other parties to work with, to raise awareness of data protection and to act as a 'focal point' in the public debate.

7.4 Different Experience

As to the precise mandate of these authorities, different models have been used in various Member States for a long time. The original approach in Sweden was based on the general need for a license. The French approach was far more selective and the German approach provided for monitoring on an *ex post* basis and powers to make recommendations rather than binding decisions. The Data Protection Directive has harmonised the roles and powers of supervisory authorities to a large extent, while adding that they must exercise their functions 'in complete independence'. However, the Directive has also introduced a few other interesting developments.

Firstly, it is evident that the Directive has encouraged a more *selective approach to supervision*, which allows a distinction between relevant cases on the basis of the risks that are involved. Only those cases likely to present specific risks are subject to prior checking by the supervisory authority. This applies regardless of the sector involved but the national law can determine which systems are considered to present specific risks.

Other systems are subject to prior notification to the supervisory authority but the Directive allows important exceptions to this principle. The possibility to develop exemptions for certain categories that do not present any risks, provided that some conditions are fulfilled, is clearly based on the experience in certain countries with similar exemptions (e.g., France and the Netherlands).

The second option – which provides for the appointment of an *internal privacy officer* – is even more interesting. This option has now been adopted in different countries following positive experiences in Germany. On the European level, there is a general obligation for Community institutions and bodies to have at least one data protection officer, with a number of specific tasks. Together, they are a valuable network of 'first line' experience, with which my office cooperates on an almost daily basis.

This can also be understood as a first important step to come to a better *distribution of roles* in data protection that allows independent authorities to concentrate on larger or more strategic issues.

In a general way, the Directive also encourages the development of *codes of conduct* for different social or economic sectors. These different instruments are designed to encourage a development in which other actors can take responsibility for an effective integration of data protection rules and principles in the normal practices of relevant organisations. Data protection is also – and not least of all – an important part of good quality where services are delivered with electronic means.

As to the relations with data subjects, the first goal for supervisory authorities should be to *raise awareness* and to *enable them to exercise their own rights*. If they do, this will gradually also encourage responsible controllers to invest more in their relations with data subjects. Investing in awareness of both controllers and data subjects is thus also a good strategy for supervisory authorities.

In my previous role as data protection commissioner in the Netherlands, I have had some valuable experience with the involvement of *intermediary organisations*, like consumer unions, trade unions, etc. The latter were quite active with data protection in employment. Under national law, these organisations also had a right to initiate legal actions in the interest of their members.

For supervisory authorities this implies a rather *complex environment* of different sectors with different needs and requirements. Independent authorities should in my view not refrain from entering into appropriate and productive relationships with these *different stakeholders*. To the contrary, many colleagues have discovered the need for partners and allies in the execution of their role and some of them have been very successful in that respect.

7.5 More Effectiveness

This overview should also deal with the question whether there are certain areas where the current role of data protection authorities might be subject to improvement in order to make their work more effective. This is an important question, since the primary mission of data protection authorities is to ensure *compliance* and to promote *effective protection*. It is *only* through these concepts that data protection rules and principles can become a reality in practice.

As a first point of attention, I would like to mention that data protection authorities should have the *possibility to set priorities* and concentrate on issues of special importance or posing special risks. Many authorities presently suffer because their activities are dominated by individual complaints. This may have different reasons but they tend to reinforce each other and limit the capacity of the authority to invest sufficient resources in important issues: firstly, a lack of alternatives for enforcement of rights by data subjects and secondly, a lack of possibility for authorities to set their own priorities and to make selections.

An efficient data protection system should allow data subjects to exercise their rights directly with responsible controllers and in case of problems choose from different alternatives for appropriate follow up. Among these alternatives, seeking help from a data protection authority would certainly be a necessary option but it should neither be the *only* one, nor a *compulsory* step before taking further legal action. Otherwise, the data protection authority would be in the position of a monopolist or develop into a bottleneck and probably both.

This would be more regrettable if the data protection authority would be obliged to deal with all complaints and requests for assistance in a similar fashion, without the possibility to exercise a reasonable discretion as to whether and how to deal with the matter. This may be a common approach for courts and understandable from the point of view of general administrative law but for data protection authorities with wide responsibilities and always limited resources, it only means that individual cases will dominate the agenda at the expense of other matters.

The appropriate remedy for these problems should thus be twofold: firstly, encourage *alternative courses of action* for enforcement of data protection rights and, secondly, make sure that data protection authorities are able to set *priorities* and develop more *flexible methods* of dealing with individual complaints, including simple procedures and using them in support of *ex officio* inquiries against responsible parties.

As to alternative courses of action, it seems appropriate to also consider introducing the possibility of *class actions*, empowering groups of citizens to jointly use litigation in matters concerning protection of personal data, as well as actions, initiated by legal persons whose activities are designed to protect the interests of certain categories of persons, such as consumer associations and trade unions. Both might be a powerful tool to facilitate the enforcement of data protection law in various situations.

It might also be interesting, in combination with these two solutions, to provide for simple ways of dealing with signals that data protection rules are being breached, without necessarily going into the details of every single case. It goes without saying that standard procedures for enforcement of data subjects' rights should be as simple as possible and should provide access to data subjects without undue formalities.

Finally, it would be interesting to invest in different means that enable organisations to *demonstrate* that 'privacy and data protection' matter for them and to use them for competition in the market. This might work in the case of 'privacy seals' for privacy compliant products and services and for third-party 'privacy audits'. Both might be good examples of 'privacy relevant services' that could be effective *in addition* to the role of data protection authorities and should not necessarily be provided by them. It would be up to the authority to decide to what extent it would be prepared to rely on the result of those services in individual cases.

These and other ideas have been mentioned in my opinion of 25 July 2007 on a better implementation of Directive 95/46/EC and are also discussed in the context of the 'London Initiative', which was launched in November 2006 and involves the sharing of 'best practices' among supervisory authorities. There is still a lot to be done but these remarks are hopefully sufficient to explain why data protection authorities are a key element in the privacy landscape and how they could be more effective.

Chapter 8
The Role of Citizens: What Can Dutch, Flemish and English Students Teach Us About Privacy?

Ronald Leenes and Isabelle Oomen

8.1 Introduction

Data protection regulation, such as the European Data Protection Directive EU/95/46 (DPD), as an instrument to protect privacy, addresses different actors. The Directive aims to regulate behaviour, in particular concerning the processing – including collection and use – of personal data. The regulation therefore addresses actors in society engaged in the process of collecting and using data – the data controllers – such as businesses and governments. It also addresses the individual whose personal data is processed, the data subjects. The regulation provides the individual a (limited) right to control the disclosure of their personal data, for instance by means of consent (Article 7.a DPD). The Directive also grants the individual a set of rights pertaining to the phases after data disclosure, including the right to inspect the data collected about them and the right to have incorrect data corrected (e.g., Article 12 DPD).

In the actual practice of personal data processing, consent increasingly seems to lose its importance or is undermined seriously. On the Internet consent is either absent, for instance because the providers claim not to collect personal data, c.f. the current search engine and behavioural targeting debates[1], or is undermined because of blanket consent provided by the individual in a take-it-or-leave it fashion for online services.

The individual as being in control over their personal data, or as the Germans phrase it having 'Informationelle Selbstbestimmung' as one of the two prongs[2] in

R. Leenes (✉)
Tilburg Institute for Law, Technology, and Society (TILT), Faculty of Law, Tilburg University, Tilburg, The Netherlands
e-mail: r.e.leenes@tilburguniversity.nl

[1] See for instance: http://googlepublicpolicy.blogspot.com/2008/02/are-ip-addresses-personal.html;http://bits.blogs.nytimes.com/2008/02/22/google-says-ip-addresses-arent-personal/;http://www.europarl.europa.eu/news/expert/infopress_page/019-19258-022-01-04-902-20080121IPR19236-22-01-2008-2008-false/default_en.htm

[2] See preamble 3 of the DPD: 'Whereas ... require not only that personal data should be able to flow freely from one Member State to another, but also that the fundamental rights of individuals should be safeguarded.'

S. Gutwirth et al. (eds.), *Reinventing Data Protection?*
DOI 10.1007/978-1-4020-9498-9_8,

the Directive seems to have lost out in comparison with the other prong: the free flow of information and enabling the information society.

The term data 'subject', probably unintended by its drafters, reflects this. Subject bears a connotation of passiveness. The data flows regulated by the Directive relate to the data subjects but the action seems to be elsewhere (with the controllers). The role of the individual in data protection seems limited. Especially considering that it is unlikely that European citizens actually know their rights regarding their personal data.[3] This can hardly be what the legislator intended.

What is the role of the citizen in a debate about reinventing data protection? Is the citizen indeed passive or even a victim of predating enterprises and governments in need of protection by regulation? Or is the individual better seen as an active entity able and willing to take up informational self control empowered by the regulation? Or, should we, in the light of discussing the reinvention of data protection, rather look at what the role of the citizen *ought* to be?

What do we actually know about what citizens think about privacy and data protection? What are their concerns and attitudes and how do they act in the information society? Is there a relation between their attitudes and their behaviour. Do the so-called privacy paradox (Norberg et al., 2007) – people say they value privacy, but act as if they do not – hold?

These are difficult questions that we can only begin to touch upon in this contribution. This paper first discusses some of the difficulties in measuring privacy attitudes by examining one of the influential privacy attitude metrics, Westin's Privacy Segmentation Index. Next, it discusses some of the early findings of a survey conducted by TILT among students in the Netherlands, Flanders and the UK. Finally, some conclusions will be drawn as input for the debate on reinventing data protection.

8.2 Measuring Privacy Attitudes

There are many studies and opinion polls regarding privacy attitudes and behaviour conducted by, or on behalf of, marketeers (Harris International for privacy & American Business (annual)), consultancy forms (e.g., PWC, 2000; Cremonini and Valeri, 2003), policy makers (e.g., Eurobarometer studies (e.g., European Commission Nos. 193 and 196, 2003); DTI, 2001; DCA, 2003), Privacy Commisioners (e.g., IC, 2004, 2006), NGOs (e.g., EPIC, 2005, Consumers International, 2001) and scientists (e.g., Zureik et al., 2008).

Many of these studies contain only a limited set of questions and aim to present a global view of the privacy concern of the population, often by means of a segmentation of the public into distinct clusters of privacy attitudes (e.g., IC, 2004, 2006; Harris Interactive, 2002).

---

[3] For instance, in the UK Information Commissioner's annual track research (IC, 2004), on a question about what the respondents have heard of the Data Protection Act, the highest ranking (unprompted) answer was 'it protects personal information' (31%), followed by 'it stops organisations passing on information about you' (18%). Only 12% says 'It allows you to see information held about you'.

8.2.1 Privacy Segmentation Index

A well-known privacy metric is the American Harris/Westin Privacy Segmentation Index (PSI) that was developed by Harris Interactive in cooperation with long standing privacy scholar Alan Westin. The index (and its precursors) has been used in many studies since the late 1970s (Kumaraguru and Cranor, 2005) and is aimed at providing a general level of privacy concern of the public. The Westin indices are also used as benchmarks for other researchers to compare their own research (e.g., Joinson et al., 2006) and its individual questions are used in many other studies as well (e.g., IC, 2004). As such, the Westin Privacy Segmentation Index is relatively influential, which makes it worthwhile to study in some detail.

The PSI ranks individuals in three groups:

- privacy fundamentalists
- privacy pragmatists
- privacy unconcerned

In recent years the index is based on the following three statements (Harris Interactive, 2002; see also for a detailed analysis of 14 Westin studies, Kumaraguru and Cranor, 2005):

- 'Consumers have lost all control over how personal information is collected and used by companies.'
- 'Most businesses handle the personal information they collect about consumers in a proper and confidential way.'
- 'Existing laws and organizational practices provide a reasonable level of protection for consumer privacy today.'

Respondents have to rank their position regarding each statement on a four point scale: strongly agree, somewhat agree, somewhat disagree, strongly disagree. The index is computed on the basis of these answers in the following way:

Privacy *Fundamentalists* are respondents who agreed (strongly or somewhat) with the first statement and disagreed (strongly or somewhat) with the second and third statements. Privacy *Unconcerned* are those respondents who disagreed with the first statement and agreed with the second and third statements. Privacy *Pragmatists* are all other respondents.

Although the index seems to provide a convenient handle on the general level of privacy concern of the public, it has also raised many concerns. The questions that make up the index are aimed at the private sector (companies), which limits the scope of the index to this sphere, while this is not always made explicit in presentations and use of the index. Second, the questions are usually used in studies commissioned by corporations aimed at influencing public policy regarding online privacy, which may bias how the segmentation is conducted (Kumaraguru and Cranor, 2005). Third, the labels associated to the three groups are pejorative (who wants to be called a fundamentalist nowadays), whereas the concerns that would put individuals in the class of fundamentalists are actually quite reasonable and the 'fundamentalists' are not merely statistical outliers that can reasonably be ignored (EPIC, 2005).

Table 8.1 Harris/Westin data sources: Harris Interactive (2002), Kumaraguru and Cranor (2005)

	1995	1999	2000	2001	2003
Fundamentalists	25	25	25	34	26
Pragmatists	55	54	63	58	64
Unconcerned	20	22	12	8	10

Apart from these concerns with the overall methodology of the PSI, there are also issues on a more detailed level. Table 8.1 shows the results of a number of the Harris/Westin studies over the last 13 years.

A first observation is that the proportion of pragmatists has risen from slightly over half of the American population to about two thirds in 2003. The source for the rise, according to the table, comes at the expense of the unconcerned. But we have to be careful drawing this conclusion. This becomes apparent when we consider other changes in the overall picture. For instance, a significant growth of the 'fundamentalists' can be observed from 2000 to 2001. The 2001 data were collected after the 9/11 attacks in the US (November 2001) making this growth counter-intuitive. The policy measures taken in response to these attacks hinged on a purported societal need to sacrifice some of the individual freedoms (including privacy) in return for public safety. The public appeared to subscribe to this idea. Yet, we see the proportion of privacy fundamentalists growing in the Harris poll. The Harris poll studies attitudes with respect to consumer privacy, so a disparity with opinions concerning a public safety versus privacy trade-off may not be entirely surprising but this may not account for the entirety of the difference.

Westin (Harris Interactive, 2002) argues that the change stems from a decline of people agreeing with statements 2 (proper business conduct regarding personal data) and 3 (adequacy of legal framework). Westin attributes these changes to three factors. First, he notes a growing aversion of the public to profiling, target marketing and information sharing. Second, he argues that privacy became political mainstream in the US; fears of over regulating the Internet gave way to State consumer protection laws. Third, he notices a decline of trust in business leaders.

This explanation is interesting in the light of the 2003 figures. These are roughly back to the pre-2001 levels, which seems odd. Are the changes in attitudes noted by Westin suddenly reversed?[4]

Another explanation of the changes in the data is around the corner though. Westin's index is based on four category responses to the three statements: strongly agree, somewhat agree, somewhat disagree, strongly disagree. For sorting the respondents into the three segments, these four categories are reduced to only two, one positive and the other negative. The effects of changing one's opinion from slightly agree to slightly disagree on the three statements has radical effects on the classification, beyond what may be warranted when we look at the actual changes in opinions. Especially when we take into account that the majority of the respondents are in the middle categories on statements 2 and 3 as Table 8.2 shows for the 2001 data.

[4] We do not know and are not aware of any analysis by Westin on the 2003 data.

Table 8.2 Privacy segmentation data 2001, taken from (Harris Interactive, 2002)

	Strongly agree	Somewhat agree	Somewhat disagree	Strongly disagree
Consumers have lost all control over how personal information is collected and used by companies	32	47	16	5
Most businesses handle the personal information they collect about consumers in a proper and confidential fashion	3	41	39	18
Existing laws and organizational practices provide a reasonable level of privacy	4	34	45	18

Brief analysis illustrates some of the problems of measuring privacy attitudes. Privacy is a complex and multidimensional concept (e.g., Solove, 2002; Bygrave, 2002). Segmentation indices and similar constructs flatten the complexity of privacy attitudes into a simple metric whose validity is an issue. When using these constructs one has to know what they mean and how they are constructed to assess their value and one has to be careful in drawing conclusions from just looking at the numbers represented by the indices. Secondly, the analysis of the evolution of the PSI data has illustrated that the construction of the index warrants special attention. The accuracy of the instrument depends on factors such as the phrasing of actual questions and statements, the number of options the respondent can choose and where cut off points are placed. The PSI seems over sensitive for relatively small changes in opinions warranting great care in the use of the outcomes.

Overall, one should be careful in using simple metrics, especially in policy debates, also because these metrics provide little guidance in what to do. Examining user attitudes and behaviour in more detail may provide more guidance.

8.3 Going into Details

8.3.1 The Prime Survey

The PRIME project is an EU sixth Framework project aimed at developing privacy – enhancing identity management solutions.[5] In order to derive requirements for such Privacy Enhancing Technologies (PETs), the Tilburg Institute for Law, Technology, and Society (TILT) is engaged in empirical research on user attitudes regarding trust,

[5] For information about the PRIME project consult http://prime-project.eu.

privacy, personal data and PETs. This paper presents a glimpse of the rich data set collected in three online surveys conducted between December 2006 and October 2007.[6]

For this study, a large sample of universities and colleges were approached in the Netherlands (26), Belgium (Flanders) (28) and the UK (334) with a request to forward an email invitation to participate in our survey to their students. Some institutions did indeed forward the invitation (including a URL to the survey web site) to their students, while others included the invitation in a newsletter or posted it on a webpage. The response rates for the email invitations were much higher than for the newsletter invitations or the web page announcements. Overall, the response rate was highest in Belgium with 3.63% (N = 2154), followed by the Netherlands with 2.31% (N = 5541) and the UK with 2.09% (N = 812). After deleting responses with more than 75% missing values, the sample comprises 7635 respondents (NL – 5139, Belgium – 1869, UK – 627).

Our sample consists in students of higher education and universities from a wide range of cultural backgrounds, fields of study and geographical locations. The data, however, certainly does not represent the general public. The sample is nevertheless valuable because we may expect students to be on the forefront of the use of new technologies and be future decision makers. Furthermore, the amount of data gathered, with over 290 variables, provides a detailed picture of the attitudes and online behaviour of the respondents in the three countries.

In the following sections we will discuss some early findings.[7]

8.3.2 Privacy Concerns

One set of questions relates to the students' concerns in general and life online more specifically. Interestingly, the general concerns (see Table 8.3) show differences between the three countries that clearly indicate that the issues on the public and political agendas in the various countries differ.

Privacy and data protection concerns (i.e., discrimination and inequality and (mis)use of personal data) rank relatively low in all three countries, while in both the Netherlands and Belgium the manifestation of privacy in discrimination and inequality ranks higher than personal data concerns. Data protection issues are clearly not on students' radars.

When zooming in on data protection concerns (Table 8.4), the three highest ranked concerns are 'invasion of one's private sphere', 'financial loss' and 'ID theft'. The first ranks highest in the Netherlands and Belgium, whereas it ranks third in the UK. Lower on the ladder are 'loss of personal freedom', 'threat to personal safety', 'unjust treatment' and 'threat to one's dignity' in the Netherlands and Belgium. The

---

[6] A detailed report will be available through the PRIME website (http://prime-project.eu) (Oomen and Leenes, 2007).

[7] See for other analysis on the data Oomen and Leenes (2008), which analyses the privacy paradox, the disparity between privacy concern and behaviour, in more detail.

Table 8.3 General concerns

Netherlands	Belgium	UK
The standards of education	Environmental issues (e.g., pollution)	The quality of health services
Environmental issues (e.g., pollution)	Discrimination and inequality	The standards of education
Crime	The standards of education	Limitation to the freedom of speech
The quality of health services	Crime	(Mis)use of personal data
Discrimination and inequality	The quality of health services	Discrimination and inequality
Limitation to the freedom of speech	Limitation to the freedom of speech	Crime
(Mis)use of personal data	Unemployment	Environmental issues (e.g. pollution)
Immigrants and asylum seekers	(Mis)use of personal data	National security/terrorism
National security/terrorism	National security/terrorism	Immigrants and asylum seekers
Unemployment	Immigrants and asylum seekers	Unemployment

rather abstract notion of dignity, which is a cornerstone for EU privacy regulation, ranks lowest in all three countries. Interesting is also that the UK students are more concerned than their Dutch and Flemish colleagues – their average scores are higher – while the Dutch score lower than the Flemish students.

Students with ethnic minority backgrounds, such as Moroccans, Turks and Surinamese in the Netherlands, unsurprisingly, are more concerned about unjust treatment than autochthonous students. Cultural differences are also visible with respect to trust.

Students were presented two standard statements regarding trust: 'Generally speaking would you say: most people can be trusted, or you can't be too careful' and 'Do you think most people would take advantage of you if they got a chance, or would they try to be fair?'.

The distribution of Dutch and Flemish respondents regarding the first statement is about equal. About 52% of these respondents claim that most people can be trusted.

Table 8.4 Data protection concerns

Netherlands + Flanders	UK
Invasion of private sphere	Possibility of identity theft
Financial loss	Financial loss
Possibility of identity theft	Invasion of private sphere
Loss of personal freedom	Threat to personal safety
Threat to personal safety	Unjust treatment
Unjust treatment	Loss of personal freedom
Threat to dignity	Threat to dignity

In the UK, only 30% say that most people can be trusted. The 1999 European Values Studies (EVS, 2007) data shows similar figures for British respondents (29.7%), who said that most people can be trusted and 70.3% said that you cannot be too careful in dealing with other people. Of the Dutch respondents in the 1999 EVS study, 59.8% said that most people can be trusted. A larger difference can be seen in the Belgian data. In the EVS, 30.7% of the Belgian respondents stated that most people can be trusted. A possible explanation for this difference is that in our survey only Flemish students participated and no Walloon students. It is possible that Flemish people look more like the Dutch and Walloon people look more like the French. This hypothesis is partly confirmed because when the Belgian respondents in the EVS are split up by language, it is clear that Flemish respondents trust other people more than Walloon respondents. Of the Flemish Belgians, 36.8% of the respondents said that most people can be trusted, whereas 63.2% stated that you cannot be too careful in dealing with other people. For the French Belgians, these were respectively 22.1 and 77.9%, which is indeed similar to France.

There appears to be no gender correlation with these figures, so male and female students hold the same opinion. However, if we look at the ethnic minority students versus autochthonous students, the differences are notable. The average of the entire sample believing that most people can be trusted of 50.3% drops to 30.2% for the ethnic groups.

The second statement, would people take advantage if given the opportunity or be fair, shows the same overall difference between Belgium and the Netherlands on the one hand and the UK on the other. About 70% of the continentals believe others would be fair, while only 42.8% of the UK students hold this view. And here too, the ethnic minority students are more pessimistic about the trustworthiness of their fellow men.

8.3.3 Attitudes

The survey contains a number of statements regarding attitudes with a five-point response scale: strongly disagree, disagree, neutral, agree, strongly agree.

A large proportion of the Flemish (48% agree and 42% strongly agree) and UK (42% agree and 27% strongly agree) students attach great importance to the protection of their personal data.[8] This in itself does not say very much, because these can be considered politically correct answers. We therefore have to make the attitudes more concrete. When we look at the willingness to limit personal data disclosure as much as possible, students tend to be less extreme. The neutral category regarding the statement ‘I want to disclose as little personal data as possible’ is significant (35% in Flanders against 32% in the UK), whereas the agree and strong agree categories score 39% and 14% respectively in Flanders and 40 and 19% respectively in the UK. The students are therefore prepared to disclose their personal data. This seems obvious.

[8] Many of the statements discussed below were only present in the Flemish and UK questionnaires.

People are considered to trade their personal data for benefits. The students show that this is not unconditionally the case. Flemish students flock around neutral, some 25% (disagree) mind disclosing personal data for benefits, 38% are neutral and 28% (agree) do not mind giving away personal data in exchange for benefits. The UK students show a different picture. Only about 9% mind giving away some data in exchange for benefits, while 27% is neutral and 53% does not mind trading their data. Although the UK students show less objection to trade their personal data, this does not mean they give away their data easily. We asked them what they would do when trying to obtain a specific online service for which they were required to provide personal data, such as name, address, gender, or age, while at the same time considering their personal data to be irrelevant for the particular service. About one third would provide the requested data, while 17% would provide false data, 36% would look for alternative sites with a different policy and some 15% said they would refrain from the service altogether.

The Flemish data also show correlations (albeit very weak ones) one would expect, students who consider data protection important mind exchanging their data in return for benefits (Kendall's Tau = .181, $p < .001$) and do provide as little data as they can (Kendall's Tau = .319).

In response to the statement 'privacy protection is for people who have something to hide', a large majority of the students in Flanders and the UK hold the opinion that this is not the case. Over a third of the Flemish students strongly disagree with the statement (as well as 30% of the UK students) and over 43% (39% in the UK) disagree with the statement. Privacy protection therefore seems to be something that benefits everyone in society.

Students do feel privacy is eroding. The students in the three countries do show differences in their assessment of the seriousness of the erosion, however. Taken together the strongly agree and agree categories score highest in the UK (69% with an emphasis on strongly agree), followed by Flanders (67% with an emphasis on agree), while the Dutch students rate at 45%. About 53% of the Dutch students rate the erosion neutral (33%) or disagree with the statement that privacy is eroding.

8.3.4 Who Is In Control?

The survey contains a group of questions regarding who is in control over personal data. The first statement is 'I decide to whom and when I disclose my personal data'. The Flemish and UK students feel very much in control, some 41% of the Flemish students agree to the statement, whereas about 40% strongly agree. The UK numbers are 48% agree and 23% strongly agree. On the question whether disclosing personal data is a de facto requirement for serious Internet activity, both UK and Flemish students centre around neutral. The proportions agreeing with the statement 'you have to disclose your personal data otherwise you will be nowhere' are about 25 and 29% per cent for the UK and Flanders respectively, while the numbers for disagree are 29 and 27%. Neutral scores 32.5% for the UK versus 33.4% for Flanders.

Students also consider themselves able to protect their own privacy. The data is skewed towards the disagree side regarding the statement 'there is little I can do to protect my privacy'. Some 36% of the Flemish students disagree or strongly disagree and so do some 43% of the UK students. Neutral amounts to 37% for Flanders versus 25% for the UK.

Once data is disclosed, the picture radically changes. Most students acknowledge they have no control over what others do with their data. About two thirds of the Dutch students agree (49%) or strongly agree (16%) to a loss of control after disclosure. The UK students feel less impotent (with 22% strongly agreeing and 38% agreeing) and the Flemish students are in between (23% strongly agree, 47% agree).

Again, correlations between the various statements are in line with expectations, for instance, for the Flanders and UK data we see that students that perceive themselves unable to protect their own privacy state that they have little control over data collection by others (Kendall's Tau .310, $p < .001$), experience little control over data use by others after data disclosure (Kendall's Tau .286, $p < .001$) and consider themselves not unlike others 'people are no longer capable to defend themselves against modern privacy invasions protect themselves' (Kendall's Tau .360, $p < .001$).

When asked for reasons why privacy is eroding, two major causes show: the technology and inadequate regulation. The majority of respondents in the Netherlands, Flanders and the UK agrees (45.5, 43.9, and 39.4%) or strongly agrees (11.3, 13.9, and 13.9%) with the statement that 'people are no longer capable to defend themselves against modern privacy invasions'. Neutral scores between 25 and 30% for the three groups. Existing legislation does not provide sufficient protection of personal data according to many students in our sample.[9] The Flemish students are most optimistic about the adequacy of the regulation, about 50% are neutral, while 30% consider the legislation inadequate and 13.5% consider it adequate. The UK students show a similar distribution, albeit slanting slightly more towards inadequacy of the regulation. The most recent UK Information Commissioner annual track research (IC, 2006) found that 49% of the respondents consider the regulation adequate. Our data shows a more pessimistic picture. The Dutch students are more negative than their Flemish and British counterparts. Here, the numbers are about 34% neutral, about 38% consider the regulation inadequate and about 20% consider it adequate.

8.3.5 Who Should Act?

Who is responsible for improving the situation? The students do not consider themselves to be the major stakeholders in this respect. The neutral category for the statement 'the protection of my privacy is mainly my own responsibility' contains

[9] Unfortunately, we have no information about their actual knowledge of the legislation.

around a third of the Dutch and Flemish respondents and slightly below 30% of the British respondents. The size of the agreeing proportions is slightly bigger than the disagreeing proportion with the British students more strongly agreeing (36.2% agree, 11.8% strongly agree) than the Flemish and Dutch who score similarly (about 31.5% agree and about 4.2% strongly agree). On average the British students consider their own role more important than the Flemish and Dutch students do.

Measures people can take by themselves to protect their privacy include behavioural and technical measures.

Among the behavioural measures are the use of anonymous email addresses, the use of pseudonyms in interactions and providing false data when personal data is requested. Table 8.5 shows how the students use these measures. Notable is that almost half of the respondents provide false answers to questions about personal data.

Table 8.5 The use of behavioural measures to enhance privacy online

	Uses it		Does not use it
Anonymous email	55.8%		44.2%
Pseudonyms	62.8%		37.2%
Incorrect answers	NL	45.3%	54.7%
	BE	45.9%	54.1%
	UK	48.8%	51.2%

When asked why they lie about these data, the irrelevancy of the requested data for the service at hand and a fear of ID theft are mentioned as the primary reasons, see Table 8.6 for the averages regarding some of the common reasons.

Among the technical measures individuals can take are the implementation of Privacy Enhancing Technologies (PETs). Here we can distinguish between basic security and privacy protection measures, such as firewalls, SPAM filters and anti-spyware, which are often also provided by Internet Service Providers and PETs that require more actions on the part of the user. Figures 8.1 and 8.2 show the familiarity and use of a number of PETs by Dutch and British students.

The data show that students are aware of many PETs but the actual use of them is relatively scarce. The level of use in the UK is slightly higher for some of the technologies than in the Netherlands, we have not looked for explanations for the differences yet.

Table 8.6 Reasons to provide false answers. Higher numbers mean more important reason, scales run from 1 to 5

	NL	BE	UK
My personal data is irrelevant here	4.08	3.96	4.5
Afraid of ID theft	3.56	3.64	4.22
Anonymity matter of principle	3.09	3.31	3.77
possible different treatment	2.59	2.43	2.77
I don't want them to know who I am	NA	3.28	3.76

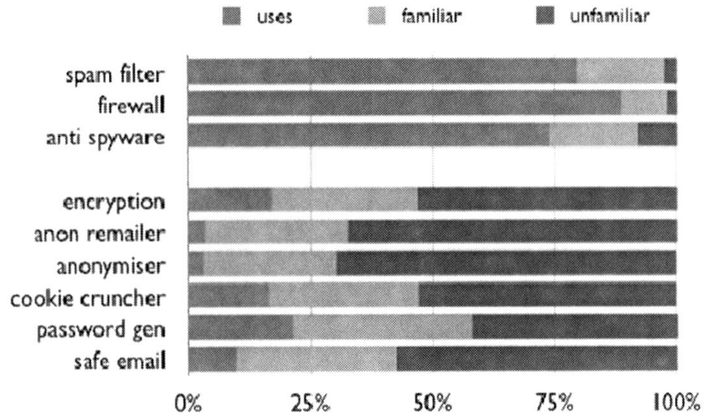

Fig. 8.1 PET use by Dutch students

Not only the individual has to play a role in improving privacy protection, also the government and new technologies can play a role. The responses to the statement 'the government ought to increase privacy protection by more legislation and enforcement' shows students from all three countries agreeing fairly strongly. A third of the Dutch students agree with this statement and a further 16% strongly agree. The Flemish score only moderately different with 42.6% agreeing and 13.5% strongly agreeing. The UK students score more radically here, 43% agree and a further 22% strongly agree.

Interestingly, given the low adoption rate for current PETs, more technology is also needed. About a third of students (in the Netherlands and Flanders) agree that more computer software is needed to protect privacy, while more than 41% of the UK students hold this position. On top of this, a further 19% of UK students strongly support this view, compared to slightly fewer for the Netherlands and Flanders.

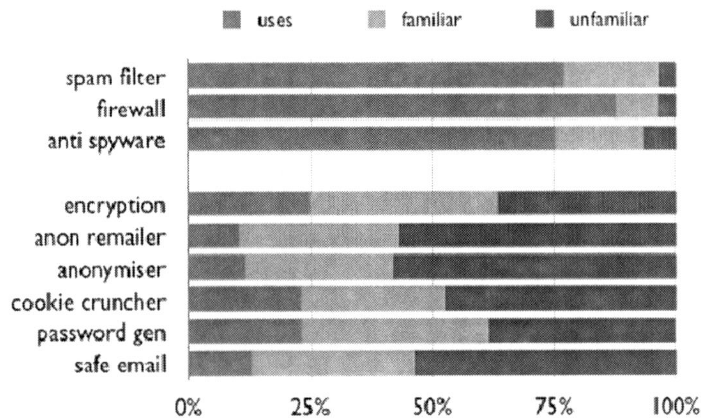

Fig. 8.2 PET use by British students

The correlations between a number of the key variables discussed in this paper show an interesting picture. Flemish and British students (we lack data for the Dutch students) who consider data protection important weakly feel that law and law enforcement are insufficient (Kendall's Tau .102, $p < .001$) while there also is a weak negative correlation between those that feel that law and law enforcement are insufficient and that protecting their privacy is their own responsibility (Kendall's Tau .136, $p < .001$) and that the government should act (Kendall's Tau .300, $p < .001$) and that more PETs are needed Kendall's Tau .197, $p < .001$). Those that feel more government action is required feel that also more PETs are needed (Kendall's Tau .197, $p < .001$).

8.4 Conclusions

What can we learn from this brief account of our survey data? First the students in our survey do care about their online privacy. The questionnaire was lengthy and took over half an hour to complete. The response rate was relatively high and many students also provided detailed answers on the open questions. This on the one hand shows a commitment to the survey's topic, while on the other hand may also show the response to be biased (those who do not value privacy may be less motivated to enter and complete the survey). We do not believe that the few iPods that we raffled among the respondents who completed the survey accounts for the high response rate; all throughout the Christmas break responses trickled in, one would expect students to have better things to do than complete a lengthy questionnaire.

Privacy concerns are not on the top of students' list of concerns but when asked in more detail, even abstract notions such as invasion of one's private sphere, next to more mundane risks such as id theft/financial loss, turn out to concern students.

The image that teenagers do not value their personal data and just disclose everything is not substantiated by our data.[10] Instead, they consider themselves to be at the helm in many cases and seem to make conscious decisions whether or not to disclose personal data. Questions as to who is requesting the data, the risks are of disclosing their data and the perceived necessity do matter here and even if data has to be provided, false data is used by many. They do not seem to simply provide data without giving it any attention, nor do they trade their data for benefits easily.

This does not mean that students feel they have full control. Control is certainly lost after disclosure and what happens after disclosure is unclear. In other words, can they make clear decisions regarding data disclosure?

There is also a clear impression that privacy is eroding and that it is increasingly difficult for individuals to protect themselves against modern infringements. Law

---

[10] Indeed, as the outcry of Facebook members over Facebook's new news feed that informed each user's friends automatically about changes in the user profile, also illustrates that privacy perceptions of teenagers are slightly more complex than 'I've got nothing to hide, so here is my data'. See for instance, Story and Stone (2007).

and technologies provide insufficient help. These findings are in line with other studies, such as those carried out by the UK Information Commissioner (2004, 2006).

In terms of addressing the issues, we notice multi-tier solutions. Students are prepared to act themselves, certainly if they are provided with tools (technology) to help them. But they clearly point out that tougher enforcement and stricter rules are also needed. This may sound as if students put the ball in the government's corner but the correlations between the various items show that the students see a role for themselves *and* technology *and* government. Let us try to work on all three fronts: improve awareness of data collection and use, build workable PETs and take enforcement of existing rules seriously, while also thinking about the adequacy of the existing framework.

Acknowledgments The research for this paper was supported by the IST PRIME project. The PRIME project receives research funding from the Community's Sixth Framework Program (Contract No. 507591) and the Swiss Federal Office for Education and Science.

References

Bygrave, Lee A. (2002), Data Protection Law: Approaching Its Rationale, Logic and Limits, Kluwer.

Consumers International (2001), privacy@net, an international comparative study of consumer privacy on the Internet.

Cremonini, L, and L. Valeri (2003), Benchmarking Security and Trust in Europe and the US, RAND Europe.

DCA (Department for Constitutional Affairs, UK) (2003), Privacy and Data-Sharing Survey of Public Awareness and Perceptions, conducted by MORI Social Research Institute.

DTI (Department for Trade and Industry, UK) (2001), Informing Consumers about e-commerce. Conducted by MORI Social Research Institute, September 2001.

EPIC (2005), *Public Opinion on Privacy.* 2005. available at http://www.epic.org/privacy/survey/default.html.

European Commission (2003a), Consumer Protection in the EU, Special Report 193, European Commission, November 2003.

European Commission (2003b), Data Protection, Special Eurobarometer 196, Wave 60.0, European Opinion Research Group EEIG.

EVS (2007), European Value Studies, Tilburg, 2007.

Harris Interactive (2002), *Privacy On and Off the Internet: What Consumers Want,* Harris Interactive conducted for Privacy & American Business.

IC (2004), Information Commissioner (UK), Annual Track Research Findings, Individuals, 2004.

IC (2006), Information Commissioner (UK), Annual Track Research Findings, Individuals, 2006, available at http://www.ico.gov.uk/upload/documents/library/corporate/research_and_reports/2006_annual_tracking_report_individuals_final.pdf.

Joinson, A. N., Paine, C., Buchanan, T., and Reips, U.-D. (2006), Watching me, watching you: privacy attitudes and reactions to identity card implementation scenarios in the United Kingdom. Journal of Information Science, 32(4), 334–343.

Kumaraguru, P., and Cranor, L. F. (2005), Privacy Indexes: A Survey of Westin's Studies (No. CMU-ISRI-5-138): Institute for Software Research International, School of Computer Science, Carnegie Mellon University.

Norberg, P., Horne, D. R., and Horne, D. A. (2007), The privacy paradox: Personal information disclosure intentions versus behaviors. Journal of Consumer Affairs, 41(1), 100–126.

Oomen, I. C., and Leenes, R. E. (2007), Privacy risk perceptions and privacy protection strategies, to appear in Leeuw, E. de., Fischer Hübner, S., Tseng, J.C., Borking, J. (Eds.) (ed), IDMan'07, Rotterdam.

Oomen, I. C., and Leenes, R. E. (2008), The PRIME survey – A study regarding privacy attitudes and behaviour of students in the Netherlands, Flanders and the UK, 2008.

PWC PriceWaterhouseCoopers (2000), e-Privacy solutions: Bridging the B2C divide e-Privacy issues among European consumers.

Solove, D. J. (2002), Conceptualizing Privacy. California Law Review, Vol. 90, p. 1087, 2002, available at SSRN http://ssrn.com/paper=313103.

Story, L., and Stone, B. (2007), Facebook Retreats in Online Tracking, the New York Times, Nov 30, 2007. available at http://www.nytimes.com/2007/11/30/technology/30face.html?ex=1354165200&en=f448f8a210da7bdf&ei=5124&partner=permalink&exprod=permalink

Zureik, E., Harling Stalker, L., Smith, E., Lyon, D., and Chan, Y. E. (2008), *Privacy, Surveillance and the Globalization of Personal Information: International Comparisons*, Forthcoming 2008, McGill-Queen's University Press: Kingston.

Part III
Regulation

Chapter 9
Consent, Proportionality and Collective Power

Lee A. Bygrave and Dag Wiese Schartum

9.1 Introduction

Who should have competence to make decisions on protection of personal data? How should that competence be exercised? How should it be distributed? It is with these questions that this paper is broadly concerned. They are fundamental questions that have been resolved differently across jurisdictions and across the years.

In this chapter, we refrain from attempting to provide complete answers to each question. Rather, we aim to examine critically aspects of the answers to them which current regulatory policies embody, particularly in Europe. Our analysis focuses on the interaction of a particular form of decision making with a particular principle for decision making. The form of decision making in focus is data subject consent (hereinafter also termed simply "consent") – i.e., decisions by data subjects signifying agreement to others being able to process personal data about them. The principle for decision making in focus is that of proportionality – i.e., a principle that sets limits on the amount and type of information that may be collected and applied in a given context to reach a given goal (or set of goals).

In this chapter, we are concerned mainly with decisions that are taken at what we term an "operative level". These are decisions made in connection with the development and/or application of relatively concrete information systems for the processing of personal data. Such decisions may be distinguished from those made by legislators when they determine the content of general statutory provisions on data protection. The latter type of decision forms, of course, much of the normative framework for the exercise of operative decisions. Thus, legislation may require that

---

L.A. Bygrave (✉)
Department of Private Law, University of Oslo
e-mail: lee.bygrave@jus.uio.no

This chapter builds upon the presentation we were asked to give at the conference, "Reinventing Data Protection?", Brussels, 12th October 2007. The topic we were asked to speak on at that conference bore the somewhat enigmatic title, "Consent versus Proportionality Principle: Are the Proportions Right?". We thank the conference organizers – particularly Yves Poullet – for presenting us with a challenging topic that stimulated us to rethink some of our conceptions of how decisions in the data protection field ought to be made.

S. Gutwirth et al. (eds.), *Reinventing Data Protection?*
DOI 10.1007/978-1-4020-9498-9_9, © Springer Science+Business Media B.V. 2009

consent be obtained in given contexts; this will lead to a range of operative decisions being taken as to how that consent requirement is to be met in a concrete situation.

The disposition of the chapter is briefly as follows. We present firstly an overview of the distribution of decision-making competence under data protection law, noting various problematic features of it. Thereafter, we examine the role of the proportionality principle in data protection law and elaborate on how the principle interacts with consent mechanisms, particularly with respect to the EU Data Protection Directive (Directive 95/46/EC – hereinafter termed simply "the Directive" or "DPD") and Article 8 of the European Convention on Human Rights and Fundamental Freedoms (hereinafter termed simply "ECHR"). Finally, we discuss the advantages and disadvantages of collective, representative forms of consent.

Our chief line of argument is that, while both consent and proportionality requirements have valuable roles to play in promoting protection of personal data, they suffer from certain weaknesses. The most glaring deficiencies appear to attach to consent requirements. Under current data protection law, data subject consent is usually formulated as a "lonely" option, with each data subject cast in the role of a solitary, independent (albeit supposedly robust and informed) decision-maker. We argue that, for a variety of reasons, this conception of consent is flawed in terms of ensuring strong data protection. We go on to argue that further attention needs to be given to developing mechanisms for the collective exercise of consent. Such mechanisms could bolster the position of the individual data subject in a situation where the data controller(s) will typically have greater bargaining strength.

9.2 Distribution of Decision-Making Competence

In data protection legislation, we can identify at least three kinds of actors with competence to decide on data protection issues at an operative level:

- Data protection authorities (hereinafter also termed simply "DPAs");
- Data controllers (i.e., those who/which determine the purposes and means of data processing);
- Data subjects (i.e., those to whom data relate).

Amongst these actors, the competence of data protection authorities is unique in that they may often have the power not just to decide on the conditions for certain forms of data processing (the case, e.g., under a licensing regime – see below) but also the power to review (i.e., consider and overturn) the decisions of another of the actors – namely, data controllers (e.g., by ordering a controller to halt a particular processing operation or to apply more extensive security measures to that operation). This latter power may be exercised independently of complaint or appeal by data subjects (Fig. 9.1).

The above three kinds of actors are not the only ones with competence to decide on data protection issues at an operative level, yet it is they who exercise such competence most commonly. Courts and tribunals may also have such competence but this will typically be exercised only on appeal from a DPA decision. In other words,

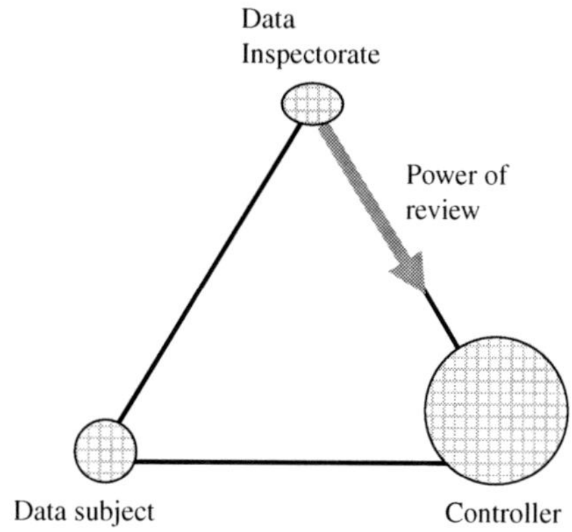

Fig. 9.1 Distribution of primary decision-making powers

the competence of the tribunal or court will typically be exercised as a power of review instigated by complaint. In many jurisdictions, this power of review tends to be exercised only exceptionally.[1] Moreover, its "operative" impact may be further lessened where the appeal body is limited to passing judgment on points of law rather than fact, or where the range of remedies that the body may apply is otherwise narrow.[2]

Many of the early data protection laws of European countries gave broad discretionary powers to national DPAs to determine the conditions for processing personal data. In some jurisdictions, such as Sweden, France and Norway, the applicable laws established licensing regimes making the ability to undertake certain forms of processing conditional upon formal approval being obtained from the relevant authority.[3] Under such regimes, data controllers and data subjects had relatively little ability to determine for themselves the conditions for processing personal data.

In subsequent years, comprehensive licensing regimes have been cut back and the decisional roles of both data controllers and data subjects enhanced. Ideological factors have partly spurred this development. Comprehensive licensing regimes have a paternalistic character at odds with the ideal of individual autonomy underpinning much of data protection policy, particularly the notion that individuals know what is best for themselves and ought to be able to decide thereafter.[4] However, the demise of such regimes has been due equally if not more to the practical problems

---

[1] See further Bygrave 2000.

[2] The case, e.g., under the US federal Privacy Act of 1974. A US federal court can only issue enforcement orders relating to the exercise of persons' rights to access and rectify information relating to themselves. The court can also order relief for damages in limited situations but cannot otherwise order US federal government agencies to change their data-processing practices. See further Schwartz and Reidenberg 1996 pp. 100, 114ff.

[3] For Sweden, see Data Act of 1973 (repealed and replaced by Personal Data Act of 1998); for France, see Act no. 78-17 on Data Processing, Data Files and Individual Liberties (since amended); for Norway, see Personal Data Registers Act of 1978 (repealed and replaced by Personal Data Act of 2000). Further on such licensing schemes, see Bygrave 2002 Chapters 4 (Section 4.2) and 18 (Section 18.4.7).

[4] See Schartum 2006.

experienced with them. In Sweden and Norway at least, extensive licensing tended to result in an excessive workload for the DPAs concerned. It inflicted upon the authorities (and many data controllers) a great deal of routine work of little direct benefit for data protection. At the same time, it drained the authorities' meagre resources, weakening their ability to carry out other important functions, such as monitoring and enforcement.

Directive 95/46/EC has cemented the shift away from reliance on comprehensive licensing schemes. On the one hand, the Directive stipulates as a general rule that data controllers may process personal data once they have notified the relevant DPA of the processing (Article 18), provided that the processing otherwise conforms to other ground rules laid down in the Directive; controllers do not have to wait for specific permission from the DPA. While the Directive also permits a system of "prior checking" by DPAs with respect to data-processing operations involving "specific risks to the rights and freedoms of data subjects" (Article 20), such a system is only to apply to a "very limited" proportion of operations (Recital 54). Thus, licensing cannot be the rule, only the exception. On the other hand, the Directive gives – at least on paper – relatively generous opportunities for data subjects to regulate, through consent mechanisms, the processing of data about themselves (Articles 7(a), 8(2)(a), 14, 15(1) and 26(1)(a)). The Directive also permits data controllers to make at least the initial decisions as to the legitimacy and justification for their processing operations (e.g., under the alternative criteria listed in Article 7(b)–(f)).

However, an increased decisional role of data subjects brings its own problems. To begin with, there are legal difficulties with properly interpreting consent requirements. For instance, consent must usually be "informed" (see, e.g., DPD Article 2(a)), yet how "informed" is "informed"? Considerable uncertainty persists as to the amount and type of information required in particular contexts (e.g., in relation to transfer of personal data across national borders – DPD Article 26(1)(a)).

Secondly, a large range of extra-legal factors undermines the privacy interests that consent mechanisms are supposed to promote or embody. The degree of choice presupposed by these mechanisms will often not be present for certain services or products, particularly those offered by data controllers in a monopoly (or near-monopoly) position. This is a problem that few if any data protection laws seem to specifically address.

Thirdly, data controllers will typically have greater knowledge about their data-processing operations than will the data subjects. This disparity can arise despite a requirement that consent is "informed" and despite the existence of other sorts of notification requirements (e.g., those arising pursuant to DPD Articles 10 and 11). The efficacy of such stipulations can be undermined by uncertainty over their interpretation – as indicated above. Further, there are indications that controllers often fail to fully comply with them.[5] Even if controllers are generous in their supply of information to data subjects, many of the latter could still suffer from inability to properly value the worth of their data in market terms or to properly gauge the long-term significance of their consent, in terms of the impact on their privacy and

[5] See, e.g., EOS Gallup Europe 2003.

autonomy. Augmenting this "privacy myopia" (Froomkin)[6] is ignorance on the part of large numbers of people of their rights under data protection law.[7]

Fourthly, problems of consensual exhaustion, laxity and apathy – in addition to ignorance and myopia – can reduce the amount of care that data subjects invest in their decisions of whether or not to consent. When frequently faced with consent requirements, many data subjects could well tire of continuously having to think carefully through the privacy-related issues inherent in each particular decision. While we are unaware of solid empirical evidence pointing to consensual exhaustion as an actual problem, it seems perfectly plausible to us to posit at least the *potential* existence of such a problem. Moreover, it seems reasonable to posit that this exhaustion will tend to be exacerbated by the increasing complexity in exploitation of personal data. Such exhaustion could quickly give way to laxity, if not apathy.

The above factors indicate that a regulatory regime giving individuals extensive room to determine for themselves the manner and extent to which data on them are processed by others, does not necessarily mean that individuals will act to limit such processing or that such processing will decrease. It would be far-fetched, though, to claim that individuals, as data subjects, generally have extensive possibilities for informational self-determination. Certainly the development of data protection laws over the last four decades – at least in Europe – has resulted in data subjects' decisional role being given greater formal prominence in the legislation concerned. Yet even under the bulk of current data protection laws, controllers are rarely hostage to consent requirements. The degree of data subject empowerment flowing from these requirements is substantially diminished by the fact that consent tends to be just one of several alternative preconditions for data processing. Article 7 of the Directive is a case in point (see Section 9.4 below).

This brings us to the question of whether the exercise of controllers' decision-making competence on data protection matters gives cause for concern. The short answer to this question is, unfortunately, yes. A growing amount of empirical evidence points to significant levels of ignorance on the part of controllers of their duties under data protection laws. Some of this evidence suggests too that compliance with the same laws is patchy. For example, a survey of Norwegian enterprises carried out in 2005 paints a discouraging picture of Norwegian data protection law in practice.[8] Fifty-four per cent of controllers covered in the survey reported that they had carried out none or only one of five selected mandatory statutory measures to protect personal data. Only 4% of the respondents answered that all five measures had been implemented.[9] When asked about their knowledge of the law concerned,

---

[6] Froomkin 2000 p. 1501.

[7] See, e.g., European Opinion Research Group 2003.

[8] Ravlum 2006.

[9] Controllers were also asked about camera surveillance. Under the Norwegian Data Protection Act of 2000, camera surveillance should be reported to the Data Inspectorate prior to start-up. The survey revealed that 20% of the controllers had not complied with this reporting requirement, while 43% answered that they did not know if notification had been sent. Again, see Ravlum 2006.

82% of the respondents answered that they had little or no knowledge. Somewhat paradoxically, though, the majority of respondents regarded data protection in a positive light. The equivalent situation of controllers elsewhere in Europe appears to be (or have been) marked by a similar mixture of ignorance, under-compliance and positive attitudes regarding data protection law.[10]

Summing up so far, a variety of problems plague the exercise of decision-making competence in the data protection field regardless of where that competence is placed. It would seem that the solution to these problems cannot lie in providing either data subjects or data controllers with even more decisional power. At the same time, reverting to a comprehensive licensing scheme administered by DPAs seems unrealistic. An important question then is whether decision-making competence can be reorganized in another way that mitigates these problems. Before dealing with that question in detail, it is worthwhile considering the impact of the proportionality principle on these decision-making processes. The pertinent issue in this respect is the extent to which application of that principle may compensate for the problems identified above.

9.3 Role of Proportionality Principle in Data Protection Law

Concern for proportionality is far from unique to data protection law and policy. Such concern is, for instance, firmly established as a basic principle in European Community (EC) law, manifesting itself in a multitude of legal instruments and judicial decisions covering a broad range of contexts.[11] In EC law, the proportionality principle is generally recognized as having three prongs:

(i) suitability – is the measure concerned suitable or relevant to realizing the goals it is aimed at meeting?;
(ii) necessity – is the measure concerned necessary to realizing the goals it is aimed at meeting?; and
(iii) non-excessiveness (proportionality *stricto sensu*) – does the measure go further than is necessary to realize the goals it is aimed at meeting?

The proportionality principle per se (as delineated above) is not included as one of the classic "Fair Information Practice" principles of data protection law,[12] yet it underpins these and shines through in their interstices. It is manifest in the criterion of "fairness" inherent in the bulk of these principles. Fairness in processing of personal data undoubtedly connotes proportionality in the balancing of the respective

---

[10] See particularly EOS Gallup Europe 2003.
[11] See generally Craig and de Búrca 2008 pp. 544–551.
[12] For a recent critical overview of these principles and their evolution, see Cate 2006.

interests of data subjects and controllers.[13] The proportionality principle – or at least aspects of it – is further manifest in a variety of relatively concrete data protection rules. The stipulation that personal data must be "relevant" and "not excessive" in relation to the purposes for which they are processed (see, e.g., DPD Article 6(c)) is a central rule on point.[14] Provisions incorporating a criterion of "necessity" also embody a requirement of proportionality. This is established most clearly in the case law of the European Court of Human Rights (ECtHR) pursuant to ECHR Article 8(2), which permits interference with the right to respect for private life in Article 8(1) if, *inter alia*, the interference is "necessary" to achieve certain enumerated interests. In the view of the Court, "necessary" implies that the interference both "corresponds to a pressing social need" and is "proportionate to the legitimate aim pursued".[15] The criterion of necessity in certain provisions of the DPD (primarily Articles 7, 8 and 13) is to be construed similarly.[16]

At the same time, elements of the classic "Fair Information Practice" principles serve to enable application of the proportionality principle. Indeed, there is a close, symbiotic relationship between the latter and elements of the former. The first element of the principle of purpose specification or finality (i.e., that personal data should be collected for specified legitimate purposes) is key in this respect. Any assessment of the proportionality of a particular action relies on identification of that action's purpose(s).

Given its manifold manifestation in data protection law, the proportionality principle must inevitably be observed by both DPAs and data controllers when exercising their respective decision-making competence. At the same time, because of its ubiquity across many codes and contexts, application of the principle to these decisions may follow not just from data protection legislation but other sets of legal norms too. For instance, a DPA decision will often have to comply with the principle as a matter of general administrative law. The same goes for decisions of data controllers that exercise public authority. Nevertheless, the precise status and content of the proportionality principle in terms of general administrative law may vary from jurisdiction to jurisdiction.[17]

---

[13] See further Bygrave 2002 p. 58.

[14] As confirmed by the European Court of Justice in its judgment of 20 May 2003 in Joined Cases C-465/00, C-138/01 and C-139/01 *Österreichischer Rundfunk and Others* [2003] ECR I-4989, particularly paragraph 91.

[15] See, e.g., *Leander v. Sweden* (1987) Series A of the Publications of the European Court of Human Rights ("A"), paragraph 58.

[16] See again the judgment of the European Court of Justice in Joined Cases C-465/00, C-138/01 and C-139/01 *Österreichischer Rundfunk and Others* [2003] ECR I-4989, particularly paragraph 91.

[17] For example, while the principle is firmly entrenched as a key norm in German and EC administrative law, its status in the respective administrative law regimes of the Scandinavian countries is less certain. See generally Bagger Tranberg 2007, Chapters 6, 7, 8 and references cited therein.

9.4 Interaction of Proportionality Principle and Consent

How does the proportionality principle interact with the consent requirements of data protection law? Is there also in this context a close, symbiotic relationship? The answer to the latter question is a qualified no. In the first place, an individual as data subject is not legally required to exercise their right of consent in conformity with the principle; indeed, there is no direct legal hindrance to consent being given or withdrawn without the data subject giving any specific consideration to proportionality whatsoever. However, the principle can have an indirect impact on the exercise of consent insofar as it influences the amount of information that a data controller must provide the data subject in order for the decision of the latter to be adequately informed. A rule of thumb is that the quality and quantity of that information must be proportional to the risks associated with the particular data-processing operation for which consent is sought. Moreover, the provision of information is intended in principle to enable the data subject to carry out their own balancing of interests and risks – a process that involves, in theory, some assessment of proportionality. Nonetheless, as indicated above, a data subject is not legally bound to undertake such an assessment.

In our view, it is worth emphasizing here that exercise of consent ought to be regarded as a process involving not simply conferral but also withdrawal of agreement. A data subject's protection of their privacy-related interests cannot be linked just to conferral of consent; their ability to withdraw consent quickly and effectively is also important. Withdrawal of consent will typically occur after the data subject has had concrete experience of the advantages and disadvantages of a particular data-processing operation. Such experience supplements the information that the data controller provided prior to the conferral of consent and can accordingly be seen as extending the informational basis that enables the data subject to undertake a sensible proportionality assessment.

Once data subject consent is given, does the proportionality principle – as found in data protection laws – cease to apply to the actions of the data controller(s)? This question raises another aspect of the interaction of consent and the proportionality principle. It is a question that teases out a *possible* difference between the Directive and the European Convention on Human Rights and Fundamental Freedoms. The Directive is structured such that the proportionality principle, as manifest in Article 6(1), must ordinarily be observed regardless of whether or not consent is given pursuant to Article 7(a), 8(2)(a) or 26(1)(a). In terms of ECHR Article 8, however, the role played in such a case by the proportionality principle, as laid down in Article 8(2), is a matter of conjecture. All decisions by the ECtHR on data protection issues have hitherto involved *non*-consensual processing of personal data. Thus, the proportionality principle (so far) has only been engaged in the absence of consent. We doubt this is due to premeditated intent on the part of the ECtHR; it is most likely due solely to the particular character of the cases that have come before the Court. We also doubt that the Court will end up construing Article 8 in a way that leaves the data protection guarantees embodied therein falling significantly short of the protection levels required by the Directive (and, as a consequence, by the laws of most European states). Still, the question remains: what may constitute interference with the right(s) laid down in Article 8(1) in the case of consensual processing of personal data? Concomitantly, to what extent will the ECtHR restrict data-processing operations which, although consented to by data subjects, nevertheless contribute to the erosion of the foundations for pluralistic, democratic society?

Yet another aspect of the interaction of consent with the proportionality principle concerns the normative relationship between the preconditions for data processing as laid down in DPD Articles 7 and 8. Article 7 lays down six sets of alternative preconditions for the processing of personal data generally; Article 8 lays down parallel, though somewhat different, sets of preconditions for processing of certain kinds of especially sensitive personal data. For present purposes, we shall focus on Article 7. Basically, it permits data processing if either the data subject consents to the processing (Article 7(a)) or the processing is "necessary" for certain specified purposes (Article 7(b)–(f)), such as concluding a contract with the data subject (Article 7(b)) or pursuing "legitimate interests" that override the conflicting interests of the data subject (Article 7(f)). It is clear that the reference to "necessary" in Article 7(b)–(f) imports a requirement of proportionality, as does the interest-balancing exercise embodied in Article 7(f).

On their face, all of these alternative preconditions carry equal normative weight – i.e., there appears to be no normative prioritization of consent relative to, say, proportionality as expressed in Article 7(f). The same can be said of the alternative preconditions for data processing specified in Article 8 (and, indeed, in Article 26 with respect to cross-border transfer of personal data in derogation of Article 25). However, in a small number of jurisdictions, the consent requirement has been given priority over the other preconditions such that a data controller must ordinarily obtain the data subject's consent to the processing unless this would be impracticable.[18] It is doubtful that the Directive, as originally conceived, mandates such prioritization. However, the Directive does not disallow it.[19] At the same time, case law of the ECtHR might provide a foundation for this prioritization and, indeed, may even require it for the processing of certain types of sensitive data, such as medical

---

[18] The case, e.g., in Estonia and, to a lesser extent, Belgium and Greece: see Beyleveld et al. 2004 p. 155 and references cited therein. In Belgium, consent is apparently given priority only with respect to processing of *sensitive* personal data: see Nys 2004 p. 36. In Norway, the prioritization has occurred pursuant to administrative practice. The Norwegian Data Protection Tribunal (*Personvernnemnda*, a quasi-judicial body handling appeals from decisions of the Data Inspectorate) has held that data controllers must ordinarily attempt to get consent unless there are reasons for waiver which are grounded in more than simply cost and convenience factors (decision in case 2004-01; followed in cases 2004-04 and 2005-08). The issue has not been the subject of court litigation in Norway.

[19] Cf. Kotschy 2006 p. 47 ("Contrary to the doctrine of 'informational self-determination" ..., Art. 7 does not overemphasize the importance of "consent": all grounds for lawful processing mentioned in Art. 7 have the same status').

data – at least in situations when the processing of such data cannot otherwise be justified under ECHR Article 8(2).[20]

9.5 Relative Strength of Consent and Proportionality Principle in Promoting Data Protection

When assessing the strength of consent relative to the proportionality principle in terms of ensuring a robust level of data protection, it is important to remember at the outset that, under the Directive at least, consent is not a stand-alone control mechanism; the proportionality principle, as manifest in Article 6(1), will also play a regulatory role. In other words, the level of data protection that is actually afforded in any particular case through applying a consent requirement, will be the result of combining the latter requirement *and* the proportionality principle. This means that it is somewhat artificial to compare the relative strength of each. Nevertheless, looking beyond the Directive, there are contexts in which consent is used as a control mechanism independently of the proportionality principle[21] and there are instances of policy discourse in which consent is promoted as an ideal regulatory tool.[22]

On the basis of the problems with consent as outlined in Section 9.2 above, it is tempting to regard consent as weaker than the proportionality principle in terms of ensuring a robust level of data protection. Yet it would be incorrect to assume that consent mechanisms are without any bite. There are numerous instances in which such mechanisms have significantly curtailed planned data-processing operations. Certain forms of direct marketing are cases in point[23]; as are certain research projects.[24]

It would be also foolish to assume that application of the proportionality principle will always afford stronger data protection than consent. The analysis has to be more contextual. The relative strength of the proportionality principle depends on a range of factors, most notably: (i) how is proportionality formulated? (ii) what are the parameters for the proportionality assessment? (iii) who undertakes the assessment?

Undeniably, though, the proportionality principle has great regulatory strength if *conscientiously* applied. Part of this strength lies in the flexible, dynamic nature of

---

[20] See particularly *Z v. Finland* (1998) 25 EHRR 371, paragraphs 95–96; *M.S. v. Sweden* (1999) 28 EHRR 313, paragraph 41.

[21] E.g., in relation to telemarketing regulation in Australia: see the federal Do Not Call Register Act of 2006.

[22] E.g., in relation to biobank research: see further Brekke and Sirnes 2006 and references cited therein.

[23] Witness, e.g., the extensive take-up – at least initially – of the National Do Not Call Registry operated by the US Federal Trade Commission: see further CBS News 2003.

[24] See, e.g., Bygrave 2002 p. 361 (footnote 1210) documenting the fate of a particular sociological research project in Norway.

the criterion of proportionality. This makes the principle highly adaptable to changes in technological and societal development. Not surprisingly, then, the principle has proven particularly useful in regulating video surveillance and the application of biometric identification and authentication schemes.[25]

When reviewing the legality of the exercise of consent, a DPA, tribunal or court has a fairly limited set of criteria for their review. They may strike down consensual processing on the basis that the consent given is not sufficiently informed, voluntary or clear. Yet they would seem to have greater flexibility in reviewing the legality of processing operations through application of the proportionality principle. The latter allows room for more general, systemic considerations about desirable levels of societal control.

However, at least in respect of *judicial* review, there are limits on the degree to which courts are willing to substitute their proportionality assessment for the equivalent assessment undertaken by a data controller, DPA or legislator. Sometimes, these limits manifest themselves in formal doctrine, such as the doctrine of margin of appreciation in Strasbourg jurisprudence.[26] Often, though, the limits appear more obliquely – for instance, when judges settle a dispute by addressing legal-technical issues only, despite the fact that proportionality considerations were pleaded during proceedings.[27] Indeed often try to avoid having, judges to address relatively controversial policy issues. This clearly tarnishes the promise of the proportionality principle as a tool of judicial review in the service of data protection.

Yet it is not just such judicial restraint that potentially tarnishes the regulatory promise of the proportionality principle. The failure of data controllers to conscientiously apply the principle is arguably of greater practical detriment, given the huge scale of their data-processing operations relative to the exercise of judicial review. Also damaging, of course, is the failure of data subjects to conscientiously apply considerations of proportionality when exercising consent. Thus, while the proportionality principle has great regulatory promise in theory, its practice is another matter. Accordingly, a question mark may be placed against its ability to compensate for the problems identified in Section 9.2 above. Can we then find another possible solution or partial solution to these problems? It is with this question that the remainder of the chapter deals.

---

[25] See further Bagger Tranberg 2007, pp. 134–153 and cases described therein.

[26] Further on that doctrine, see, e.g., Yourow 1996.

[27] As occurred in the decision of the European Court of Justice on the transfer of airline passenger name records (PNR data) to US border-control agencies: see judgment of 30 May 2006 in Joined Cases C-317/04 and C-318/04, *European Parliament v. Council of the European Union and Commission of the European Communities*. Here, the ECJ nullified the initial decisions of the European Commission and Council allowing such transfer, simply on the basis that they were *ultra vires*. The court did not go on to address the privacy-related arguments that were raised during litigation. These included an argument that the decisions at issue were in breach of the proportionality principle.

9.6 Organisation of Decisional Competence Regarding Data Protection

The three main actors with primary decisional competence on data protection issues (as described in Section 9.2 above) are organisationally very different. A data protection authority has typically a relatively large number of staff, who are hierarchically organised. A controller is also often a collective entity (large or small) but can be an individual, physical/natural person. A data subject, however, is always an individual, physical/natural person – at least under most data protection laws.[28] As organisations, DPAs and controllers will typically have multiple persons involved in the interpretation and application of data protection rules and in the preparation of decisions connected to those rules. Data subjects are, in principle, solitary decision makers.

Regardless of whether an actor is a collective entity or not, they may compensate for their possible lack of expertise, insight or other resources by co-operating with and/or seeking advice from, other bodies. Indeed, in some situations, DPAs and controllers in the public sector may be *required* to do so – e.g., pursuant to general administrative law.[29]

Yet, as far as the actual exercise of decisional competence is concerned, there are differences between the actors. Data protection authorities in the EU/EEA "shall act with complete independence in exercising the functions entrusted to them" (DPD Article 28(1)). This requirement of independence means that they cannot be instructed by another administrative body on how their decisional competence is to be exercised. It probably also restricts their ability to enter into legally binding agreements with other regulatory authorities that place extensive limits on the exercise of that competence.

On the other hand, controllers are generally assumed to be able to exercise their decisional competence in close co-operation with others – as indicated in the Directive's definition of "controller" (Article 2(d)). Such co-operation may arise, for instance, in connection with the administration of a common platform for identity management involving various companies. The co-operation may involve daily exercise of controller competence without each and every one of the controllers continuously keeping, as it were, their hand on the steering wheel. We shall not elaborate further on precisely what procedural routines must be observed in such a co-operative framework; it suffices to note that a fair degree of organisational freedom appears to exist.

Data subjects, though, do not seem to enjoy an equivalent degree of organisational freedom when exercising their decisional competence. In principle, their

---

[28] The data protection laws of a small number of countries – e.g., Austria, Italy and Switzerland – extend expressly to processing of data on organized collective entities, such as corporations. For in-depth treatment of the issue of data protection for such entities, see generally Bygrave 2002 Part III.

[29] See also DPD Article 28(6) mandating increased cooperation between the various national DPAs within the EU.

consent is exercised individually. This is in keeping with much of the ideological basis for data protection law and policy, which accords a central place to the autonomy and integrity of the individual *qua* individual.

Before we proceed further, it is pertinent to elaborate on the current legal limitations, under the Directive, regarding data subjects' ability to organise themselves. As indicated above, there are no legal limitations placed on the ability of data subjects to obtain advice from others in advance of, or after, exercising their decision as to whether or not to consent to a particular processing operation. Those persons that are in agreement with each other may also organise themselves as a collective entity and appoint someone to represent their viewpoint on a particular issue. For instance, all employees in a firm can agree amongst themselves whether or not they want photographs of each of them published on the firm's website and appoint a person to communicate their decision to the management. This would also be possible even if there were initial disagreement between the employees, as long as each employee had freely and unambiguously accepted the compromise reached. However, a data subject is probably not allowed to transfer the exercise of their decisional competence to an organisation that is intended to act on behalf of them and other data subjects if the organisation is permitted to make a decision that is binding on *all* the persons for whom the organisation acts, even if some (a minority) of those persons disagree with it. This is probably also the case even if the organisation is established precisely in order to protect the privacy and related interests of a group of individuals. Such an arrangement is in tension, if not conflict, with the definition of consent in DPD Article 2(h), which refers to a "*freely given*, specific and informed indication of *his* wishes by which the data subject signifies *his* agreement to personal data ... being processed" (emphasis added). This definition emphasises strongly both the independence of the data subject and the personal, individual nature of their consent.

Notwithstanding these apparent legal limitations, it is worth discussing their desirability (see Section 9.8 below). And it is worth considering how a collective consent mechanism could work, were these limitations relaxed. We undertake such a consideration in the next section.

9.7 Collective Consent

We employ the term "collective consent" to denote consent exercised on behalf of a group of data subjects but without these persons individually approving each specific exercise of that decisional competence. In other words, it denotes a mechanism involving collective conferral or withdrawal of consent, which is binding on all of the group members, even when some of these disagree with the particular decision. In the following, we consider how such a mechanism could be organised in a way that would seem most favourable for the data subjects' privacy and related interests.

Such a mechanism is probably most relevant and realistic to establish where individuals have already organised themselves to safeguard or promote a set of common interests. Relevant organisational forms are, for example, trade unions, environmental protection organisations, sports clubs, student associations and the like. The purpose behind each such organisation will influence how collective consent is exercised. Collective consent is likely to be exercised in conformity with that purpose. A trade union, for instance, could quite likely refuse to agree to extensive logging of employees' computer usage because it views such logging as detrimental for the social-psychological work environment. Similarly, an environmental protection organisation could quite easily withdraw its agreement to a particular company processing data on its members, as a reaction to the company's plans to invest in an environmentally unsound business venture. Moreover, as these two hypothetical examples indicate, organisations could very well find adoption of a collective consent mechanism attractive because it increases their power in negotiating etc. with other organisations.

Naturally, a collective consent mechanism must be subject to certain legal requirements in much the same way as is the case when consent is exercised individually. This means that the requirements that consent be informed, voluntary and clear must apply as far as possible to such a mechanism. Further, these requirements must apply not just to the initial conferral of consent but also to its possible withdrawal (cf. our comments in Section 9.4 above).

Collective consent must be organised such that it does not result in a narrower set of choices for individuals than they would otherwise have. To begin with, it must be completely up to each individual member of the organisation to decide whether or not to transfer the exercise of their consensual competence to that organisation. In other words, membership of the organisation must not be made conditional on such competence actually being transferred. Concomitantly, a decision to transfer such competence must be freely revocable. This means, *inter alia*, that revocation may occur without detrimental consequences for the person's continued membership. Moreover, each member must retain the right to exercise their consensual competence at odds with the decision adopted by the organisation regarding a particular processing operation. For example, if a trade union consents to the processing of data on its members by a particular bank and a union member objects to this, the latter would be able to withdraw consent with respect to the processing of data on themselves (though not data on other members). And the person would be able to do so without jeopardising their trade union membership.

As far as provision of information is concerned, there must be a requirement that each member of an organisation be fully informed about the consequences of a collective consent regime before they decide whether or not to transfer their consensual competence to the organisation. The information provided must comprehensively cover the issue of voluntariness, including the right to revoke a decision to transfer competence and the right to exercise that competence at odds with organisational policy.

Just as the exercise of data subject consent must ordinarily be unambiguous (DPD Article 7(a)) so too must be the decision to transfer consensual competence. Indeed, in our opinion, the gravity of the decision necessitates that it be *expressly* made – preferably in writing. Moreover, the decisional process on this point – and evidence of that process – should be kept formally separate from the decisional process regarding membership of the organisation. This follows from the observation above that organisational membership is to be treated separately to the issue of transferral of consensual competence.

9.8 Pros and Cons of Collective Consent

In this section, we aim to assess the strengths and weaknesses of a possible regime based on collective consent as outlined in the preceding section. To what extent is such a regime desirable? Wherein lies its value? What are its flaws? The assessment is necessarily tentative – exactly what practical impact such a regime will have is, of course, uncertain.

Naturally, the problems with individualized consent as outlined in Section 9.2 above – power imbalance, privacy myopia, consensual exhaustion, etc. – constitute the principal grounds in favour of collective consent. Concomitantly, it is plausible to envisage that, under a collective consent regime, the privacy-related interests of data subjects will be administered more carefully than would be the case were each data subject to exercise consent individually. For instance, greater attention may well be given to the proportionality principle; an organisation is probably more likely to undertake and act upon a realistic proportionality assessment than is any one of its individual members.

Individualized consent is not just problematic in terms of safeguarding the long-term privacy-related interests of data subjects. Data controllers experience problems with individualized consent too. Obtaining consent on an individualized basis is frequently expensive and time consuming for controllers. Thus, many controllers are prone to circumventing – or attempting to circumvent – consent requirements. In principle, a collective consent regime could cut costs by permitting a controller to negotiate with just one actor rather than numerous data subjects. This could enhance, in turn, the willingness of controllers to utilize and observe consent requirements.

At the same time, though, it is quite probable that a collective consent regime will result in a tougher bargaining process for controllers. They are likely to negotiate with a counterpart that is more resilient and offensive than an individual data subject would typically be. This could dampen controllers' willingness to utilise a collective consent regime. Yet, in so far as they do utilise such a regime, there could well be a windfall for privacy and data protection interests. For instance, controllers are likely to be put under greater pressure to factor privacy and data protection considerations into their plans – indeed, to factor these in at an early stage so as to minimise the risk of conflict. It is plausible to envisage, for example, a company that wishes to develop a new yet possibly controversial system for processing data on its employees, entering into negotiations with the trade union that administers the employees' consent, at or near the beginning of the development, precisely in order to avoid subsequent conflict that would put the company's investment in the information system at risk.

The possibility to administer their members' consensual decision-making powers could well stimulate greater engagement by trade unions and other like organisations in data protection issues. This increased organisational engagement, however, could lead to increased *dis*engagement in such issues by their individual members. The latter might feel that as their data protection interests are apparently looked after by the organisation, they do not need to get personally engaged in the issues involved. On the other hand, though, a collective consent regime might well help to activate individual members' consciousness about the general societal relevance of data protection in as much as it links the matter to other sets of issues (workplace relations, consumer protection, environmental protection, etc.). Further, if it actually delivers a significant, tangible degree of data protection, such a regime could engender a feeling of greater empowerment on the members' part ("yes, our voice counts!").

From the perspective of DPAs, the possible increase in engagement in data protection issues noted above would be welcome – at least in principle. There might be one practical drawback, however: an increase in engagement could lead to increased levels of conflict which could lead in turn to an increased workload for DPAs. This possibility, however, deserves minimal emphasis in weighing up the pros and cons of collective consent.

When exercising consent on their own, data subjects are not obligated to put weight on simply the privacy-related aspects of their decision. Indeed, they are not obligated to place any weight on privacy-related factors. It could also be that an organisation exercises collective consent based on a consideration of factors ranging further than the privacy and data protection interests of its members. For example, an environmental protection organisation could withdraw consent it has given to an oil company to process data on the organisation's members (who have otherwise entered into a customer relationship with the company) primarily in order to pressure the company to adopt a "greener" business policy. Some might view this sort of behaviour as an abuse of the data protection agenda. We feel, however, that such use of a collective consent mechanism is legitimate and, in many cases, positive. Data controllers can make decisions regarding data protection that are based on a range of factors other than data protection (profit margins, organisational efficiency, crime control, etc.). Thus, it ought to be acceptable that organisations which exercise consent on behalf of their members make decisions on data protection (also) in order to achieve other goals that they (and the bulk of their members) view as important.

9.9 Conclusion

Our suggestions regarding a collective consent regime should not be taken to mean that we wish to dispense entirely with individualized consent. Despite its weaknesses, individualized consent ought not to – and, realistically, will not – disappear from data protection law and policy; it will and should remain an integral part of regulatory regimes in the field. At the same time, its inherent problems must be recognized and greater effort needs to be put into devising rules and other measures to strengthen the bargaining position of individuals in their role as data subjects. Collectivization of consent is one possible means of strengthening that position. It could also be one means of ensuring that the proportionality principle is given greater practical bite. Thus, it merits further attention.

References

Bagger Tranberg, C. 2007. *Nødvendig behandling af personoplysninger*. Copenhagen: Forlaget Thomson.

Beyleveld, D., Townend, D., Rouillé-Mirza, S., Wright, J. 2004. *The Data Protection Directive and Medical Research Across Europe*. Aldershot: Ashgate.

Brekke, O.A. and Sirnes, T. 2006. Population Biobanks: The Ethical Gravity of Informed Consent. *BioSocieties* 1: 385–398.

Bygrave, L.A. 2000. Where have all the judges gone? Reflections on judicial involvement in developing data protection law. In *IT och juristutbildning. Nordisk årsbok i rättsinformatik 2000*, ed. Peter Wahlgren, 113–125. Stockholm: Jure AB.

Bygrave, L.A. 2002. *Data Protection Law: Approaching its Rationale, Logic and Limits*. London: Kluwer Law International.

Cate, F.H. 2006. The Failure of Fair Information Practice Principles. In *Consumer Protection in the Age of the 'Information Economy'*, ed. Jane K. Winn, 341–377. Aldershot: Ashgate.

CBS News. 2003. "Do-Not-Call" Still A Big Hit. 1 July 2003. http://www.cbsnews.com/stories/2003/03/11/politics/main543573.shtml. Accessed 1 March 2008.

Craig, P. and de Búrca, G. 2008. *EU Law*. Oxford: Oxford University Press.

EOS Gallup Europe. 2003. Data Protection in the European Union. Flash Eurobarometer 147. http://ec.europa.eu/public_opinion/flash/fl147_data_protect.pdf. Accessed 1 March 2008.

European Opinion Research Group. 2003. Data Protection. Special Eurobarometer 196. http://ec.europa.eu/public_opinion/archives/ebs/ebs_196_data_protection.pdf. Accessed 15 January 2008.

Froomkin, A.M. 2000. The Death of Privacy? *Stanford Law Review* 52: 1461–1543.

Kotschy, W. 2006. Commentary to Directive 95/46/EC. In *Concise European IT Law*, ed. Alfred Büllesbach, Yves Poullet, Corien Prins, 42–54. Alphen ann den Rijn: Kluwer Law International.

Nys, H. 2004. Report on the Implementation of Directive 95/46/EC in Belgian Law. In *Implementation of the Data Protection Directive in Relation to Medical Research in Europe*, ed. Deryck Beyleveld, David Townend, Ségolène Rouillé-Mirza, Jessica Wright, 29–41. Aldershot: Ashgate.

Ravlum, I.-A. 2006. *Behandling av personopplysninger i norske virksomheter*. Oslo: Transportøkonomisk institutt.

Schartum, D.W. 2006. Data Protection: Between Paternalism and Autonomy. In *Festskrift till Peter Seipel*, ed. Cecilia Magnusson Sjöberg, Peter Wahlgren, 553–568. Stockholm: Norstedts juridik.

Schwartz, P.M. and Reidenberg, J.R. 1996. *Data Privacy Law: A Study of United States Data Protection*. Charlottesville, Virginia: Michie.

Yourow, H.C. 1996. *The Margin of Appreciation Doctrine in the Dynamics of the European Court of Human Rights Jurisprudence*. The Hague: Martinus Nijhoff Publishers.

Chapter 10
Is a Global Data Protection Regulatory Model Possible?

Cécile de Terwangne

10.1 Introduction

On 14 September 2007 Peter Fleischer, Google's global privacy counsel, pleaded at a UNESCO conference for the setting up of global international privacy standards. At the same time, in parallel, he posted the following text on Google Public Policy Blog:

'Google is calling for a discussion about international privacy standards which work to protect everyone's privacy on the Internet. These standards must be clear and strong, mindful of commercial realities, and in line with oftentimes divergent political needs. Moreover, global privacy standards need to reflect technological realities, taking into account how quickly these realities can change.'

Such an advocacy of privacy was clearly an essay from Google's officials to regain prestige notably after the revelation that Google had been keeping and using huge amounts of personal data collected from users' web researches.[1] Anyway, whatever the strategy and the sincerity of the appeal, it has had a worldwide repercussion due to the fact that it emerged from the largest web search engine company.

Precisely two years before, on 14 September 2005, a similar call for global harmonization of the protection of information privacy was launched by the world's

C. de Terwangne (✉)
Faculty of Law, University of Namur, Namur, Belgium
e-mail: cecile.deterwangne@fundp.ac.be

[1] At the same time Google was trying to buy DoubleClick, the largest cyber-marketing company. This prospect of merging two huge data bases mobilized (real) privacy advocates who put forward the severe risk for privacy that such an operation would represent: 'On April 20 2007 the Electronic Privacy information Center (EPIC) filed a complaint with the US Federal Trade Commission to block Google's planned acquisition of Internet advertiser DoubleClick. [...] Google is the internet's largest search company. DoubleClick is the internet's largest advertising company. Neither has done a particularly good job protecting online privacy and the combined company would pose a unique and substantial threat to the privacy interests of internet users around the globe.' M. Rotenberg, 'Google's proposals on internet privacy do not go far enough', *Financial Times*, 24 September 2007.

S. Gutwirth et al. (eds.), *Reinventing Data Protection?*
DOI 10.1007/978-1-4020-9498-9_10,

privacy and data protection Commissioners at their annual international conference in Montreux, Switzerland. They adopted the Montreux Declaration entitled 'The protection of personal data and privacy in a globalized world: a universal right respecting diversities'.

In this text, the privacy Commissioners stated that 'It is necessary to strengthen the universal character of this right in order to obtain a universal recognition of the principles governing the processing of personal data whilst respecting legal, political, economical and cultural diversities'. In addition, the Commissioners have agreed to work towards this recognition of the universal nature of data protection principles. They committed themselves to work with governments as well as international and supranational organisations with a view to adopting a universal convention on data protection.

This declaration did not reach a wide public for sure but there is no doubt about the sincerity and conviction of its authors.

In fact one could advocate that such international privacy standards have already been defined since more than a quarter of century.[2] On 22 September 1980, the Organisation for Economic Co-operation and Development (OECD) published its Guidelines on the Protection of Privacy and Transborder Flows of Personal Data.[3] And on 28 January 1981 the Council of Europe adopted the Convention for the protection of individuals with regard to automatic processing of personal data.[4] These international texts contain what can be considered as the fundamental information privacy principles.

So the question can be put whether there is still a need of global harmonization of privacy/data protection standards. And if such a need exists, what could be the content of such a global data protection model?

10.2 Is There a Need of Global Harmonization of Data Protection Regimes Throughout the World?

The answer to the question about the real necessity of a harmonised and universal protection of personal data is linked to the characteristics of the world in which we live today, the so-called 'information society'. We are facing an ever-increasing need of free flows of data (1.1.) whereas new risks and threats arise from the development of information technologies (1.2.).

---

[2] See for example Marc Rotenberg's sarcastic reaction to Google's proposal for international standards of privacy protection online: 'This is an interesting proposal, since countries from America, Europe and Asia announced global privacy standards more than 25 years ago.' (op. cit.).

[3] Available at: <http://www.oecd.org/document/18/0,3343,en_2649_34255_1815186_1_1_1_1,00.html.

[4] Available at: http://www.coe.int/t/e/legal_affairs/legal_cooperation/data_protection/documents/international_legal_instruments

10.2.1 Increased Need of Free Flows of Data

Globalization of business and extensive developments of global information networks have intensified a need that was already identified in 1980. In fact, at that time when the OECD Guidelines were adopted, it was already with a view of guaranteeing the free flows of personal information so that business activities could be run properly. A need of sharing personal data, communicating them across boundaries was already induced by the international movements of goods and services, multi-place economic activities and the deploying of multinationals.

This trend of internationalizing business, marketplaces and organisations has been accelerating these last decades and has lead to the phenomenon of 'globalization'. In a concomitant way, the need to have personal data free to be transferred through national frontiers grew as well. Data are effectively linked to the flows of goods, services, finance, to the movement of persons and workers, etc.

We live nowadays in a globalized but also in a networked society. Technical interconnection has brought with it human interconnection (for professional, social, economic, political, personal, etc., reasons). The deployment of the Internet has drastically increased the possibilities of exchange of information. The technical means of international exchanges are now available to ordinary individuals. We see official as well as private websites, blogs, forums, social network sites and virtual communities flourish. Moreover, information and communication technologies – the Internet in the first place – generate additional and most of the time hidden flows of data, some of which are necessary for the offer of the information service or help to the management of the service while others are exploited for their potential economic value.

Finally, since the events of the 11th of September 2001 the globalized and networked society has become a cross-border surveillance society. Henceforth flows of personal data concern national and trans-national police and surveillance services more and more interested in the sharing and the communication of personal information.

10.2.2 Higher Risks and Threats

International flows of personal data are a clear reality as well as the need for such flows not to be disrupted. But this reality goes together with higher or even new risks and threats with regard to the individuals' freedoms and rights.

The globalization of economic activities has caused the intensification of cross-borders information exchanges. This means a practical difficulty for the data subjects to follow the personal information concerning them, to control who does what with it and to verify the quality of data and its relevance as regards the aim of the processing. Geographical distance goes with loss of track of data, difficulty to find the right interlocutor, language difficulties and difficulty to be listened to and respected. In addition to this reduction – in fact deprivation – of mastery over one's personal data, means of redress are not always available or affordable in countries where data are transferred.

Information networks and especially the Internet, have in a certain measure suppressed any geographical dimension, which increases the difficulty to be aware of things and to keep control over one's personal data once they have been communicated through the network.

Besides that risk of control deprivation, one watches the multiplication of uses of intrusive technologies of data processing and of hidden collections and uses of personal data. The Internet surfer leaves a trail of personal details, which are captured by computer logs. This involuntary mine of information notably allows personalized cyber-marketing. Surveillance at work through telecommunications control or through cameras has rapidly followed technical progress. The introduction of Internet connections and of e-mail possibilities in the offices has been accompanied by surveillance of web surf and of e-mail use.[5] Localization data, behaviour data and biometric data are also being processed for different purposes among which is surveillance. The spread of RFID (Radio Frequency Identification[6]) offers an additional way of invading individuals' privacy.

The increase of security concern has also brought with it an intensive recourse to invasive control technologies. Video surveillance has expanded everywhere and is more and more refined (with zoom possibilities, night vision, face recognition technology, detection of unusual behaviour or suspect profile etc.). Travel is a major opportunity for control either through the processing of localization data or through the collection and long-term storing of huge quantity of details about each traveller (air passengers, see the PNR problem).[7]

10.3 Disparities Between Legal Data Protection Regimes

In response to the technological progress and developments, to the reality of ever-increasing uses and movements of personal data and to the ensuing risks for civil liberties and rights, especially for privacy, answers can be found in data protection legislation. However, existing models of data protection are pretty diverse.

---

[5] For a detailed overview of technological control on workplace see Electronic Privacy Information Center and Privacy International, *Privacy and Human Rights 2006, an International Survey of Privacy Laws and Developments*, Washington, DC, EPIC, 2007, pp. 65–79.

[6] See 'What is Radio Frequency Identification (RFID)?', AIM Global, Association for Automatic Identification and Mobility, http://www.aimgobal.org/technologies/rfid/what_is_rfid.asp

[7] See Article 29 European Data Protection Working Party, Opinion 2/2004 on the Adequate Protection of Personal Data Contained in the PNR of Air Passengers to be Transferred to the United States' Bureau of Customs and Border Protection (US CBP), January 29, 2004, available at http://ec.europa.eu/justice_home/fsj/privacy/ workinggroup/wpdocs/2004_en.htm; Privacy International et alii, *Transferring Privacy: The Transfer of Passenger Records and the Abdication of Privacy Protection*, February 2004, available at http://www.privacyinternational.org/issus/terrorism/rpt/transferringprivacy.pdf

10.3.1 The Comprehensive Model

The European Union has adopted a comprehensive regulatory model. The common legal framework for the 27 EU Member States lays mainly in the general Directive 95/46/CE[8] elaborating the general data protection regime, completed by specific Directives 2002/58/CE[9] on privacy and electronic communications and 2006/24/EC[10] , the so-called Data Retention Directive. These texts aim at warranting the free flow of personal data inside the European Union together with offering guarantees as to the protection of those data in name of the protection of an authentic human right.[11]

On the basis of these texts harmonized and comprehensive data protection legislation has been enacted in all the 27 EU Member States. This legislation sets rules concerning the legitimacy of data processing, data quality, the protection of sensitive data, transborder data flows, the accountability and enforcement ways and notably, the role of independent data protection authorities. It grants specific rights to the data subjects and imposes duties to data controllers as regards data processing.

10.3.2 The Piecemeal Model

The United States have followed a totally different approach far from the European model of an all-encompassing protection regime. The U.S. system is complex, associating federal and state level regulations and self-regulatory and co-regulatory measures. Adopted legislations are sector-oriented (for example ruling the health[12] or the financial sector[13]) or address specific and sometimes narrowly-targeted privacy issues (for instance the video privacy Protection Act).[14] This fragmented system of protection presents the disadvantage of inevitable gaps in protection and

---

[8] Directive 95/46/EC of the European Parliament and of the Council of 24 October 1995 on the protection of individuals with regard to the processing of personal data and on the free movement of such data, *OJ* L 281, 23.11.1995, p. 31–50.

[9] Directive 2002/58/EC of the European Parliament and of the Council of 12 July 2002 concerning the processing of personal data and the protection of privacy in the electronic communications sector (Directive on privacy and electronic communications), *OJ,* L 201, 31.7.2002, p. 37–47.

[10] Directive 2006/24/EC of the European Parliament and of the Council of 15 March 2006 on the retention of data generated or processed in connection with the provision of publicly available electronic communications services or of public communications networks and amending Directive 2002/58/EC, *OJ,* L 105, 13.4.2006, p. 54–63.

[11] See Article 8 of the Charter of Fundamental Rights of the European Union recognizing the 'right to the protection of personal data' aside from the 'right to respect for [one's] private and family life, home and communications' (Article 7 of the Charter).

[12] Health Insurance Portability and Accountability Act ('HIPPA'), 45 C.F.R. §§ 160–164.

[13] Right to Financial Privacy Act of 1978, 12 U.S.C. §§ 3401–3422; Fair Credit Reporting Act, 15 U.S.C. §§ 1681 et seq.; Gramm-Leach Bliley Act, 15 U.S.C. §§ 6801–6809.

[14] Video Privacy Protection Act, 18 U.S.C. 2710. see J. R. Reidenberg, 'Privacy Wrongs in search of Remedies', 47 *Hastings L.J.* 877 (2003).

in enforcement or leads to anomalies.[15] Enforcement mechanisms particularly raise criticisms since some regulations exclude the possibility of direct complaint by individuals. Launching complaint is reserved to organizations acting on behalf of the consumer: the Federal Trade Commission (FTC) or the Federal Communications Commission (FCC), for instance.

Labelling schemes offer an example of self-regulation (such as TRUSTe or BBBOnline). They have been developed to certify and monitor privacy policies adopted by a labelled organisation.

The Safe Harbor Principles agreement signed between USA and EU[16] illustrates the co-regulation phenomenon. Organisations are only submitted to the principles contained in the agreement if they decide so. Official bodies like FTC are entitled to sue infringements to the principles.

10.3.3 The sector-Oriented Model

Some other countries like Japan, Australia or New Zealand, have focused on sector specific and local rules: they have adopted relatively comprehensive laws establishing general fair information principles (on the OECD model) and have subsequently elaborated these principles in numerous sectors regulations. They equally foster self-regulation.

10.3.4 The 'Risk-Burden Balance' Model

Japan's and Australia's model is also characterised by the fact that their legislation exempts ranges of activities because they consider them as presenting no danger that would deserve an answer in terms of protection of individuals. The Australian Privacy Act 1988 exempts all the small businesses from respecting the National Privacy Principles.[17] In Japan, entities that have been holding personal information on less than 5,000 individuals or for less than 6 months are exempt from regulation.[18]

10.4 Disparities in the Ways of Considering Data Protection

There are various ways to consider data protection. These divergent considerations have an impact on the attitude adopted towards the problem of data protection.

Data protection can be seen as a fundamental right. That is clearly the Council of Europe's approach and the European Union's approach in general: the Council of

---

[15] For example, cable service providers are regulated differently from Internet service providers.

[16] Decision 2000/520/CE, *J.O.C.E.*, 25 August 2000, L 215, pp. 0007–0047.

[17] See Section 6D of the Privacy Act 1988 that defines what is to be considered as 'small business'.

[18] Act No. 57 on the Protection of Personal Information, May 30, 2003.

Europe Convention 108 and Article 8 of the EU Charter of fundamental rights are evident human rights instruments. The EC directives on data protection are the result of the necessity to manage a human right in the framework and with the constraints of a global market.[19]

Far from this perspective, data protection can be considered as a consumer concern. Following this point of view, personal data are marketable goods and the protection of this data is to be balanced with private interests. This leads to no real rights being guaranteed to the data subject: individual access to one's personal information may be refused when there is an overriding private interest or when the burden it would lead to would be disproportionate to the risks. This is the perception underlying the model of APEC Privacy Framework[20,21] as well as the EU-US Safe Harbour agreement.[22]

Data protection can also be perceived as just a problem of trust. Data protection is then reduced to a question of security. The World Summit on the Information Society Declaration in 2003[23] follows this point of view and treats data protection as part of cyber-security. Data protection coincides with confidentiality and confidentiality breaches are the problem to tackle.

---

[19] See Article 1 of the Directive 95/46: '1. In accordance with this Directive, Member States shall protect the fundamental rights and freedoms of natural persons and in particular their right to privacy with respect to the processing of personal data.

2. Member States shall neither restrict nor prohibit the free flow of personal data between Member States for reasons connected with the protection afforded under paragraph 1.'

[20] Asia Pacific Economic Countries (APEC) Privacy Framework, November 2004 – Available at <http://www.apec.org/content/apec/apec_groups/som_special_task_groups/electronic_commerce.html>

[21] The VIIIth APEC's privacy principle entitled 'Access and Correction' avoids the word 'right'. It states 'Individuals *should be able to*: (a) obtain from the personal information controller confirmation of whether or not the personal information controller holds personal information about them; (b) have communicated to them, after having provided sufficient proof of their identity, personal information about them [...]; (c) challenge the accuracy of information relating to them and, if possible and as appropriate, have the information rectified, completed, amended or deleted.

Such *access and opportunity for correction* should be provided *except where:* (i) *the burden or expense of doing so would be unreasonable or disproportionate to the risks to the individual's privacy in the case in question*; (ii) the information should not be disclosed due to [...] or *to protect confidential commercial information*; or (iii) [...].'

[22] Decision 2000/520/CE, *J.O.C.E.*, 25 August 2000, L 215, pp. 0007–0047.

[23] World Summit of the Information Society, Declaration of Principles – Building the Information Society: a global challenge in the new Millennium, Document WSIS-03/GENEVA/DOC/4-E, Geneva, 12 December 2003: 'B 5 Building confidence and security in the use of ICTs 35. Strengthening the trust framework, including information security and network security, authentication, privacy and consumer protection, is a prerequisite for the development of the Information Society and for building confidence among users of ICTs. A global culture of cyber-security needs to be promoted, developed and implemented in cooperation with all stakeholders and international expert bodies. These efforts should be supported by increased international cooperation. Within this global culture of cyber-security, it is important to enhance security and to ensure the protection of data and privacy, while enhancing access and trade.'

10.5 A Universal Data Protection Model?

10.5.1 Existing International/Regional Standards

10.5.1.1 OECD's Guidelines

As mentioned in the Introduction of this paper, OECD is the first international arena where a consensus between several states, major economic actors and as such intensive users of (personal) information, could be reached. This has lead to the publication of the 1980 Guidelines on the Protection of Privacy and Transborder Flows of Personal Data.[24] These Guidelines contain what is known as the fundamental fair information principles, eight principles that have inspired many legislation or self-regulation documents around the world. These principles are the following ones: (1) collection limitation, (2) data quality, (3) purpose specification, (4) use limitation, (5) security safeguards, (6) openness, (7) individual participation and (8) accountability.

The 'Recommendation on Cross-border Co-operation in the Enforcement of Laws Protecting Privacy' adopted by the OECD Council on 12 June 2007 also stresses the need to reach a common protection of personal data throughout the world. It states 'This Recommendation is intended to foster international co-operation among Privacy Enforcement Authorities to address the challenges of protecting the personal information of individuals wherever the information or individuals may be located. It reflects a commitment by member countries to improve their enforcement systems and laws where needed to increase their effectiveness in protecting privacy.'[25]

10.5.1.2 Council of Europe's Convention

The second multi-national instrument dealing with data protection, already mentioned in the Introduction as well, was adopted only four months later. It is the Council of Europe Convention 108 (28 January 1981) for the protection of individuals with regard to automatic processing of personal data. This text promotes basic principles for data protection. Unsurprisingly these principles are in the line of those proclaimed by OECD. Some divergences are noticeable. The Council of Europe instrument establishes special categories of data, provides additional safeguards for individuals and requires countries to establish sanctions and remedies. The Convention has been completed ten years later by an additional Protocol[26] to insist on the role of independent supervisory authorities and to take into consideration the increase in exchanges of personal data across national borders.

---

[24] See Sjaak Nouwt's contribution in the present book.

[25] Point 2 of the Annex. Available at <www.oecd.org/sti/privacycooperation>

[26] Additional Protocol to the Convention for the Protection of Individuals with regard to Automatic Processing of Personal Data regarding supervisory authorities and transborder data flows, 8 November 2001.

10.5.1.3 United Nations' Guidelines

UN Guidelines for the Regulation of Computerized Personal Data Files (Resolution 45/95 1990) have been adopted on 14 December 1990. These guidelines contain minimum guarantees in data protection field that should be provided in national legislation. These guarantees are expressed in a set of general principles pretty similar to the fair information principles already recognized in the previous international/regional instruments. These principles are:

1. Principle of lawfulness and fairness;
2. Principle of accuracy;
3. Principle of the purpose-specification;
4. Principle of interested-person access;
5. Principle of non-discrimination: special categories of information should not be collected;
6. Admissible exceptions;
7. Principle of security;
8. Supervision and sanctions;
9. Transborder data flows: they should be free to countries with comparable guarantees.

10.5.1.4 Asia Pacific Economic Cooperation (APEC)'s Privacy Framework

Peter Fleisher, Google's global privacy counsel, added in his pleading for the adoption of information privacy protection universal standards 'To my mind, the APEC privacy Framework is the most promising foundation on which to build. The APEC framework already carefully balances information privacy with business needs and commercial interests. And unlike the OECD guidelines and the European Directive, it was developed in the Internet age.' Are APEC principles really good global data protection standards?

Graham Greenleaf does not share Peter Fleisher's enthusiasm about the APEC Framework 'The privacy principles are at best an approximation of what was regarded as acceptable information privacy principles 20 years ago when the OECD Guidelines were developed', he stated.[27] Neither does Marc Rotenberg, convinced that 'APEC Framework is backward looking. It is the weakest international framework for privacy protection, far below what the Europeans require or what is allowed for trans-Atlantic transfers between Europe and the U.S.', particularly because it focuses on the need to show harm to the consumer.[28]

In fact APEC's Privacy Framework, even if based on the OECD Guidelines consensus, does not reproduce all the content of these Guidelines: it has dropped the

---

[27] G. Greenleaf, 'Asia-Pacific developments in information privacy law and its interpretation', *University of New South Wales Faculty of Law Research Series* 5 (19 January 2007).

[28] Marc Rotenberg, op. cit.

Openness Principle[29] and has lowered the content of other principles such as the Purpose Specification Principle[30], for example. It has also not reproduced principles present in other international instruments or in national laws of many countries among which are APEC's Member States.[31,32]

Moreover, new principles have appeared, testimony of the influence the USA have had on APEC's negotiation process. The principle of 'Choice' for instance that could already be found in the EU-US Safe Harbour Agreement. It provides that 'Where appropriate, individuals should be provided with clear, prominent, easily understandable, accessible and affordable mechanisms to exercise choice in relation to the collection, use and disclosure of their personal information. It may not be appropriate for personal information controllers to provide these mechanisms when collecting publicly available information'. This principle can present a danger of lessening the protection if implemented in certain ways, notably if it mainly means 'opt-out principle.'[33] The 'Preventing harm' principle is also a new 'protection' principle susceptible of dangerous application. It says that 'Personal information protection should be designed to prevent the misuse of such information. Further, acknowledging the risk that harm may result from such misuse of personal information, specific obligations should take account of such risk, and remedial measures should be proportionate to the likelihood and severity of the harm threatened by the collection, use and transfer of personal information'. Such a principle can be used to justify exempting whole sectors of activities (as the small businesses sector in Australian law) because of not sufficiently dangerous, or only providing piecemeal remedies in 'dangerous' sectors (as in the USA).[34] It can also lead to

---

[29] 'Openness Principle (12). There should be a general policy of openness about developments, practices and policies with respect to personal data. Means should be readily available of establishing the existence and nature of personal data, and the main purposes of their use, as well as the identity and usual residence of the data controller.'

[30] 'Purpose Specification Principle (9). The purposes for which personal data are collected should be specified not later than at the time of data collection and the subsequent use limited to the fulfilment of those purposes or such others as are not incompatible with those purposes and as are specified on each occasion of change of purpose.' In contrast, the APEC Information Privacy Principle entitled 'Notice' provides that clear statements should be made accessible by information controllers, disclosing the purposes of collection, possible types of disclosures, controller details and means by which an individual may limit use and disclosure and access and correct their information. 'All reasonably practicable steps shall be taken to ensure that such notice is provided either before or at the time of collection of personal information. Otherwise, such notice should be provided as soon after as is practicable'.

[31] For instance, it does not limit collection to lawful purposes.

[32] On all the critiques about the weaknesses of APEC Privacy Framework, see G. Greenleaf, 'APEC's Privacy Framework sets a new low standard for the Asia-Pacific', in M Richardson and A Kenyon (Eds) *New Dimensions in Privacy Law: International and Comparative Perspectives,* Cambridge University Press, 2006, pp. 91–120; G. Greenleaf, 'Asia-Pacific developments in information privacy law and its interpretation', op. cit.

[33] In the FAQ linked to the Safe Harbor Principles, it is clearly stated that choice means opt-out, except for sensitive data.

[34] G. Greenleaf, 'APEC's Privacy Framework sets a new low standard for the Asia-Pacific', op. cit., p. 100.

the necessity for individuals to prove the risk of harm to obtain the benefice of protection.[35]

Finally, APEC Framework excludes information that may be used to enter into contact with somebody from the scope of the definition of 'personal information'. This is 'an illustration of where APEC's principles look to the past and do not deal with problems of the present and future.'[36] Indeed, among the information not covered by the protection fall phone numbers, email addresses and IP addresses.

Even if the last born of the international instruments that govern data protection, the APEC's Privacy Framework should not serve as a model for a universal set of data protection standards.

Having observed the international panorama of data protection instruments, we can conclude that there are commonly accepted core principles, certain of which could be called 'content principles' while others address the problem of enforcement of the content principles. But these principles have appeared in the two last decades of the XXth century, before the expansion of world-wide networks like the Internet. A positive and a negative point can be made about this. These long-lasting data protection principles have proved to be capable of adapting to the evolution of technology and reality. They are still an adequate answer to the problems and risks arisen from the technological developments. However, they do not answer to all the new threats induced by these developments. In the last paragraphs of this contribution we will list the admitted core principles, content ones and enforcement ones and evoke the emerging additional principles that should be soon part of the universal data protection standards.

10.5.2 Universal Standards: Content Principles

10.5.2.1 Collection Limitation Principle

There should be limits to the collection of personal data. Only personal data that are relevant to the purposes for which they are to be used should be collected.

Moreover, personal data should be collected lawfully and in a fair manner, which means that data should be collected transparently, not about data subjects who would not be aware of the operation.

10.5.2.2 Data Quality Principle

In addition to be relevant as regards the collection purposes, data should be accurate, complete and kept up-to-date to the extent necessary for those purposes.

---

[35] 'He would also place on Internet users the burden of showing how and where harm occurred, which is particularly unfair since so little is known about how companies that collect personal data make use of the information.' M. Rotenberg, op. cit.

[36] G. Greenleaf, APEC's Privacy Framework sets a new low standard for the Asia-Pacific', op. cit., p. 100.

10.5.2.3 Purpose Specification and Limitation/Use Limitation Principle

The purposes for which personal data are collected should be specified. It should not be allowed to store data for undefined purposes. The subsequent use must be limited to the fulfilment of those purposes or such others as are not incompatible with the initial purposes.

10.5.2.4 Non Discrimination (Sensitive Data)

Certain categories of personal data more likely than others to give rise to unlawful or arbitrary discrimination, including information on racial or ethnic origin, colour, sex life, political opinions, religious, philosophical and other beliefs as well as membership of an association or trade union, should not be compiled except in certain limited cases.

10.5.2.5 Security Principle

Data should be offered adequate security safeguards with regard to the risk involved and the nature of the data. Organisational measures (for instance the restriction of access to the information within the organisation, or requirements concerning long-term storage) as well as technical measures have to be taken. They should be based on the current state of the art of data security methods and techniques in the field of data processing.

10.5.2.6 Openness Principle

Personal data controllers should provide clear and easily accessible statements about their practices. Individuals should be provided with information as to the identity of the data controller, the purpose of the processing and the categories of disclosures of the data.

10.5.2.7 Individual Participation Principle (Right of Access and of Correction)

Everyone who proofs his/her identity must be recognized the right to know whether information concerning him/her is being processed and to obtain it in an intelligible form, without undue delay or expense. He/she must have the right to have erroneous or inappropriate or unlawful data rectified or erased.

10.5.2.8 Responsibility/Accountability Principle

Personal data controllers should be responsible for unlawful data processing.

10.5.2.9 Proper Level of Protection in Case of Transborder Flows

Transborder data flows to countries that offer comparable safeguards for the protection of personal data should not be hampered.

10.5.3 Universal Standards: Enforcement Principles

'If you haven't got compliance, you haven't got much.'[37]

10.5.3.1 Independent Supervision

Each country is invited to designate an authority responsible for supervising observance of the principles set forth above. These authorities shall offer guarantees of impartiality and independence vis-a-vis persons or agencies responsible for processing data.

10.5.3.2 Legal Sanctions and Remedies

In the event of violation of the provisions of the national law implementing the aforementioned principles, criminal or other penalties should be envisaged together with the appropriate individual remedies.

10.5.4 Additional Principles

10.5.4.1 Minimisation Principle

The collection limitation principle should be rewritten to integrate also a dimension already present in various national legislations: the minimisation of collection of data. The obligation to reduce to a minimum the data collected to feed a data processing has become especially important, notably to guide technical developers of information products.

10.5.4.2 Proportionality Principle

Unlike the APEC's approach that could be seen as using the proportionality principle to restrict the scope of data protection regulation, we propose to integrate this principle inside the scope of the protection.

The purpose should be specified (purpose specification principle) but it should also be asked that the purpose be legitimate. This requirement is present in the Council of Europe Convention 108, in the EU data protection general Directive (and consequently in the national legislation of the 27 European Member States) and in the UN Guidelines. This is the expression of the proportionality principle. It means that to be considered as legitimate a data processing should not cause more harm to the data subject than it presents interest to the data controller.

---

[37] Peter Hustinx at the International Conference 'Reinventing Data Protection?', Brussels, 12 and 13 October 2007.

The proportionality principle has also implications on the collected data. Only non excessive data should be collected. Data although relevant as regards the purpose of the processing, should not be collected if its collection or use would cause too much harm to the data subject.

10.5.4.3 Right to Know the Logic

At the Brussels Conference, Marc Rotenberg said in a fairy tale way: 'There is a giant sleeping in the EU directive. That is the right to know the logic of a data processing'. He meant Article 12 of the 95/46 EU Directive that states: 'Right of access:

Member States shall guarantee every data subject the right to obtain from the controller: (a) without constraint at reasonable intervals and without excessive delay or expense:

- confirmation as to whether or not data relating to him are being processed and information at least as to the purposes of the processing, the categories of data concerned, and the recipients or categories of recipients to whom the data are disclosed,
- communication to him in an intelligible form of the data undergoing processing and of any available information as to their source,
- *knowledge of the logic involved in any automatic processing of data concerning him at least in the case of the automated decisions referred to in Article 15 (1)*; (...).'[38]

It is true that what was introduced in the EU directive was an answer to the development of automated decisions. But such a right should not be restricted to automated decision. It should be effective towards any personal data processing. Individuals should be given the right to know the logic involved in any processing of data concerning them. This is extremely important in presence of profiling activities.

10.6 Conclusion

There already exist commonly accepted data protection standards. They have been tested for more than twenty years and have proved to be adaptable to technological change. The last international instrument about data protection, the APEC Privacy Framework, is however a weakening of these standards, certainly due to the influence of the USA in the negotiation process. The US have a market-oriented approach to the question and hardly accept imposing 'burdens' on economic activities in the name of the protection of personal data. This last instrument, even with its imperfections, is nevertheless a sign of the expansion throughout the world of

[38] Our italics.

the concern about data protection. The development of the Internet has rendered this concern critical. ICT developments in general and the tremendous growth of their use in all human activities (social, economic, political, etc.) have also shown the necessity to enrich the fundamental data protection principles with additional principles meant to maintain the balance between the efficiency of the technological tools and the power of their users on the one hand and the rights and interests of the individuals, data subjects, on the other.

Chapter 11
Technical Standards as Data Protection Regulation

Jane K. Winn

11.1 Introduction

European data protection law establishes certain basic minimum requirements for the collection and processing of personal data. Although data protection laws apply to information without regard to its form, some of the most sensitive issues related to data protection law arise in the context of personal information stored in digital form within computer systems. When individual computer systems form part of information and communications technology (ICT) networks, then data protection issues may be even more challenging. The 1995 Data Protection Directive, which provides for the free flow of information within the EU within a harmonized framework of national data protection laws and blocks cross-border data flows to jurisdictions that lack adequate protections, creates a legal framework to protect the privacy of personal information within global ICT networks. But because the growth of global ICT networks may erode the authority of national governments within their geographical borders, it is possible that the practical impact of the Data Protection Directive may be diminished.

Technical standards are the foundation of ICT networks because they make interoperability possible. One of the success stories of European integration is the "New Approach" to the development of technical product standards to support harmonized product safety legislation (Egan, 2001; Schepel, 2005). Although the Data Protection Directive does not explicitly provide for the harmonization of ICT standards and data protection law in the same manner that New Approach directives do, such a strategy of harmonizing law and technical standards might help to restore some of the regulatory authority lost by national governments as a result of the globalization of ICT networks. Just as technical standards make networked communications possible, increasing the risk that data may be processed without regard to the requirements of data protection law, they may also lower the cost of compliance with data protection laws and increase access to privacy-enhancing technologies. Standards developed in support of data protection law would be ICT standards,

J.K. Winn (✉)
University of Washington School of Law, Seattle, Washington, USA
e-mail: jkwinn1@u.washington.edu

S. Gutwirth et al. (eds.), *Reinventing Data Protection?*

DOI 10.1007/978-1-4020-9498-9_11,

however, which differ significantly from the product standards associated with the New Approach. The rapid pace of innovation and the truly global scope of information networks make the process of developing ICT standards much more challenging than the process of developing traditional product standards, which itself was not an easy task. Coordinating the development of standards under conditions of rapid technological innovation and dynamic business models in global markets with regional and national law reform efforts raises major governance challenges.

In the European context, the notion of "better regulation" may provide some guidance with regard to how those challenges might be met (Hodges, 2007). Efforts to improve European regulation are part of a broader strategy to assure the competitiveness of European economies under conditions of global competition. In the context of developing and implementing ICT standards, European formal de jure standard-setting efforts face serious challenges from informal de facto efforts with roots in the US standards system. The institutional differences between European and US standards systems is due in part to the greater deference of US regulators to market-oriented private-sector standards bodies known as consortia or fora. Informal de facto standard-setting efforts based in the US private sector can respond more nimbly to emerging trends in global markets because they may be less encumbered with institutional processes designed to assure transparency and political accountability. If EU regulators decide they want to integrate ICT standards into the existing framework of EU data protections laws, then they may have no choice but to find a way to out-manoeuvre US efforts to minimize government intervention in global information networks.

11.2 Standards and Regulation

Under appropriate circumstances, adoption of technical standards can enhance the effectiveness of either economic regulation or social regulation (Miller, 1995).[1] The OECD defines economic regulations as those that intervene directly in market decisions such as pricing, competition, market entry, or exit (OECD, 1997). Economic regulations support the goal of increasing economic efficiency by reducing barriers to competition and innovation, often through deregulation and by improving regulatory frameworks for market functioning and prudential oversight. By contrast, social regulations protect public interests such as health, safety, the environment and social welfare. Because their primary purpose is the achievement of social objectives, the economic effects of social regulations may be secondary concerns even though they may be substantial (OECD, 1997).

Although standards have been used as a mechanism to regulate economic behaviour for thousands of years, formal standard-developing institutions did not emerge until the end of the 19th century (Spivak and Brenner, 2001). The idea that standards should be used to support both social and economic regulations emerged during late

[1] Tying standards to legislation under inappropriate circumstances may result in "technology forcing legislation", which may lead to inefficient and unintended results.

19th century and early 20th century reform movements aimed at halting the excesses of the Industrial Revolution and insuring that economic development serves public as well as private purposes. A major theme in the modern standards movement that began in the 19th century was a naïve belief that science and technical standards based on science, could improve the quality of life in a way that transcends ideological conflicts (Krislov, 1997). By the 1940s, such naïve beliefs had been superseded by a more pragmatic focus on using standards to evaluate products for safety and conformity with the claims of producers (Krislov, 1997).

Before World War II, most formal standardisation institutions were organized and regulated at the national level.[2] Many countries, including Great Britain, Germany, France and Japan, adopted a more centralized approach to standards policy by promoting a close relationship between an officially recognized national standards body, government regulators charged with oversight of the economy and private industry (Spivak and Brenner, 2001). By contrast, the US adopted a more decentralized approach to standards development by allowing hundreds of different private standard-developing organizations to compete in private-sector markets, while maintaining a standard-developing agency within the Federal government to meet public-sector demand for standards. The work of competing private standards bodies in the US is coordinated by the American National Standards Institute, which "accredits" those standards bodies that comply with "ANSI Essential Requirements" for fair and transparent procedures. In 1947, ISO was established as a non-governmental organization to promote the publication and distribution of international standards by working with national standards bodies.

As world trade recovered following World War II, trading nations established the General Agreement on Trade and Tariffs (GATT) in 1947 to provide a foundation for multilateral cooperation in reducing tariffs and other obstacles to trade created by national governments. Technical standards as a barrier to trade were not addressed in GATT, however. Following the Tokyo Round of GATT negotiations in 1980, the Standards Code was introduced as a voluntary agreement among 32 nations to reduce technical barriers to trade (Belson, 2002). The Standards Code permitted member states to require compliance with technical standards in support of health, safety, environmental or other social objectives, provided that barriers to trade were avoided, or at least minimized. Barriers to trade could be minimized by assuring transparency in regulatory reliance on standards and supporting international standards whenever possible, as well as through the use of standards specifying performance requirements rather than describing specific designs. The Standards Code also required signatories to guarantee national treatment for foreign trading partners in the application of technical standards and non-discrimination in product testing and certification programmes. Adherence with the Standards Code was not mandatory for GATT members, so only 39 members ever ratified it, limiting its impact on world trade.

[2] The International Telecommunications Union would be an exception, having been established in 1865 as the International Telegraph Union.

In 1995, the World Trade Organization (WTO) was established; and provisions of the Standards Code were expanded and placed in the Agreement on Technical Barriers to Trade (TBT), which members are now required to ratify. Article 3 of the TBT requires WTO members to take reasonable measures to ensure that private standards bodies comply with requirements regarding non-discrimination and transparency. Within the US system of competition among private standard-developing organizations, ANSI-accredited standards bodies would be in compliance with these WTO obligations. In addition, Annex 3 to the TBT contains a "Code of Good Practice for the Preparation, Adoption and Application of Standards," but compliance with this Code is voluntary and lacks a compliance mechanism (National Research Council, 1995). At least in principle, the TBT has created a framework within which multilateral cooperation to develop and implement technical standards to strengthen data protection rights is now possible. While some forms of national laws targeting various health and safety issues routinely incorporate references to technical standards, this has not been the case with data protection laws.

Although the obligation to protect sensitive personal information is embodied in many different bodies of law, few contain explicit references to technical standards and none provide an effective institutional framework for coordinating the information privacy rights created by law with technical standards designed to achieve the same goal. In 1950, Article 8 of the European Convention on Human Rights recognized a general "right to respect for his private and family life, his home and his correspondence." In response to the challenges of protecting this right in the face of growing use of computer networks across national boundaries, the OECD issued Guidelines on the Protection of Privacy and Transborder Flows of Personal Data in 1980. Although the OECD Guidelines developed the concept of "data controller" to assign responsibility for compliance with data protection laws and refers to the Guidelines as establishing minimum "standards," they provided guidance to controllers in general terms and did not recognize a role for technical standards per se in improving compliance.[3] Even though the Data Protection Directive was finalized 15 years later, it shares many structural characteristics with the OECD Guidelines, including the absence of any reference to technical standards.

In the early years of European integration, technical barriers to trade created significant obstacles to the expansion of the Internal Market. The EU developed a form of co-regulation to coordinate law reform efforts with standard-developing efforts known as the "New Approach" to standardisation.[4] Before the New Approach, the process of harmonizing standards to remove technical barriers to trade had been slow and ineffective because it attempted to regulate all product-specific details at the highest political level (Falke, 1997). The New Approach consists in the following basic principles:

---

[3] The 1981 Council of Europe Convention for the Protection of Individuals with regard to Automatic Processing of Personal Data also omits any reference to technical standards.

[4] Council Resolution of 7 May 1985 on a new approach to technical harmonization and standards (85/C 136/01).

- Harmonization is limited to essential safety requirements, which are defined in an EU directive;
- The appropriate European Standards Organization (CEN, CENELEC or ETSI) is assigned the task of developing technical standards that meet the essential requirements of the directive;
- Conformity with those standards is not mandatory because producers may always show they are in compliance with the law without reference to the standards; and
- Producers that can show their products conform to the standards enjoy the benefit of a rebuttable presumption of compliance with the requirements of the law.

The New Approach has played an important role in creating a single market by removing technical barriers to cross-border trade within Europe but it has proven difficult to adapt this framework to the special circumstances of ICT standards development. This is in part because the New Approach process of developing standards in support of legislation may be much slower and more politicized than the relatively streamlined, focused processes of informal standard-developing efforts often used to develop ICT standards. Furthermore, the importance of standards and the effectiveness of the New Approach model of co-regulation are not as widely recognized as they might be even in Europe. The Data Protection Directive was developed by the Commission's Internal Market DG, not by the Enterprise DG, which has primary authority for industrial policy and standards policy and so it was not classified as a New Approach directive because the connection between privacy law and standards was not well recognized at the time it was drafted. As a result, the Directive does not provide the Commission with a formal legislative mandate to work with an EU standards body to develop standards in support of information privacy.

11.3 Special Challenges of ICT Standards

With regard to activities that take place within information networks, strong positive and negative externalities produce "network effects" that in turn create strong pressure for convergence around a single network, product or standard (Shapiro and Varian, 1999). The pursuit of positive network externalities by network users often produces a "first mover advantage" for the promoter of a technology that helps to define a network. This first mover advantage may give one party a decisive advantage over its competitors that enter the market later with equivalent or even superior products. With regard to ICT standardisation, delay by one standard-developing effort in finalizing its work product may cede the first mover advantage to a competing effort, condemning its own standard to irrelevance. With regard to global ICT networks, the rewards of achieving first mover status have triggered competition among various economic powers including the United States, the European Union and the People's Republic of China, to promote the development of ICT standards that will favour their domestic economies (Winn, 2007; Kennedy, 2006).

The EU approach to ICT standards emphasizes multilateral cooperation, transparency and accountability (Van Eecke et al., 2007). Processes that embody these values, however, are complicated by political manoeuvring, which may delay the completion of projects or produce more complex deliverables. If more narrowly focused efforts by informal US standardisation bodies can finalize standards and bring them to global markets more quickly, then they may succeed in excluding European ICT standards from those markets. This is not always the case, however: the GSM standard for mobile phones is an important but rare "success story" for European ICT standardisation efforts (Pelkmans, 2001). Although the EU was behind the US in adoption rates for analogue mobile phones, it managed to overtake the US with GSM standards for digital phones, notwithstanding its adherence to the EU approach to ICT standards development. This is due in part to the US decision to move away from government mandates to private-sector competition to set standards for digital mobile telephony. This resulted in several competing standards, which fragmented the US market, causing US consumers to pay high prices for bad service, while EU consumers enjoyed more reasonable prices for much better service under the GSM system. Several other factors that contributed to the success of the GSM standard within Europe, such as the transition from national monopoly providers to competitive telecommunications markets, are unlikely ever to be repeated, making it difficult for EU policy makers to treat the GSM process as a model.

While European regulators may feel more comfortable coordinating legislation and technical standards by working with recognized European Standards Organizations (ESOs) such as the European Committee for Standardisation (Comité Européen de Normalisation or CEN), European Committee for Electrotechnical Standardisation (CENELEC) and European Telecommunication Standards Institute (ETSI), many of the ICT standards used in global markets are the product of more informal standard-developing organizations. These include the Internet Engineering Task Force (IETF)[5] and World Wide Web Consortium (W3C).[6] These de facto international standards bodies do not have the kind of formal de jure mandate that bodies like ISO, the International Telecommunications Union, or the International Electrotechnical Commission have, but as a practical matter their impact on the development of global ICT network standards is enormous. However, not all informal international standard-developing organizations have the transparency and openness of the IETF and W3C, which are committed to lowering barriers to participation and using the Internet to make records of their standard-developing efforts accessible to a global public. Many informal international efforts are organized as "consortia," "fora" or "alliances" that may place restrictions on membership and treat their proceedings as confidential (European Committee for Standardisation, 2008; The ConsortiumInfo.org, 2008).[7]

[5] IETF was created in 1986 to help coordinate the development of standards to support the future growth of the Internet.

[6] W3C was created in 1994 to help coordinate the development of standards to support the further growth of the World Wide Web.

[7] CEN and US attorney Andrew Updegrove each maintains a list of consortia that is updated regularly.

While the US economy and legal system support the development of standard-developing consortia[8], there are relatively few successful consortia based in Europe.

The US has clarified the application of its antitrust laws to joint research and standard-development efforts among competitors, which has had the effect of removing legal obstacles to the growth of consortia, with the 1984 National Cooperative Research Act, the 1993 National Cooperative Research and Production Act and the 2004 Standards Development Organization Advancement Act. Consortia often enjoy a decisive competitive advantage over more traditional, ANSI-accredited standards bodies if they can respond more quickly to market demands for new standards by completing and implementing standards more quickly. While the members of successful consortia may enjoy significant economic benefits, the lack of transparency of the procedures of many consortia has raised concerns about their impact on more traditional standard-setting bodies (Egyedi, 2003; Cargill, 2001). It is unclear whether standards developed by informal de facto standards bodies can be recognized as "international standards" for purposes of determining compliance with national obligations under the WTO TBT.

One effort to address the need for ICT standards within a "New Approach" type of framework can be found in the area of electronic signatures. The Electronic Signature Directive combines the technology-neutral general enabling provisions with the technology-specific, public-key infrastructure (PKI) focused provisions derived from the national digital signature laws enacted in some EU countries such as German and Italy. PKI authentication systems are described in the legislation as "advanced electronic signatures" and are given a stronger form of legal recognition than less powerful authentication systems. Although the Directive was initially conceived of as a New Approach directive, its structure was soon changed into a less demanding variation of the New Approach format. The Electronic Signature Directive did not require the development of a formal "European Standard" by CEN, CENELEC, or ETSI but instead was intended to respond to market demand by referring to "generally recognized standards for electronic signature products." This weaker requirement was chosen because it was recognized that it was premature to attempt to develop a European Standard when the market for PKI technologies had not yet matured. The work of developing standards to meet this requirement was undertaken by the European Electronic Signature Standardisation Initiative, an ad hoc body organized by ICT Standards Board, which in turn was a joint venture of ETSI, CEN and CENELEC. The EESSI standards development work was undertaken with financial support from the Commission, as well as some European and foreign stakeholders and was completed in 2003. Some of the EESSI deliverables were published in the Official Journal in much the same manner that

[8] In recent years, the US may be suffering from an overpopulation of consortia, which leads to redundancy, waste and the risk of fragmentation of ICT markets if no single consortia standard can achieve market dominance.

European Standards developed in connection with New Approach Directives are published.

In principle, the kind of sustained public/private cooperation used to develop the EESSI standards combined with a clear legislative framework should now be encouraging the widespread deployment of strong authentication technologies in Europe. The Electronic Signature Directive and the EESSI project were an effort to bring some of the benefits of standard-developing by consortia to Europe but it now appears that this effort was at best a very modest success. A study by the Commission in 2006 conceded that market adoption of e-signatures had not developed as expected, however (EC, 2006b). The 2006 Commission study identified as possible factors contributing to this failure the complexity of the technology and the reluctance of certification service providers to act as "trusted third parties" out of liability concerns. A 2007 study undertaken at the request of the Commission on the standardisation aspects of e-signatures expanded on the 2006 study finding that the following factors contributed to the slow adoption rates for e-signature technologies in Europe: complexity of PKI systems, high initial investments required to establish smart card-based authentication systems, lack of sophisticated off-the-shelf software products, focus on single-application solutions and lack of interest in standard-based solutions among business users and lack of interoperability among national systems within Europe (EC, 2007b). Because some European countries require "advanced electronic signatures" to access e-government services or to participate in e-invoicing schemes, e-signature technologies may eventually achieve widespread adoption for business-to-government applications but there is no evidence that they will ever achieve widespread adoption in commercial transactions among businesses or between businesses and consumers.

In 1999, DG Enterprise engaged in a dialogue with stakeholders to learn whether there would be private-sector support for the Commission to play a role in promoting data protection standards similar to the role it plays in promoting the development of industrial standards under the New Approach (ITPS, 1999). Some experts expressed optimism that EU standards processes might be compatible with private-sector efforts at self-regulation with regard to data protection obligations, including development of standards at the regional level and providing a presumption of compliance with legal obligations as an incentive to adopt the resulting standards. Others called into question the ability of government-sponsored efforts to respond to rapidly developing technical and economic issues and advocated deferring to industry-led sector-specific efforts unless there was clear market demand for such government efforts. In the absence of strong support from stakeholders, the Commission adopted a cautious stance by providing support for continued exploration of the issues within Initiative for Privacy Standardisation in Europe (IPSE) organized by CEN Information Society Standardisation System (CEN/ISSS). A final report of the IPSE effort (CEN and ISSS, 2002) noted that there was sufficient consensus to proceed with several efforts. These efforts have proceeded in two phases and are designed to produce analysis and voluntary guidance for data controllers. The first phase ended in 2005 after five informal standards known as CEN Workshop

Agreements had been published (CEN, 2008)[9]; the second began in 2008 and is discussed further below.

11.4 Privacy-Enhancing Technologies

Under appropriate circumstances, market pressures might push data controllers to implement technologies or standards that allow end-users to protect their privacy, or improve their own compliance with data protection laws. One indication that market pressures in the absence of social regulation might promote the effective technologies to safeguard information privacy would be the growth of markets for effective "privacy enhancing technologies" (PET) (Hes and Borking, 1998).[10] PET have been defined as:

> A technology whose primary purpose is to enhance the privacy of a user. They can be defined as a coherent system of ICT measures that protects privacy by eliminating or reducing personal data or by preventing unnecessary and/or undesired processing of personal data, all without losing the functionality of the information system (CEN, 2005).

A study for the Dutch Ministry of the Interior notes that PET "are about the translation of 'soft' legal standards into 'hard' system specifications" (KPMG et al., 2004). Yet in more than a decade of discussion about PET, there seems to be little evidence a market for PET is emerging on a scale adequate to protect the public interest in information privacy. One of the examples of a PET highlighted in the 2004 report for the Dutch Data Protection Authority that is also a standard is the Platform for Privacy Preferences (P3P) specification. Given the large amount of attention that the P3P standard received, it may be useful to try to identify factors that might have contributed to its failure to achieve widespread adoption.

In 1997, the W3C began working on a technical standard that would allow web site operators to communicate with potential visitors about the type of information they collect about visitors and how that information is later used. In 2002, the P3P specification was issued as a formal W3C recommendation (P3P1.0, 2008). Web site operators can use P3P standards to develop machine-readable descriptions of their practices regarding the collection and use of data and Internet users can deploy "P3P

---

9 The five deliverables are: CWA 15499-1 Personal Data Protection Audit Framework (EU Directive EC 95/46) Part I: Baseline Framework – The protection of Personal Data in the EU; CWA 15499-2 Personal Data Protection Audit Framework (EU Directive EC 95/46) Part II: Checklists, questionnaires and templates for users of the framework - The protection of Personal Data in the EU; CWA 15262 Inventory of Data Protection Auditing Practices; CWA 15263 Analysis of Privacy Protection Technologies, Privacy- Enhancing Technologies (PET), Privacy Management Systems (PMS) and Identity Management systems (IMS), the Drivers thereof and the need for standardisation; CWA 15292 Standard form contract to assist compliance with obligations imposed by article 17 of the Data Protection Directive 95/46/EC (and implementation guide).

10 An early investigation of the idea of PET was the 1995 study by Netherlands and Ontario data protection agencies, published in revised form by the Dutch Data Protection Authority.

user agents" software to assist them in analyzing the privacy practices of different web sites.

Microsoft and AOL Time Warner were early adopters of the P3P standard, releasing P3P 1.0 compliant versions of their Internet Explorer and Netscape Navigator browsers in 2002. Not long afterward, a survey of the top 500 web sites indicated that only 17% had chosen to publish their privacy policies in machine-readable form using the P3P standard. Later in 2002, it became clear that there was little industry support for the standard (Festa, 2002). Mozilla Firefox, an open source browser, did not provide a P3P user agent. In 2004, in a discussion among Firefox developers, Michael Kaply of IBM recommended not implementing P3P with the following explanation:

> Ah the memories.
> We (IBM) wrote the original P3P implementation and then Netscape proceeded to write their own.
> So both our companies wasted immense amounts of time [on what] everyone thought was a crappy proposal to begin with (Kaply, 2004).

Some web site operators who implemented P3P encountered unexpected technical problems caused by glitches in how the P3P user agent was configured in the browser (Hacker, 2002). After conducting a survey of more than 100,000 unique web sites in 2005, researchers at the University of Alberta concluded that P3P adoption is stagnant, errors in P3P documents are a regular occurrence and very little maintenance of P3P policies is apparent (Reay et al., 2007).

The failure of P3P to achieve the market acceptance its US supporters hoped it would have may be due to a variety of factors. The simplest explanation might be that P3P did not provide data subjects with a service that they value, so they "voted with their feet" by not demanding it. Another relatively straightforward explanation might be that it did not provide enough data protection to be interesting to data subjects: P3P was criticized by privacy advocates in Europe and the US for promoting the notice and consent model of information privacy that provides scant protection to data subjects (Electronic Privacy Information Center and Junkbusters, 2000). It is also possible that too many data subjects suffer from forms of bounded rationality such as optimism bias, which leads them to underestimate the risks that their information privacy will be infringed, or the harm that they will suffer as a result. In this scenario, lack of widespread deployment of P3P would be due to market failure caused by lack of rationality among potential users of P3P technology. Another possible explanation might be that the goals of data protection laws, like human rights generally, are not appropriately the subject of commerce at all and so can only be protected with effective social regulations that are imposed on commercial actors notwithstanding their cost. In this case, expecting self-regulation through private standard-developing efforts under competitive market conditions to produce a socially acceptable level of data protection is a category error.

11.5 Better Regulation, Standards and Data Protection

In 2000, the EU launched "the 'Lisbon Agenda' with the goal of making Europe the most competitive and dynamic knowledge-driven economy in the world" (EC, 2000). While the results of the Lisbon Agenda have been disappointing in many regards, one element of the strategy that may have a positive impact on European economies is a new emphasis on "better regulation" (EC, 2006a). While EU policies to promote better regulation focus on simplification of existing legislation, reduction of administrative burdens and greater use of impact assessments during the preparation of legislation, Member States also have better regulation initiatives. The UK approach to better regulation in particular emphasizes a risk-based approach to regulation and incorporating new governance notions such as "responsive regulation" (Ayres and Braithwaite, 1992; Parker and Braithwaite, 2005). This approach requires regulators to maximize the use of less coercive forms of regulation while retaining credible enforcement mechanisms that can be used selectively in order to achieve legislative goals. A "better regulation" approach to data protection in this broader sense would take advantage of market-based and self-regulatory institutions whenever possible combined with the ability to impose significant sanctions where warranted. Harmonizing data protection law with technical standards might improve the effectiveness of market-based and self-regulatory efforts to improve compliance throughout ICT networks subject to EU law.

Although the failure of unregulated markets to embrace privacy-enhancing technologies on a voluntary basis suggests a need for regulation, the problems encountered in implementing the Electronic Signature Directive show how difficult it will be to update the New Approach to meet the challenges of the information society. If a way to update it can be found, however, the rewards in terms of reducing the cost of private compliance and public enforcement efforts could be enormous. Designing effective enforcement mechanisms is an essential part of "smart regulation" schemes because resources for enforcement are often spread thin and errant behaviour is difficult to detect. In addition, lack of clarity of regulatory objectives and distribution of enforcement functions across a number of regulators whose activities are not well coordinated may undermine enforcement efforts (Baldwin and Black, 2008).

Reliance on a single form of regulation is often inadequate to achieve modern policy goals, so "regulatory pluralism" or combining different policy instruments so that strength in some areas can offset weakness in others, may provide better results (Gunningham and Sinclair, 1999). In some contexts, the range of policy instruments available to regulators may be thought of as falling into a hierarchical order, from the most frequently used and least invasive to the most severe and rarely invoked forms of government intervention (Braithwaite, 1985). Coordination of regulation and technical standards can improve the effectiveness of more collaborative forms of regulation, minimizing the need to resort to more punitive forms.

In order to avoid repeating the problems encountered with the Electronic Signature Directive in the realm of data protection, it will be necessary to develop a framework for determining which social and economic goals can be better achieved by coordinating technical standards and social regulations and in appropriate cases, how the legislative mandate referring to technical standards should be drafted. In addition, the process for developing ICT standards in support of legislation will need to be more responsive to market demands than was the EESSI. In 2008, the CEN/ISSS Data Protection and Privacy Workshop (DPPW) announced a new work plan, which included three new projects designed to develop such market-oriented standards that will also support European data protection law. One project would identify a common European set of voluntary "Best Practices" for data protection management; a second would develop privacy audit tools to permit managers to perform self-assessments of their compliance with data protection laws; and a third would establish a "voluntary technology dialogue system" to maintain open lines of communication between regulators and private enterprises developing new technologies that may affect data protection rights. While the CEN/ISSS DPPW efforts target "soft" management standards rather than "hard" technical standards, the success of other CEN ICT workshop efforts at meeting market demand in other areas suggests that these new efforts may also have a positive impact.

Several US laws now mandate a risk-management approach to the security of sensitive personal information, thus embodying "soft" management process standards rather than the kind of "hard" technical standards associated with the New Approach, the Electronic Signature Directive or P3P. In 1999, Congress enacted the Gramm-Leach-Bliley Act (GLB), a major reform of US banking law that included new financial information privacy provisions. These provisions require that whenever a financial institution opens an account for a consumer and on an annual basis thereafter, the institution must provide the consumer with a notice regarding what personal information it collects about its customers, what it proposes to do with that information and how the individual can "opt out" of unacceptable proposed uses of that information.[11] GLB also requires that these notices be given in language that is comprehensible to consumers, although experience with the legislation indicates that most US consumers either do not or cannot read and understand them. The protections in GLB were further undermined by the fact that consumers may not stop transfers of data among the subsidiaries of financial conglomerates. GLB is regarded in many quarters as unsuccessful: it imposes high compliance costs on financial institutions by requiring that they mail incomprehensible annual privacy notices to their customers while providing little real privacy protection to US consumers.

The information privacy provisions of GLB require US financial institutions to adopt management process standards designed to minimize the risk that the security of sensitive customer information will be breached. These standards reflect a risk-management perspective and require the implementation of appropriate management processes to cope with information system security challenges as they emerge. Under GLB, financial institutions must develop and implement appropriate physical, technical and management process safeguards to protect their customers' personal information. The GLB Safeguards Rule issued by the Federal Trade

[11] 16 C.F.R. §§313.5–313.7.

Commission requires institutions other than regulated depository institutions that handle consumer financial information to:

- designate one or more employees to coordinate the safeguards;
- identify and assess the risks to customer information in each relevant area of the company's operation and evaluate the effectiveness of the current safeguards for controlling these risks;
- design and implement a safeguards programme and regularly monitor and test it;
- select appropriate service providers and contract with them to implement safeguards; and
- evaluate and adjust the programme in light of relevant circumstances, including changes in the firm's business arrangements or operations, or the results of testing and monitoring of safeguards.[12]

In 2003, the Department of Health and Human Services issued the HIPAA Security Rule imposing similar obligations on health care providers.[13] In 2007, the UK Gambling Commission followed this model by requiring remote and software gambling operators to implement security procedures based on ISO 27000, an information security risk-management standard (United Kingdom Gambling Commission, 2007).

The dominance of informal standards bodies such as consortia in the realm of ICT standards for global information networks poses serious challenges to the political legitimacy of any attempt to integrate standards with European legislation if those standards are produced by consortia that do not meet the WTO requirements for standard-developing processes. In a 2008 discussion document prepared by DG Enterprise, minimum criteria that an informal standards body should be required to meet before any of its standards might legitimately be considered as possible subjects of regulation were:

- Proceedings should be open, so all interested parties should have access and should be maintained by a non-profit organization.
- Decision-making processes should favour consensus outcomes.
- Participation from all interested parties should be structured to promote balanced outcomes.
- Proceedings should be transparent, so that records of discussions and decision making are available to all interested parties and responses are provided to comments.
- Provisions should be made to maintain standards over a long period of time.
- Standards should be made available for implementation without charge or for a reasonable fee.
- Intellectual property rights necessary to implement standards should be made available on a fair, reasonable and non-discriminatory basis.
- Standards should respond to market demands and be effective and relevant.

---

[12] Standards for Safeguarding Customer Information, 16 C.F.R. § 314.1–314.5 (2005).

[13] 68 Fed. Reg. 8334 (February 20, 2003); 45 C.F.R. Parts 160, 162 and 164.

- Standards should be neutral, based on the best available technology and permit competition; performance standards should be preferred over descriptive standards.
- The quality and level of detail should be sufficient to permit the development of competing, interoperable implementations (EC, 2007a; WTO TBT Committee, 1995).

While many of the informal standards bodies currently producing standards will not meet these requirements, the Commission's strategy of "constructive engagement" may still have an impact if it motivates some successful consortia to embrace transparent, fair processes in order to increase the chances that their standards will be recognized in Europe.

11.6 Conclusion

European regulators are taking modest steps toward integrating technical standards into the framework of data protection laws. While less ambitious than the reforms in the 1980s of procedures for harmonizing product standards that led to the New Approach, these efforts are informed by a similar commitment to supporting the continued growth of the internal market with effective social regulations. The expansion of global ICT networks and competition from informal standards bodies organized outside Europe, have complicated the challenges facing EU regulators considerably since the New Approach was developed.

Effective use of technical standards to support data protection laws may be possible if the goals and techniques of social and economic regulation are clearly distinguished. Private-sector efforts to promote PET standards such as P3P may have failed in part because an economic regulation approach was taken to address a social regulation problem. Even if the policy goals of legislation are clearly understood, a further problem will be to determine whether support can be given to appropriate standards developed outside the European standards system, or whether independent standard-development efforts should be undertaken. "Appropriate" in this context would refer not only to the technical qualities of a standard but the political accountability of the processes by which it was developed.

References

Ayres, I. & Braithwaite, J. (1992). *Responsive regulation: Transcending the deregulation debate*. New York: Oxford University Press.

Baldwin, R. & Black, J. (2008). Really responsive regulation. *Modern Law Review*, 71(1), 59–94.

Belson, J. (2002). *Certification marks*. London: Sweet & Maxwell.

Braithwaite, J. (1985). *To punish or persuade: Enforcement of coal mine safety*. Albany, NY: State University of New York.

Cargill, C. (2001). The informal versus the formal standards development process: Myth and reality. In S. M. Spivak & F. C. Brenner (Eds.), *Standardisation essentials: Principles and practice* (pp. 257–265). New York: Marcel Dekker.

Egan, M. (2001). *Constructing a European market: Standards, regulation and governance*. New York: Oxford University Press.
Egyedi, T. M. (2003). Consortium problem redefined: Negotiating 'democracy' in the actor network on standardisation. *Journal of IT Standards & Standardisation Research,* 1(2), 22–38.
Electronic Privacy Information Center & Junkbusters (2000). Pretty poor privacy: An assessment of P3P and internet privacy. Report. http://epic.org/reports/prettypoorprivacy.html. Accessed March 27, 2008).
European Commission (EC) (2000). Challenges for enterprise policy in the knowledge-driven economy. COM 256. Brussels: European Commission.
European Commission (EC) (2006a). A strategic review of better regulation in the European Union. COM 689. Brussels: European Commission.
European Commission (EC) (2006b). Report on the operation of Directive 1999/93/EC on a community framework for electronic signatures. COM 120 Final. Brussels: European Commission.
European Commission (EC) (2007a). European ICT standardisation policy at a crossroads: A new direction for global success. Discussion document for 2008 open meeting. Brussels: European Commission. http://ec.europa.eu/enterprise/ict/policy/standards/cf2008/080206-dispaper.pdf. Accessed March 27, 2008.
European Commission (EC) (2007b). The study on the standardisation aspects of eSignatures. http://www.esstandardisation.eu/study.php. Accessed March 27, 2008.
European Committee for Standardisation (CEN) (2005). Analysis of privacy protection technologies, privacy-enhancing technologies (PET), privacy management systems (PMS) and identity management systems (IMS), the drivers thereof and the need for standardisation. CWA 15263. Brussels: CEN. ftp://ftp.cenorm.be/PUBLIC/CWAs/e-Europe/DPP/CWA15263-00-2005-Apr.pdf. Accessed March 27, 2008.
European Committee for Standardisation (CEN). Data protection and privacy. http://www.cen.eu/cenorm/sectors/sectors/isss/cwa/dppcwa.asp. Accessed March 27, 2008.
European Committee for Standardisation (CEN). ICT standards consortia. Updated list of standards consortia. http://www.cen.eu/cenorm/businessdomains/businessdomains/isss/consortia/index.asp. Accessed March 27, 2008.
European Committee for Standardisation (CEN) & Information Society Standardisation System (ISSS) (2002). Initiative on privacy standardisation in Europe. Final report. Brussels: CEN/ISSS. http://www.cen.eu/cenorm/sectors/sectors/isss/activity/ipsefinalreportwebversion.pdf. Accessed March 27, 2008.
Falke, J. (1997). Achievements and unresolved problems of european standardisation: The ingenuity of practice and the queries of lawyers. In C. Joerges, K.-H. Ladeur, E. Vos (Eds.), *Integrating scientific expertise into regulatory decision-making: National traditions and European innovations* (pp. 187–224). Baden-Baden, Germany: Nomos Verlagsgesellschaft.
Festa, P. (2002). Promise of P3P stalls as backers regroup. CNET News.com. http://www.news.com/2100-1023-963632.html. Accessed March 27, 2008.
Gunningham, N. & Sinclair, D. (1999). Regulatory pluralism: Designing policy mixes for environmental protection. *Law & Policy*, 21(1), 49–76.
Hacker, S. (2002). P3P in IE6: Frustrating failure. O'Reilly Mac Devcenter.com. www.oreillynet.com/mac/blog/2002/06/p3p_in_ie6_frustrating_failure.html. Accessed March 27, 2008.
Hes, R. & Borking, J. (1998). Privacy enhancing technologies: The path to anonymity. Revised edition. Dutch Data Protection Authority. http://www.dutchdpa.nl/documenten/EN_av_11_Privacy-enhancing_technologies.shtml. Accessed March 27, 2008.
Hodges, C. (2007). Encouraging enterprise and rebalancing risk: implications of economic policy for regulation, enforcement and compensation. *European Business Law Review*, 18(6), 1231–1266.
Institute for Prospective Technological Studies (ITPS) (1999). Data protection: Devising a framework for standardisation. Report on the Workshop. cybersecurity.jrc.ec.europa.eu/docs/data%20protection%20standardisation/DataProt991025final.doc. Accessed March 27, 2008.

Kaply, M. (2004). Bug 225287 – Remove p3p from the default build, Comment #12. https://bugzilla.mozilla.org/show_bug.cgi?id=225287#c12. Accessed March 27, 2008.

Kennedy, S. (2006). The political economy of standards coalitions: Explaining China's involvement in high-tech standards wars. *Asia Policy*, 2, 41–62.

KPMG, et al. (2004). Privacy-enhancing technologies: White paper for decision makers. Ministry of the Interior and Kingdom Relations, The Netherlands. http://www.dutchdpa.nl/downloads_overig/PET_whitebook.pdf. Accessed March 27, 2008.

Krislov, S. (1997). *How nations choose product standards and standards change nations*. Pittsburgh, PA: University of Pittsburgh Press.

Miller, A. S. (1995). Environmental regulation, technological innovation and technology-forcing. *Natural Resources & Environment*, Fall, 64–69.

National Research Council (1995). *Standards, conformity assessment and trade into the 21st century*. Washington, DC: National Academy Press.

Organization for Economic Co-operation and Development (OECD) (1997). The OECD report on regulatory reform: Synthesis. Paris: OECD. www.oecd.org/dataoecd/17/25/2391768.pdf. Accessed March 27, 2008.

Parker, C. & Braithwaite, J. (2005). Regulation. In P. Cane & M. Tushnet (Eds.), *Oxford Handbook of Legal Studies* (pp. 119–145). New York: Oxford University Press.

Pelkmans, J. (2001). The GSM standard: Explaining a success story. *Journal of European Public Policy*, 8(3), 432–453.

Platform for Privacy Preferences. 1.0 (P3P1.0) Specification. www.w3c.org/p3p/. Accessed March 27, 2008.

Reay, I. K., Beatty, P., Dick, S., & Miller, J. (2007). A survey and analysis of the P3P protocol's agents, adoptions, maintenance, and future. *IEEE Transactions on Dependable and Secure Computing*, 4(2), 151–164.

Schepel, H. (2005). *The constitution of private governance: Product standards in the regulation of integrating markets*. Portland: Hart Publishing.

Shapiro, C. & Varian, H. R. (1999). *Information rules: A strategic guide to the network economy*. Cambridge, MA: Harvard Business School.

Spivak, S. M. & Brenner, F. C. (2001). *Standardisation essentials: Principles and practice*. New York: Marcel Dekker.

The ConsortiumInfo.org. Standard setting organization and standards list. Updated list of organizations that create or promote standards. http://www.consortiuminfo.org/links/. Accessed March 27, 2008.

United Kingdom Gambling Commission (2007). Remote and gambling software technical standards, Annex C. http://www.gamblingcommission.gov.uk/Client/mediadetail.asp?mediaid=130. Accessed March 27, 2008.

Van Eecke, P., Pinto Fonseca, P., Egyedi, T. (2007). EU Study on the specific policy needs for ICT standardisation: Final report. Brussels: European Commission. http://ec.europa.eu/enterprise/ict/policy/standards/piper/full_report.pdfa. Accessed March 27, 2008.

Winn, J. K. (2007). US and EU regulatory competition and authentication standards in electronic commerce. *Journal of IT Standards and Standardisation Research*, 5(1), 84–102.

WTO Committee on Technical Barriers to Trade (WTO TBT Committee) (1995). Decisions and Recommendations adopted by the Committee since 1 January 1995, G/TBT/1/Rev.8, 23 May 2002, Section IX.

Chapter 12
Privacy Actors, Performances and the Future of Privacy Protection

Charles Raab and Bert-Jaap Koops

12.1 Background

A large proportion of the scholarly work on privacy and data protection has focused attention on the instruments or 'tools' that are, or that could be, used for regulating the processing and flow of personal data. This important research has generated considerable debate, criticism and (re)conceptualisation of the means whereby rights or claims to privacy can be defended or promoted. Much of the discourse around data protection has had to do with the merits or shortcomings of laws, directives, codes of practice, privacy statements and seals, privacy-enhancing technologies (PETs), contracts, binding corporate rules, international agreements and treaties and so on (e.g., Bennett and Raab, 2006).

Discussions of the instruments are sometimes partisan, reflecting, for example, preferences for or against state control and pressures for self-regulation or for technological solutions. This should serve to remind us that designing the instruments that are the 'how' of data protection is not a dispassionate technocratic process of choosing tools to do a job but a political process in which there are many conflicts and interests, in which more than data protection is at stake. In particular, the merits of, and relationship between, legal instruments and system architecture or 'code' has held centre-stage as a principal topic of analysis (Lessig, 1999). The emphasis on some instruments (e.g., self-regulatory codes of practice), which was strong in American policy discourse, has faded somewhat from prominence in the debates of the new century, although market-based or property solutions retain their vigour to a large extent, in part reflecting frustration with the difficulty of regulating privacy through supra-individual institutional processes in a global information environment.

The value of tools-oriented analysis is that it helps to clarify the 'how' and 'what' of information privacy protection and perhaps also the 'what works?' orientation of policy-makers and practitioners. The expected further development of information

C. Raab (✉)
School of Social and Political Science, University of Edinburgh, Edinburgh, Scotland, UK
e-mail: c.d.raab@ed.ac.uk

Bert-Jaap Koops wrote this paper as part of a project on law, technology and balances of power that was funded by NWO, the Dutch Organisation for Scientific Research.

S. Gutwirth et al. (eds.), *Reinventing Data Protection?*
DOI 10.1007/978-1-4020-9498-9_12,

and communication technologies (ICTs), as well as innovations in the application of ICTs in economic production and consumption, in public administration and in law enforcement and public order domains, are likely to bring forth new regulatory instruments or new variations on older ones. No doubt, these will keep the scholarly industry alive. Although the pursuit of understanding in terms of regulatory instrumentation is far from exhausted, we need to know more about the array of instruments *as an ensemble*, or how each one functions as a component of a holistic regulatory regime, both descriptively and in terms of possible improvements in regulatory design (Bennett and Raab, 2006; Raab and De Hert, 2007, 2008).

But whilst further exploration of this is necessary, it is insufficient for achieving the aim of understanding regulation without bringing in a further dimension of the analytical paradigm: the ‘who’ of privacy protection, considering both who are the protectors and who are the protected. Moreover, just as we cannot understand tools without seeing them in relation to each other, we cannot understand these actors without understanding *action*; that is, the relationships and processes through which actors come together in co-operation or conflict, whether to shape the tools, use them, or avoid them. Regulators and other practitioners may understand these dimensions very well and no doubt have well-developed views on who *ought to* take part in the process, when and where.

If we are to point to the future, it may well be important to look a bit more systematically at these dimensions, in order to see how improvements could be made in the existing processes of decision-making, the patterns of responsibility and accountability and the relationships amongst participants. It is arguable that the problems of data protection, as well as the successes, are attributable in considerable part to the participants or policy actors, to the roles they play and to the institutions in which action takes place and not only to the instruments or tools that are used to protect personal data. The focus of attention here is therefore on the policy actors and the institutions they inhabit. It is also concerned with where these actors and institutions are located in ‘policy space’, which comprises the governmental or political arenas that exist within particular jurisdictions and at different levels from the local to the global. We might say that that is the ‘where’ of privacy protection. Moreover, because these relationships take place in real time, there is also a question about ‘when’, which points up the element of ‘process’ more than just an account of actors who do certain things. Whether it is the ‘what’, the ‘who’, the ‘where’ or the ‘when’ of regulation that is under investigation, we should not lose sight of the *exercise of power* as a crucial dimension of these phenomena. This points towards other, more normative, aims of this paper: to consider the responsibilities of actors and to evaluate performances, even if only in broad-brush terms, in order to show the way to possible changes.

12.2 Mapping the Landscape of Actors

In regard both to instruments and levels or arenas, there is a very disjointed landscape that defies simple description or the easy reading of trends. This paper cannot provide a comprehensive account of the expanding policy community for privacy and data protection but the available evidence is of a complex patterning of a highly diverse and shifting array of groups, networks and other comings-together, some more institutionalised than others, that have barely emerged as the subject of contemporary systematic research. There may be a prospect of effective global regulation or, on the other hand, an increasing incapability of existing and foreseeable instruments and regulatory strategies. There is a range in-between these poles, in which path-dependent patchworks of *ad hoc* tools, organisations and strategies cope with problems, with some, but limited, success. These reflect the generations of privacy protection from the 1970s to the present and thus encompass the historic responses to major technological change, as well as accommodations or resistances to privacy-unfriendly political and commercial initiatives.

It is now some 39 years since the establishment of the first regime for the protection of personal data, that of the German *Land* of Hesse, which included a regulatory agency headed by a privacy commissioner (Bennett, 1992). Since then, there has been a proliferation of such organisations and officials across the world, in individual countries and in smaller jurisdictions (i.e., within federal countries). The history of developments in these jurisdictions need not be rehearsed here; nor does the way each such regime has mixed and matched particular instruments according to its own politically-driven estimate of the relative value of laws, codes of practice, technological instruments and other tools or mechanisms in protecting information privacy (see Bennett and Raab, 2006). These policy 'choices' have often been driven by international legal requirements, policy learning and borrowing, regulatory traditions and other pressures, as well as, perhaps, chance.

In the present context, it is more important to note that regulatory policies and legislation have taken place at several *levels*, or jurisdictional arenas, which are substantially, albeit disjointedly, interrelated. Early on, information privacy protection became a 'project' of an international informal group of prominent public officials and academics in the 1970s and continued with a further concretisation of rules, principles and guidelines established by institutions, notably the Council of Europe and the Organisation for Economic Co-operation and Development in 1980–1981. These rules and principles shaped subsequent national and sub-national legislation and continued into the second generation when national laws were aligned with a further trans-national landmark in privacy protection, the European Union (EU) Directive 95/46/EC in 1995, itself influenced by national practices and legal provisions. These activities and rules have borne not only upon national jurisdictions but upon sub-national ones as well and on the activities of the private (or at least, non-state) sector of the economy in which personal data are processed. They, and perhaps especially in recent years, the EU, have impinged upon many old members of the club of information privacy regulation, such as the USA and Canada and on many new entrants when they set up their laws and regulatory machinery for the first time, such as the countries of Eastern and Central Europe and the non-Commonwealth countries of the Pacific Rim.

As has just been indicated, there are prominent players in arenas above that of the individual country: international formal organisations have been important from early days onward and have generated some of the main international, authoritative documents having regulatory force. These have helped to set the parameters for regulation, the understandings of privacy-related issues and the very means of regulation themselves. But new players among international organizations have come along. At the global level, the World Trade Organization (WTO) has played a part in shaping privacy protection in a context of international trade policy. The United Nations, although not a new player, has also lent its moral force to the cause of privacy protection, although it has played little part in practical activity. Regionally, the Asia-Pacific Economic Co-operation (APEC) group of countries have formed regular relationships concerning information privacy protection, from which the APEC privacy framework, albeit much criticised, has been a tangible outcome. In addition, international organisations of other provenances have come into view as participants: global and European standardisation organisations are among the prominent participants, although movement towards the development of world-wide privacy standards has been halting. The movement for the creation of a privacy standard has had its manifestations at national (e.g., Canada), European (CEN/ISSS) and broader international (ISO) levels. Particularly in the ICT context, organisations like the World Wide Web Consortium (W3C) have also aimed at developing privacy standards, such as the Platform for Privacy Preferences (P3P), although the degree of success has not been very high.

Other international mechanisms fall somewhere between formal organisations and networks; or rather, the same members operate in both kinds for different purposes. It is in this context that account must be taken, not only of who does what at what level but at the *interaction* of players across levels as they shape policy and regulatory instruments. Under the European Data Protection Directive 95/46/EC, the so-called Article 29 Working Party has been very prominent on the regulatory landscape in the past decade. As a body that includes representatives of the EU Member States' supervisory authorities, it has produced many reports, opinions and other relevant documents concerning a host of technological, policy and information practice-related issues and operates in relation to other EU institutions. This is also the place to note the formal establishment of the role and office of the European Data Protection Supervisor (EDPS) within the EU, thus underlining the importance of the European level of data protection activity and pointing towards an EU spokesperson role vis-à-vis the rest of the world.

The most visible and long-standing network of wide extent, going back some thirty years, is the circle of the *world's privacy commissioners* that has met annually to compare experiences, to examine regulatory and technological developments and to respond to (or perhaps procrastinate in the face of) immediate issues. This is the maximal grouping, so far, for global regulation of privacy-invasive information practices and of surveillance but it has yet to achieve an organisational presence that persists from year to year. This perhaps exemplifies and signifies the general inhibitions on the formation of global regulation and, in this example, the effect of financial and organisational resource limitations, as well as national political and legislative constraints upon the further development of commissioners' roles. Particularly among some national commissions, it may also reflect a certain reluctance to promote further institutionalisation and the pressures of collective decision-making that such institutionalisation would entail. Over the years, in fact, the annual commissioners' conference, held in different places across the globe, has produced final communiqués and resolutions but often with apparent difficulty in concerting views on issues of the day that affect the working of all in their national contexts, or in agreeing on the very propriety of such concertation.

Just what the difficulties here have been, what explains them, and the perceived prospects for overcoming them as international data protection moves into a future marked by increasing surveillance-related threats to the privacy that the regimes have been constructed to protect, should be among the main subjects of future policy-oriented research. There are, however, some signs that this network may become more institutionalised and bureaucratised, possibly spawning its own secretariat and thus potentially operating in a more visible and regular way between the annual occasions that have been hitherto organised on a rotating *ad hoc* basis. There may possibly be a pay-off in terms of greater influence, or at least voice, in the world's arenas where policies are made that pose threats to privacy. These include a number of data-gathering and surveillance activities that have proliferated at least since the events of 11 September 2001 and that have put privacy protection on the defensive (see, e.g., EPIC, 2006).

Within its orbit but not organisationally connected to it are smaller groupings or networks of regulators taking a special interest in, for example, the field of telecommunication and its privacy implications. There are also gatherings of European privacy commissioners (or similar titles) in larger or smaller groupings for mutual learning and comparing experiences, based on regional, historic or other affinities. These interactions include those of EU Member States, of the EEA and of sub-jurisdictions in Germany, Switzerland and Spain, as well as of Jersey, Guernsey, Cyprus, Malta and the Isle of Man; the expansion of the EU to include new Member States in East and Central Europe has further ramified these patterns of interaction. The first European Congress on Data Protection was held in March, 2006 in Madrid. At the level of EU and European or world-level institutions, there are many other comings-together of commissioners for various purposes: besides the activities of the Article 29 Working Party, important data-protection work is conducted within Europol, Eurojust and Interpol. In all these processes and contexts there have been many other participants apart from information or privacy commissioners but the latter have been the most identifiable category or grouping, with some degree of continuity and coherence manifested through their networks and more formal arrangements.

Thus, during the decades in question, there have been increasing efforts to create roles, networks and organisations of regulatory bodies and individual actors across jurisdictional lines, with a particular concentration within Europe but with important intercontinental linkages as well. There are also significant affinities and interchange among agencies within particular linguistic groupings in the Francophonic and Spanish-speaking worlds. Networks and ad hoc concentrations of a more specialised sort have also been evident in domains in which privacy issues are prominent in relation to new ICT (e.g., telecommunications; radio frequency identification (RFID)) or other developments in the fields of business and government. Taken together, these and other formal or less formal arrangements beyond the national state resemble a *kaleidoscope*, in which the same pieces group and regroup periodically in the course of time; the 'usual suspects' have the chance to come together frequently in the rounds of meetings and other means of communication they use for dialogue, deliberation and common action. Some of this club-like behaviour is carried out publicly and transparently and the network boundaries are fairly penetrable by other persons, who may work in privacy-related roles in other public bodies, private-sector companies, academia and interest groups and who have relatively easy access to some meetings and to the members of the 'club'. We may note, also, the emergence of international gatherings of the world's freedom-of-information commissioners, in ways that resemble their privacy counterparts; in some cases, these may be the same persons (or at least the same regulatory authorities) wearing different hats.

Beyond those developments of the past few decades and of very recent years, new roles and, indeed, careers and formal qualifications have proliferated in a host of organisations such as firms and public agencies. These include data protection or privacy officers, chief information officers and the like, who are charged with responsibility for the legal compliance and good practice of their organisations and who have developed institutional bases for their training, common learning, interest co-ordination and representation. Their activities emanate from organisations, both private and public, within countries and among prominent multinational firms and represent a movement towards professionalism as well as policy interest and collective representation. There are now many thousand such persons on the scene; many of them also intersect with, or even double up as, the officials responsible (in some countries) for compliance with freedom-of-information in their organisations, given the close relationship between, and even mutual entailment of, these two aspects of information policy.

Further afield in the regulatory universe are the groupings of privacy advocates in and among a number of countries, such as the Electronic Privacy Information Center (EPIC) and Privacy International, whose members and spokespersons play significant parts in pressure-group and advisory activities that flow into the shaping of regulation.[1] They have well-publicised, regular conferences and meetings (e.g., the annual Computers, Freedom and Privacy conference) and host active websites, e-mail discussion and information networks and blogs. Of particular interest is the European combination of national privacy-advocate organisations, European Digital Rights (EDRI), founded in 2002 by a few national groups and now boasting 29 privacy and civil-rights groups in 18 European countries, resulting in a significant increase in sharing and spreading information on impending surveillance and privacy-threatening measures, if not necessarily in lobbying power, as many of the constituent groups operate largely independently at their own national levels. These privacy groups overlap with a host of citizens', consumers' and human rights bodies that act nationally, regionally or internationally, often concerting views and activities across national boundaries and attempting to influence policies at several levels. Counterposed to those, of course, are groups and networks that seek to *limit* privacy

---

[1] Systematic research on privacy advocates is reported in Bennett (2008).

protection by shaping regulatory rules or instruments in ways that, they believe, will properly minimise the impediments to the commercial or state activities that make extensive or intensive use of personal data. Yet there are signs that, among these mainly industrial and commercial interests, privacy and data protection are coming to be seen as 'good business' and therefore as something to be accommodated and shaped rather than resisted. Understanding all these actors' relationships with others in policy space and the policy-process dynamics in which they are engaged is especially important for an analytic framework that incorporates conflict and negotiation as major processes and that does not necessarily seek to tell stories either about the onward march of privacy protection or the inevitable erosion of privacy.

12.3 The 3D-Landscape: Multi-Level Governance?

Thus, since the inception of privacy protection as a felt responsibility of states in regard to their citizens and inhabitants, we have been witnessing the development of a rich but variegated pattern of connections of a variety of frequencies and densities in and around the issues, instrumentation and practices of privacy protection. The *effectiveness* of this regulatory activity is a crucial but different question that defies attempts at measurement and evaluation, as Bennett and Raab (2006) have argued. Be that as it may, it is nonetheless appropriate to consider how far this phenomenon constitutes, or promotes, the institutionalisation of a multi-level governance (MLG) infrastructure (Bache and Flinders, 2004; Hooghe and Marks, 2003) to regulate information practices in line with a framework of laws, human rights and other principles that aim at the control of surveillance (defined broadly) and the protection of privacy. To the extent that the politics of privacy protection is becoming the *international relations* of privacy protection, it is open to question what the relevant analytical frameworks or 'theories' may be for investigating them. MLG seems to bridge the politics and the international relations but only systematic study would show its usefulness or its need for modification, or perhaps rejection, for the purpose of understanding information-policy regimes such as that for the protection of privacy or personal data.

If one is talking about groups, networks, roles, circles, clubs, bodies and so on, one is not necessarily talking about discrete *levels* in a jurisdictional or geographical sense, although those levels are important as targets or sources of regulatory activity and many of the policy actors can be located at one level or another. Although the meaning of 'level' is far from clear in the relevant theoretical literature, 'levels' as a term referring to place or jurisdiction is, in any case, too tidy a concept to embrace activity that is so scattered in time and space and that takes place in ways that do not conform to the nesting, hierarchical and sometimes inter*governmental*-relations implications of MLG approaches. But these implications are not intrinsic to such approaches, although there may be some important hierarchical arrangements within a looser set of relationships and these may properly attract the label 'multi-level': for example, the formal relationship between institutions of the EU and those of the Member States is such that, in the privacy field, EU Directives are binding on national governments and are supposed to generate compliant activity at that level and within it.

Nor is it to be assumed that MLG involves only *public-sector* actors or organisations. This is because one of the characteristics of 'governance' *tout court* is the involvement of a mixture – obviously different in specifics within different fields – of policy participants of varied provenance. One of the consequences of the shift from the study of government to the study of governance is that – corresponding to the complexity of the world – there is little collective or individual behaviour that can be ruled out, *a priori*, as candidates for inclusion in accounts of the policy processes for the particular subject at hand, whether it is the health or education services, transport, public order – or information privacy. The involvement of standardisation bodies, technology and retail firms, or activist groups in the shaping of regulation in the privacy field are examples of this. Other examples of a more traditional kind can be found in the privacy-related activities of individual firms nesting within the framework of similar activity undertaken at a higher level for an industry as a whole, such as a sectoral trade association (e.g., a direct-marketing association), although the efficacy of such self-regulation through, for example, private-sector industrial codes of practice, at and between private-sector levels, arouses scepticism. In any case, the 'governance' part of MLG betokens a vast research endeavour, not only to 'name the parts' that are involved but to comprehend their relationships and contributions toward producing a regulatory output and outcome. As with the study of governance in other fields and also more generally, the risk of losing sight of the contribution and sometimes the pre-eminence, of central states is ever-present, especially if one were to adopt the unsustainable position that the Internet, for example, is ungovernable, not least by state activity.

12.4 How Does the Landscape Function?

An important next step in analysis is to look more closely at policy actors and at their different roles. By looking at the various roles and responsibilities that all policy actors are given or take on themselves, we can assess any gaps in the distribution of all aspects of privacy protection across the range of actors. Table 12.1 attempts this in a generalised and basic fashion[2]:

This table does not necessarily imply that there is a strict one-to-one relationship between actors and roles, nor can it show that, for the most part, there are complex interdependencies amongst actors, just as there are for policy instruments or tools. A more elaborate – multi-dimensional – table, including a time dimension, would be necessary for a realistic picture of these relationships that would show how

[2] Bennett and Raab (2006: 220) draw an analogous diagram of actors but do not explicitly indicate their roles.

Table 12.1 Actors and their privacy roles and responsibilities

Actor	Responsibility
Constitution-maker	Stipulate the right to privacy
Legislature	Make privacy-compliant laws and data protection acts
Data protection authority	Supervise and enforce compliance, encourage good practice, raise awareness in public and politics
Court	Decide cases involving privacy breaches
Government department or agency	Compliance, staff training in privacy protection
Private company	Compliance, staff training in privacy protection
Privacy activist organisation	Campaign for privacy, propose regulations, raise public awareness
Academic	Explain privacy and data protection, discern long-term developments
Journalist	Highlight issues and events, explain policies and developments
Consumer	Protect own privacy, complain
Citizen	Protect own privacy, complain
Technology developer	Implement privacy-enhancing technologies (PETs), educate IT professional staff about privacy

role-performance, for any actor, is a collaborative project. However, that is beyond the scope of this paper.

What interests us now is a broad-brush and general assessment of actors' actual performance. A brief roll-call of the actors and how they perform their roles and handle their responsibilities seems to suggest a fairly bleak picture. However, we must start with a *caveat* about any such judgments. As Bennett and Raab (2006: Chapter 9) note, the evaluation of data protection systems is no mean undertaking and is fraught with problems of conceptualisation, criteria, evidence and measurement. As they argue, '[s]ummary statements about effectiveness owe more to the discourse of engaged policy debate and advocacy than to that of reasonably detached analysis' (Bennett and Raab, 2006: 235). Therefore, the judgments made in this paper should not be taken as arising from a base of systematic, intensive and extensive research, which we cannot pretend to have; nor can we say that it exists anywhere. Moreover, they are not tied to any specific country or data protection regime. Judgments will also depend on the criteria or benchmarks that are chosen; these are controversial and not universally established, and it is questionable how far they could be applied fairly to countries and privacy regimes that reflect a great variety of histories, cultures, institutional structures and values. Therefore, the remarks in this paper are indicative best-guesses, sometimes reflecting what can be taken to be conventional wisdom, which may stimulate not only debate but further comparative research in depth. That said, what does the roll-call indicate?

First, constitution-makers have generally created a good basis for privacy protection by including privacy in the constitutional make-up of most national and international legal systems. However, it should be noted that the exceptional grounds for infringing privacy are quite broadly formulated, or at least can be interpreted quite broadly by the courts, as in the case of Article 8 of the European Convention on Human Rights (ECHR), so that the actual privacy protection at the constitutional level is not very solidly rooted. Perhaps that is inevitable, as the prevailing doctrine is that privacy often needs to be balanced against a variety of competing rights, so that it needs to be flexibly formulated at the constitutional level.

Be that as it may, the result is that at the level of legislatures, both national and supranational (EU), many laws are drafted that are, even if compliant with a constitution, distinctly privacy-unfriendly. The trend in many Western countries, already visible in the 1990s and reinforced after 9/11, is that legislatures, in a piecemeal fashion, consider privacy less important when deciding upon some anti-terrorist, anti-crime, or public-service measure. Legislators seem to pay less attention to, and have increasingly less patience for, the needs of privacy protection, as compared to two or three decades ago. On the other hand, a large number of countries throughout the world have passed significant data protection laws over the past decades and legislatures seem to take their responsibility seriously to create a firm legal basis for data protection in the national and supranational legal systems. One might debate whether the actual form of the resulting data protection legislation, which varies across countries to a significant degree within the framework of universally respected principles, is actually the most suitable for data protection, but that is a different issue. On balance, however, the net effect of privacy-unfriendly and of data protection laws seems to us to be fairly limited from the perspective of privacy protection: with considerable simplification, legislatures currently tend to attack rather than protect privacy in legislation and it is not difficult for them to follow populist and media demands to erode privacy in favour of, for example, security and law enforcement purposes. Yet we should also acknowledge the argument that even the 'best' data protection and privacy laws are weak instruments to regulate technological changes that have privacy implications, sophisticated commercial uses of personal data, government policy imperatives, and – perhaps especially – the Internet and global information flows (Koops and Leenes, 2005).

Let us move on to consider data protection authorities (DPAs) or privacy commissions. As we described above, they are very active on many fronts, including in overlapping cross-border networks and appear to work conscientiously to fulfil their responsibilities. Having said that, one must also be critical of the DPAs' actual effect on privacy protection, although the fault for this may lie elsewhere, in the legislation that established their roles, responsibilities, powers and resources. Thus many DPAs are understaffed, have too few financial and staff resources and sometimes too few powers to be able adequately to supervise and enforce compliance with data protection legislation. Moreover, while some DPAs focus more on supervision, others tend to pay more attention to awareness-raising and lobbying and within the EU, there seem to be some differences in opinion between the various DPAs on crucial issues like transfer of Passenger Name Record data to the USA. This diversity does not seem to enhance the power of the privacy supervisors in Europe – or elsewhere – when it comes to influencing heavily politicised regulatory measures such as the ones we mentioned. So, although DPAs are diligent, they face a difficult job in meeting their heavy responsibility for supervising privacy compliance and for influencing privacy debates and decision-making processes.

Then, there are the courts. An overall impression is that the courts are not acting as a significant or consistent protector of privacy. Partly, of course, this is caused by the quite lenient laws that some legislatures have passed but it is also in part owing to the infrequency of privacy-infringement cases coming before the courts. But the latter argument may also be reversed: as long as the courts do not clearly and seriously punish privacy infringements – and to our knowledge, there are actually few cases in which a privacy breach led to significant civil or criminal sanctions[3] – citizens and consumers have little occasion to go to the courts if their privacy is violated. We could also point out certain cases where the courts have done privacy a distinct disservice; for example, *Khan* v. *United Kingdom*[4] and the European Court of Justice's Passenger Name Record judgment[5] but perhaps these are equally exceptional as cases that substantially punish privacy violators (cf. Bygrave, 2002 for an overview of data protection decisions).

The next category of actors includes public and private organisations that use personal data. Are they as privacy-compliant as they should be and do they sufficiently train their staff in privacy protection? On the whole, although these questions, as with all others, require a depth of empirical research that is not readily available, many would adopt a lenient stance and say that organisations are not doing a bad job when it comes to being privacy-compliant, although almost any except the most scrupulous organisation is bound to violate a few data protection rules. They would argue that shortcomings should probably be blamed more on the extreme complexity, vagueness and the absurdity of certain data protection rules in real-life situations, than on the willingness or effort of organisations to protect personal data. However, there are exceptions to this sanguine picture: in Europe, these might be found perhaps somewhat more in the public than in the private sector, with certain ministries and surveillance agencies consistently downplaying the importance of privacy and data protection. In the United States, it is arguably in the private sector that the most notorious privacy violators are to be found, such as certain data brokers and search-engine providers. On the whole, we could be satisfied with the way that most organisations live up to their privacy responsibilities, if it were not the case that the relatively few exceptions are likely to cause a majority of privacy threats that we face today. It should also be considered that a more nuanced evaluation should distinguish between large and small or medium-sized companies, between government agencies of very different kinds (e.g., some are for law enforcement, others are for providing welfare benefits) and between different types of information

[3] With the exception, of course, of physical privacy violations, like rape and burglary; our argument here refers rather to violations of informational privacy.

[4] [2000] ECHR 195 (12 May 2000). In this case, it was decided that a breach of Art. 8 ECHR (privacy) did not need to have consequences for evidence exclusion in light of Art. 6 ECHR (right to a fair trial); the case therefore effectively condones privacy-violating behaviour by police authorities.

[5] ECJ 30 May 2006, C-317/04. In this case, the – privacy-unfriendly – PNR Agreement with the USA (Council Decision 2004/496/EC of 17 May 2004) was annulled on procedural grounds. The result was that a new PNR Agreement was negotiated with the USA, which was even more privacy-unfriendly than the first one.

activity (e.g., simple use of data, or more sophisticated data-mining and profiling) and different kinds of data flow (e.g., used strictly within one organisation, or shared widely across a range of agencies).

We now come to 'third parties': activists, academics and the media. Most activists are indefatigable and imaginative in approaching their tasks seriously, even against heavy opposition and a few examples, such as EPIC, show that privacy groups can actually make a difference in the shaping of privacy policy. However, the effectiveness of organisations such as EPIC seems exceptional: most privacy groups have few resources and are dependent on volunteers and good intentions rather than a solid popular or political basis on which to build a consistent fight for privacy rights.[6] Privacy activists seem particularly important in the current landscape, where privacy is on the defensive against the threats posed by identity measures, DNA databases and technologies for tracking and recording human movement and transactions and needs active and perhaps combatant spokespersons, However, unless they are based in countries like the US that have a tradition of large-scale private charity, they find it difficult to live up to their task in countries where people are reluctant to contribute substantial financial support.

Academics present a rather ambivalent picture. There is a fairly consistent if rather small group of privacy academics around the world who participate in and add to privacy debates and privacy discourse. They are based in legal, technical, philosophical and social scientific disciplines and a number of them go beyond privacy itself to investigate surveillance and the other values that are affected by it. Almost all of them try to explain and keep abreast of developments in privacy and data protection and several try to influence policy by writing opinions and giving expert statements. On the conceptual side, although 40 years of privacy research have provided useful insight into what privacy actually is, what the relationship is between privacy and data protection and why privacy is so important, academics often have difficulty in getting these conceptual insights across to politicians or to the public. This is not to criticise the academics as a group or individually: we know from experience how hard it is to give convincing answers to the questions raised in a language that fits the frame of reference of politicians and the public. But academics should also realise that as long as such convincing answers, in understandable language, remain absent in public and policy debates, privacy is hard to defend in the current climate. In mounting this defence, an additional problem for many academics is that it is easy for politicians and others to point out that empirical findings about public attitudes towards privacy invasions do not always strengthen the case against excessive surveillance. We refer again to this below.

As to the media, the picture is also mixed. They may be part of the solution but they are certainly part of the problem, as privacy invasion by the media into the lives of celebrities as well as 'ordinary' people seems to sell papers and boost ratings.

[6] An illustrative example is the Dutch group Bits of Freedom, which for several years was one of the most well-informed and vociferous groups in Europe but which had to be disbanded for lack of funding in 2006.

The popularity of the 'big brother' television series also attests to the profits to be gained from lives lived in a goldfish bowl. With a few exceptions, most media tend to neglect or downplay privacy as an issue, and particularly the tabloid press and popular commercial television broadcasters have a tradition of not taking privacy seriously in the context of policy issues where 'security' is an overriding concern. But the 'quality press' has a somewhat different tradition and seems to have taken up privacy as an issue that is worthy of news and of concern. Over the past year or two, a shift seems to be slowly taking place, from privacy as a culprit in an 'If-you-have-nothing-to-hide, you-have-nothing-to fear' discourse (cf. Solove, 2007) towards privacy as a vulnerable good in a 'surveillance society' discourse. This only occurs in a small part of the media, albeit in some of the more influential ones but it may be a significant development that indicates that some journalists are shouldering their responsibility in noticing and critically describing societal developments, in this case, the threat to privacy of the increasingly surveilled Western society.

What can be said about the privacy bearers themselves: citizens and consumers as 'data subjects'? They are, to a certain extent, responsible for protecting their own privacy – the proverbial closing of the curtains if they want to hide in-house activity. In some ways, quite a number of citizens certainly do protect their privacy as far as it lies in their power to do so. However, most citizens have little notion of the threats to their privacy that current society poses, particularly since privacy is increasingly infringed by covert, complex and distant technological applications of which citizens have little knowledge. Moreover, many of these technologies cannot be blocked by closing curtains – the counter-technologies, if they exist, lie beyond the power (both in terms of awareness and of availability and cost) of most citizens to apply; many of them must be built into the design of technologies in ways that citizens cannot control.

On top of this, citizens in general do not have as high a regard for privacy as they had a few decades ago, for example, in discussions and surveys about 'security versus privacy'. The 'I have nothing to hide' mantra is often heard – and used by politicians to pass privacy-infringing laws – because many citizens seem to think it unproblematic to decrease privacy by measures aimed at solving crimes and preventing terrorism, on the – erroneous – assumption that the measures will be applied to criminals and terrorists but not to themselves, since they are doing nothing wrong (cf. Solove, 2007). They do not realise that the enhanced surveillance measures often target the population at large and scan unsuspected, ordinary citizens for possible 'uncommon' behaviour that matches 'risk profiles'. What holds for persons as citizens applies more or less equally to them as consumers. Perhaps consumers are, generally, even less concerned over privacy than citizens are, since they see immediate benefits of providing personal data to businesses and hardly any threats of abuse of these data, apart from perhaps being pestered by direct marketing, which is hardly threatening to most people. As a result of the relatively low privacy-awareness and privacy appreciation of citizens and consumers and the consequent ease with which they accept infringements, both actual and potential, of their privacy, the protection of privacy as a core value of society is not particularly advanced, and possibly even weakened, by the privacy bearers themselves.

Then, there is the final actor on our stage: the technology developers. It is commonly assumed that they have no responsibility for privacy protection and it is therefore usually considered that they make no effort to make the technology they develop more privacy-friendly, or at least less privacy-threatening. Although academic literature has started to suggest that, in order to keep privacy alive, privacy-enhancing technologies (PETs) must be used (Lessig, 1999), there is a long way to go before this suggestion will be fully listened to and accepted in the community of technology developers. The attempts to develop and market PETs so far have largely been made by privacy activists, lobby groups, DPAs, or other privacy protectors, with the help of technology developers working in commission but there are only infrequent indications that technology industries are aware of a need or value to pay attention to privacy in the development process. Although a 'business case' for privacy protection can be made, such an enlightened approach is not common; nor is privacy protection, apart from data security – which is, of course, highly important – sufficiently incorporated into public procurement processes. As a consequence, most technology that emerges on the market enables privacy infringement much more than privacy protection, since technology tends to facilitate data collection and merging rather than data shielding (Koops and Leenes, 2005).

12.5 Conclusion

We have mapped the landscape of privacy actors, showing a remarkable range of diverse and versatile actors with many potential interconnections and interrelationships. This suggests that privacy is an object of much attention, action and policy-making and there is indeed an impressive range of activities developed by the array of actors. At the same time – although we must repeat our *caveat* that empirical research is lacking here – a roll-call of actors to survey the way in which each responds to and deals with privacy should not make us optimistic that privacy is well protected across the board. Many actors are diligent and make good efforts to protect privacy, although they often face not only resource limitations that limit their success but also public, commercial and political indifference or hostility. Moreover, quite a number of actors seem to pay less attention to privacy than it deserves, perhaps through an underrating or lack of understanding of its value.

Overall, the cast of privacy actors, despite (or perhaps because of?) the many interconnecting and co-operative roads, gives the impression of being too varied and too fragmented to be able to function well. Since there are so many actors, each with her own responsibility, the risk looms large that each individual actor downplays her own responsibility. Pluralism of regulatory activity is one thing but dilution is the other side of the coin, particularly if there is no director to guide the actors. Individual activities are likely to fail to achieve the available synergies without a strategy that cumulates them into a joint performance that achieves its goal.

If privacy is to be adequately protected – and it is vital for society that it is – some shifts may have to be made among the company of players; we only highlight a few here. The actors could do with better direction and a better script, which emphasises the characteristics of an overall 'play', or regime, beyond the individual characters and their performances. The government is probably the most important actor to take on more responsibility for championing privacy: they can strengthen its presence in policies, provide more funds to privacy-protecting actors, sharpen and orchestrate the implementation of privacy instruments and co-ordinate and facilitate joint policies and activities. In present and foreseeable political circumstances, however, governments are unlikely to be able to perform these regime-sustaining tasks and international or global governance structures are still embryonic and intermittent. A shift is probably also needed in the responsibilities of technology developers: as long as they are able to dismiss privacy as something that 'society' should take care of once their technology emerges on the market, privacy-threatening technologies will continue to be developed, marketed and applied, with few countervailing technologies that can protect privacy. PETs should be taken seriously as a stronghold in the privacy landscape but they can only become a success if privacy awareness and appreciation become ingrained in the minds of technology developers and embedded in business and governmental decisions and requirements. A more privacy-supportive public opinion is also necessary but there are no clear signs of its emergence despite occasional promising fluctuations. In short, there are many challenges that privacy research, policy and practice face and they are likely to keep us busy in the coming years.

References

Bache, I. and Flinders, M. (eds.) (2004) *Multi-level Governance*, Oxford: Oxford University Press.

Bennett, C. (1992) *Regulating Privacy: Data Protection and Public Policy in Europe and The United States*, Ithaca, NY: Cornell University Press.

Bennett, C. (2008), *Privacy Advocates: Resisting the Spread of Surveillance*, Cambridge, MA: MIT Press.

Bennett, C. and Raab, C. (2006) *The Governance of Privacy: Policy Instruments in Global Perspective* (2nd edn.), Cambridge, MA: MIT Press.

Bygrave, L. (2002) *Data Protection Law: Approaching Its Rationale, Logic and Limits*, The Hague/London/New York: Kluwer Law International.

Electronic Privacy Information Center (2006), *Privacy & Human Rights. An International Survey of Privacy Laws and Developments*, EPIC 2006.

Hooghe, L. and Marks, G. (2003), 'Unraveling the Central State, but How? Types of Multi-level Governance', *American Political Science Review*, 97(2): 233–243.

Koops, B.-J. and Leenes, R. (2005), ' "Code" and the Slow Erosion of Privacy', *Michigan Telecommunications & Technology Law Review* 12(1): 115–188, http://www.mttlr.org/voltwelve/koops&leenes.pdf.

Lessig, L. (1999), *Code and Other Laws of Cyberspace*, New York: Basic Books 1999.

Raab, C. and De Hert, P. (2007) 'The Regulation of Technology: Policy Tools and Policy Actors', Tilburg University Legal Studies Working Paper No. 004/2007 (TILT Law & Technology Working Paper Series No. 003/2007).

Raab, C. and De Hert, P. (2008) 'Tools for Technology Regulation: Seeking Analytical Approaches Beyond Lessig and Hood', in Brownsword R. & Yeung K., *Regulating Technologies*, Oxford, Hart Publishers, Oxford: Hart Publishing.

Solove, D. (2007) ' "I've Got Nothing to Hide" and Other Misunderstandings of Privacy', *San Diego Law Review*, 44:745.

Part IV
Specific Issues

Chapter 13
First Pillar and Third Pillar: Need for a Common Approach on Data Protection?

Diana Alonso Blas

13.1 Introduction

During international discussions on data protection the question is regularly raised as to the need of a European Union instrument covering the third pillar and, if so, as to the desirability of such an instrument being fully consistent with Directive 95/46/EC.[1]

Back in 2004 the Committee on Citizens' Freedoms and Rights, Justice and Home Affairs of the European Parliament issued a report[2], drafted by MEP Cappato, which contained the following statements:

The European Parliament:

1. *Urges the Commission, in the short term, to propose, as announced, a 'legal instrument' on the protection of privacy in the third pillar; this instrument should be binding in nature and aimed at guaranteeing in the third pillar the same level of data protection and privacy rights as in the first pillar; it should harmonise, according to these high standards, the current rules on privacy and data protection concerning Europol, Eurojust and all other third-pillar organs and actions, as well as any exchange of data between them and with third countries and organisations;*

D. Alonso Blas (✉)
Data Protection Officer, Eurojust (European Union's Judicial Cooperation Unit), The Hague, Netherlands
e-mail: dalonsoblas@eurojust.europa.eu

Diana Alonso Blas is the Data Protection Officer of Eurojust since November 2003. The opinions expressed in this article are however her personal ones and do not necessarily represent those of the organisation.

[1] Directive 95/46/EC of the European Parliament and of the Council of 24 October 1995 on the protection of individuals with regard to the processing of personal data and on the free movement of such data, Official Journal of the European Communities L 281, p. 31, Volume 38, 23 November 1995, often referred to as 'the Directive'.

[2] Report of 24 February 2004 on the First Report on the implementation of the Data Protection Directive (95/46/EC) (COM(2003)265 – C5-0375/2003 – 2003/2153(INI)), Committee on Citizens' Freedoms and Rights, Justice and Home Affairs. Rapporteur: Marco Cappato.

S. Gutwirth et al. (eds.), *Reinventing Data Protection?* 225
DOI 10.1007/978-1-4020-9498-9_13, © Springer Science+Business Media B.V. 2009

2. *Considers that, in the long term, Directive 95/46/EC should be applied, following the appropriate modifications, to cover all areas of EU activity, so as to guarantee a high standard of harmonised and common rules for privacy and data protection;*

Similar statements have been heard during the (still ongoing) discussions regarding an envisaged framework decision on data protection in the third pillar.[3] Often a call is made for harmonisation of rules with the wish to avoid proliferation of regulations covering the diverse institutions and bodies in all pillars or even within the third pillar field.

13.2 Present Situation Regarding Data Protection in the Third Pillar Area: The Role of Council of Europe Convention 108

The frequent calls for a European Union instrument regulating data protection in the third pillar based on the same principles of the Directive could be read as implying a lack of rules in this sector; this is however not the case.

In fact, there is one international data protection instrument generally applicable: the Convention for the Protection of Individuals with regard to Automatic Processing of Personal Data.[4] This Convention has been, as of 31 March 2008, ratified by 39 countries and signed by another four.[5]

The general application of Convention 108 derives clearly from its Article 3, which reads as follows: *The Parties undertake to apply this Convention to automated personal data files and automatic processing of personal data in the public and private sectors.* The explanatory report to the Convention underlines the fact that *Article 3 imposes obligations on the member States to apply data protection principles even when they process public files – as is usually the case – entirely within their national borders.*

The application of Convention 108 is therefore not limited to the first pillar, as it is the Directive[6]; in fact the pillars are an 'EU invention', not a Council of Europe one. Actually, the Convention plays a fundamental role in the third pillar sector. For instance, Article 14.2 of the Eurojust Decision[7] underlines the role of the

---

[3] Proposal for a Council Framework Decision on the protection of personal data processed in the framework of police and judicial cooperation in criminal matters, CRIMORG 153 DROIPEN 94 ENFOPOL 170 DATAPROTECT 47 ENFOCUSTOM 102 COMIX 901.

[4] Convention opened to signature on the 28th January 1981 in Strasbourg, often referred to as 'Convention 108'.

[5] See for a full overview of the ratifications and signatures: http://Conventions.coe.int/Treaty/Commun/ChercheSig.asp?NT=108&CM=1&DF=&CL=ENG

[6] See Articles 3 and 13 of the Directive.

[7] Council Decision 2002/187/JHA of 28 February 2002 setting up Eurojust with a view to reinforcing the fight against organised crime, OJ L 63, 6.3.2001, p.1, as last amended by Decision 2003/659/JHA (OJ L 245, 29.9.2003, p.44), often referred to as 'the Eurojust Decision'.

Convention as a benchmark for the organisation regarding data protection: *Eurojust shall take the necessary measures to guarantee a level of protection for personal data at least equivalent to that resulting from the application of the principles of the Council of Europe Convention of 28 January 1981 and subsequent amendments thereto where they enter into force in the Member States.* A similar statement is also contained in recital 9 of the preamble to the Eurojust Decision. The Convention is also referred to in the Europol Convention[8]; for instance, in its Article 10.1, when dealing with the processing of special categories of data in the work files for the purposes of analysis.

Convention 108 is so far the most important reference text regarding data protection in the third pillar; one could however wonder if there is a need for a more detailed instrument as the Convention is quite general, containing general principles but not detailed regulation.

In the first pillar Convention 108 has served as the basis for more detailed European legislation. In fact, the Directive built on the principles of the Convention, as it is clearly stated in recital 11 of its preamble: *Whereas the principles of the protection of the rights and freedoms of individuals, notably the right to privacy, which are contained in this Directive, give substance to and amplify those contained in the Council of Europe Convention of 28 January 1981 for the Protection of Individuals with regard to Automatic Processing of Personal Data.*

13.3 Is It Possible to Go Further than Convention 108 Does in the Third Pillar Area?

13.3.1 The Proposal for a Council Framework Decision on the Protection of Personal Data Processed in the Framework of Police and Judicial Cooperation in Criminal Matters as a Test-Case

The wish to have a European Union instrument regulating data protection in the third pillar has been there for many years. After several failed attempts of previous presidencies, substantial progress has been made, especially under the recent Portuguese presidency, regarding a Proposal for a Council Framework Decision on the protection of personal data processed in the framework of police and judicial cooperation in criminal matters.

The purpose of this envisaged framework decision is defined in recital 5 of its preamble, as it presently stands[9]: *The exchange of personal data in the framework*

---

[8] The Convention based on Article K.3 of the Treaty on European Union, on the establishment of a European Police Office (Europol Convention), Official Journal C 316, 27/11/1995 P. 0002–0032.

[9] A political agreement regarding this instrument was achieved under the recent Portuguese presidency, in Autumn 2007. As the framework decision is still not adopted, references to it are made on

of police and judicial cooperation in criminal matters, notably under the principle of availability of information as laid down in the Hague Programme, should be supported by clear binding rules enhancing mutual trust between the competent authorities and ensuring that the relevant information is protected in a way excluding any obstruction of this cooperation between the Member States while fully respecting fundamental rights of individuals. Existing instruments at the European level do not suffice. Directive 95/46/EC of the European Parliament and of the Council of 24 October 1995 on the protection of individuals with regard to the processing of personal data and on the free movement of such data does not apply to the processing of personal data in the course of an activity which falls outside the scope of Community law, such as those provided for by Title VI of the Treaty on European Union, or, in any case, to processing operations concerning public security, defence, State security and the activities of the State in areas of criminal law.

The intention of this new instrument is therefore to create a harmonised level of protection in the third pillar field, building on the basis of Convention 108, which is not affected by this instrument[10] but providing more specific and developed rules. The final result risks however not to provide such a positive outcome; in fact, serious doubts have been raised as to the compliance of the (politically agreed) text with Convention 108. This concern had already been raised by Michael Kennedy, President of the College of Eurojust at the time, in a letter to Commissioner Vitorino in May 2004[11], when the European Commission was working on the draft instrument.

The European Data Protection Supervisor (EDPS), Peter Hustinx, has in his various opinions, of 19 December 2005, 29 November 2006 and 27 April 2007[12], voiced his concerns that developments in the negotiations were leading towards a level of protection of personal data not only below the standards laid down in Directive 95/46/EC but also incompatible with the more generally formulated Council of Europe Convention No 108. According to the EDPS, the proposal even falls below the level of protection afforded by Convention 108 in many aspects. It is thus unsatisfactory and will even be incompatible with international obligations of the Member States.

The latest opinion of the EDPS regarding this initiative, of April 2007, is extremely clear in pointing out the poor quality and the low level of protection

---

the basis of the latest draft available at the moment of writing this article: document of the Council 11365/3/07 REV 3.

[10] See recital 25 of the preamble to this instrument, which reads as follows: *This Framework Decision does not affect the Council of Europe Convention of 28 January 1981 for the Protection of Individuals with regard to Automatic Processing of Personal Data, the Additional Protocol to that Convention of 8 November 2001 or the Council of Europe Conventions on judicial co-operation in criminal matters.*

[11] Letter of Michael Kennedy to Commissioner Antonio Vitorino of 13 May 2004: *It is our opinion that the draft may not be compatible with some of the provisions of the Convention and its additional protocol.*

[12] Third opinion of 27 April 2007 on the proposal for a Council Framework Decision on the protection of personal data processed in the framework of police and judicial co-operation in criminal matters, OJ C 139, 23.06.2007, p. 1; the first Opinion can be found in the OJ C 47, 25.2.2006, p. 27; the second Opinion is available on EDPS website: www.edps.europa.eu.

offered by this proposal: *The EDPS is concerned because the current text takes out essential provisions for the protection of personal data which were included in the Commission proposal. By doing so, it significantly weakens the level of protection of the citizens. Firstly, it fails to provide the added value to Convention 108 which would make its provisions appropriate from a data protection point of view, as required by Article 30(1) of the EU-Treaty. Secondly, it also fails to meet in many aspects the level of protection required by Convention 108. Therefore, the EDPS believes that this proposal would need substantial improvements before it could be the basis for the discussion of an adequate general framework on data protection in the third pillar.*

The difficulties in trying to reach political agreement regarding this initiative have obviously played a role in these negotiations leading to a result that is far from satisfactory, as the EDPS expresses in unambiguous terms in its third opinion: *The EDPS is well aware of the difficulties in reaching unanimity in the Council. However, the decision making procedure cannot justify a lowest common denominator approach that would hinder the fundamental rights of EU citizens as well as hamper the efficiency of law enforcement.*

The result achieved so far in these negotiations is by no means encouraging from the data protection perspective. The text is indeed a compromise based on the lowest common denominator, containing several important limitations in its scope and numerous exceptions. Taking this instrument as a test-case one can therefore conclude that achieving a general level of protection higher than the one of the Convention in the third pillar is indeed not an easy target.

13.3.2 The Position of Eurojust Regarding the Proposal for a Council Framework Decision on the Protection of Personal Data Processed in the Framework of Police and Judicial Cooperation in Criminal Matters

Eurojust has been involved in the discussions regarding this proposal since 2004, when the European Commission started working on this draft framework decision. From the beginning the position of Eurojust was favourable regarding the purpose of this initiative but, at the same time, concerned about the consequences it could have for the processing of personal data at Eurojust.[13] In that context it is important to mention that Eurojust has in place very comprehensive data protection rules,

---

[13] See in that sense the above-mentioned letter of Michael Kennedy to Commissioner Vitorino of May 2004: *I have recently become aware of the DG JAI proposals to harmonise data protection measures in the third pillar. This is undoubtedly an area in which greater clarity would be most welcome and Eurojust will be pleased to support initiatives to achieve this objective provided always that our operational capacity and effectiveness are not compromised. We share your interest in ensuring that appropriate levels of data protection are in force. We are concerned about the potential impact such a sensitive initiative will have on the operational capacity of our organisation.*

contained not only in the Eurojust Decision itself but also reinforced and further developed through the adoption of tailor-made rules of procedure on the processing and protection of personal data at Eurojust, adopted by the College of Eurojust unanimously in October 2004 and by the Council in Brussels in February 2005.[14]

The data protection regime at Eurojust is far more protective than the proposed framework decision. Leaving aside the issue of the weakening of the text during the various rounds of negotiations, it is in itself not surprising that a first EU instrument regarding data protection in the third pillar can, given the sensitivity of the topic and the national interests at stake, not be too far-reaching. Therefore, the application of this new regime to well-established data protection systems, like the ones of Eurojust and similarly Europol, would have only brought with it a decrease of the level of protection offered so far.

This point was made very clear in the letter of 11 May 2006 of Michael Kennedy to Madame Roure, rapporteur at the European Parliament: *We would particularly like to draw your attention to the fact that the Eurojust data protection rules contain enhanced safeguards for personal data of victims and witnesses, more strict time limits for storage of personal data than those foreseen in the draft decision, very extensive security provisions including organisational arrangements and technical measures provided by the automated case management system that ensure automatic compliance with most of the data protection rules, as well as additional control systems such as extensive log files and audit trails and a two-level monitoring by the Data Protection Officer and the Joint Supervisory Body.*

In the light of these considerations, we would like to let you know that Eurojust would not oppose the introduction of an obligation for Eurojust to ensure a level of protection equivalent to that resulting of the application of the framework decision (now or in the near future), in order to enhance consistency and effectiveness of the legal framework on data protection in the third pillar. We would however be gravely concerned if an obligation to make our rules 'fully consistent with the decision' (as it is worded in your proposed amendments 6 and 61) would be introduced as this could be interpreted as imposing a full harmonisation that would in practice result in a decreasing of the level of protection we presently offer and we are sure that this is not the purpose you envisage with your proposal, as we understand from the content of your letter.

Finally, the explanations given by Eurojust seemed to be convincing enough as the final text (so far) contains a clear limitation of the scope of application of the envisaged framework decision. This is made particularly clear in the preamble (recital 24a): *Several acts, adopted on the basis of Title VI TEU, contain specific provisions on the protection of personal data exchanged or otherwise processed pursuant to those acts. In some cases these provisions constitute a complete and coherent set of rules covering all relevant aspects of data protection (principles of data quality, rules on data security, regulation of the rights and safeguards of data subjects, organisation of supervision and liability) and they regulate these*

[14] OJ C 68, 19.3.2005, p. 1.

matters more in detail than the present Framework Decision. The relevant set of data protection provisions of those acts, in particular those governing the functioning of Europol, Eurojust, the SIS and the CIS, as well as those introducing direct access for the authorities of Member States to certain data systems of other Member States, will not be affected by the present Framework Decision.

The maintenance of these already existing and more protective regimes is in my view a very positive development. Having said that, it is worth underlining the fact that Eurojust welcomes the idea behind the envisaged framework decision: *Eurojust has been involved from the very beginning in the discussions around this draft framework decision and welcomes the adoption of an instrument providing for a basic level of protection for personal data in the third pillar.*[15]

13.4 Would It Be Desirable to Put in Place an Instrument Regulating Data Protection in the Third Pillar Area Based on the Regime of Directive 95/46?

In the previous section the example of the envisaged framework decision regarding data protection in the third pillar has been used to underline the difficulties of reaching a political consensus regarding such an instrument. Leaving aside the question of the feasibility of such an initiative, a more general question remains to be answered: would it be desirable to put in place an instrument regulating data protection in the third pillar based on the regime of the Directive, as was suggested in the report of the LIBE committee of 2004?[16]

The Directive has become de facto the standard of data protection, not only in Europe but even worldwide, given the somehow 'extraterritorial effects' of it due to the regime applicable to third countries[17], which are strongly encouraged to adopt data protection legislation similar to the Directive to fit within the concept of 'adequate protection'.[18] It would therefore be very difficult to imagine the Directive not playing any role in the third pillar field.

In fact, several Member States have implemented the Directive also in the third pillar area[19] and also other European regimes created after the Directive have taken its provisions into account to ensure coherence between the applicable regimes. This

---

[15] Quote from the letter of 11 May 2006 of Michael Kennedy to Madame Roure, rapporteur at the European Parliament.

[16] See footnote number 2.

[17] See in that respect Alonso Blas, D., *Universal effects of the European Data Protection Directive* in Dumortier J., Robben F. and Taeymans M. (editors), *A decade of research @ the crossroads of law and ICT*, Larcier, p.23–32, 2001.

[18] See in respect of the concept of 'adequate protection' document WP 12 'Transfers of personal data to third countries' from the Article 29 Working Party of European Data Protection Authorities, adopted on 24 July 1998.

[19] See for further information Report from the Commission – First report on the implementation of the Data Protection Directive (95/46/EC) /* COM/2003/0265 final * as well as the technical analysis on which such report was partially based: http://ec.europa.eu/justice_home/fsj/privacy/

is surely the case regarding the Eurojust rules: *Such rules were drafted taking full account of the existing European and international instruments such as the Council of Europe Convention 108 and the European Directive 95/46/EC and build on the same principles while taking into account the specific situation and needs of Eurojust in order to be able to perform its operational tasks fully and efficiently. We would like to underline the fact that we do not foresee any problems of lack of coherence due to the exclusion of Eurojust from the scope of application of the draft framework decision, as the Eurojust rules are based on the same existing European data protection principles (see recital 6 of the preamble to the draft framework decision).*[20]

However, a full implementation of all provisions of the Directive in the third pillar would face quite a few difficulties. Without attempting to be exhaustive in mentioning all problematic areas, it is worth exploring some examples of provisions of the Directive whose application is far from being easy in the third pillar sector; this is often the case regarding the rights of the data subjects.

- Articles 10 and 11 of the Directive deal with the information to be given to the data subject at the moment of collection of personal data or, at least, at the time of recording such data.
  - One of the typical examples of cases which Eurojust deals with is the so-called 'controlled delivery' in which law-enforcement authorities are aware of the fact that a certain vehicle is transporting drugs from one country to another and decide to let that vehicle cross the border without being arrested, to be able to find out where the delivery leads to and possibly get hold of the whole organisation behind the drug trafficking activities. To be able to carry out such an operation, often several surveillance mechanisms are put in place such as telephone tapping, devices to follow the vehicle and so forth, on the basis of the required authorisation of the judicial authorisations of the countries involved. Needless to say, it is by all means impossible to inform the data subject in advance or at the time of recording of such processing operation/s without jeopardising the investigation.

---

docs/lawreport/consultation/technical-annex_en.pdf: *The laws in all Member States apply, in principle, to matters both within and outside of the scope of Community law, even though they also often contain specific exemptions concerning typical 'third pillar' issues such as police or state security matters, as regards the information provided to the data subject. Thus, Member States have generally not availed themselves of the possibility to limit the scope of the national laws to matters within the scope of Community law.*

Member States have also made rather limited use of the possibility to fully exclude from these laws processing related to the matters listed in Art. 3 (2), first indent, of the Directive. The Irish, and Spanish laws have such full exceptions for areas such as police, security and/or terrorism and serious organised crime. Other Member States subject some or most processing in the areas listed in Art. 3 (2), first indent, to separate laws, but to be compatible with the principle of the Directive. Such laws in the Netherlands, Germany, Italy and Luxembourg touch on police, security and sometimes defence matters.

[20] Quote from the letter of 11 May 2006 of Michael Kennedy to Madame Roure, rapporteur at the European Parliament.

- A similar example is the case of telephone tapping, a not uncommon practice in preliminary phases of an investigation, in which obviously information can not be given to the data subject/s at the moment in which the telephone interception has been authorised by the judicial authorities. One could even wonder if it is reasonable, as seems to be the case under German legislation, to inform all people who have called or who have been called by a certain person of the fact that their conversations were tapped in the course of an investigation at a later stage, even if this investigation led to no action by the judicial authorities. The fact that persons would receive notice that the telephone of somebody they knew was at a certain moment tapped in the course of an investigation could have a substantially negative impact on the reputation of that person, even if the investigation did not have any judicial consequence for the person as such.

- Articles 12 and 13 of the Directive deal with the issue of access to personal data. In the practice of international investigations, the sole fact of confirming that a certain authority has data on one person can have a negative impact on ongoing investigations. For instance, if a person receives confirmation of the fact that Eurojust processed information on him/her, he/she receives de facto confirmation of the existence of an ongoing international investigation regarding him/her and possibly, where relevant, regarding the organisation in which he/she operates and this might lead to a change of pattern of actions of the organisation, jeopardising the ongoing investigation. In practice, exceptions are used very often and practices such as indirect access are relatively common in the third pillar sector and will still be allowed even if the third pillar draft framework decision comes into place.[21] The Eurojust Decision contains in its Article 19.7 a provision dealing with the cases in which access is denied or when no personal data concerning the applicant are processed by Eurojust: in such a case Eurojust shall just notify the applicant that it has carried out checks, without giving any information that could reveal whether or not the applicant is known.
- It seems quite obvious why Article 14 of the Directive, dealing with the right of the data subject to object to the processing of personal data, could not possibly be implemented in the third pillar sector.

These are just some examples related to the rights of the data subjects' provisions but one could think of other important differences regarding data protection in the

---

[21] See in that respect recital 24 a of the preamble to this instrument: *Some Member States have ensured the right of access of the data subject in criminal matters through a system (...) where the national supervisory authority, in place of the data subject, has access to all the personal data related to the data subject without any restriction and may also correct, erase or update the inaccurate data. In such a case of indirect access, the national law of those Member States may provide that the national supervisory authority will only inform the data subject that all the necessary verifications have taken place. However, those Member States also provide for possibilities of direct access for the data subject in specific cases, such as access to judicial records, to obtain copies of own criminal records or of own hearing by the police services.*

first and the third pillar fields, such as the practical impossibility of using consent as a legal ground for police and justice processing operations. The rules of procedure on the processing and protection of personal data at Eurojust[22] are a good example of third pillar rules that were drafted taking full account of the provisions of the Directive but also of the activities that Eurojust has to perform to achieve its tasks in the field of judicial cooperation and coordination.

13.5 What Will the Future Bring: Data Protection After the Treaty of Lisbon

At the moment of writing this article little is known as to what the Treaty of Lisbon[23] will bring about in the field of data protection.

It is clear in any case that the extension of the co-decision procedure to a higher number of policy areas in which the elected members of the European Parliament will have to approve EU legislation along with the Member States, particularly in the areas of justice, security and immigration, can be seen as an improvement of the democratic process in Europe. And that this procedure, in combination with the fact that the Treaty allows decision-making in more policy areas by qualified majority voting, notably in the area of justice and home affairs, instead of unanimity as it was required so far, will hopefully lead to a higher level of protection of human rights, as has been pointed out by the Committee on Civil Liberties, Justice and Home Affairs of the European Parliament[24]: *The qualified majority system will facilitate negotiations in the EU institutions and lead to the adoption of higher standards of fundamental rights protection (by contrast, the unanimity principle favours the adoption of a minimum common denominator and in several cases raises questions as to the added value of EU legislation).*

The end of the pillar structure as it has been traditionally known is another important element of this reform treaty. It should however be pointed out that this does not automatically imply that the Directive will also apply to the processing of personal data in the area of police and judicial cooperation in criminal matters. The Directive includes a specific provision laying down that these rules shall not apply to the processing of personal data in the course of an activity that falls outside the scope of Community law, such as those provided for by Titles V and VI of the Treaty on European Union and in any case to processing operations concerning public security, defence, state security (including the economic well-being of the state when the processing operation relates to state security matters) and the activities of the state

[22] See footnote number 14.

[23] Treaty of Lisbon amending the Treaty of the European Union and the Treaty establishing the European Community, signed at Lisbon, 13 December 2007 (2007/C 306/01), OJ C 306 of 17.12.2007, p.1. See for more information: http://europa.eu/lisbon_treaty/index_en.htm

[24] Opinion of the Committee on Civil Liberties, Justice and Home Affairs included on the report of the Committee on Constitutional Affairs on the Treaty of Lisbon (2007/2286(INI)), of 29.1.2008, Rapporteurs: Richard Corbett and Iñigo Mendez de Vigo.

in areas of criminal law. Therefore, in order for the Directive to apply generally, such provision would have to be repealed.[25]

It is significant to mention that a declaration was adopted together with the treaty[26] with the following wording: *The Conference acknowledges that specific rules on the protection of personal data and the free movement of such data in the fields of judicial cooperation in criminal matters and police cooperation based on Article 16B of the Treaty on the Functioning of the European Union may prove necessary because of the specific nature of these fields.*

The European Data Protection Supervisor had in its letter of 23 July 2007 to the Intergovernmental Conference[27] put forward a number of detailed suggestions to extend and give more substance to the content of this declaration but these suggestions have not been taken on board. The EDPS presented in this letter his views regarding this matter in the following way: *It has also to be noted that the processing of personal data in the area of police and judicial cooperation in criminal matters can require provisions specific to this area. Those specific provisions include safeguards for the data subject as well as exceptions to the protection, in order to reconcile the protection of the data subject with the public interest of the State in criminal matters. It is understood that the European Parliament and the Council shall, on the proposal of the Commission, adopt a proposal for a sector specific Directive in this area which will apply in addition to the general Directive on the protection of personal data (currently: Directive 95/46/EC) and which aims to ensure the widest possible application of the data protection principles contained in this general Directive.*

13.6 Conclusion: Common Approach?

It is time now to return to the question posed at the beginning of this article: would a common approach, possibly based on the Directive, be recommended for the first and third pillar regarding data protection?

As mentioned earlier, Convention 108 already offers a basic common approach that needs to be fully respected. Any new instrument should respect the Convention as well as the basic principles contained in the Directive, which are essentially the same. An overall instrument would have to be relatively general but, if it has to have any added-value, it should go further than Convention 108; however, as we have seen, this result has not been achieved regarding the envisaged framework decision in the third pillar. We have also seen that the application of the Directive as such

[25] See in that respect the interesting letter of the EDPS to the President of the Intergovernmental Conference, of 23 July 2007: http://www.edps.europa.eu/EDPSWEB/webdav/site/mySite/shared/Documents/Consultation/Comments/2007/07-07-23_Letter_IGC_EN.pdf

[26] Declaration number 21. Declaration on the protection of personal data in the fields of judicial cooperation in criminal matters and police cooperation.

[27] See footnote 25.

does not automatically work in the police and justice field and that there is therefore a need to adapt the rules to the reality of these sectors.

There is in my view a need for clear, unambiguous and specific tailor-made rules for the third pillar field and, even within this sector, for the various areas of activity within it. There are important differences in the work for instance of the police and the judiciary, which also bring with them different needs in terms of processing of personal data. Putting in place very general rules to be able to cover everything would in all probability create unregulated areas and uncertainty and not lead to a high level of protection. The particular nature of the police and judicial work needs to be taken into account.

It is also crucial to develop, within any set of rules, specific provisions for the protection of the various categories of data subjects. The Eurojust Decision contains rules[28] offering particular protection when personal data on persons who are suspect of a criminal investigation or prosecution, victims and witnesses are processed. The data that might be processed regarding victims and witnesses are limited and additional guarantees are put in place for its protection. Similar provisions could be introduced in a broader way at European level.

The Treaty of Lisbon offers some positive perspectives for the future by introducing co-decision procedures and replacing the requirement of unanimity by qualified majority, allowing hopefully for a higher level of protection to be achieved in future negotiations regarding data protection in the police and justice sector. However, having followed closely the negotiations regarding the framework decision, I am not optimistic as to the chances of adoption of a European Union instrument offering adequate data protection in the third pillar field in the near future. The framework decision is disappointing as a result; with a bit of luck it will be a first step that might have the value of encouraging Member States to improve the protection of personal data in this field but, even if there is some positive evolution in the future, this will take time.

Therefore, in the light of my experience, I think that including Eurojust, Europol, the Schengen Information System (SIS) and the Customs Information System (CIS) in the scope of application of any potential new and probably rather basic, instrument in this sector implies a risk of lowering the level of protection of personal data, which is presently high. There is of course no objection to the inclusion of an obligation for Eurojust, Europol and other third pillar bodies to keep a level of protection as high as that resulting from any new instrument in this field. This will for the time being not pose any challenges for these organisations but, should the future bring at some point an improvement of the level of protection generally imposed, it will oblige these organisations to keep up with the developments.

Proliferation of regulations is often seen as something negative, creating confusion and a patchwork of rules that are difficult to oversee and apply. Indeed, having several sets of rules might have disadvantages but I am of the opinion that having a collection of different sets of rules offering high protection and sufficient

[28] See Article 15 of the Eurojust Decision, in particular paragraphs 2, 3 and 4.

oversight mechanisms, such as in the case of Eurojust the existence of an independent Data Protection Officer and an external Joint Supervisory Body monitoring the compliance with the rules, is a much better option than trying to put in place general instruments containing too general and vague provisions and offering low protection. It is crucial of course to ensure that existing rules are compatible with each other but this is in my view the case so far.

I am therefore in favour of sticking to the good systems already existing in the third pillar sector such as the ones of Europol, Eurojust, the SIS and the CIS, which, as stated in the preamble to the framework decision, *constitute a complete and coherent set of rules covering all relevant aspects of data protection (principles of data quality, rules on data security, regulation of the rights and safeguards of data subjects, organisation of supervision and liability) and they regulate these matters more in detail than the present Framework Decision,* not only because they are there and have proved to work but also because they contain detailed and tailor-made provisions that relate directly to the work carried out by the institutions or bodies applying them and allow them to operate in a well-defined and clear framework. This fits in my view thoroughly with an environment in which data controllers are generally used to operate within very defined and detailed rules: one should not forget that a crime is only a crime if it is typified as such in the criminal code. Police and judiciary are there to apply the law: the more specific, clear and related to their activities that the rules on the processing of personal data are, the better they will be understood and applied.

Chapter 14
Who is Profiling Who? Invisible Visibility

Mireille Hildebrandt

14.1 Why Protect Personal Data?

The assumption of the conference on 'Reinventing Data Protection?' was that data protection and privacy are not the same thing, though they may overlap. One of the questions raised by advanced data processing techniques like data mining and profiling is whether the assumption that it is *data* that need to be protected still holds.[1] The data protection directive of 1995 builds on the concept of personal data, defined as data that relate to an identified or identifiable natural person.[2] When looking into the consequences of extensive profiling – the precondition for e.g., Ambient Intelligence and other smart applications – we may come to the conclusion that the difference

M. Hildebrandt (✉)
Law Science Technology & Society, Vrije Universiteit Brussel, Brussels, Belgium Erasmus School of Law, Erasmus University Rotterdam, the Netherlands
e-mail: mireille.hildebrandt@vub.ac.be

Mireille Hildebrandt is Associate Professor of *Jurisprudence* at Erasmus University Rotterdam. She has been seconded to the centre for *Law Science Technology and Society* studies as the Vrije Universiteit Brussels, from which position she is coordinator for profiling technologies in the EC funded Network of Excellence (NoE) for the *Future of Identity in Information Society* (FIDIS). From her position in Rotterdam she is Dean of Education of the research school on *Safety and Security*, an interuniversity network for the study of security and justice.

[1] An interesting analysis of how data protection legislation was actually negotiated can be found in Bonner and Chiasson (2005). 'If fair information principles are the answer, what was the question? An actor-network theory investigation of the modern constitution of privacy.' *Information and Organization* **15**: 267–293, demonstrating that changes in the socio-technical landscape have made the assumptions about individual control over one's personal data and 'policing' by a supervisory authority dubious. As regards the European Data Protection Directive D 95/46 EC it should be clear that both the purpose of facilitating cross-border data flows and the purpose of the protection of personal data were directed to harmonisation of the internal market.

[2] D 95/46 EC, Article 2 sub a: 'personal data shall mean any information relating to an identified or identifiable natural person ('data subject'); an identifiable person is one who can be identified, directly or indirectly, in particular by reference to an identification number or to one or more factors specific to his physical, physiological, mental, economic, cultural or social identity'. About the contextual and casuistic complexity of the concept of personal data, see Opinion 4/2007 of the Article 29 Working Party on the concept of personal data (WP 136).

S. Gutwirth et al. (eds.), *Reinventing Data Protection?*
DOI 10.1007/978-1-4020-9498-9_14, © Springer Science+Business Media B.V. 2009

between data and personal data is no longer crucial, because profiling technologies can infer highly sensitive information (even knowledge) out of seemingly trivial and/or anonymous data. In this contribution I will argue that, in as far as the objective of data protection legislation has been the protection of privacy, equality of arms (transparency), non-discrimination and a relatively unobstructed flow of information, we need a paradigm shift from data to knowledge to sustain such protection.[3]

To argue my case I will move to the core challenge of profiling: the occurrence of an invisible visibility (Section 14.2). After an explanation of what is meant with profiling technologies (Section 14.2.1) I will discuss two potentially hazardous consequences: first, social sorting, refined discrimination and the autonomy trap (Section 14.2.2) and second, the implications of physical and behavioural biometrics for what have been called the secrets of the self. Social sorting, refined discrimination and the autonomy trap will discuss privacy as autonomy, taking into account the pitfalls of consent as an instrument of protection (Section 12.2.2.2); after which the section will move beyond privacy, explaining how profiling facilitates a new type of segmented society with far reaching consequences for individual autonomy (Section 14.2.2.3). The implications of physical and behavioural biometrics for the secrets of the self will discuss privacy as opacity, focusing on the extent to which the hiding of personal data interferes with the accuracy of such biometrics and on the extent to which the hiding of such data can protect against transparency of the self (Section 14.2.3.2); after which the section moves beyond privacy, acknowledging that the self is always already a relational self, constituted in relation to other selves and things (Section 14.2.3.3). These sections will start by mining the implications of profiling as a new type of knowledge. The inventory of challenges generated by the status of the profiles as a new type of knowledge will then be followed by an investigation of the legal status of profiles (Section 14.3), having made the case that we need to shift our attention from personal data to data in a much wider sense and the profiles inferred from them. An analysis of Articles 15 and 12 of the directive will be made, to assess whether they are of any help regarding the implications of profiling (Section 14.3.1). To remedy the present loss of protection, which is caused by the unjustified focus on personal data, I will propose a set of new legal transparency rights, claiming the need to articulate these rights in the technological infrastructure against which they aim to protect (Section 14.3.2). We shall end with some concluding remarks.

14.2 Invisible Visibility[4]

14.2.1 Profiling: Detecting the Difference that Makes a Difference

The profusion of digital data, collected, stored and processed in public and private contexts (professional, business, retail, transport, governmental, Internet commerce,

---

[3] Hildebrandt (2006a).

[4] This phrase, highly evocative of the crucial significance of profiling today, was coined by Keymolen (2006).

virtual communities etc.), is taking on paralysing proportions. The competitive advantage of data collection no longer resides in the amount of data but in finding the data that make a difference:[5] discriminating information from noise, while holding on to the data that are noise today in case they turn out to be information tomorrow.

Profiling, defined as the process of knowledge discovery in data bases (KDD), seems the only technology capable of detecting which data make a difference. It achieves such salience by means of pattern recognition: instead of mining data on the basis of predefined classes (which would produce a query that does *not* provide what one does not already know), profiling uses algorithms to locate unexpected correlations and patterns. KDD is described as:

> Knowledge discovery in databases is the non-trivial process of identifying valid, novel, potentially useful, and ultimately understandable patterns in data.[6]

These patterns emerge in the process of data mining and after interpretation, application and testing they can be used for matching with new data. Pattern recognition, based on 'blind' correlations (i.e., correlations that do not derive from predefined hypotheses and do not necessarily imply causes or reasons) allows those that use the ensuing profiles to anticipate the state or behaviour of the objects or subjects that are being profiled. Profiling makes visible patterns that are invisible to the naked human eye, highlighting – on the basis of mathematical techniques – previously unknown structures of reality in flux. One could thus say that they render visible the invisible. Many authors have claimed that profiling thus produces a new type of knowledge. The novelty is generated by the fact that unlike traditional sociological research it is not based on a sample or a query (which both presume predefined hypotheses), as well as on the fact that it has few pretensions as to causal or psychological underpinnings.[7] In fact, the groundwork for profiling was not performed by sociology but by marketing research, e.g., multiple regression analysis.[8] The knowledge inferred is not foundational but pragmatic and can best be understood in reference to Peirce's definition of what he calls the Maxim of Pragmatism:

> Consider what effects that might conceivably have practical bearings we conceive the object of our conception to have: then, our conception of those effects is the whole of our conception of the object.[9]

This conception of knowledge, meaning or truth is of course not pragmatic in the naïve or utilist sense; it is pragmatic in the sense that it avoids understanding knowledge in a general, universal or foundational way.[10] Profiles provide (local)

---

[5] Cf. Lévy (1990), at 157.

[6] Fayyad et al. (1996), at 6.

[7] About the fact that profiling produces a new type of knowledge e.g., Custers (2004), Zarsky (2002–2003).

[8] About the difference between traditional sociological research, which entails 'empirical statistical research with self-chosen hypothesis' and data mining or profiling, which entails 'the automated generating and testing of hypotheses', see Custers (2004), at 56.

[9] Peirce (1997), at 111.

[10] Whether the pragmatist maxim concerns knowledge, meaning or truth and how we should understand these terms was the object of intense debate between – amongst others – Peirce and William James.

knowledge relevant within the relationship between a certain organisation and its environment,[11] requiring real time monitoring of the environment and real time updating of the relevant profiles. On the basis of that knowledge profilers can determine which data contain information, thus detecting '*the difference that makes a difference*', the crucial feature of 'a "bit" of information', as explained by George Bateson, one of the founding fathers of cybernetics.[12] Cybernetics as 'the science of communication and control in animal and machine' or 'control theory as it is applied to complex systems'[13] depends on profiling technologies to seek out the differences that – in a specific context, at a specific moment in time, from a specific perspective – make a difference for the profiler, turning data into either noise or information.

14.2.2 Social Sorting, Refined Discrimination, Autonomy Trap

14.2.2.1 Implications of a New Type of Knowledge

When suggesting that profiling renders visible patterns invisible to the naked human eye, we confront the core of what makes profiling both interesting and dangerous. Because of being invisible to the naked eye, these patterns are only visible to those that profile, not to those that are being profiled. They thus constitute an *invisible visibility* for most citizens that are the object of profiling. One of the implications of such invisibility is that consumers are making decisions without being aware of the knowledge held by commercial enterprise (government agencies, health care organisations, social security offices), raising the issues of individual consent, self-determination and autonomy on the one hand and of refined dynamic social sorting on the other hand.

14.2.2.2 Privacy as Autonomy: The Pitfalls of Consent

Loyal to the tenet of liberal democracy consent plays an important role in the data protection directive, seemingly empowering citizens to choose whether or not to leak their personal data, thus legitimising the collection and processing of personal data for which no other legitimisation can be found. However, as we can not have our cake and eat it too, refusing to disclose personal data may cause serious disruption of one's socio-economic existence since many transactions require such disclosure. Besides that, the sheer amount of occasions in need of consent turn the requirement

[11] Hildebrandt (2008a).

[12] Kallinikos (2006) at 60 and 70, referring to Bateson (1972). See Bateson (1972) in the section on 'The Epistemology of Cybernetics', at 315.

[13] Cybernetics. Encyclopaedia Britannica. 2008. Encyclopaedia Britannica Online. 20 Jan. 2008 <http://www.britannica.com/eb/article-9028365>, referring to Wiener, N. (1948), *Cybernetics or Control and Communication in the Animal and the Machine*, Paris, Hermann et Cie - MIT Press, Cambridge, MA.

into a hoax, as nobody has either the time or the willingness to seriously investigate the consequences of leaving one's traces with the providers that are mining them.

This state of affairs is seriously aggravated in the case of widespread profiling, because the consequences of handing over one's data are unclear (due to the invisibility of one's visibility). On top of that the link between disclosing one's personal data and the application of what has been called 'group profiles' is complex. First, group profiles that are applied to me have been inferred from masses of (personal) data that are *not* mine (hiding my data will not stop the process of group profiling); second, they are applied because my (personal) data match the profile, which does not imply that the profile actually applies (the problem of non-distributive profiles)[14]; third, sophisticated profiling technologies like e.g., behavioural biometric profiling (BBP) do not require identification at all,[15] thus falling outside the application of the directive.

For these reasons, informed consent is a wholly inadequate legitimisation in the case of group profiling: the invisibility of the patterns that become visible to the profiler and the inability to anticipate the consequences of the application of profiles derived from other people's data clearly rule out *informed* consent. Even if I could anonymise my data, or work with pseudonyms, the lack of information on how I am being categorised and what the consequences are turns the idea of self-determination into ridicule. Zarsky, for instance, speaks of the autonomy trap, depicting how profilers can easily manipulate a person into certain choices of actions, due to the fact that she is not aware of the knowledge about herself. One of Zarsky's salient examples of potential manipulation concerns online profiling:

> Mr. Orange often purchases through an e-commerce grocer and has recently stopped buying cigarettes. The grocer, anxious to cash in on potentially lucrative tobacco sales, notices that Mr. Orange has just purchased a 'nicotine patch' and concludes that he is trying to quit smoking. Mr. Orange is then presented with cigarette ads at the websites he visits and even receives a 'complementary' cigarette pack in his most recent grocery shipment.[16]

One could imagine more creative tactics, like putting banners on Mr. Orange's favourite website that refer to scientific research about the diminishing chance to develop dementia for cigarette smokers. One can also anticipate that professional profilers will mine such information and sell it to whoever expects to make a profit on the sale of cigarettes. The point is not that Mr. Orange is provided with free cigarettes or informed of specific scientific research. The point is that he is not aware of what is known about his smoking habits, by whom this knowledge is mined, to whom it is sold or distributed, nor how this knowledge is being used to

---

[14] Saliently discussed by Vedder (1999).

[15] Yannopoulos, A., A. Vassiliki and T. Varvarigou, (2008) 'Behavioural biometric profiling and Ambient Intelligence', in: Hildebrandt, M. and S. Gutwirth (eds.), *Profiling the European Citizen. A Cross-Disciplinary Perspective*, Dordrecht Springer 2008: 89–103.

[16] Zarsky (2002–2003), at 20.

influence his behaviour. One could of course object that such attempts to influence customers are not really very new, being part of our economic system. However, the extent to which such personalised knowledge can be inferred and distributed is new and increasing exponentially, making a relevant difference to our capacity to act on informed consent.

14.2.2.3 Beyond Privacy: The Segmented Society Revisited

Manipulation such as this will be based on the refined and dynamic categorisations produced by increasingly autonomic profiling. In fact profiling seems the postmodern version of a premodern phenomenon: the segmentation of society into different groups that allows profilers to associate and identify their potential clients as members of a group with well-defined characteristics. An observation of Lawrence Lessig comes to mind, whereas he refers to the fact that urbanisation and the increasing mobility it entailed had as a consequence that it was more difficult to locate and identify people, thus providing a kind of freedom absent in premodern segmented societies. One of the results of profiling technologies may well be that it will once again be easy to locate and identify people, restricting their freedom to move around anonymously, not having to account for their whereabouts to whatever authority takes an interest.[17] Are we turning our urbanised societies into a global village, reinstalling the preconditions for intensive social control by means of transnational socio-technical infrastructures with an unprecedented potential for dataveillance,[18] social sorting and refined segmentation?[19]

Obviously profiling technologies do not reproduce premodern segmented societies: the segmentation is dynamic and personalised, profiles are continuously updated and a person is identified as a member of a variety of groups or categories. But even though the segmentation is customised, it ends up making visible what became invisible in the processes of urbanisation and globalisation, rendering every person traceable to a previously unthinkable extent.

The result is the possibility to engage in refined price discrimination,[20] actuarial justice and highly problematic social sorting. This raises the issues of non-discrimination and due process,[21] rather than just privacy and requires remedies beyond written opacity or transparency rights.

---

[17] Lessig (1999) at 155.

[18] Cf. Clarke, R., 'Profiling: A Hidden Challenge to the Regulation of Dataveillance' Int'l J. L. & Inf. Sc. 4,2 (December 1993). At http://www.anu.edu.au/people/Roger.Clarke/DV/PaperProfiling.htm, downloaded 19th January 2008.

[19] Cf. Lyon, D. (ed.) (2002), *Surveillance as Social Sorting. Privacy, Risk and Automated Discrimination*, Routledge.

[20] Cp. Odlyzko, A. (2003), Privacy, Economics, and Price Discrimination on the Internet, available at: http://www.dtc.umn.edu/~odlyzko/doc/privacy.economics.pdf, downloaded 19th January 2008.

[21] Steinbock, D.J. (2005), Data Matching, Data Mining, and Due Process, *Georgia Law Review* (40) 2005-1:60. Citron, D.K. (2007), Technological Due Process, *Washington University Law Review*, 85:1249–1313.

14.2.3 *Secrets of the Self:*[22] *Physical and Behavioural Biometrics*

14.2.3.1 Implications of a New Type of Knowledge

Returning to the fact that the profiles produced by mathematical data mining techniques are invisible to the naked eye and thus invisible for most citizens that are being profiled, we now confront the fact that profilers may come to know intimate things about us, some of which we may not even know about ourselves.

14.2.3.2 Privacy as Opacity:[23] Hiding of Personal Data

Biometric profiling is usually associated with DNA matching, which entails the comparison of DNA profiles found as traces at a crime scene and the DNA profiles of one or more suspects.[24] More interesting, however, are the samples of DNA kept in DNA data bases, providing access to all intimate knowledge of a person's biological constitution, based on DNA profiling in the science of human genetics. Depending on the state of the art in medical science, the sample may contain information about hereditary diseases (both physical and mental), hair colour, skin colour, ethnical background, etc., as well as information about family relations (parenthood, indications of hereditary diseases that may implicate relatives etc.). One can imagine the interest insurance companies would take in such materials, as it would allow refined and personalised risk analysis and price discrimination – blowing up the principle of solidarity that was partly based on ignorance about who runs which risks.

Another interesting field is behavioural biometric profiling, like key stroke behaviour, gait analysis, which facilitates identifying a person as the same person without having to identify the person in terms of name or address.[25] Such identification – a matter of re-recognition[26] – makes it possible to correlate the biometric behaviour with e.g., transactional behaviour, health risks or whatever other states or behaviours are found to correlate with a certain behavioural biometric.

If many people hide their personal data this will imply that the group profiles built on such data will be based on inaccurate input, making them less precise in their application. It may also render the application of profiles more difficult because in hiding one's personal data one could prevent matching with a profile.

---

[22] Hudson (2005).

[23] For an analysis of privacy as a legal right that aims to provide opacity *of* citizens and data protection as a set of legal rights and obligations that aim to provide transparency *to* citizens of the processing of their personal data, see De Hert and Gutwirth (2006).

[24] Schneider, P.M. and P.D. Martin, Criminal DNA databases: the European situation, *Forensic Science International* (119) 2001-2: 232–238.

[25] Rejman-Greene, M., 'Biometrics – real identities for a virtual world', BT Technology Journal (19) 2001-3: 115–121. Jain, A.K., A. Ross and S. Prabhakar, An Introduction to Biometric Recognition, *IEEE TRANSACTIONS ON CIRCUITS AND SYSTEMS FOR VIDEO TECHNOLOGY*, (14) 2004-1: 4–20.

[26] Dötzer (2005).

Translating privacy in the hiding of personal data thus effects two things: smart things will be less smart because the input of data in the profiling process is less accurate and those that manage to avoid the application of profiles may avoid the consequences of refined discrimination. As soon as profiling becomes wide-spread, however, hiding one's data will inevitably result in being categorised as such, which will have consequences anyway – like e.g., receiving less service, being attributed more risk, paying higher prices, etc. It seems to me that leaving the choice to hide one's personal data to individual citizens in the end forces everybody to conform to indiscriminate leaking of personal data, because – as mentioned earlier – you can not have your cake and eat it too. Solutions may need to be designed at another level of protection, keeping in mind that the protection of a public good like privacy, should not be left to a market that is regulated by insurmountable transaction costs on the side of individual citizens. As Paul Schwartz has aptly argued in his discussion with Lawrence Lessig on the commodifation of privacy, the 'market' for personal data suffers a structural market failure due to a set of constraints that concern – amongst others – the inability to gain access to secondary and tertiary data processing or profiling, resulting in an enduring asymmetry between individual citizens and those organisations that profile them.[27]

14.2.3.3 Beyond Privacy: Oneself as Another

Understanding informational privacy as the hiding of personal data easily turns privacy into a private good, traded in an unfair market.[28] To confront the challenges of profiling technologies I would rather quote Agre's and Rotenberg's definition of the right to privacy, linking privacy to identity-building:

> the freedom from unreasonable constraints on the construction of one's own identity.[29]

The attraction of this definition is that it avoids the defensive undertone of much privacy debate. The reduction of informational privacy to non-disclosure of personal data and the subsequent focus on the development of privacy enhancing technologies (PETs) that enable anonymisation and user-centred identity management (working with contextual pseudonyms) all target *data minimisation*, thus presenting us with a paradigm that is incompatible with the advent of smart applications that thrive on data maximisation in order to detect which data is information in which context, at which point in time and for which user. Instead of seeing privacy exclusively in terms of negative freedom (freedom from), Agre and Rotenberg's definition emphasizes the positive freedom inherent in privacy: the freedom to construct one's own identity in the face of the many identifications that are possible. Such a

---

[27] Schwartz (2000), at 763–776. The other constraints that result in a marked failure are the collective action problem, bounded rationality and limits to exit from certain practices (see idem at 766–771).

[28] About the pitfalls of commodification of personal data see Prins (2004).

[29] Agre and Rotenberg, 2001, at 7. Cf. Hildebrandt (2006b). cp. Rouvroy (2008), downloaded 19th January 2008.

conception of privacy also enables one to face the challenge of profiling, because the constitution of one's identity is always mediated by what G.H. Mead called the gaze of the other.[30] Referring to Ricoeur's *Oneself as Another* it becomes pertinent to acknowledge that the invisible visibility produced by profiling technologies will have a major impact on our capacity to construct our own identity.[31] If one cannot anticipate how one is being profiled it may become very difficult to reconstruct the self in any meaningful way: the mediation of the gaze of the other is lacking as we have no access to it. Though the gaze is fixed on our every movement, *we do not see it*, as it is part of the hidden complexity of an environment in which the things themselves have become the interface.[32] The secrets *of* the self (the invisible) remain a secret *to* the self, while being mined by others (who made the invisible visible).

This, however is not the only problem engendered by profiling technologies that construct intimate knowledge of – for instance – our biological constitution or of certain parts of our personality that we are not aware of. At some point doctors, insurance companies, social security providers, employers and even friends may disclose knowledge to us we would rather not be aware of. Some authors argue that our selves depend on the secrets they build on, potentially destabilising our sense of self once they are revealed to us.[33]

One could claim that invisible visibility creates a twofold – paradoxical – burden on the relationship between profiler and profiled: to disclose the secret may disrupt the life of the person who was unaware of it, while to use the knowledge without sharing it would be in disrespect of the person's autonomy.

14.3 The Legal Status of Profiles[34]

14.3.1 Article 15 D 95/46 EC

Having made the case for a paradigm shift *from data to knowledge* protection, we now come to the question of how to make such a shift operable. For a start, we could point to Article 15 of the data protection directive, which grants 'a right to every person not to be subject to a decision which produces legal effects concerning him or significantly affects him and which is based solely on automated processing of data intended to evaluate certain personal aspects relating to him' and to Article 12,

---

30 Mead (1959/1934).

31 Ricoeur (1992).

32 Another point is that the gaze is not the gaze of another human subject, it is the gaze of a profiling machine. Especially in the case of autonomic computing, which tries to rule out human intervention as much as possible, this presents novel challenges to the construction of the self: what happens to our self-constitution via the gaze of the other when we begin to anticipate the gaze of machines instead of humans? About profiling machines see Elmer, G. (2004), Profiling Machines. *Mapping the Personal Information Economy*, MIT Press.

33 Hudson (2005).

34 Bourcier (2001).

which grants the right to every data subject 'to obtain from the controller knowledge of the logic involved in any automatic processing of data concerning him at least in the case of the automated decisions referred to in Article 15 (1)'. Note that the right of Article 15 is granted to every person, while the transparency right of Article 12 is given only to the data subject. The wording of Article 12, however, suggests that when Article 15 is at stake the person concerned is a data subject because the automated processing of data can only apply to her if she is identifiable as such.

The problem with Article 15 (and Article 12) is threefold.[35] Firstly, many decisions taken on the basis of profiling require some form of human intervention, even if routine, in which case Article 15 is no longer applicable. Second, paragraph 2 of Article 15 provides two grounds for lawful application of decisions based on automated processing of data, severely restricting the applicability.[36] Third, because even if the law attributes such rights of transparency and the right to resist automated decision making, these rights remain paper dragons as long as we lack the means to become aware of being profiled. If we do not know that we are being categorised on the basis of a match with a group profile that was not derived from our personal data, how should we contest decisions regarding insurance, credit rating, employment, health care?

Interestingly, the draft framework decision on data protection in the third pillar, originally contained no similar rights, suggesting that the application of automated profiles is no problem in the case of policing and criminal justice. Keeping in mind the objective of interoperability of police data bases across the European Union, the absence of rights like the ones in Article 15 and 12 should be a source of serious concern. The Council has, however, provided protection against such decisions by inserting Article 8, which states that 'A decision which produces an adverse legal effect for the data subject or seriously affects him and which is based solely on automated data processing for the purposes of assessing individual aspects of the data subject shall be permitted only when the legitimate interests of the data subject are safeguarded by law.' This is a curious rearticulation, providing a right not to be subject to such decisions but basically providing grounds for such decisions as long as the legitimate interests of the affected person are safeguarded by law. Compared to Article 15 of the data protection directive this provision echos the ground of exception of paragraph 2, which states that a person may be subjected to an automated decision if it 'is authorized by a law which also lays down measures to safeguard the data subject's legitimate interests'. The protection provided by Article

[35] Cp. Bygrave (2001), who detects another problem, whereas he suggests that Article 15 only protects those citizens who *exercise* the right not to be subject to automated decisions.

[36] Paragraph 2 of Article 15: Subject to the other Articles of this Directive, Member States shall provide that a person may be subjected to a decision of the kind referred to in paragraph 1 if that decision: (a) is taken in the course of the entering into or performance of a contract, provided the request for the entering into or the performance of the contract, lodged by the data subject, has been satisfied or that there are suitable measures to safeguard his legitimate interests, such as arrangements allowing him to put his point of view; or (b) is authorized by a law which also lays down measures to safeguard the data subject's legitimate interests.

8 does not forbid these decisions; it rather provides the legal authorization, on condition that legitimate interests are safeguarded by law. Who decides about the extent of the legitimate interests of the affected person as well as what counts as a legal safeguard here is unclear, while it may in fact be the case that a person will never find out that she was the target of such a decision.

14.3.2 *Effective Legal Remedies: Rethinking the Legal Status of Profiles*

A shift from the protection of data to the protection of knowledge should focus on the proliferation of profiles that may at some point in time be applied to a person whose data match with a profile. What is needed here is a set of two interrelated rights and obligations. First, an *effective* right of access to profiles that match with one's data and are used to categorise one, including the consequences this may have. To ensure an effective right we may need to articulate it in the technological infrastructure that enables extensive profiling. In other work we have coined the term Ambient Law for the articulation of legal rights in the technologies against which such rights aim to protect.[37] The right of access right should be complemented with an obligation for the profiler to communicate which profiles are being constructed that match with a person's data, including the consequences thereof. Like the right of access to profiles, such obligations should also be articulated in the technological architecture that facilitates profiling. It should be obvious that many objections can be raised to these rights and obligations, from claims concerning intellectual property on profiles (or trade secrets)[38] to claims that granting this right would be technically impossible to implement. Though I can see the reality of the objections, I am not impressed. If we want smart things and Ambient Intelligence while safeguarding public goods like privacy, equality of arms and due process we cannot do without a right to know what is known about us. We need to provide the legal and technological infrastructure to make invisible visibility open to scrutiny by those concerned. This means that, secondly, a person should have the right to contest the accuracy and the applicability of a profile, including the right to contest application on grounds of unjustified discrimination. Should such protections not be feasible, the question arises whether we should want to invest in a technological infrastructure that could change the fabric of checks and balances between

[37] Hildebrandt and Koops (2007), Hildebrandt (2008b).

[38] See recital (41) of the preliminary section of D 95/46 EC: 'Whereas any person must be able to exercise the right of access to data relating to him which are being processed, in order to verify in particular the accuracy of the data and the lawfulness of the processing; whereas, for the same reasons, every data subject must also have the right to know the logic involved in the automatic processing of data concerning him, at least in the case of the automated decisions referred to in Article 15(1); whereas this right must not adversely affect business confidentiality or intellectual property and in particular the copyright protecting the software; whereas these considerations must not, however, result in the data subject being refused all information'.

governments and commercial enterprise on the one hand and individual citizens on the other. Considering the massive impact on our *freedom from* unreasonable constraints as well as our *freedom to* develop and celebrate our personal identity, the decision on the construction of this socio-technical architecture cannot be left to a failing market or an ambitious executive. Such decisions belong to the democratic legislature, taking into account the public consequences of private actions,[39] or if the legislator does not do its job here, publics should be formed to address the issue and to put it on the agenda of policy makers, computer engineers and business enterprise.[40]

Though I do not think we should take the objections for granted, I do agree that they require serious attention and call for a joint effort of lawyers and computer engineers to figure out how to reconfigure the legal and technological infrastructure to make such rights possible. An interesting option could be to think more explicitly about the legal status of group profiles: do we want to think in terms of property law, personality rights or tort law? Do we want group profiles to be owned by commercial enterprise, or should they be owned by those whose data were used to construct them or, even more to the point: by those to whom they may be applied? Obviously political decisions are at stake here, belonging in the domain of the legislator. But as lawyers we need to investigate how such property rights could fit into the legal system, without violating the legitimate claims of others.[41] Alternatively, we could think of profiles in terms of personality rights that aim to protect our privacy, perhaps even granting the right to demand the destruction of certain profiles because they imply a serious violation of the private sphere. At this point we should ask the computer engineers whether such destruction is feasible and effective in the reality of an interconnected world. Yet another option would be to resort to tort law and in specific instances to criminal law to specify in which cases a profiler is liable for harm caused by the application of group profiles that do not apply to all the members of the group (non-distributive groups), or by the unfair application of group profiles that boil down to unjustified discrimination. In this case the technological infrastructure would need to expose the application of profiles whenever harm occurs, otherwise the victim simply has no way of knowing that the use of a group profile made a difference.

14.4 Concluding Remarks

Data protection takes personal data as its exclusive focus. Profiling technologies challenge the wisdom of such exclusion. Group profiling, based on knowledge discovery in databases, is not necessarily based on the personal data of whoever suffers

---

39 Lessig (2006), at 338.

40 Cf. Dewey (1927), see Hildebrandt and Gutwirth (2007).

41 About the specific role of lawyers, who must invent legal solutions to new problems while keeping in mind how they could fit the existing fabric of legal statutes, case law, doctrinal positions, principle and policies, see Gutwirth and De Hert elsewhere in this volume.

or enjoys the application of group profiles. Group profiles may disclose knowledge and information about lifestyles, personal preferences, shopping and travel habits, web surfing behaviour, health risks, security risks, ethnic origin, sexual preferences and religious belief. To mine and even to apply such knowledge a person need not be identified in the regular sense of the term; biometric behavioural profiling allows re-recognition without knowing who you actually are. The impact of profiling technologies – against which data protection legislation does not protect in as far as it only applies to the processing of personal data – may soon be far greater than the impact of sharing your personal data. This contribution explains the implications of widespread profiling for privacy as autonomy and for the right to non-discrimination and explores ways to rethink the legal status of the profile. Two rights are proposed to empower citizens over and against the profiles that may impact their lives: first, the right of access to profiles that may be applied to them; second, the right to contest the validity or the fairness of the application of a profile. To be effective, these rights need to be complemented with legal obligations for those that construct and apply profiles and – equally important – they need to be inscribed in the technological infrastructure against which they aim to protect. Without such inscription access to profiles is not feasible and awareness of wrongful application of profiles highly unlikely. Instead of aiming for data minimisation, this contribution argues the need for a minimisation of knowledge asymmetry that will allow profiling technologies to flourish, while providing citizens with the legal-technological instruments to gain access to profiles and challenge their application.

This will evidently not solve all the problems related to the advent of smart applications, proactive computing, genetic profiling and ambient intelligence. If our concern is a right to oblivion and/or a right not to know what is inferred about ourselves, we still need a set of effective opacity rights allowing us to unplug from the permanence of knowledge construction. Such opacity rights will require careful calibration with the transparency rights needed to sustain a smart environment that allows anticipation of the knowledge that will be applied to us.

References

Bateson, G. (1972). *Steps to an Ecology of Mind*. New York, Ballantine

Bonner, W. and M. Chiasson (2005). "If fair information principles are the answer, what was the question? An actor-network theory investigation of the modern constitution of privacy." *Information and Organization* **15**: 267–293

Bourcier, D. (2001). "De l'intelligence artificielle à la *personne virtuelle*: émergence d'une entité juridique?" *Droit et Société* **49**: 847–871

Bygrave, L. (2001). *Minding the Machine. Article 15 and the EC Data Protection Directive and automated profiling. Computer Law & Security Report.* **17**: 17–24

Custers, B. (2004). *The Power of Knowledge. Ethical, Legal, and Technological Aspects of Data Mining and Group Profiling in Epidemiology*. Nijmegen, Wolf Legal Publishers

De Hert, P. and S. Gutwirth (2006). Privacy, Data Protection and Law Enforcement. Opacity of the Individual and Transparency of Power. *Privacy and the Criminal Law*. E. Claes, A. Duff and S. Gutwirth. Antwerpen Oxford, Intersentia

Dewey, J. (1927). *The Public & Its Problems*. Chicago, The Swallow Press

Dötzer, F. (2005). Privacy Issues in Vehicular Ad Hoc Networks. *Workshop on Privacy Enhancing Technologies*. Dubrovnik, available at: http://www13.informatik.tu-muenchen.de/personen/doetzer/publications/Doetzer-05-PrivacyIssuesVANETs.pdf

Fayyad, U. M., G. Piatetsky-Shapiro, et al., Eds. (1996). *Advances in Knowledge Discovery and Data Mining*. Meno Park, California, Cambridge, Mass., London England, AAAI Press / MIT Press

Hildebrandt, M. (2006a). "From Data to Knowledge: The challenges of a crucial technology." *DuD – Datenschutz und Datensicherheit* **30**: 548–552

Hildebrandt, M. (2006b). Privacy and Identity. *Privacy and the Criminal Law*. E. Claes, A. Duff and S. Gutwirth. Antwerpen – Oxford, Intersentia: 43–58

Hildebrandt, M. (2008a). Defining Profiling: A New Type of Knowledge. *Profiling the European Citizen. A Cross-disciplinary Perspective*. M. Hildebrandt and S. Gutwirth, Springer: 17–30

Hildebrandt, M. (2008b). A Vision of Ambient Law. *Regulating Technologies*. R. Brownsword and K. Yeung. Oxford, Hart: 175–191

Hildebrandt, M. and S. Gutwirth (2007). "(Re)presentation, pTA citizens' juries and the jury trial." *Utrecht Law Review* **3** (1): http://www.utrechtlawreview.org/

Hildebrandt, M. and B.-J. Koops (2007). *A Vision of Ambient Law*. Brussels, FIDIS

Hudson, B. (2005). Secrets of Self: Punishment and the Right to Privacy. *Privacy and the Criminal Law*. E. Claes and A. Duff. Antwerp Oxford, Intersentia

Kallinikos, J. (2006). *The Consequences of Information. Institutional Implications of Technological Change*. Cheltenham, UK Northampton, MA, USA, Edward Elgar

Keymolen, E. (2006). *Onzichtbare Zichtbaarheid. Helmuth Plessner ontmoet profiling. Bachelor Thesis Faculty of Philosophy*. Rotterdam, not published

Lessig, L. (1999). *Code and Other Laws of Cyberspace*. New York, Basic Books

Lessig, L. (2006). *Code Version 2.0*. New York, Basic Books

Lévy, P. (1990). *Les technologies de l'intelligence. L'avenir à l'ère informatique*. Paris, La Découverte

Mead, G. H. (1959/1934). *Mind, Self & Society. From the Standpoint of a Social Behaviorist*. Chicago – Illinois, The University of Chicago Press

Peirce, C. S. (1997). *Pragmatism as a Principle and Method of Right Thinking. The 1903 Harvard Lectures on Pragmatism*. Albany, State University of New York Press

Prins, J. E. J. (2004). "The Propertization of Personal Data and Identities." *Electronic Journal of Comparative Law, available at http://www.ejcl.org/* **8**(3)

Ricoeur, P. (1992). *Oneself as Another*. Chicago, The University of Chicago Press

Rouvroy, A. (2008). "Privacy, data protection and the unprecedented challenges of Ambient Intelligence." *(2) Studies in Ethics, Law and Technology, Issue 1, available at SSRN: http://ssrn.com/abstract=1013984*

Schwartz, P. M. (2000). "Beyond Lessig's *Code* for Internet Privacy: Cyberspace Filters, Privacy-Control and Fair Information Practices." *Wisconsin Law Review* **4**: 743–788

Vedder, A. (1999). "KDD: The challenge to individualism." *Ethics and Information Technology* **1**: 275–281

Zarsky, T. Z. (2002–2003). "'Mine Your Own Business!': Making the Case for the Implications of the Data Mining or Personal Information in the Forum of Public Opinion." *Yale Journal of Law & Technology* **5** (4): 17–47

Chapter 15
Challenges in Privacy Advocacy

Gus Hosein

Though it is rarely ever said, there is much to be optimistic about within the field of privacy advocacy. The amount of news coverage to privacy issues is ever-increasing. The number of privacy experts and professionals is on the increase as government and companies are recognising the need to consider privacy principles. Survey after survey shows that citizens and consumers are deeply concerned about their privacy and the use of their personal information by others. Companies are increasingly adapting their collection practices to cater for privacy concerns, as consumers are ever-more privacy conscious, aided by the constant news-flows regarding data breaches and other privacy failures. Regulators and commissioners, often working together, issue strong opinions and judgments in the defence of privacy.

Parliamentary and congressional scrutiny is growing as well. Committee hearings have followed on quickly from policy developments, investigating policies such as the transfer of passenger data to foreign governments, the interception, collection and retention of communications-related data and the introduction of biometric identity documents. Even just recently, the UK Parliament's Joint Committee on Human Rights lambasted the government for ignoring data protection for many years leading to its loss of 25 million records on British families; the US House of Representatives ensured that the Stimulus Package of February 2009 contained privacy protections for electronic medical records; continues to resist the Bush Administration's pressure to immunise telephone companies from lawsuits because of their complicity in wide-scale surveillance programmes; the new Australian government has rejected the previous government's plans for an identity card; amongst others.

Scrutiny may arise from other sources as well. Tim Berners-Lee articulated his concern about online tracking for advertising purposes[1]; airlines protested against

G. Hosein (✉)
Information Systems and Innovation Group, Department of Management, The London School of Economics and Political Science, Houghton Street, London, GB
e-mail: i.hosein@1se.ac.uk

[1] Rory Cellan-Jones, 'Web creator rejects net tracking', BBC News, March 17, 2008.

S. Gutwirth et al. (eds.), *Reinventing Data Protection?*
DOI 10.1007/978-1-4020-9498-9_15, © Springer Science+Business Media B.V. 2009

US government plans to require them to fingerprint passengers[2]; the Indian government had to concede that it could not ban Blackberry services even though they are equipped with higher-grade encryption services than government policy dictates[3]; and a UK company conducted research using open-government rules to discover that all UK government departments lack basic systems for proving compliance with privacy law.[4]

These, and many other initiatives around the world, are strong indications that there is an increasing level of activity privacy to complement (though not proportionately) surveillance policy.

There is now a strong consensus that privacy is essential to a well-functioning and ethical society, democracy and marketplace.

- Privacy's links with freedom of expression is becoming clear as we discovered how companies are complicit in disclosing the names of dissenters to oppressive governments, as was discovered in the case of Yahoo! aiding the Chinese government. High profile incidents have also highlighted how the right to peaceful assemble is being infringed, as protesters in a number of countries have been filmed, questioned, fingerprinted and even had their DNA taken despite never having broken any law.
- Corporate social responsibility mechanisms are now recognising the importance of privacy, even as scandals emerge around spying in the workplace, from the boardrooms to the factory floors.
- Data breach legislation has shown to the public that you need not be paranoid just because you are concerned about organisations collecting your personal information, when this information may be abused by others.
- Cases of extradition, rendition and torture have emerged because of errors in the handling of personal data by law enforcement and intelligence agencies. For instance, Maher Arar was wrongfully designated a terrorist through data-sharing errors, as discovered by the judicial inquiry into how the US extraordinarily rendered him to Syria, through Jordan.

There are now hundreds of thousands of cases of privacy abuses through negligence and maliciousness that have raised the profile of this issue to an unprecedented level. The great tragedy is that just as privacy is becoming recognised and actionable, the supporting infrastructure is at its most fragile state since the post-war era. Never have the threats been so obvious, the errors and challenges so clear and yet we are less prepared now than we have ever been before.

---

[2] Thomas Frank, 'Airlines blast plan to fingerprint foreign fliers', USA Today, March 16 2008, available at http://www.usatoday.com/travel/flights/2008-03-16-fingerprints_N.htm

[3] Amit Bhattacharya, 'Look who wants to read your emails', The Times of India, March 16 2008, available at http://timesofindia.indiatimes.com/Special_Report/Look_who_wants_to_read_your_emails/articleshow/2869684.cms

[4] John Leyden, 'UK government data protection is a shambles', The Register, March 10 2008, available at http://www.theregister.co.uk/2008/03/10/uk_gov_data_protection_shambles/print.html

15.1 Changes in Privacy Campaigning

Over the past decade the landscape for privacy protection has transformed.

A decade ago, privacy groups were focused on a number of policing and national security campaigns (e.g., closed-circuit television cameras), communications surveillance (e.g., surveillance being designed into the infrastructure), communications security (the 'crypto-wars') and free expression issues (particularly on-line issues). Privacy campaigners also focused on the private sector surveilling its customers, whether through collecting medical records (e.g., US laws on health insurance), financial records (e.g., credit records), or the then-budding area of electronic commerce.

Campaign successes were achieved through coalition building and educational campaigns on the importance of privacy. Media organisations were becoming more aware of these challenges and began regularly covering some of these issues, though they were often too arcane for the general population. Politicians were coming to terms with the new political realities of the globalisation of markets, the movement of people and data across borders and technological advancements. It was still a nascent field in many ways, with a few strong leaders and small groups making the most out of their small resources.

In the last ten years, the challenges grew, the coalitions fragmented and the moods of the public and the media fluctuated. The level of uncertainty rose, along with the stakes. Privacy groups were caught in the storm of trying to research the policies while rushing out responses to media and political developments.

A number of successful 'response' strategies emerged. Media organisations around the world documented the greater incursions upon the private lives of the individual, with a particular focus on the actions of the US government even if it meant ignoring domestic programmes. Parliaments and privacy commissioners issued condemnations and damning analyses of proposed plans to collect, profile and share data. Legal and academic institutions released studies assessing proposed policies and identifying the fault lines. Some national constitutional courts released opinions that upheld the right to a private life, though surprisingly the number of cases brought before these courts dwindled.

Despite these response strategies there have been practically no clear 'wins' in the past decade. Indeed, some amendments to policies have increased oversight and reduced harms. Some policies have withered, such as the data profiling of US citizens, whether under the 'Total Information Awareness' project (TIA) or the 'Computer Aided Passenger Pre-Screening Program' (CAPPS II), though the creators of these systems are insisting that these programmes be offered lifelines. Meanwhile, Europe seems set to become the next home of data-mining as these systems are the subject of government-funded research and play a key component in future government plans. As examples, the EU-funded iTRACS consortium is conducting research into data mining techniques that can be applied to financial, travel and communications data, albeit in a privacy protective way (if this is possible); and the EU plans for next generation border management that involves the collection and mining of travel, biographic, biometric and behavioural data.

Just as bad policies travel worldwide, rarely has a privacy-invasive bill not become law, a technological infrastructure not been developed, a data collection scheme abandoned. Even the withering programmes and policies have returned under new guises. As examples, data profiling systems re-emerged in the US to be applied at the border under the 'Automated Targeting System'; UK Parliamentary initiatives to reduce the invasiveness of plans to analyse communications records were corroded when the UK government managed to push a more invasive policy through the European Union; data breach legislation is being watered down to minimise the impact upon companies while disarming the rights of consumers.

Many of these surveillance initiatives outlast the campaigns to oppose them. Often the decisions to implement surveillance systems take place behind closed doors, after controversies have subsided to some extent. The Passenger Name Record debate is a key example of this: original campaigns in 2003 against the US plans seem to lead somewhere as the EU was rejecting US demands for data from EU carriers. By 2004 a limited agreement was settled upon and another campaign followed that questioned the legality of the agreement. Many twists and turns later, we ended up in 2006 with an interim agreement that was worse and in 2007 with an agreement that was even worse than that. In the end, the EU agreed to an expansive regime of data sharing with the US because, behind closed doors, the EU was hoping that the US would offer data from its own carriers to the EU for its own expansive purposes. Campaigners tried as much as they could to follow this arcane issue during its 5 year gestation period but they were eventually shut out of a negotiations process involving secret agreements and oversight arrangements that involved non-disclosure agreements.

These dynamics are not necessarily unique to privacy. Other policy areas such as copyright, national security and free expression face similar challenges. There are a number of challenges that are unique to privacy and the remainder of this chapter will focus on these.

15.2 Crossing Political Lines

Amongst privacy campaigners' greatest strengths is their ability to appeal across traditional political boundaries. This is because privacy is appealing to political groups of all stripes. Yet this great advantage is also our greatest vulnerability: no political movement is a natural home to privacy protection.

Images of totalitarian governments often involve far-right political movements dominating the political machinery. In this right-wing dystopia surveillance is used to advance policing, to identify anti-social behaviour (and increasingly before it even occurs) and to segment the population by race, nationality, creed, sexuality, amongst other categories. Alternatively, the capitalist-dystopia imagines market-led societies where individuals' personal information is owned by companies who manage our health, finances and access to services. In the former system, questioning surveillance policy becomes unpatriotic while in the latter, democratic rights no longer exist as they are subsumed by the market.

A dystopia of the 'left' also exists. Here all policies would pursue the common good where the needs of the many outweigh the privacy rights of the few. Ownership of information is given to the state to use as it sees fit. Rather than discriminate through the collection of information on certain groups the state collects information on all. This renders everyone equal, under surveillance. Decisions are made by bureaucrats and co-ordination and co-operation with other jurisdictions takes precedence over democratic process.

These dystopias are simplistic but they serve a point: to show how privacy can be a casualty on both sides of the political spectrum. While we are fortunately not dealing with such realities, every day we see how political alliances are fickle. Politicians who prefer a smaller and less intrusive state are less likely to support campaigns calling for the regulation of the use of personal information by the private sector. These same politicians on the 'right' are often pro-surveillance when it involves national security and the management of borders and immigration. For instance, many of the Republicans in the US that opposed Clinton-era policies to embed surveillance into communications standards, amongst them former Senator John Ashcroft, became strong advocates of greater surveillance after 9/11. Similarly, otherwise principled advocates of democratic rights are sometimes the very same people who oppose adherence to international human rights standards on the grounds of state sovereignty. That is, these conventions may 'interfere' with the sovereign right of states to decide when and how to conduct intrusive surveillance.

Politicians on the left who worry about surveillance discrimination may also part ways with privacy advocates. For instance, in the UK, we are well on the way to having the profiles of 50% of the black male population in the National DNA database by 2010. In response, left-wing thinkers have joined the police in calling for a mandatory DNA database containing the profiles of all citizens, possibly at birth. The left's concern with discrimination has converged with the police's precautionary approach to data collection. Similarly, opposition to US government programmes that fingerprinted foreign visitors from Arab and Muslim nations subsided when the US-VISIT programme began fingerprinting all foreign visitors. Finally, the left's fondness for multi-lateralism left us dumbfounded when UK politicians who opposed national fingerprint-based identity cards supported similar European Union initiatives that would mandate them across the union.

Political expediency and 'bipartisan' initiatives also often enhance surveillance policy. An EU policy requiring the retention of communications transaction logs of all European-based communications was approved by the European Parliament on the legislation's first reading vote because the two largest party-coalitions from the left and the right agreed to the policy out of political expediency. In the UK local councils led by any and all three political parties have vastly expanded CCTV surveillance because the measure is politically attractive, despite the fact that the effectiveness of this policy has been cast into doubt even by UK Government research. Recently a police official expressed despair that a small town with little crime installed CCTV costing £10,000 despite no clear need to do so. Political forces from all sides of the spectrum came to the town's defence. Similarly, in Toronto the privacy commissioner of Ontario agreed with the transit network's plans for expanding the network of cameras by 11,000 to act as a deterrent against crime, despite extensive research showing otherwise.

15.3 A Proactive Agenda

Unlike some advocacy domains, privacy is (for many countries) already established in law. Privacy exists in constitutions and in parliamentary actions around the world. But as all advocates recognise, regardless of their domain, getting the law on the statute books merely gives it a legal phrasing. For a right to have life it needs constant protecting. If we fail to do that, it becomes merely a statement upon a piece of paper, to which governments and corporations pay mild attention.

It is now common for governments to open their legislative dialogues over surveillance policies by promising that the new policies are in adherence to constitutional and international treatises. They know full well that this 'compliance' is merely spin but more importantly they are confident that few people will question the assertion. Many companies have privacy policies that state their intent to protect privacy and then follow on by ambiguously declaring how they interfere with consumers' private lives. Law and policy and often their associated enforcement mechanisms being courts and regulators, are clearly insufficient. These various institutions appear to be merely applying principles and concepts blandly with little care and lacking in fervour.

Privacy requires constant and passionate campaigning. We have seen countries declare nearly unanimously that privacy must be protected only to see that just a few years later privacy is nearly revoked. There were marches on the streets in the 1970s and 1980s against national censuses and databases and even national commissions establishing the need for privacy but now we all live under surveillance.

While the old battles still must be fought against such things as national databases and the use of marketing data by firms, we must simultaneously focus our attention on areas of upcoming interest, perhaps even before they garner the public attention they deserve. Doing so will keep privacy protection current while also setting a standard for norms and values as technologies and conditions change. Particularly important, for this goal, is to focus our attention on the younger generations and how systems are being developed almost as though institutions were trying to rid them of privacy expectations. Over 70,000 school children in the UK have been fingerprinted in order to take out library books and to pay for school lunches; it is expected that they will not see moral quagmires around national fingerprinting schemes in the way that their grandparents often refer to them as tools of totalitarian states. A spokesman for the UK's Association of Chief Police Officers recently argued that primary school children should be eligible for the DNA database if they exhibit behaviour indicating that they may become criminals in later life. He argued that because of the aforementioned programmes we have been able to desensitise children to fingerprinting, the same can happen to DNA collection, making it acceptable.[5]

As with any complex and highly political policy domain, constant advocacy is necessary, particularly as those who wish to promote surveillance are not imagining, even for a moment, a cessation of their hostilities. In times of peace and times of war, in both bull and bear markets, for both the advancement of the common good and political glory privacy is always under siege.

15.4 A Fuel Crisis in Privacy Action

Despite all of this, privacy activism is possibly the poorest funded form of political activity on such an important issue. Outside of the US there are no full-time funded privacy organisations. Privacy campaigners have to fund their work through other jobs, whether as academics, lawyers, journalists and a myriad of other professions. When funded, privacy advocates only get funding to look at specific issues, e.g., 'privacy and terrorism', 'privacy and communications surveillance' and thus miss out on the broader policy issues.

This has a number of other ramifications, including

1. Privacy advocates can not even afford to travel to meetings and keep regular contact with institutions around the world. We are therefore locked out of essential decision-making processes and forced to adapt to whatever we are served when mere ideas are transformed into policies that cause laws. We are left to comment, or snipe, from the outside and we are then criticised for not having participated in 'open' deliberations that led to agreements.
2. The public discourse is in many ways dictated by what is of interest to the media instead of our own media campaigns. Privacy campaigners must be able to raise the quality of our actions in order to capture the public's interest and imagination. To date we have relied too much on the work of a few experts who are known to international media, who are dogged by journalists around the world but who receive no recognition for all of their hard work. In turn the media organisations decide the stories and privacy advocates are called on to react, rather than trying to dictate future events. In a similar vein, modern media campaigning involves using alternative media that are quite expensive, e.g., generating online video content, so while our opponents are able to generate content to promote their views using new media, we remain at the end of a telephone line waiting for it to ring.

[5] Mark Townsend and Anushka Asthana, 'Put young children on DNA list, urge police', The Observer, March 16 2008, available at http://www.guardian.co.uk/society/2008/mar/16/youthjustice.children/print.

Privacy and surveillance are key components of many modern policy issues today. We need to start broadening our areas of work in order to cater for this spread, or else we will wake up in ten years from now, having fought law enforcement policies for a decade and may be won some and lost others and yet still find ourselves in a surveillance society. It is completely understandable that proponents of next-generation invasive ID cards point to the fact that consumers have never rejected grocery-store loyalty cards and therefore have no problem with invasive systems. Of course they carry those cards because we have never been able to mount campaigns against them while we focus on a myriad of other funded issues. But every proposal submitted to funders to fund action in broader issues has been rejected.

This does not bode well for the future of privacy. As the issue broadens out we remain stuck in old mindsets, forced by the media, by the volume of issues and policies from the law enforcement and online worlds, or by the inability to gain funds to broaden our work.

But we must shift our focus from viewing privacy as a 'technology and society' issue and rather we must recognise that it is a key political issue of our times. Most other policies rely on privacy and surveillance, ranging from environmental policies, homeless policies, health and genetics policy, policing, immigration policy, etc. As such, privacy advocates must start becoming experts in these other issue areas and start engaging in the policy debates on immigration, carbon footprints, genetic issues, etc.

This branching out for privacy can only be enabled if we can devise a way of perceiving privacy not merely as a human right, nor merely as a consumer right. We must find a way to see privacy as effective public policy. Doing so will probably not fix the funding problem but would at least cover the breadth issue. If we can find a way of arguing that privacy enhances the likelihood of a public policy being effective then we can find many more opportunities to weigh in to policy debate and perhaps we may find many more friends.

Our 'friends' to date have been mostly from the political sphere, which as I have mentioned earlier, is fraught with conflict and challenges. But if we can perceive privacy protection as effective public policy that can enhance consumer confidence, reduce likelihood of security breaches and costs, ensure proportionality and necessity, a creator or trust-builder in new markets and products, amongst others, then our alliances may grow. We could then reach out to regulators outside of the traditional privacy space, consumer groups who have focused on ethics as quality and sustainability rather than as civil liberties and industry representatives who see privacy adherence as an obligatory passage point to the hearts, minds and pockets of consumers. At long last we could have a positive agenda for moving forward and be able to engage in debates that put our opponents on their back feet as they will appear to be conflicting with consumer and citizen interests.

This is not supposed to be some revelation. In a way we have all been doing this for some time now. My own organisation has spent the past two years actively engaging with companies, many of them the very same companies that we are campaigning against. We are reaching out to consumer groups to promote privacy as a confidence issue. We meet with Parliamentarians and government officials who want to hear the weaknesses in their policies and how they can engage with citizens to promote good policy. In sum we are contending that privacy protection is not merely good for the protection of the rights of individuals but also because it is merely good sense. While we continue to be poorly funded in our tasks, we do feel like we are accomplishing something. And after twelve years in this field, it feels good to finally write those words.

Chapter 16
Developing an Adequate Legal Framework for International Data Transfers

Christopher Kuner

With the EU Data Protection Directive[1] (hereinafter referred to as the "General Directive") having been in force now for over ten years, it is wise to examine the basic concepts and assumptions on which the Directive is based, to determine whether it is functioning properly.[2] It is the thesis of this paper that the present EU legal framework for "adequacy" decisions for the international transfer of personal data is inadequate, in both a procedural and substantive sense, and needs reform.[3]

16.1 Procedural Problems and the Mathematics of Adequacy

An examination of the current adequacy system shows that it is cumbersome, expensive, slow, and sends the wrong message to third countries. Under Article 25(1) of the General Directive, "the Member States shall provide that the transfer to a third

C. Kuner (✉)
Partner, Hunton & Williams, Brussels, e-mail: ckuner@hunton.com. Chairman, Task Force on Privacy and the Protection of Personal Data of the International Chamber of Commerce (ICC).
This article is written in the author's personal capacity. It reflects the legal status as of January 2008.

[1] Directive (EC) 95/46 of the European Parliament and of the Council of 24 October 1995 on the protection of individuals with regard to the processing of personal data and on the free movement of such data [1995] OJ L281/31.

[2] As Wagner's Hans Sachs sings in Act One, Scene Three of *Die Meistersinger von Nürnberg*: "Gesteht, ich kenn' die Regeln gut, und dass die Zunft die Regeln bewahr', bemüh' ich mich selbst schon manches Jahr. Doch einmal im Jahre fänd' ich's weise, dass man die Regeln selbst probier', ob in der Gewohnheit trägem Gleise ihr' Kraft und Leben nicht sich verlier' !"/"You'll admit I know the rules well; and to see that the guild preserves the rules I have busied myself this many a year. But once a year I should find it wise to test the rules themselves, to see whether in the dull course of habit their strength and life doesn't get lost".

[3] Unless otherwise noted, this chapter will deal solely with adequacy decisions and the concept of "adequate protection" under Article 25 of the General Directive, but not with "adequate safeguards" under Article 26 of the same Directive, so that it will not deal with issues such as binding corporate rules or the use of standard contractual clauses for international data transfers.

S. Gutwirth et al. (eds.), *Reinventing Data Protection?*
DOI 10.1007/978-1-4020-9498-9_16,

country of personal data which are undergoing processing or are intended for processing after transfer may take place only if, without prejudice to compliance with the national provisions adopted pursuing to the other provisions of this Directive, the third country in question ensures an adequate level of protection." A formal finding of adequacy is carried out by the Member States and the European Commission following the procedure set out in Article 30(1) of the General Directive, with the advice of the Article 29 Working Party.[4] So far only a handful of adequacy determinations have been rendered by the European Commission[5], which cover, for example, Argentina[6], Canada[7] the Bailiwick of Guernsey[8], the Isle of Man[9], Switzerland[10] and the US safe harbor system.[11] In addition, on 23 July 2007 the European Council approved an agreement reached between the European Union and the US Department of Homeland Security (DHS) recognizing that the DHS provides an adequate level of protection for airline passenger (PNR) data transferred from the EU.[12]

---

[4] General Directive, Article 25(6). See General Directive, Article 30(1)(b) regarding advice by the Article 29 Working Party. In theory EU Member States may also make formal adequacy determinations; see General Directive, Article 25(3), stating "the Member States and the Commission shall inform each other of cases where they consider that a third country does not ensure an adequate level of protection...". However, in practice greatest importance is attached to decisions made at a pan-EU level by the European Commission.

[5] In 2000, the European Commission also issued an adequacy decision for Hungary, but this is no longer in force following Hungary's accession to the EU. Commission Decision (EC) 2000/519 of 26 July 2000 pursuant to Directive (EC) 95/46 of the European Parliament and of the Council on the adequate protection of personal data provided in Hungary [2000] OJ L215/4. Since this chapter was finalized, an additional adequacy decision has been issued covering the Bailiwick of Jersey. Commission Decision of 8 May 2008 pursuant to Directive 95/46/EC of the European Parliament and of the Council on the adequate protection of personal data in Jersey (2008/393/EC) [2008] OJ L138/21.

[6] Commission Decision C(2003)1731 of 30 June 2003 pursuant to Directive (EC) 95/46 of the European Parliament and of the Council on the adequate protection of personal data in Argentina [2003] OJ L168.

[7] The adequacy decision applies to Canadian organizations subject to the Canadian Personal Information Protection and Electronic Documents Act (PIPED Act). See Commission Decision (EC) 2002/2 of 20 December 2001 pursuant to Directive (EC) 95/46 of the European Parliament and of the Council on the adequate protection of personal data provided by the Canadian Personal Information Protection and Electronic Documents Act [2002] OJ L2/13.

[8] Commission Decision 2003/821 of 21 November 2003 on the adequate protection of personal data in Guernsey [2003] OJ L308.

[9] Commission Decision 2004/411 of 28 April 2004 on the adequate protection of personal data in the Isle of Man [2004] OJ L151/1.

[10] Commission Decision (EC) 2000/518 of 26 July 2000 pursuant to Directive (EC) 95/46 of the European Parliament and of the Council on the adequate protection of personal data provided in Switzerland [2000] OJ L215/1.

[11] Commission Decision (EC) 2000/520 of 26 July 2000 pursuant to Directive (EC) 95/46 of the European Parliament and of the Council on the adequacy of the protection provided by the safe harbor privacy principles and related frequently asked questions issued by the US Department of Commerce [2000] OJ L215/7.

[12] Council Decision 2007/551/CFSP/JHA of 23 July 2007 on the signing, on behalf of the European Union, of an Agreement between the European Union and the United States of America on

Reaching an adequacy determination is a lengthy process that is complicated by political factors. One can better understand the difficulty of reaching adequacy decisions if one considers how long it would take for the remaining countries in the world to be found adequate. There are currently 192 Member States of the United Nations, and if one subtracts the 27 EU Member States and the three countries of the European Free Trade Association (EFTA) (Iceland, Lichtenstein, and Norway) that have ratified the General Directive, this leaves 162 countries eligible for adequacy. One can then subtract the six further countries that have already been found adequate, leaving 156 countries.[13] For the sake of argument, one can then assume that perhaps half of these remaining countries would never be found adequate for various reasons, such as they do not have a democratic system of government, a functioning legal system, or other basic requirements for adequacy, thus leaving 78 possible adequacy candidates. If one assumes that future adequacy decisions will be approved at the same rate as they have been since the Directive came into force (namely at a rate of six countries approximately every ten years), then it would take approximately one hundred and thirty years for these 78 countries to be found adequate. While 130 years may be a reasonable timescale for building the Pyramid of Cheops or the Great Wall of China, it is clearly absurd with regard to passing adequacy decisions, and shows the flaws in the present system.

The system of adequacy determinations seems to be so slow for various reasons. First of all, one of the first steps in an adequacy decision is the preparation of a study on the legal system of the country in question by the European Commission. Such studies are difficult and time-consuming, since they require highly specialized linguistic, legal and data protection expertise. As both the European Commission and the national data protection authorities lack the necessary resources to perform such studies, they have to turn to outside contractors, which slows down the process. The problems in carrying out such studies are particularly acute with regard to countries that have legal and linguistic structures radically different from those in Europe (such as Asian countries), and for which very little specialized expertise is available. Political factors can also sometimes enter into the process of negotiating adequacy determinations; an example of this is the decision concerning Argentina, where a number of data protection authorities had misgivings as to whether the Argentine system should be found adequate, but the decision was ultimately approved because of politics.

These factors also explain why adequacy decisions are much easier to pass for smaller countries than for large complex ones; unfortunately, it is precisely these larger countries for which there is a greater need for adequacy decisions, since data

---

the processing and transfer of Passenger Name Record (PNR) data by air carriers to the United States Department of Homeland Security (DHS) (2007 PNR Agreement) [2007] OJ L204/16.

[13] The Working Party 29 has found that the Faroe Islands and Jersey offer an adequate level of data protection. Article 29 Working Party, Opinion 9/2007 on the level of protection of personal data in the Faroe Islands (WP 142, 9 October 2007); Opinion 8/2007 on the level of protection of personal data in Jersey (WP 141, 9 October 2007). Since this chapter was finalized, an additional adequacy decision has been issued covering the Bailiwick of Jersey. See supra footnote 5.

controllers are more likely to seek to transfer personal data to large countries with great economic importance than to small countries. This is demonstrated by examining the gross domestic product (GDP) of countries for which adequacy decisions have already been rendered.[14] For 2006, the GDP of the six countries for which adequacy decisions have so far been rendered equals approximately 31% of global GDP. While this is an impressive figure, the vast majority of it comprises the GDP of the USA, and when one subtracts US GDP from this figure, only 3.8% of world GDP is covered by the remaining five adequacy decisions. This means that most of the countries for which adequacy decisions have been rendered are not of the greatest economic importance and the large, dynamic economies to which data are increasingly being transferred (such as China, India and Japan) are currently not covered by adequacy decisions. Indeed, it is questionable whether an adequacy decision could ever be passed for any of these countries, because of the extreme complexity of evaluating their legal and cultural systems against the requirements of EU data protection law.[15] In addition, some third countries resent the EU sitting in judgment of their legal structure as being "adequate" or "inadequate", which has led to political tensions.[16]

16.2 Substantive Problems with Adequacy

In evaluating substantive problems with the adequacy concept, it is important to consider the legal status of "adequacy" in data protection law. The prohibition against transferring personal data to third countries without an adequate level of data protection seems to have a different legal quality than do basic data protection principles, such as proportionality, security and purpose limitation. This can be seen by looking at the General Directive, in which rules on data processing are contained in Chapter II ("General rules on the lawfulness of the processing of personal data"), whereas restrictions on international data transfers are contained in a separate Chapter IV ("Transfer of personal data to third countries"). It is also striking that in its own adequacy decisions, the European Commission does not always require that third countries found adequate themselves prohibit the transfer of personal data to non-adequate countries. For example, the Canadian Personal Information Protection and Electronic Documents Act (PIPED Act (PIPEDA)) has been found adequate, even though the Act itself contains no such prohibition. Similarly, the Article 29 Working

---

[14] Figures are taken from the World Bank, see http://siteresources.worldbank.org/DATASTATISTICS/ Resources/GDP.pdf.

[15] The author is aware of a case in which a study concerning adequacy for a large Asian country had to be abandoned since it proved impossible to put together a team for the study with the necessary qualifications.

[16] E.g., tensions arose between Australia and the EU concerning the Article 29 Working Party's evaluation of Australian privacy law published in March 2001. Article 29 Working Party, Opinion 3/2001 on the level of protection of the Australian Privacy Amendment (Private Sector) Act 2000 (WP 40, 26 January 2001).

Party has not included restrictions on international data transfers based on adequacy as one of the key factors in evaluating whether third countries offer an adequate level of data protection.[17]

Thus, restricting data transfers to non-adequate countries seems not to be considered a fundamental principle of data protection law. The rationale behind the adequacy concept is the desire to maintain a high level of data protection throughout the EU by preventing circumvention of EU rules through the transfer of processing to third countries with a lower standard of data protection.[18] As such, the concept serves a political end (preventing circumvention of EU law), rather than being a principle of data processing in itself. However, there are other ways to prevent circumvention of EU law that are more efficient and effective than the adequacy concept.

16.3 Possible Improvements to the Adequacy System

Before considering alternatives to the adequacy approach, it is useful to consider changes that could be made in the short term to make the present system more efficient. The following are some suggestions along these lines:

- First of all, if the present system of rendering adequacy decisions for entire countries is to be maintained, more financial and personnel resources will have to be made available for this purpose. At the present time, the relevant units of the European Commission and most national data protection authorities are understaffed and under-resourced,[19] and this situation will have to be improved if the

[17] See Article 29 Working Party, Working Document on Transfers of personal data to third countries: Applying Articles 25 and 26 of the EU data protection directive (WP12, 24 July 1998), page 6, where the Working Party lists six key factors to be taken into account when evaluating adequacy (purpose limitation; data quality and proportionality; transparency; security; rights of access, rectification and opposition; and restrictions on onward transfers), and does not include data transfer restrictions to non-adequate countries among these principles.

[18] See U Dammann and S Simitis, *EG-Datenschutzrichtlinie* (Nomos Verlagsgesellschaft, 1997) 270. See also Article 29 Working Party, Discussion Document: First Orientations on Transfers of Personal Data to Third Countries – Possible Ways Forward in Assessing Adequacy (WP4, 26 June 1997), page 12, in which the Article 29 Working Party states regarding Council of Europe Convention 108 that "a missing element of the Convention in terms of the content of its substantive rules is the absence of restrictions on transfers to countries not party to it. This creates the risk that a Convention 108 country could be used as a 'staging post' in a data transfer from the Community to a further third country with entirely inadequate protection levels." An adequacy rule was later added to the Convention 108 as an additional protocol: Convention for the Protection of Individuals with regard to Automatic Processing of Personal Data, January 28, 1981, ETS 108 (1981), Additional Protocol to the Convention for the Protection of Individuals with regards to Automatic Processing of Personal Data, regarding Supervisory Authorities and Transborder Data Flows, November 8, 2001, ETS 181 (20001), Article 2.

[19] See L Speer, "Variable Funding of EU Privacy Law Means Uneven Enforcement Across European Union" (January 2007) *World Data Protection Report*, page 24.

institutions responsible for making adequacy determinations are to do so on a more efficient scale.

- The procedures for adequacy decisions should be better communicated to third countries. At present, little information is available about the procedures that countries must go through to be declared adequate. There seems also to be general confusion among third countries as to what they have to do to initiate an adequacy review: while the European Commission often states that it only initiates an adequacy proceeding based on a request by a third country, many third countries seem to believe that it is up to the EU to approach them about an adequacy review.
- The adoption of tools and "best practices" for adequacy decisions could also help. Thus, the European Commission could adopt standardized checklists that countries would use in preparing for an adequacy review; could prepare a written document setting forth the procedure for determining adequacy and the steps that countries have to follow; could set standardized deadlines for the various steps in an adequacy determination; and could make these materials available on the Internet. All of these measures would help streamline the adequacy process.
- Greater use should be made of partial or sectoral adequacy decisions. It is not clear why at the present time the European Commission has been concentrating on adequacy decisions covering an entire country, which are necessarily more complex and difficult to reach than more limited decisions. In many countries there are specific laws covering data processing in different sectors and the level of protection may differ substantially among different sectors.[20] Thus, greater use could be made of adequacy decisions covering a specific industry, a specific type of data processing, or a specific law or regulation. Examples of such decisions already exist, such as those concerning the US safe harbor system (which covers those companies that have voluntarily joined safe harbor) or the Canadian PIPED Act (which only covers data processing that falls under that Act). Such limited adequacy decisions would be quicker and easier to reach than those covering entire countries, and could be fine-tuned to cover types of data transfers and data processing where there is the greatest need for adequacy decisions.

[20] See Article 29 Working Party, Working Document on Transfers of personal data to third countries: Applying Articles 25 and 26 of the EU data protection directive (WP12, 24 July 1998), page 26, in which the Article 29 Working Party recognized that many third countries have different levels of data protection in different economic sectors. See also See Charles D. Raab, Colin J. Bennett, Robert M. Gellman, Nigel Waters, "Application of a methodology designed to assess the adequacy of the level of protection of individuals with regards to processing personal data: test of the method on several categories of transfer", Final Report, European Commission tender No. XV/97/18/D, September 1998, which study examines the level of data protection in six selected third countries and concludes that in many of them, the level of protection differs among various sectors.

16.4 Accountability: An Alternative Standard for International Data Transfers

Following these criticisms of the present adequacy system, one might ask if it would not be better to scrap the system altogether and simply allow the international transfer of data outside the EU with no legal restrictions. In fact, experience since enactment of the General Directive has shown that there is a need for legal principles to ensure that personal data remain protected once they are transferred outside of national borders. Allowing personal data to be transferred outside of the EU with no protection would deal a significant blow to the confidence of European citizens in the processing of their personal data, which could have grave repercussions for e-commerce and the economy. Thus, there is a need for some legal structure to ensure that personal data are not deprived of protection once they are transferred outside the EU. However, such protection need not necessarily be achieved through the use of an adequacy standard. In fact, there is another principle that could provide such protection more efficiently, namely the principle of accountability. Under an accountability standard, the data exporter remains responsible for personal data once they are transferred outside his country or region and must take measures ensuring that the data are protected when processed in third countries. Furthermore, the data exporter remains liable for any damage or harm resulting from misuse of the personal data outside of its country or region.

Accountability has several advantages over an adequacy standard:

- First, accountability does not require the enactment of adequacy decisions covering an entire country or sector in a lengthy and cumbersome process, but is determined for each individual data transfer based on the precautions taken by a particular data exporter. It is thus more flexible than an adequacy standard.
- Second, the accountability principle ensures that there is always a party in the individual's own country who remains liable and to whom the individual may turn if there is a problem with regard to the processing of the personal data outside of the EU.
- Third, the accountability standard avoids quixotic attempts to convince third countries to conform their laws to EU standards, which process tends to be lengthy and to lead to tensions with such countries.

An accountability standard is already recognized in data protection law. For example, the 28th International Data Protection Commissioners Conference held in London approved on November 3, 2006 a "Global Privacy Standard" (GPS) that attempts to find a set of data protection principles that are consistent with and reflect the laws of different countries around the world. The GPS endorses an accountability approach.[21] The Canadian PIPED Act also contains an accountability

[21] See A Cavoukian, Creation of a Global Privacy Standard, page 3, http://www.ipc.on.ca/images/Resources/up-gps.pdf: "2. Accountability: Collection of personal information entails a duty of care for its protection. Responsibility for all privacy related policies and procedures shall be documented and communicated as appropriate, and assigned to a specified individual within the organization.

approach to ensure that personal data are protected once they are transferred outside of Canada by private sector entities.[22] The accountability approach is also accepted by many third countries, such as the APEC countries.[23] An accountability approach would thus be seen as less paternalistic than the present EU adequacy approach and would be more likely to find global acceptance. The accountability approach has already been used in some countries in enforcement cases involving international data transfers.[24]

It would exceed the boundaries of this paper to explain all the details of how an accountability approach would work in practice. However, as a first step it would be necessary to investigate what legal mechanisms could ensure that the data exporter remained accountable and responsible for data processing once such data have been transferred outside the EU. This might include reliance on liability concepts under national law, or use of data transfer mechanisms that are already recognized, such as binding corporate rules or the use of standard contractual clauses. Any such mechanisms would hopefully be harmonized to the greatest extent possible (e.g., through guidance issued by the European Commission, or decisions issues by the Commission recognizing certain mechanisms to ensure accountability) to prevent a splintering of the law. Some, but not all, of these steps would likely require amendment of the General Directive.

Another possible approach would be to keep the present adequacy system but introduce elements of an accountability approach into it. This could mean, for example, that greater emphasis would be put on data transfer protections that offer

---

When transferring personal information to third parties, organizations shall seek equivalent privacy protection through contractual or other means."

[22] See Section 5, 4.1.3 of PIPEDA: "An organization is responsible for personal information in its possession or custody, including information that has been transferred to a third party for processing. The organization shall use contractual or other means to provide a comparable level of protection while the information is being processed by a third party."

[23] APEC Privacy Framework, Accountability Principle, http://www.apec.org/apec/apec_groups/committees/committee_on_trade/electronic_commerce.MedialibDownload.v1.html?url=/etc/medialib/apec_media_library/downloads/taskforce/ecsg/pubs/2005.Par.0001.File.v1.1: "A personal information controller should be accountable for complying with measures that give effect to the Principles stated above. When personal information is to be transferred to another person or organization, whether domestically or internationally, the personal information controller should obtain the consent of the individual or exercise due diligence and take reasonable steps to ensure that the recipient person or organization will protect the information consistently with these Principles."

[24] See, e.g., Canadian Commissioner's Findings, PIPEDA Case Summary #313: Bank's notification to customers triggers PATRIOT Act concerns (October 19, 2005). In this case, the Office of the Privacy Commissioner of Canada received a number of complaints after the Canadian Imperial Bank of Commerce (the CIBC) sent a notification to its VISA customers in the fall of 2004, amending its credit cardholder agreement. The notification referred to the use of a service provider located in the United States and the possibility that US law enforcement or regulatory agencies might be able to obtain access to cardholders' personal information under US law. The Commissioner found that such transfers did not violate PIPEDA, since the CIBC had been transparent about its personal information handling practices and had protected personal information in the hands of foreign-based third-party service providers to the extent possible by contractual means.

realistic hope of redress for data subjects and less emphasis would be put on protections that are difficult or impossible to enforce. Taking the set of approved standard contractual clauses for controller-to-controller transfers approved by the European Commission in 2004 as an example[25], certain obligations of the data importer (e.g., Clause II(f) stating that the data importer will provide the data exporter with evidence of financial resources sufficient to fulfil its responsibilities under the Clauses, or Clause V(c) stating that the data importer will abide by a decision of a competent court of the data exporter's country) could be eliminated, or could be transferred to the data exporter, since they are difficult or impossible to enforce against a party outside the EU.

Use of an accountability approach need not in practice result in a lessening of the level of data protection for international data transfers. Adequacy decisions are at best approximate determinations of a country's level of data protection, and inevitably result in compromises that are open to interpretation. For example, Argentina was found adequate in 2003, but in the same year Amnesty International expressed concerns about serious human rights abuses in the country.[26] Thus, adequacy decisions are far from always being objective and logical, and do not provide a watertight standard of data protection. Indeed, international law places strict limits on the ability to enforce foreign data protection law outside national borders,[27] and no adequacy decision can change that. Thus, while adequacy purports to provide a strong level of protection for personal data, such protection is actually difficult to enforce outside the borders of the EU. By contrast, an accountability standard concentrates on effective protections that are workable in practice, and on granting individuals a remedy against a data exporter in their own country.

Use of an accountability standard does not mean that no regard should ever be paid to the data protection standards in the country of data import; indeed, such standard could be relevant in determining whether the data exporter could be held fully accountable for any violation of data protection rights. Both the GPS and PIPEDA take into account the level of data protection offered in the country of data import, but evaluate the data transfer on a case-by-case basis, rather than making a blanket decision as to whether legal protection in the country is "adequate" or

[25] Commission Decision (EC) 2004/915 of 27 December 2004 amending Decision (EC) 2001/497 as regards the introduction of an alternative set of standard contractual clauses for the transfer of personal data to third countries [2004] OJ L385/74.

[26] See Amnesty International Report 2003, Argentina, http://web.amnesty.org/report2003/Arg-summary-eng: "Hundreds of people were arrested during massive and widespread demonstrations and demonstrators were killed by police in circumstances that suggested that they had been extra judicially executed. Human rights defenders, journalists and social activists were reportedly harassed and assaulted. Reports of killings and ill-treatment by police continued. During a mass raid on an indigenous community, police ill-treated and racially abused indigenous people. Judicial decisions in Argentina and new initiatives abroad to investigate past human rights violations were announced."

[27] See Christopher Kuner, European Data Protection Law: Corporate Compliance and Regulation, page 125 (2nd edition Oxford University Press 2007).

"inadequate".[28] A "fail safe" clause could be incorporated into any accountability arrangement that would give data protection authorities the power to intervene when it was clear that there would likely be a serious risk of the misuse of personal data, such as in cases of data transfers to pariah states, or if there was a sudden and drastic deterioration in the level of democracy or legal protection that the data would be afforded in the country of import.[29]

16.5 Conclusions

The present adequacy standard is clearly inadequate, both from a procedural and substantive point of view. The standard was created for a world in which the Internet was not widely used, and in which data did not flow as easily across national borders as they do now. The present system of adequacy decisions has been grievously overloaded by the great increase in data flows in the past few years, and also drains resources that could better be used in other areas of data protection.

An accountability approach would be more efficient and would also provide for more effective protection for transborder data flows than the adequacy standard. Adequacy is not a fundamental principle of data protection law, but rather a political principle that was adopted in order to prevent the circumvention of EU rules by transferring data processing to third countries. Accountability would also provide incentives for data controllers not to circumvent EU rules, since they would remain responsible for data processing in any event even if the data are transferred outside of the EU. Furthermore, accountability requires that there is a party based in the EU that would remain liable for data processing, so that both individuals and data protection authorities always have someone to turn to in their own jurisdiction if a problem arises.

A comparison of the present adequacy system and a possible accountability system for international data transfers demonstrates that often the best can be the enemy of the good. The difficulty of reaching adequacy determinations has meant that such decisions have mainly been rendered for smaller countries with similar

---

[28] The GPS requires that organizations seek "equivalent privacy protection through contractual or other means", while Section 5. 4.1.3 of PIPEDA provides that "the organization shall use contractual or other means to provide a comparable level of protection while the information is being processed by a third party".

[29] This approach was used by the Canadian Federal Commissioner in PIPEDA Case Summary #313: Bank's notification to customers triggers PATRIOT Act concerns (October 19, 2005). In that case, the Commissioner found that PIPEDA had not been violated by data transfers to the US that could be accessed by US law enforcement authorities, but seemed to base this conclusion at least in part on the fact that the US offers a "comparable level" of privacy protection to that in Canada, thus leaving the door open to take action in the case of data transfers to countries that do not offer such a comparable level. However, note that this case was decided not only under PIPEDA, but also under subsection 245(1) of the Canadian Bank Act, which requires in the case of outsourcing of data processing by banks outside of Canada that such data transfers receive the approval of the Canadian Office of the Superintendent of Financial Institutions (OSFI).

legal systems to those of the EU, so that data transfers to other countries are often left to take place without any legal protection at all. An adequacy standard seems to create a watertight legal structure protecting the processing of personal data outside of the EU, but in practice such protection is often impossible to ensure, given the fact that the enforceability of EU law stops at the borders of the EU Member States. An accountability approach may seem to lack some of the more detailed protections of the adequacy systems, but it does provide effective protection, since it ensures that there is a party in the EU against which enforcement may be taken. Even if an accountability standard is not adopted, at least some basic steps should be taken to make the process of issuing adequacy decisions more effective, such as granting more resources to the data protection authorities and the data protection unit of the European Commission, providing increased transparency about the adequacy process, and developing standardized tools for countries that are working toward adequacy.

It can only be hoped that European policy makers will take a hard look at the current adequacy system and its present failings and reform the system in a way that more effectively protects the interests of data controllers, individuals, and data protection supervisory authorities.

Chapter 17
Towards a Common European Approach to Data Protection: A Critical Analysis of Data Protection Perspectives of the Council of Europe and the European Union

Sjaak Nouwt

17.1 Introduction

In this contribution I will focus on the background of Data Protection (DP) regulations in Europe. The question whether a common approach exists for data protection in Europe can, in my opinion, be answered with "No", at least: "Not yet". This lack of a common approach is probably mainly caused by the fact that the development of DP legislation in Europe has been based on different aims and perspectives. This is a result of the existing difference in characters of the institutions that are responsible for DP legislation. Furthermore, there are also differences on how DP legislation in case law is applied at European and national levels. This is caused by differences in interpretations of the rules and definitions in the Member States.

National DP legislations have, for example, been drafted under the influence of regulations by the European Union (EU), the Council of Europe (CoE) and the Organisation for Economic Co-operation and Development (OECD). The EU and OECD and the DP regulations they drafted, especially EU Directive 95/46/EC and the OECD Privacy Guidelines 1980, were based on economic factors. The DP regulations made by the CoE, especially the Convention for the Protection of Human Rights and Fundamental Freedoms, Convention No. 108 and several Recommendations, have been drafted from a human rights perspective. National legislations have been established under the influence of both perspectives. First of all, national DP legislations have been drafted so that Convention No. 108 could be ratified. Not every EU Member State had ratified Convention No. 108 at the beginning of the nineties so the EU decided to draft a DP Directive. Directive 95/46/EC has had more effect in the EU Member States because of the legal obligation to implement

S. Nouwt (✉)
Royal Dutch Medical Association (KNMG), Utrecht, and Privacy Consultant, Tilburg, The Netherlands (formerly: TILT, Tilburg University, Netherlands)
e-mail: s.nouwt@fed.knmg.nl

S. Gutwirth et al. (eds.), *Reinventing Data Protection?*
DOI 10.1007/978-1-4020-9498-9_17,

this Directive into national legislation. Can we therefore conclude that the economic perspective has more influence on DP legislation in Europe than the human rights perspective?

At national level, every EU Member State has now implemented Directive 95/46/EC, although the European Commission thinks that the application of this Directive at national level can be improved. The application of EU DP regulations also differ as a result of different interpretations of definitions and applications in national case law. Examples of such cases are the Durant-case (UK) and the Dexia-case (NL). Finally, self-regulatory DP initiatives also exist at national level and there is only one at EU level.

I will conclude with the following questions:

- Would DP be better from a human rights approach or an economic approach?
- Money makes the world go around but what about Data Protection?
- Google calls for Global Privacy Standards: a Devil in Disguise?

17.2 Data Protection from an Economic Perspective

17.2.1 The Organisation for Economic Co-Operation and Development

The Organisation for Economic Co-operation and Development (OECD) is an economic organization and is not involved in human rights activities. Its roots lie in the Marshall Plan.[1] On a vast range of economic issues, the OECD provides analysis and advice. The OECD drafts internationally agreed instruments, decisions and recommendations to promote the rules of the game in many areas, like combating bribery in international business transactions, taxation, environment and information and communications policy. However, the OECD has more (30) and other members than the EU. Among the OECD members are big non-European countries like Australia, Canada, Japan, New Zealand and the USA. As a result, the scope of these Guidelines is worldwide.

The OECD published its Guidelines on the Protection of Privacy and Transborder Flows of Personal Data (1980) at the beginning of the 1980s.[2] These Guidelines are still valid and contain the famous eight basic privacy principles:

1. Collection Limitation Principle
2. Data Quality Principle
3. Purpose Specification Principle
4. Use Limitation Principle

---

[1] See also: OECD, Annual Report 2007, p. 7. Available at: <http://www.oecd.org/dataoecd/1/53/38484866.pdf> (last visited, January 11, 2008).

[2] The OECD Privacy Guidelines are available at: <http://www.oecd.org/document/18/0,3343,en_2649_34255_1815186_1_1_1_1,00.html> (last visited, January 11, 2008).

5. Security Safeguards Principle
6. Openness Principle
7. Individual Participation Principle
8. Accountability Principle.

In 1985, the OECD published the Declaration on Transborder Data Flows.[3] Considering the OECD Privacy Guidelines (1980), the OECD pays attention to policy issues related to the so-called transborder data flows. These international flows of computerised data and information are considered an important consequence of technological advances and they play an increasing role in national economies. At the same time, data protection can be considered a guarantee for the cross border free flow of personal data, by creating an equivalent level of protection in the Member States.

In this Declaration, the OECD expresses the intention to:

- Promote access to data and information and related services and avoid the creation of unjustified barriers to the international exchange of data and information;
- Seek transparency in regulations and policies relating to information, computer and communications services affecting transborder data flows;
- Develop common approaches for dealing with issues related to transborder data flows and, when appropriate, develop harmonized solutions;
- Consider possible implications for other countries when dealing with issues related to transborder data flows.

At the conference, "A Borderless World: Realising the Potential of Global Electronic Commerce" in Ottawa, Canada on 7–9 October 1998, the OECD Ministers accepted the Ministerial Declaration on the Protection of Privacy.[4] This Declaration has served as the basis for the OECD privacy protection work since 1998. In this Declaration, the Ministers stated that they will reaffirm their commitment on the protection of privacy on global networks in order to ensure the respect of important rights, build confidence in global networks and to prevent unnecessary restrictions on transborder flows of personal data. The Ministers also declared that bridges should be built to ensure privacy protection on global networks based on the OECD Guidelines and that they will take necessary steps to ensure that the OECD Privacy Guidelines are effectively implemented on global networks.

In 2002, the OECD published the report: "Privacy Online: OECD Guidance on Policy and Practice". This report offers policy and practical guidance to help implement the OECD Privacy Guidelines for the online processing of personal data. The report draws together work on alternative dispute resolution, privacy-enhancing technologies, online privacy policies, enforcement and redress, in relation to e-commerce. The guidance includes a practical tool in the form of a privacy policy

---

[3] This Declaration is available at: <http://www.oecd.org/document/25/0,3343,en_2649_34255_1888153_1_1_1_1,00.html> (last visited, January 11, 2008).

[4] Available at: <http://www.oecd.org/dataoecd/39/13/1840065.pdf> (last visited, January 11, 2008).

statement generator to help organisations develop privacy policies and statements for display on their websites.[5]

In June 2006 the OECD Working Party on Information Security and Privacy (WPISP) published the report: "Making Privacy Notices Simple: an OECD Report and Recommendations".[6] The WPISP recognises that a privacy notice on a website is an excellent tool to disclose an organisation's privacy practices and policies. However, many notices are too lengthy, confusing and contain complex legal language. In this report the WPISP recommends that privacy notices should be short, simple and usable for individuals to assimilate the information they contain and to compare the privacy practices of the organisations processing their personal data.

In 2006, the OECD started to examine the cross-border aspects of privacy law enforcement. After the Report on "Cross-border Enforcement of Privacy Laws" (October 2006), the OECD published in 2007 the "Recommendation on Cross-border Co-operation in the Enforcement of Laws Protecting Privacy". The recommendation contains a framework for co-operation in the enforcement of privacy laws. The purpose is that governments improve their domestic frameworks for privacy law enforcement to better enable their authorities to co-operate with foreign authorities and to provide mutual assistance to one another in the enforcement of privacy laws.[7]

From these OECD initiatives we can conclude that from an economic perspective, data protection should be considered as a guarantee for the transborder flow of personal data.

17.2.2 The European Union

The European Union (EU) also has an economic background. Before 1993 (the Treaty on European Union, signed at Maastricht, came into force on November 1, 1993), the EU was known as the European Economic Community (EEC). The EEC originated from the European Coal and Steel Community (ECSC), which was established in 1952.

At EU level, the DP Directive 95/46/EC was drafted by DG Internal Market. The DP Directive is applicable to the first pillar (Community-pillar) of the EU.[8] From the fact that DG Internal Market drafted this Directive and because of the EU's originally economic background, it is easy to understand this Directive's important economic purpose, namely to level privacy for the transborder flow of personal data

[5] The privacy policy statement generator is available at: <www.oecd.org/sti/privacygenerator> (last visited, January 11, 2008).

[6] Available at: <http://www.olis.oecd.org/olis/2006doc.nsf/LinkTo/NT00003A7E/$FILE/JT03212212.PDF> (last visited, January 11, 2008).

[7] See also: <www.oecd.org/sti/privacycooperation> (last visited, January 11, 2008).

[8] The second pillar is Common Foreign and Security Policy (CFSP) and the third pillar is Police and Judicial Co-operation in Criminal Matters (PJCC). The second and third pillar are characterised by autonomy of the Member States.

within the internal market of the EU. This also follows from the title of the Directive: "Directive 95/46/EC on the protection of individuals with regard to the processing of personal data and on the free movement of such data". The scope of Directive 95/46/EC is not only to protect the right to privacy with respect to the processing of personal data (Article 1, par. 1) but also to remove obstacles for the free flow of personal data (Article 1, par. 2). The latter demonstrates the fundamental economic perspective of this Directive.

Other EU DP Directives are Directive 2002/58/EC (privacy and electronic communications) and Directive 2006/24/EC (Data Retention Directive). The EU has also undertaken other related initiatives like: the Proposal for a Council Framework Decision for Police and Judicial Co-operation in Criminal Matters, the Europol information systems, Eurojust, Eurodac, Schengen Information System, the Prüm Treaty (or Schengen III), etc. It would be interesting to examine how these information systems and regulations are related to each other and how they relate to the general DP principles in Directive 95/46/EC. However, this goes beyond the scope of this contribution.

17.3 Data Protection from a Human Rights Perspective

17.3.1 The United Nations

After the "war by terror" (1940–1945)[9], the United Nations (UN) provided a world wide better protection of human rights, including a "right to privacy". The right to privacy was established in Article 12 of the Universal Declaration of Human Rights (1948)[10]:

> No one shall be subjected to arbitrary interference with his privacy, family, home or correspondence, nor to attacks upon his honour and reputation. Everyone has the right to the protection of the law against such interference or attacks.

Later, the UN considered that freedom, justice and peace in the world can only be guaranteed when the dignity and the equal and inalienable rights of all members of the human family are recognized. The recognition of these rights derives from the inherent dignity of the human person. The UN also recognized that after the experiences of WW-II, the ideal of free human beings enjoying civil and political freedom and freedom from fear and want can only be achieved if conditions are created whereby everyone may enjoy his civil and political rights, as well as his economic, social and cultural rights. As a result, in 1966, the UN adopted the International Covenant on Political and Civil Rights.[11]

---

[9] Other than the "War on terror", following the September 11, 2001 attacks in the United States.

[10] The Universal Declaration of Human Rights is available at: <http://www.un.org/Overview/rights.html> (last visited, January 11, 2008).

[11] See also the preamble of the International Covenant on Political and Civil Right, at: <http://www2.ohchr.org/english/law/ccpr.htm> (last visited, January 11, 2008).

More specifically related to the processing of personal data, in 1990 the UN adopted the Guidelines Concerning Computerized Personal Data Files.[12] These guidelines contain minimum guarantees that should be provided in national legislation by a set of general principles. These principles are:

1. Principle of lawfulness and fairness;
2. Principle of accuracy;
3. Principle of the purpose-specification;
4. Principle of interested-person access;
5. Principle of non-discrimination;
6. Power to make exceptions;
7. Principle of security;
8. Supervision and sanctions;
9. Transborder data flows.

These principles should be made applicable in the national legislations to all public and private personal data files.

17.3.2 The Council of Europe

Not long after World War II, in 1950, the Council of Europe (CoE) established the right to private life from a human rights perspective.[13] Article 8 of the European Convention on Human Rights says:

> 1. Everyone has the right to respect for his private and family life, his home and his correspondence.
> 2. There shall be no interference by a public authority with the exercise of this right except such as is in accordance with the law and is necessary in a democratic society in the interests of national security, public safety or the economic well-being of the country, for the prevention of disorder or crime, for the protection of health or morals, or for the protection of the rights and freedoms of others.

The human right to private life has been elaborated by the CoE in the Data Protection Treaty 1981 (ETS No. 108). This Treaty introduced eight DP principles as a legal framework for DP as an element of "private life". These principles are the same basic privacy principles as the ones formulated in the OECD Privacy Guidelines 1980.

The DP Treaty has been elaborated in several Resolutions and Recommendations by the CoE[14]:

---

[12] Available at: <http://www.unhchr.ch/html/menu3/b/71.htm> (last visited, January 11, 2008).

[13] Other than what resulted from the 9/11 attacks, WW-II gave cause for a European-wide improvement of the protection of human rights, including the right to private life.

[14] Source: Council of Europe, Data Protection "Recommendations and Resolutions of the Committee of Ministers". On the internet: <http://www.coe.int/t/e/legal_affairs/legal_co-operation/ data_protection/documents/international_legal_instruments/2Recommendations%20and %20resolutions%20of%20the%20Committee%20of%20Ministers.asp#TopOfPage> (last visited, January 11, 2008).

Recommendations:
Recommendation No.R(2002) 9 on the protection of personal data collected and processed for insurance purposes (18 September 2002).
Recommendation No.R(99) 5 for the protection of privacy on the Internet (23 February 1999).
Recommendation No.R(97) 18 on the protection of personal data collected and processed for statistical purposes (30 September 1997).
Recommendation No.R(97) 5 on the protection of medical data (13 February 1997).
Recommendation No.R(95) 4 on the protection of personal data in the area of telecommunication services, with particular reference to telephone services (7 February 1995).
Recommendation No.R(91) 10 on the communication to third parties of personal data held by public bodies (9 September 1991).
Recommendation No.R(90) 19 on the protection of personal data used for payment and other operations (13 September 1990).
Recommendation No.R(89) 2 on the protection of personal data used for employment purposes (18 January 1989).
Recommendation No.R(87) 15 regulating the use of personal data in the police sector (17 September 1987).
Recommendation No.R(86) 1 on the protection of personal data for social security purposes (23 January 1986).
Recommendation No.R(85) 20 on the protection of personal data used for the purposes of direct marketing (25 October 1985).
Recommendation No.R(83) 10 on the protection of personal data used for scientific research and statistics (23 September 1983) [replaced by Recommendation No. R(97) 18 with regard to statistics].
Recommendation No.R(81) 1 on regulations for automated medical data banks (23 January 1981) [replaced by Recommendation No. R (97) 5].

Resolutions:
Resolution (74) 29 on the protection of individuals vis-à-vis electronic data banks in the public sector.
Resolution (73) 22 on the protection of privacy of individuals vis-à-vis electronic data banks in the private sector.

An interesting research question would be what the effect is of these Recommendations. Has or can their effect be measured? This question also goes beyond the scope of this contribution.

An important criterion in the case law by the European Court on Human Rights (ECHR) is whether, according to the second paragraph of Article 8, an interference with someone's private life is "necessary" in a democratic society and in the interest of national security, public safety or the economic well-being of the country, for the prevention of disorder or crime, for the protection of health or morals, or for the protection of the rights and freedoms of others. According to the Court, "necessary" means that there must be a pressing social need for an interference with a human right.[15] In most case law about Article 8, the Court concludes that there is an interference with the right to one's private life but then the Court checks whether this interference is:

1. in accordance with the law, and
2. necessary in a democratic society in the interests of national security, public safety or the economic well-being of the country, for the prevention of disorder or crime, for the protection of health or morals, or for the protection of the rights and freedoms of others.

For example in the case of *Peck v. The United Kingdom*, the Court considered "whether, in the light of the case as a whole, the reasons adduced to justify the disclosure (*of personal data, SN*) were "relevant and sufficient" and whether the measures were proportionate to the legitimate aims pursued".[16] In § 87 of *Peck v. The United Kingdom*, the Court continues: "Accordingly, the Court considers that the disclosures by the Council of the CCTV material in the CCTV News and to the Yellow Advertiser, Anglia Television and the BBC were not accompanied by sufficient safeguards to prevent disclosure inconsistent with the guarantees of respect for the applicant's private life contained in Article 8. As such, the disclosure constituted a disproportionate and therefore unjustified interference with his private life and a violation of Article 8 of the Convention." What follows from this judgment is, that the necessity test consists in a proportionality (does the aim justify the means?) and subsidiarity test (are there other less intrusive means available?).[17] According to De Hert, the European Court does not impose the necessity test with regard to Article 8, because it does not require blood to violate one's privacy.[18] However, limited by what is "relevant and sufficient" and proportionate, the court leaves the Member States a "margin of appreciation" in considering the pressing social need for an interference with the right to private life.

17.4 Data Protection at National Level

At a national level, the right to privacy is constitutionally protected as a human right, when it is explicitly mentioned in the Constitution (e.g., the Netherlands, Belgium) or when it is recognised as being a part of the constitutional heritage

---

[15] Case of *Handyside v. The United Kingdom*. Judgment of 7 December 1976, § 48.

[16] Case of *Peck v. The United Kingdom*. Judgment of 28 January 2003, § 76. Also available at: <www.privacynetwork.info> (last visited, January 11, 2008).

[17] See also: Paul De Hert, Balancing security and liberty within the European human rights framework. A critical reading of the Court's case law in the light of surveillance and criminal law enforcement strategies after 9/11. *Utrecht Law Review*, Vol. 1, Issue 1 (September) 2005, especially pp. 91–94.

[18] Ibid. p. 89.

(e.g., Canada, USA, France, Germany, Sweden). The Right to Data Protection is also explicitly mentioned in some constitutions, like in those of Sweden and in the Netherlands.[19] This makes data protection at least sound as though it is also a human right. But is it? At the moment, DP legislation in all EU Member States implements the DP Directive. According to the evaluation of the implementation, carried out by the European Commission, the EC sees that no changes are necessary in the Directive but recognises that the application of the Directive should be improved. However, some Member States have still failed to incorporate a number of important provisions of the Directive. "In other cases, transposition of practice has not been conducted in line with the Directive or has fallen outside the margin of manoeuvre left to Member States".[20] Despite the harmonizing character of Directive 95/46/EC, differences in the implementation of the Directive in national legislation still exist.

Also at national level, important case law exists that has effect on the interpretation and application of the Directive. An example is the *Durant-case* (UK).[21] In this case, the Court of Appeal in the United Kingdom considered for example the following question: "What makes 'data' 'personal' within the meaning of 'personal data'?". According to the Information Commissioner, the answer to this question can be interpreted as follows:

> Where an individual's name appears in information the name will only be 'personal data' where its inclusion in the information affects the named individual's privacy. Simply because an individual's name appears on a document, the information contained in that document will not necessarily be personal data about the named individual.

As a result, the fact that your name is on a list, does not as such give you a right to a copy of your personal data.

Another example is the *Dexia-case* (NL). On June 29, 2007 the Dutch Supreme Court published the Dexia decision, about the right of access to one's personal data.[22] The most important question for the Supreme Court was whether a bank is obliged to provide copies of documents and transcriptions of phone calls to the data subjects. In general, the Court concluded that a data subject has a right to copies of such documents and transcriptions of phone calls that contain his or her personal data. According to the Supreme Court, this is the most effective way of providing

---

[19] See also: Paul De Hert, Bert-Jaap Koops and Ronald Leenes, Conclusions and Recommendations. In: Ronald Leenes, Bert-Jaap Koops, Paul De Hert (eds.), *Constitutional Rights and New Technologies. A Comparative Study*. The Hague: T.M.C. Asser Press, 2008, pp. 269–273. IT&Law Series 15.

[20] Commission of the European Communities, *Communication from the Commission to the European Parliament and the Council on the follow-up of the Work Programme for better implementation of the Data Protection Directive*. Brussels, 7 March 2007, COM(2007) 87 final, p. 5. Available at: <http://ec.europa.eu/justice_home/fsj/privacy/docs/lawreport/com_2007_87_f_en.pdf> (last visited, January 11, 2008).

[21] *Michael John Durant v Financial Services Authority* [2003] EWCA Civ 1746, Court of Appeal (Civil Division) decision of Lord Justices Auld, Mummery and Buxton dated 8th December 2003. Also available at: <www.privacynetwork.info> (last visited, January 11, 2008).

[22] Hoge Raad, 29 juni 2007, LJN AZ4664. See also P.J.A. de Hert, M. Hildebrandt, S. Gutwirth, R. Saelens, De WBP na de *Dexia*-uitspraken. *Privacy & Informatie*, 2007/187.

data subjects with information so that they are able to control the legitimacy and correctness of the processing of their personal data. However, the Supreme Court continues, a data subject should not abuse his right of access and, realising this right should not lead to a disproportionate burden for the data controller (the bank) or interfere with the rights and interests of others. As a result, the Dutch Supreme Court has broadly interpreted the right of access.

From the *Durant-case* and the *Dexia-case* it can be concluded that the interpretation of Directive 95/46/EC by national judges can differ. Despite the harmonisation of data protection law by this Directive, differences in the application at national levels still exist.

17.5 Self-Regulation

For a good understanding of self-regulation: there are a lot of self-regulation instruments. Self-regulation instruments can be divided into five clusters: technology-oriented instruments, behaviour-oriented instruments, information instruments, contractual instruments and dispute resolution instruments.[23] The following table shows some examples of self-regulation instruments within each cluster:

Technology-oriented	Behaviour-oriented	Information	Contractual	Dispute resolution
Normalisation	Code of conduct	Hallmark	Terms and conditions	Arbitration
Technical agreements	Protocol	Certification	Standard regulations	Binding recommendation
Regulation by techniques	Gentlemen's agreement	Approval regulation		Mediation
	Covenant	Chain guarantee system		Ombudsman
	Cartel	Visitation		Disciplinary law

The best known example of self-regulation with respect to data protection is perhaps the Code of Conduct. At EU level, only one European Code of Conduct has been approved. This is the Code of Conduct of the Federation of European Direct and Interactive Marketing (FEDMA). This indicates that there is very little interest for self-regulation of data protection at a European level. Self-regulation of data protection ("self-regulation" in the meaning of substitute for state regulation) seems to be deficient. This can also be illustrated by the decline of WebTrader in the Netherlands and in the United Kingdom. According to an EC study[24], the Safe

[23] See also Sjaak Nouwt, *Privacy voor doe-het-zelvers. Over zelfregulering en het verwerken van persoonsgegevens via internet*. Den Haag: Sdu, 2005. ITeR nr. 73. (*Privacy for hobbyists. About self regulation and the processing of personal data on the Internet*).

[24] Commission Staff Working Paper, *The application of Commission Decision 520/2000/EC of 26 July 2000 pursuant to Directive 95/46 of the European Parliament and of the Council on the*

Harbor Program has also been unsuccessful: several companies that adhered to the Safe Harbor Program do not comply with the openness and enforcement principles. Lack of openness, legal certainty and compliance seem to be important deficiencies in the Safe Harbor Program. In the United States there also seems to be a shift from industry self-regulation to government regulation for online privacy.[25] According to privacy polls, this opinion is shared by the majority of the interviewed customers.

17.6 Interesting Developments

With respect to the main question in this contribution, some interesting developments can be mentioned:

1. The Data Protection website of the European Commission has been moved from DG "Internal Market" to the European Union's "area" of "Freedom, Security and Justice".[26] Does this illustrate that within the European Union, Data Protection is moving from the economic approach to the human rights approach? Perhaps it would not be a bad idea to shift Data Protection further to "The EU's Human Rights & Democratisation Policy"?
2. The publication of the EU "Proposal for a Framework Decision on the protection of personal data processed in the framework of police and judicial cooperation in criminal matters" (June 12, 2007). The conclusions of the Council meeting of 12–13 June 2007 are that the new framework decision will be based on the Council of Europe established minimum data protection principles set by the Convention of 28 January 1981 for the protection of individuals with regard to automatic processing of personal data and its Additional Protocol of 8 November 2001, including Recommendation (87)15 regulating the use of personal data in the police sector. The EU is now seriously dealing with data protection in the third pillar and is trying to implement the human rights approach of the Council of Europe.
3. In 2006, the Court of Justice of the European Communities published two judgments on PNR-data (Passenger Name Records).[27] The Court concluded that the transfer of personal data for purposes of public security and criminal law falls outside the (economic) scope of Directive 95/46/EC. According to the European

---

adequate protection of personal data provided by the Safe Harbour Privacy Principles and related Frequently Asked Questions issued by the US Department of Commerce. Brussels, 13.02.2002 SEC(2002) 196. Available at: <http://ec.europa.eu/justice_home/fsj/privacy/docs/adequacy/sec-2002-196/sec-2002-196_en.pdf> (last visited, January 11, 2008).

[25] Joseph Turow, *Americans and Online Privacy. The System is Broken*. A Report from the Annenberg Public Policy Center of the University of Pennsylvania, June 2003. Available at: <http:// www.asc.upenn.edu/usr/jturow/internet-privacy-report/36-page-turow-version-9.pdf> (last visited, January 11, 2008).

[26] See: <http://ec.europa.eu/justice_home/fsj/privacy/index_en.htm> (last visited, January 11, 2008).

[27] C-317/04 and C-318/04.

Data Protection Supervisor (EPDS), these judgments have created a loophole in the protection of European citizens.

As a result, there seems to be a shift for data protection within the EU from the original economic approach, to a human rights approach, influenced by new EU activities with regard to law enforcement issues.

Another interesting general initiative was taken by Peter Fleischer, Google's Global Privacy Counsel. In his blog on September 14, 2007 he called for Global Privacy Standards for online privacy worldwide. According to Fleischer, the APEC-Privacy Framework (2005)[28] could be a promising foundation to build this on. In 2005, the Asia-Pacific Economic Cooperation (APEC) published their Privacy Framework. The APEC Privacy Framework should contribute to a consistent approach to information privacy protection, avoid the creation of unnecessary barriers to information flows and prevent impediments to trade across APEC member economies. It offers technical assistance to those APEC economies that have not yet addressed privacy from a regulatory or policy perspective.[29] Fleischer considers the APEC Privacy-Framework as a "modern approach to the OECD Privacy Principles". Especially interesting in the APEC Privacy-Framework is that privacy should also help to protect citizens against misuse of their personal data and the consequent harm of individuals. However, it should be noted that important people and institutions have also criticized the APEC Privacy-Framework.[30]

Also in 2005, the Data Protection and Privacy Commissioners published their Montreux Declaration: The protection of personal data and privacy in a globalised world. The Montreux Declaration also illustrates the existing interest in a new common approach to data protection.

17.7 Towards a Common Approach in Europe

From the foregoing sections, it appears that the EU is shifting towards the DP regime of the CoE. This is for example illustrated by the conclusion of the Council that the data protection framework for police and judicial cooperation in criminal matters will be based on the CoE data protection principles. However, this shift is also illustrated by the Amendments to Convention 108 (1999), allowing the accession

---

[28] Asian-Pacific Economic Cooperation, APEC Privacy Framework. APEC#205-SO-01.2, ISBN 981-05-4471-5, 36 pp. Available at: <http://www.apecsec.org.sg/content/apec/publications/all_publications/telecommunications.html> (last visited, January 11, 2008).

[29] See also: <http://www.apec.org/content/apec/apec_groups/committees/committee_on_trade/electronic_commerce.html>(last visited, January 11, 2008).

[30] For example: Graham Greenleaf, the Australian Privacy Foundation (APF) and the Asia-Pacific Privacy Charter Council (APPCC). See also: Electronic Privacy Information Center and Privacy International, *Privacy & Human Rights 2006. An International Survey of Privacy Laws and Developments*. Electronic Privacy Information Center and Privacy International, 2007, pp. 13–14. Also available at: <www.privacyinternational.org> (last visited, January 11, 2008).

of the European Communities to the Convention.[31] As a result, the EU seems to be shifting from an economic approach to a human rights approach. This could be a positive shift. But what are the differences and similarities of data protection in "the two Europes"?

One of the differences is that the data protection activities within the EU seem to be taken more seriously than those within the CoE. This is for example illustrated by the fact that the Article 29 Working Party has published over 145 documents with regard to EU Directive 95/46/EC, while the Data Protection Committees of the CoE has published only 10 reports and studies and only 5 reports and studies by experts have been published.[32]

The reports and studies by the Data Protection Committees are:

Progress report on the application of the principles of Convention 108 to the collection and processing of biometric data (2005);
Guiding principles for the protection of personal data with regard to smart cards (2004);
Report containing guiding principles for the protection of individuals with regard to the collection and processing of data by means of video surveillance (2003);
Guide to the preparation of contractual clauses governing data protection during the transfer of personal data to third parties not bound by an adequate level of data protection (2002);
Report on the Impact of Data Protection Principles on Judicial Data in Criminal Matters including in the framework of Judicial Co-operation in Criminal Matters (2002);
Third evaluation of Recommendation N° R (87) 15 regulating the use of personal data in the police sector (2002);
Model contract to ensure equivalent protection in the context of transborder data flows with explanatory report (1992);
The introduction and use of personal identification numbers: the data protection issues (1991);
Data protection and media (1990);
New technologies: a challenge to privacy protection? (1989).

---

[31] Council of Europe, Amendments to the Convention for the Protection of Individuals with regard to Automatic Processing of Personal Data. Approved by the Committee of Ministers, in Strasbourg, on 15 June 1999. Available on the Internet: <http://conventions.coe.int/Treaty/en/Treaties/Html/108-1.htm> (last visited 3 April 2008).

[32] In 1976, the Committee of Ministers set up a Committee of experts from each of the Member States of the Council of Europe, which subsequently became the Project Group on Data Protection (CJ-PD) in 1978. Over the years, the Committee of experts published a series of recommendations, studies and reports. In 2003, the Committee of experts and the Consultative Committee, consisting in representatives of parties to the Convention, merged and became a single enlarged committee (T-PD).

The following reports and studies by experts have been published:

Report on the application of data protection principles to the worldwide telecommunication networks (Poullet et al., 2004);
Report on the protection of personal data with regard to the use of smart cards (Neuwirt, 2001);
Study contracts involving the transfer of personal data between Parties to Convention Ets 108 and third countries not providing an adequate level of protection (Huet, 2001);
Protection of personal data with regard to surveillance (2000) and Guiding principles for the protection of individuals with regard to the collection and processing of data by means of video surveillance (Buttarelli, 2000); and
Revisiting Sensitive Data (Simitis, 1999).

In my opinion, these reports are not very well-known, not even by privacy advocates. Also my personal experience is that literature and official documents more often refer to EU documents, including documents from the Article 29 Working Party, than to documents from CoE Experts or Data Protection Committees. This could be explained by the fact that national data protection legislation within the European countries has a more direct link to Directive 95/46/EC than to Convention 108. It is also possible that the EU directives and documents receive more attention because Convention 108 is not self-executing, although it has a binding force but is "only" addressed to the Member States.[33]

Are there any differences in content? Convention 108 consists in three main parts[34]:

- substantive law provisions in the form of basic principles;
- special rules on transborder data flows;
- mechanisms for mutual assistance and consultation between the Parties.

The basic principles (see also Section 17.3.2) in Chapter II of the Convention must guarantee the data subjects in all contracting countries a minimum protection against the automatic processing of their personal data. At the same time, these basic principles should result in the harmonisation of data protection laws in the contracting states.

Directive 95/46/EC is, at least partly, based on the Convention. This is confirmed in preamble 11 of the Directive: "*Whereas the principles of the protection of the*

[33] The addressees are not just Member States because non-European states are also allowed to access the Convention.

[34] Convention for the Protection of Individuals with regard to Automatic Processing of Personal Data (ETS No. 108), Explanatory Report, § 18. Available at: <http://conventions.coe.int/treaty/en/Reports/Html/108.htm>.

rights and freedoms of individuals, notably the right to privacy, which are contained in this Directive, give substance to and amplify those contained in the Council of Europe Convention of 28 January 1981 for the Protection of Individuals with regard to Automatic Processing of Personal Data."

The following table illustrates the provisions where elements of the basic data protection principles can be found in the Convention and in Directive 95/46/EC:

Data protection principle	Convention 108	Directive 95/46/EC
Collection limitation	5(a)	5, 6(1a,b), 7, 8, 9
Data quality	5(c,d)	6(1c,d)
Purpose specification	5(b,e)	6 (1b,e), 10, 11
Use limitation	5(b)	5, 6(1b,c,d,e), 7, 8, 9, 25, 26
Security safeguards	7	16, 17
Openness	8(a)	10, 11, 12, 18, 19, 20, 21
Individual participation	8(b,c)	12, 13, 14, 15
Accountability	8(d)	6(2), 22, 23, 24

The rules on transborder data flows in Chapter III of the Convention must guarantee the free flow of personal data between the contracting countries. This can be guaranteed by the fact that all contracting countries offer a minimum level of protection by means of the basic principles.

Directive 95/46/EC also has a separate chapter relating to the transfer of personal data to third countries (Chapter 4). Like the Convention, the Directive guarantees the free flow of personal data between the Member States by the basic principle that the transfer of personal data is only allowed to a third country with an adequate level of protection.

In the Convention, mechanisms for mutual assistance and consultation between the Parties refer to individual cases (Chapter 4) and to the Convention as a whole (Chapter 5).

The Directive also provides mechanisms for mutual assistance and consultation between the Member States. Preamble 64 of the Directive says: "*Whereas the authorities in the different Member States will need to assist one another in performing their duties so as to ensure that the rules of protection are properly respected throughout the European Union.*" This has been formulated in Article 28. Furthermore, Article 29 establishes "Article 29 Working Party". One of the tasks of Article 29 Working Party is to contribute to the uniform application of the national measures that implement the Directive.

From this overview, we can conclude that the Convention and Directive 95/46/EC have a lot in common and, more specifically, are focused on the same three main parts. However, both documents also differ from each other. The main difference is perhaps the fact that Directive 95/46/EC is much more detailed, by providing administrative obligations, than the Convention. An example is the notification procedure (Chapter 2, Section 9 of the Directive) that has been criticised because of the burden it imposes.[35] The Convention is less detailed but provides principles, which by definition have a more abstract level.

The "engagement" between the data protection frameworks of "the two Europes" is well illustrated by the recent proposal of the Justice and Home Affairs Council of the EU for a Framework Decision for data protection within the context of the police and judicial cooperation in criminal matters.[36] This Framework Decision for the third pillar is supposed to be built upon the Council of Europe's basic data protection principles.[37] In April 2007, a revised version of the proposal was submitted to the European Parliament for consultation. In his third Opinion, the European Data Protection Supervisor (EDPS) concludes that, despite the intention to build the Framework upon Convention 108, the revised proposal fails to meet the level of protection required by the Convention.[38] Although the EDPS is convinced that the proposal could mean a considerable step forward for the protection of personal data[39], he concludes that the revised proposal needs substantial improvements to be consistent with the first pillar data protection principles (Directive 95/46/EC) and to be in line with Convention 108 and Recommendation R(87)15 regulating the use of personal data in the police sector.[40]

The opinion of the EDPS stresses how important it is for an adequate level of data protection to tune the economic approach of the EU with the human rights approach of the CoE. Because the EU is currently extending the legal framework on data protection to the third pillar, the human rights approach is also becoming important for the EU. A common approach for data protection by the CoE and the EU has thus become inevitable for the level of data protection in Europe in the public and private sector. Such a common approach could, in the end, lead to a worldwide

---

[35] Commission of the European Communities, *Communication from the Commission to the European Parliament and the Council on the follow-up of the Work Programme for better implementation of the Data Protection Directive*. Brussels, 7.3.2007. COM(2007) 87 final, p. 6. See also the Commission's *First report on the implementation of the Data Protection Directive (95/46/EC)*. Brussels, 15.5.2003. COM(2003) 265 final.

[36] Commission of the European Communities, *Proposal for a council framework decision on the protection of personal data processed in the framework of police and judicial cooperation in criminal matters*. Brussels, 4.10.2005. COM(2005) 475 final. 2005/0202 (CNS).

[37] Press Release, Brussels 12 June 2007. IP/07/808. Available on the Internet at: <http://europa.eu/rapid/pressReleasesAction.do?reference=IP/07/808>.

[38] European Data Protection Supervisor, *Third opinion of 27 April 2007 on the proposal for a Council Framework Decision on the protection of personal data processed in the framework of police and judicial co-operation in criminal matters*, OJ C 139, 23.06.2007, p. 1. Available at: <http://www.edps.europa.eu/EDPSWEB/edps/lang/en/pid/247>.

[39] See the EDPS' *first Opinion of 19 December 2005 on the Proposal for a Council Framework Decision on the protection of personal data processed in the framework of police and judicial co-operation in criminal matters* (COM (2005)475 final), OJ C 47, 25.02.2006, p. 27. Also available at: <http://www.edps.europa.eu/EDPSWEB/edps/lang/en/pid/194>.

[40] *Recommendation No R (87) 15 of the Committee of Ministers to Member States regulating the use of personal data in the police sector*, adopted on 17 September 1987 and available at: <www.coe.int/dataprotection/>.

data protection standard, while it also meets the standard data protection principles accepted by the OECD and the APEC.

17.8 Conclusion

The main conclusion is that, now that data protection within the EU is extending to the third pillar, data protection within the EU more than ever needs to be in line with the human rights approach of the CoE. This also follows from the opinion of the EDPS. Therefore, a common approach by the EU and the CoE seems inevitable. This means structural co-operation between the EU and the CoE in this field. As a result, the work of the CoE will be better known and will also be better implemented because the implementation mechanism of the EU appeared to be more effective. A common human rights approach by the EU and the CoE could promote trust between governments and citizens and prevent national member states from becoming police states.

I also promised to conclude this contribution with the following questions:

Would DP be better from a human rights approach or an economic approach?

I would say that both approaches are important. International institutions have been dealing with data protection for a long time now (since the 1980s). The OECD and the EU have an economic approach whereas the UN and the CoE have a human rights approach. However, data protection is important for citizens in their relationship with the public sector (human rights approach) as well as in their relationship with the private sector (economic approach). It is important that the EU is now also dealing with data protection from a human rights perspective.

Money makes the world go around but what about Data Protection?

The title of this contribution has a question in it: Is or should there be a common approach to data protection? My conclusion is that there is no common approach for data protection. So far, data protection has been the result of both an economic approach and a human rights approach. However, I think that there should be a common approach to data protection. Such a common approach is not only important as a guarantee for a fair processing of personal data by industries all over the world but also for a fair processing by governments. Especially the tendency within the public sector to collect every kind of personal (communication) data[41], makes the need to protect our human rights even more important. Do we really feel safer when "they" know everything about us?

Google calls for Global Privacy Standards: a Devil in Disguise?

[41] See for example the Data Retention Directive 2006/24/EC.

It is true that Google has a dubious reputation on data protection.[42] However, a global standard for online privacy is not a bad idea. Consistency of data protection regulations, in the private sector and in the public sector, is always in the interest of legal certainty for citizens (consumers), industries (companies), organisations (governments) and law enforcement agencies. So why not give Google, or at least Peter Fleischer, the benefit of the doubt and help this initiative to lead to a common approach for data protection?

[42] See for example: Electronic Privacy Information Center, *Privacy? Proposed Google/ DoubleClick Deal*. On the internet: <http://epic.org/privacy/ftc/google/> (last visited, January 11, 2008).

Chapter 18
Freedom of Information Versus Privacy: Friends or Foes?

Ivan Szekely

18.1 On the Relationship Between the Two Concepts

Behind the anomalies currently besetting the notion of privacy – anomalies that arise from different cultural, political and social milieus both at the group and at the individual level – there lies a common conceptual element: individuals and small communities carry an increasing weight vis-à-vis the external world. This conceptual element is reflected in the various manifestations of privacy, whether as a social phenomenon, or as a value, or as a right, written or unwritten, or as a political goal, or even as a marketable commodity.

The notion of freedom of information (FOI) shows similar anomalies, whether we look at it in a historical context or study it from a geographical, cultural or political perspective; and, these, too, share a common element, which is the pivotal role assigned to individuals in their dealings with one of the fundamental actors of the external world: the modern state.

The view whereby these two concepts clash and mutually limit each other has been gaining popularity.[1] In other words – according to this view –, a legal system or a social establishment must decide whether it prefers freedom of information (together with the associated concepts of transparency and accountability) at the expense of respecting and protecting people's right to privacy, or the other way around. In black and white, one should envisage it as a zero-sum game, in which we must take away the same amount from the implementation of one concept that we

I. Szekely (✉)
Open Society Archives at Central European University, Budapest, Hungary
e-mail: szekelyi@ceu.hu

[1] In some cases this view is based on misunderstanding of at least one element of this relationship: even a 'Comprehensive Information Assurance Dictionary' can contain expressions relating to data protection in a misleading sense (Schou et al. 2002), or a European law firm in its statement seems to confuse data protection legislation and secrecy legislation (Louis 2006); similarly, the notions of confidentiality, data protection and freedom of information seem to be muddled in the health sector (see for example Theale Medical Centre 2007). In other cases the approach is correct but the analyses emphasize the conflict between the two areas (e.g. Pitt-Payne 2007, Singleton 2002).

S. Gutwirth et al. (eds.), *Reinventing Data Protection?*
DOI 10.1007/978-1-4020-9498-9_18,

add to the implementation of the other and it is entirely up to us where we actually draw the line.

This approach is based on a fundamentally flawed interpretation. If we were to ask what were the ultimate goals of the two 'competing' concepts from the viewpoint of the individual, then we would come to the conclusion that it was the same one: both are meant to protect the individual citizen from excessive information power.

18.1.1 The Citizen and the State

Our current notions of privacy and FOI are strongly related to the power relations between state and the citizen, although none of them can entirely be reduced to that. In the case of privacy, it is evident that the boundaries cannot be limited to the state, as we also have the business world, the civil organizations and even other individuals to consider. The freedom of information – in short, the individuals' freedom and fundamental right to accessing public information – is, in theory, only meaningful vis-à-vis the public sector but in reality the borderlines are beginning to blur: in the practice of modern state administration, several of the state's functions are outsourced to the business and even the civil sector.[2]

In the field of information, any relationship, even a momentary one, has a stronger and a weaker side. The stronger party always has more information about this relationship; typically, the weaker parties cannot even be sure what it is exactly that the stronger side knows about them. It is sufficient to remember only the day-to-day power relations between state and citizen or service provider and customer.

If we study the changes from the abstract viewpoint of power relations, rather than from a purely legal aspect, then we shall find that the application of modern information technology has greatly altered the earlier balance: the stronger side has mostly become even more powerful, the weaker even more vulnerable. One branch of the arising problems originates from the changes in the information boundaries of the private sphere, i.e., from the concentration of information power *as a factor in monitoring and influencing the individual,* while the other main branch stems from the changes in the information status of the individuals, which determines their participation in society, i.e., from the concentration of information power *as a monopoly on handling public information.*

The guaranteeing of privacy, most notably of information privacy, serves – in tandem with the European system of laws and regulations, as well as with data protection and other available means and methods to carry out data handling – to counter-balance the former of these two influences. The freedom of information helps dampening the latter. What they share in common is that they constitute an essential element in the information autonomy of the individual. On the one hand, this is assuming that data protection functions as an active right of informational

[2] See: Alasdair S. Roberts: Structural pluralism and the right to information (Roberts 2001)

self-determination, going well beyond its traditional, protective legal character; in other words, the individual should be able to decide when, how and to what extent the information on his or her person can be accessed by others. On the other hand, a similarly fundamental element of information autonomy is the ability of the individuals to access information in the public sphere – even to the extent that he or she should be able to decide, within the possibilities available, what information to receive and what to reject – in other words, the option of rejecting unwelcome information (propaganda, marketing) should be left open. It is evident that the state and its citizens (analogously, of the business sphere and the customers) should have significantly different information utopias and in its purest forms, neither can be implemented. But the key factor in both scenarios is the extent to which each side, i.e., the stronger and the weaker, has the ability to access information about the other.

18.1.2 Cultural and Political Dichotomies

From the above it follows that, rather than being diametrical opposites, the concepts of information privacy and freedom of information in fact complement each other. The ideals behind them – the transparent and accountable state and the autonomous, self-determining citizen – are interdependent sister concepts. Although they were undeniably produced by the Western cultural hemisphere in modern history, these sister concepts in some sense constitute outstanding achievements in social and legal developments. From a Western perspective it may appear that these two elements of the twin concepts are fundamentally alien to the cultural East. Since the notion of *individuum* does not have the same importance in the East as it does in the West, individual autonomy in the field of information is not a fundamental demand of the citizens living in Eastern societies – and vice versa: the eastern citizens do not want to hold their leaders, sovereigns and state bureaucracy to account. While such a sweeping generalization is not entirely unfounded, it is not entirely true, either. On the basis of my brief experience in Korea, in cultures rooted in Confucian traditions the respect of individuals also includes the respect of the 'information self'. From the analysis of Western observers there emerges a tradition, which I personally would describe as 'virtual privacy': if the physical environment does not permit the implementation of privacy, then the participants will achieve it by the wilful elimination of mutual perception.[3] The respect of the individual is also reflected by the use of modern information and communication technologies in the countries of the cultural East.[4]

The dichotomy of dictatorial regimes and democratic establishments offers a different comparison (although here, too, we rarely see the extremes appear in their

[3] For more details, see Crane [1967] 1999, especially p. 62, on the encounter of the master and his disciple.

[4] This is the topic of a recent study by a Hungarian student following a field trip in Japan: Vincze, B., Protection of privacy in using modern information technologies in Japan.

purest forms), which is manifested in a grotesque symmetry. While the transparent, accountable state and the autonomous, self-determining citizen are the ideals of the democratic establishments, those of the dictatorial regimes are the autonomous, self-determining state and the transparent, accountable citizen. The elderly and the middle-age generations living in Europe's 'new democracies' had ample opportunity to experience the difference between the two.

18.2 Conflicting Areas

If we accept that in a democratic society privacy and freedom of information are two concepts that complement each other, instead of competing with each other, than there is no need to 'balance' the two concepts in general – and the present paper could end here. However, although the two concepts do not clash head on, they have certain interfaces or conflict zones. While the existence of these zones does not question the complementary nature of the two concepts, marking the borderline between the implementation of the two is not always easy in practice.

Of these conflict zones, we would like to focus on two in particular. We can outline them with the help of the following questions: Firstly, does a public servant have a private life? Secondly, does the information about collaborators of former (dictatorial) regimes constitute 'data of public interest'?

18.2.1 Public Service and Private Life

In everyday usage, public service refers to a form of employment, which in theory implies a dedication to serving the public and in practice means a job with the associated duties in some government institution. The democratic state – we are still speaking theoretically – executes the will of the people through representatives elected by the public and these representatives entrust various organizations with the job of carrying out the 'will of the people'. These organizations are financed by the taxpayers' money to carry out a public mandate – and so the public has every moral right to monitor their activities and to hold the people in charge to account. In the majority of the democratic states this moral right has been transformed into codified rights and freedoms, or in the case of their most advanced form, a universal right of everyone to access public information or 'data of public interest': the freedom of information.

If we take the data belonging to the domain of information privacy – i.e., personal data – to be a well-defined set, then we shall be able to place right next to it the set of data of public interest, which includes the data that constitute the domain of the freedom of information (Fig. 18.1). Actually, by doing that we have also defined the most fundamental categories of information about the state and the citizen.

The dischargers of public service are, naturally, not merely abstract legal entities and institutions but real people who work in these institutions – people who are entitled to the rights to privacy, including the right to information privacy in particular.

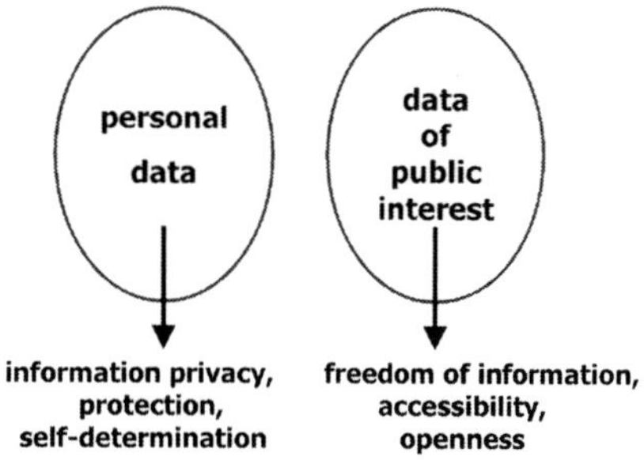

Fig. 18.1 Fundamental categories of information about the state and the citizen

To what category does their personal data belong? Or to put it differently: Do public servants need to surrender the rights that they are otherwise entitled to as private persons or as individuals? We can approach this problem from two directions. On the one hand, in modern societies individuals fill various positions in various communities and, in accordance with that, they perform various roles, including the written and unwritten rights and duties that are associated with those roles.[5] Public service is one of these distinguished roles, which may be associated with different (written and unwritten) rights and obligations. On the other hand, we could say that a public servant is quite simply not a 'private person' but a representative of the people and at the same time a servant of the state. And in that capacity, he is subjected to rules and regulations that are different from the ones that apply to private individuals in general.

Once we have adopted the latter approach, our problem apparently becomes a very simple one: in all activities one carries out in his or her capacity as a public servant, he or she cannot be regarded as a private person and, therefore, all the information that are produced in connection with that activity are 'data of public interest', to be handled according to the principles and rules associated with FOI. So does it follow from this that the personal data of public servants are actually not personal data, they belong to the domain of data of public interest?

It should be pointed out however that a public servant also has a private life and the two roles belong to the same individual: the information generated in the course of performing the two different roles can be associated with the same person. Therefore, the two sets will partially overlap and an intersection will be created (Fig. 18.2).

Here, too, a seemingly simple solution presents itself: The data protection rules, which have been introduced in order to guarantee information privacy, should not apply to those data, which are created in connection with public service activities. So does that mean that these data do not constitute personal data? No, it does not mean that: according to European legal philosophy and dogma, personal data do not lose their personal character on account of their public service environment. These are personal data, to which the principles and practical rules of data protection

[5] The preservation of this multi-role character constitutes one of the most important questions in the protection of privacy in the era of surveillance society and integrated information systems.

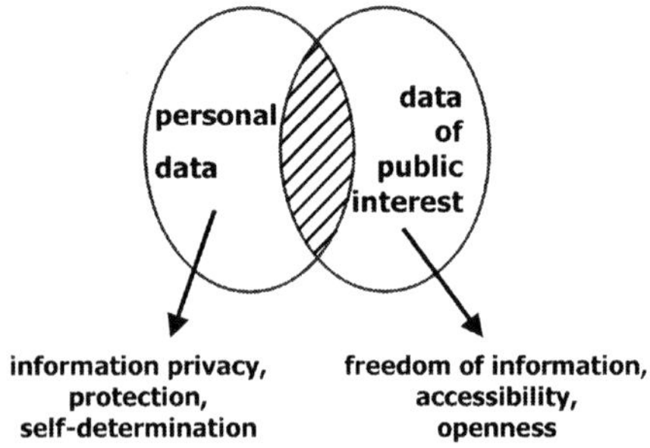

Fig. 18.2 The same individual, different roles

and informational self-determination do not apply, or do not apply entirely. If the main principles regarding public service are transparency and accountability, then the main principles regarding these personal data should be openness and public access (Fig. 18.3).[6]

However, drawing the borderline is not always easy. On the one hand, in numerous countries the information rights associated with these two domains are regulated in separate laws and bylaws and sometimes they do not fully cover the overlaps or intersections. On the other hand, the day-to-day practice of public service often throws up problems that do not lend themselves to trivial solutions on principles and they are not covered in the relevant legal articles.

Where do the boundaries of the overlap lie? Or to rephrase the question: Where do the boundaries of a public servant's private life lie? I personally know public servants who take great care to make sure that their private lives are well separated from their professional capacity. By the same token, I also know public servants who take their work home with them, allowing it to become part of their private lives, thanks

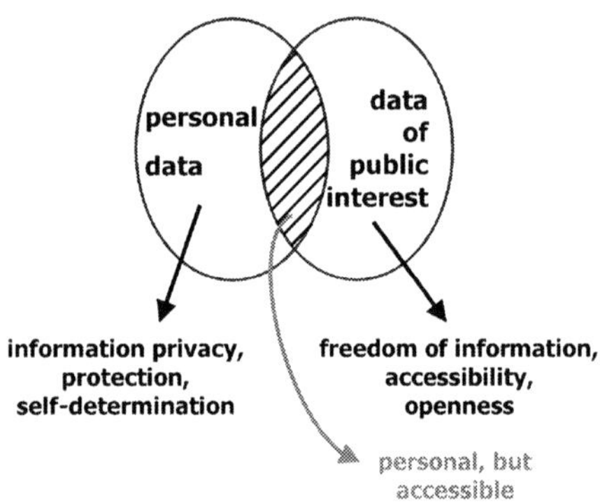

Fig. 18.3 Personal data in public function

[6] In Hungary, where data protection and freedom of information are regulated by a joint law, certain public servants tried to abuse their data protection rights immediately after the enactment of the law (in the early 1990s): they refused to release documents to applicants on the ground that these documents bore their official signature – their personal data.

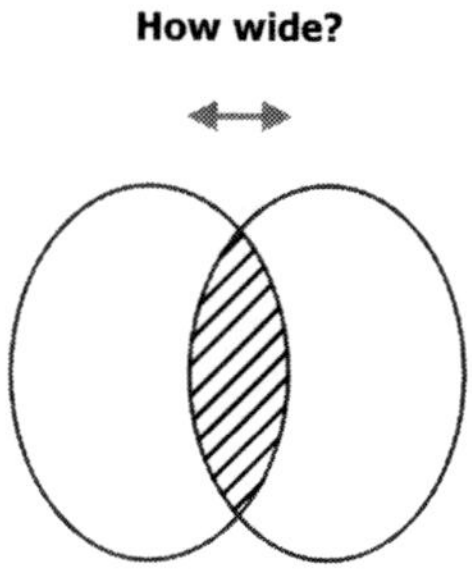

Fig. 18.4 The overlapping area: How wide?

to the blessings – or curses – of modern information and communication technologies. And I also know public servants, whom people on the street recognize, thanks to their high-ranking status or public appearances, with journalists stopping them for an interview while shopping. However, I know of no such laws or legislations, which adequately regulate either these situations or the handling of personal data under these circumstances. I can only confirm the existence of a linear relationship between the position of a public servant and the size of the overlap: the higher position a public servant has, the greater is the overlap and also, by implication, the narrower is the extent of his or her private life (Fig. 18.4).

In an authoritarian society or social milieu even the journalists tend to subscribe to the view that the private life of a prime minister is sacred, because he is a very important person, while the private life of his secretary is less so, because she fills a less important position. In reality, quite the opposite is true. The private life of a secretary is more important, because her role and lifestyle more closely approximates that of a private individual. And as for all the things that 'important persons' can do to secure the physical boundaries of their private life (surrounding their residences with stone walls, hedges or security guards), it is important to remember that they cannot do the same regarding the information about their private life (notably: their personal data), at least not in principle.

What about the time scale of the overlap's pertinence? The most obvious frame of reference in this could be the duration of the working hours. According to this, all the data generated in the life of a public servant on workdays before 8 am and after 5 pm and all day on weekends, are private information and should be beyond public scrutiny. However, even after deducting the hours spent working overtime or working at home, there exists a much longer cycle, too: the duration of a public service career. Can someone's status as a public servant legitimate public scrutiny of personal data relating to an earlier period? The accountability of a minister is more far-reaching than that of a clerk but what happens when a clerk becomes a minister at a later stage? Can he be called to account about events that took place before his appointment as a minister? The same dilemma presents itself in relation to a minister who has been retired for years but the tabloid press sustains an interest in him on account of his former position (Fig. 18.5).

And finally: Is it possible at all to separate a person's identity as a private individual from his/her capacity as a public servant during working hours while doing

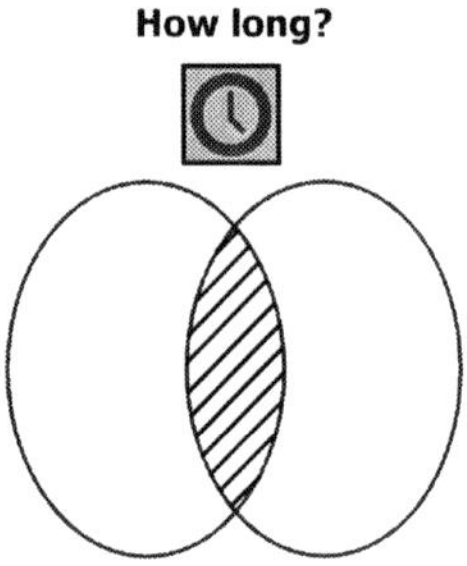

Fig. 18.5 The overlapping area: How long?

public service work? Like every other employee, a public servant takes private telephone calls, writes private e-mails and conducts private affairs during work, not mentioning occasional visits to a café or to the restroom. It is quite obvious that his/her personal data related to these activities should not concern the public – except for the cases, when the taxpayers‘ money is being squandered for private purposes, or when one is found in gross neglect of one duties, or when one abuses one's official power (Fig. 18.6).

The key element in all the numerous questions raised above is *public function*. We can declare that the main clause of the freedom of information applies to all the personal data, which are related to the conduction of public service – irrespective of the actual location and time, i.e., whether it is done during or outside working hours, at the workplace or at home; furthermore, it is clear that the higher the position the public servant in question occupies, the broader is the range of personal data that should be made open to public scrutiny.[7] On the other hand, the possible range of private data can vary according to the social, political and cultural traditions and tastes, as manifested, for example, in the differences between the public scrutiny given to the health condition and sexual life of a US President or a presidential

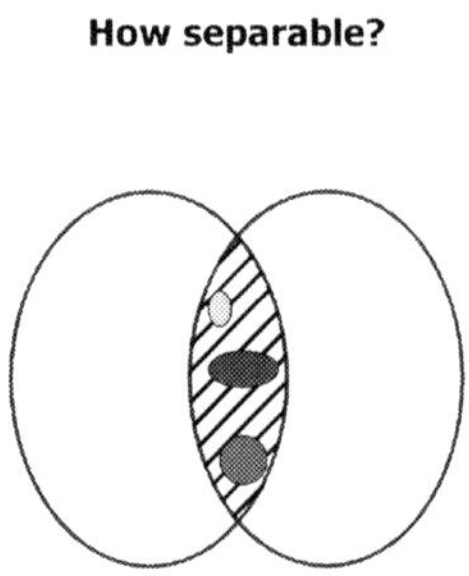

Fig. 18.6 The overlapping area: How separable?

[7] The logic behind this reasoning can appropriately also be applied to employees working in the private sector but in that case it is not the freedom of information that limits the private life of the employees but the employers' thirst for information, which leads to the tapping of telephone conservations, the monitoring of private e-mails and occasionally even the use of polygraphs. However, here, too, the activities carried out on behalf, or in the name, of the company can be separated from private life, the representation of the company's interests from activities conducted as private individuals.

candidate on the one hand and that of the heads of states in Europe, not to mention Eastern Europe, on the other.

18.2.2 Lustration

This expression gained currency in the new European democracies during the years immediately after the political transition. It was introduced in reference to the process of 'cleansing': the attempt to screen out persons who had participated in the activities of the Communist state security forces, either as paid informers or as enlisted personnel.[8] It is not the aim of the present paper to discuss the various motives, personal interests and moral justifications of people who took part in those activities, either as official members of the organization or as writers or readers of surveillance files but the lustration laws apply to all of them equally. The actual model chosen to find a solution for the problem varied from country to country.

The screening process has three main objectives: the first one is lustration, which aims at ridding the public life of the persons who had carried out activities irreconcilable with the democratic legal system (this is the penal element); the second is the unveiling of the activities of the secret police under the one-party state system (this is the element of information restitution); and the third is the provision of access to personal files for the individuals concerned (this is the element of informational self-determination). The three objectives received different emphasis in the legislation and practice of the various countries: in some countries, the main objective was to unmask the former informers and oust them from positions of influence; other countries focused on the retroactive implementation of informational self-determination; and the rest assigned priority to unveiling the system of spying.

One of the sanctions introduced had a bearing on information rights: the clandestine activities of the perpetrators were published. This elicits the following question: Should, therefore, the relevant activities of unpaid collaborators be treated as 'data of public interest'? Is the disclosing of these data a question of freedom of information at all? In our view, public access to information regarding the collaborators' activities as a *social phenomenon* (and also the operation of the secret police) belongs to the realm of FOI. By contrast, information about the activities of individual collaborators already belongs to the overlap: to the domain of *personal* data, however, governed by the main principles of transparency.[9] The grey area this time

---

[8] I would like to point out that in the controversial and murky waters of retroactive justice-making the only reason why retroactive sanctioning can legally be justified is that the activities of the previous political regime's secret police had violated the constitutional requirements of even *that* establishment.

[9] This is why, in my opinion, the Constitutional Court's resolution 60/1994 (XII.24.) caused severe damage in the conceptual framework of Hungarian information rights, when it declared that, according to the Constitution, the information concerning the earlier activities of people presently active in public service or politics, activities that are irreconcilable with the democratic legal system, were *'data of public interest'*. It could have declared that these were personal data, the

is outlined by the boundary between the mandatory publication of personal data and the limitations on the publication of data of public interest (for example, state secrets).

In a paradoxical manner, in weighing the options about the publication of personal data, here, too, the key element is the public function. An officially employed secret policeman naturally filled a public function – he was a 'public servant' in the broader sense of the word – even though the public was not able to learn about his work; according to our current notions, this is what justifies the publication of his personal data. But the private citizen who wrote the reports voluntarily was not employed by these organizations and quite often received no salary or any other rewards for his acts. But through his act he rendered a form of public service – again, in a broader sense and with an ironic overtone – and so (besides the social justice) this could justify the publication of his personal data.

18.3 Evolution or Erosion?

Viewing it from a historical perspective – and leaving aside the wartime or dictatorial excesses – freedom of information and information privacy seem to be moving in the opposite directions: in fully fledged democracies, more and more people are being aided by more and more rights and more and more technological means to access public information; parallel with that, they more and more seem to be losing the capacity to dispose over their personal data.

In the history of rights to public information, the first agents to gain the right to disseminate information were the intermediaries between the source of information and the end users. Such intermediaries were the representatives and the media. At the next stage, the intermediaries, in addition to passing on information, also won the right to demand information. In other words, people in possession of a press card or a delegate's card received privileges in accessing information. Finally, the end users themselves gained the right to ask for and to receive answers directly. This is where we are at the moment in the case of the majority of the most advanced democracies, at least in theory. Therefore, the legal development of access to public information can be presented by an evolutionary model.

By contrast, the traditional boundaries of private life have continued to erode, precisely on account of the changes in information relations, the overall result being that, when seen from the viewpoint of the earlier value systems, the spread of new information technologies has produced negative rearrangements at a social level. First the technology of *acquiring* information about individuals went through revolutionary changes (telephony, photography)[10]; next it was the element of

disclosure of which lied in the public's interest; alternatively, it could have said that these were personal data, which would need to be published by force of law; or that the decision to give public access to these data did not lie with the person concerned. The actual wording of the resolution, however, implicitly stripped these data of their personal nature.

[10] The environment that led to the initial conceptualization of privacy by Warren and Brandeis.

information *processing* that led to fundamental changes (computerized data processing)[11]; and finally, the two elements mixed irreversibly, creating a new dimension in the handling of personal information (let us simply call it the Internet world).[12] Naturally, the development of privacy and data protection legislation reveals positive, evolutionary tendencies, while the practical enforceability of the rights thus codified shows clear signs of an erosion.

The processes outlined above mainly characterize the most developed countries, which are often described as traditional democracies. In the case of the new democracies, the dynamics of both the evolution and the erosion is different. While before the Second World War, the countries now referred to as the 'new European democracies' were *not yet able* to reach that stage of democratic legal development, which could have organically allowed the development of a full catalogue of human rights, along with the modern system of new information rights (including the legal and institutional guarantees of ensuring privacy and FOI), in the decades that followed it[13] they were *no longer able* to do the same.

It is quite apparent in the case of these countries that the euphoria of the democratic transition engendered an ardent demand to curb the state's omnipotence in information power. This demand concerned the creation of the state's transparency and accountability (with a special emphasis on the disclosure of and access to, documents of recent history), as well as the restraint of its power to monitor people's private life. Despite the adverse effects of society's over-politicization, human rights in general became more important throughout this period and this created a favourable environment both for the legal codification of information privacy and FOI and for the creation of the institutional system monitoring their implementation. But the euphoria subsided after a few years, the new or reformed legal system was put in place; the public could witness the emergence of new or restored government structures; and a new generation grew up, for whom the new values of capitalism, such as the belated original accumulation of capital, the enjoyment of material possessions, career and political power, enjoyed priority over respect for human rights, including information rights. In this regard, the countries, which took advantage of the historic opportunity and rode the tidal wave of democratic transition to install the legal and institutional guarantees for the implementation of information rights, can count themselves lucky. In summary, therefore, the development of information privacy and FOI in the new democracies has shared common dynamics, characterized by rapid development first and followed by gradual erosion.

And if we were asked to identify the source of influences *simultaneously* working towards development and erosion in the new democracies, then we would have to name the advanced democracies of the West, which had exerted a paradoxical influence on them. The new international relations, the obligations and the commitments

---

[11] The environment that led to the promulgation of classical data protection laws.

[12] The environment that led to the need of 'reinventing data protection'.

[13] In the case of the republics of the former Soviet Union, during the period between the two World Wars.

together had a controversial effect on the implementation of the information rights in the countries undergoing democratic transition. On the one hand, the international community expects the new democracies to provide legal guarantees for the realization of individual rights and freedoms, including the free access to public information and the protection of information privacy. On the other hand, their newly conferred NATO membership, the urgency to join the Schengen zone – along with the additional tasks that would entail – as well as the cooperation with Europol and other international investigative agencies, not to mention the economic and political ties with the United States, all tend to put pressure on the above mentioned countries to limit self-determination over personal data, to extend the laws on classified information and to be cooperative in anti-terrorism campaigns, all of which assumes the curbing of the recently granted information rights.

18.3.1 Further Similarities and Differences

If we consider the phylogenesis and the ontogenesis of data protection and freedom of information legislation (i.e., the historical processes of the creation of the two codified laws and their respective careers in the various countries), it will immediately be quite clear that the group of newcomers, which only recently joined the community of countries with legal guarantees of data protection and FOI, have gone through more or less the same stages as the pioneers had. Moreover, the steps taken are remarkably similar in the two areas under scrutiny.

The first step in the area of privacy protection (usually prompted by some external actuality) is the start of scholarly research. Ahead of their time, a few advocates, specialists and scholars issued warnings, which were usually followed by the various national governments' decision to set up committees, made up by serious scholars and specialists, with a mandate to investigate the consequences of computerization on people's private lives.[14] The 'late-coming countries' usually skipped this stage in their national development, although even in the case of the new democracies those few scholars and specialists, who were familiar with the topic and had contact with the specialist of the developed democracies, were helping the work of the drafting committees behind the scenes.

In the area of FOI, the phase of scholarly committees was skipped and the development began after the Second World War with the appearance of advocacy and

[14] A classic example is the British government's decision to set up the Younger Committee, which incorporated in its 1972 Report the results of a highly advanced sociological survey, as well as a study of the evolution of the notion of privacy. A similar committee was founded in France, which published its findings – the Tricot Report – in 1975; then back in Great Britain the Lindop Committee was set up, which published the results of its research in 1978; the task of these committees was, among others, to lay the grounds for the legislative work. In the US, the House of Representatives Special Subcommittee on Invasion of Privacy held hearings as early as 1965, while the Secretary's Advisory Committee on Automated Data Systems, commissioned by the Department of Health, Education and Welfare submitted its report entitled 'Records, Computers, and the Rights of Citizens' in 1973, providing ammunition to the birth of the USA Privacy Act.

lobby groups.[15] The formation of informal coalitions determined to exert pressure on legislation soon followed both in the area of FOI and that of information privacy and DP alike.[16] Their members typically included advocates, civil organizations, sympathetic MPs, a considerable faction of the press and the prominent representatives of the legal and the informatics professions; the opponents were made up by government officials and representatives of the counter-interested business sector. Subsequent to this phase, in each country where the work of drafting the bills took place in a calm social and political milieu, the debates remained within the bounds of professional discussions, while on each occasion that they were accompanied by social tensions and political quarrels they assumed the character of a party political campaign: one of the political sides stepped forward as a resolute champion of information rights.[17]

The actual passage of the law has come to constitute some kind of a watershed in the development of both information privacy and FOI, as not every one of the countries that set themselves the task to guarantee the information rights actually reach this stage: in a legal sense, this implies the establishment of sectoral laws and regulations, as well as the creation of independent, monitoring institutions. Several countries have got stuck at the level of a 'single act', which makes the system extremely vulnerable, even where the fundamental principles have been incorporated in the constitution. Parliaments can quite simply modify or limit a single act and in the case when the constitutional guarantee is lacking, the incumbent administration can easily introduce modifications. (Sweden offers an extremely positive example concerning the constitutional guarantees of freedom of information: its FOI Act actually forms part of the country's Constitution.)[18] Typically, the countries that imported the idea and the legal guarantees of data protection and freedom of information relatively late – some new European democracies included – passed only one law, either in one or both of the two areas. In the implementation of the law, this also means that the administrators regard it as a one-off and exotic piece of legislation, which should be used only in special cases; in other respects, numerous questions regarding its application, minor points and harmonization with other legislations are left open. By contrast, in countries, which decided to put in place

---

[15] Here is a cursory list: one such group in the 1960s was the Ralph Nader Center for Study of Responsible Law in the United States; another one was Campaign for Freedom of Information, founded in 1984 and still active in Great Britain; National Campaign for People's Right to Information (NCPRI), a national platform set up in India in 1996, which led to the birth of the Right to Information Act in the various Member States first and eventually nationwide in 2005.

[16] Among the coalitions, we can also find some formal organizations, such as the earlier mentioned NCPRI in India, or Citizen's Initiative in Slovakia, with the latter becoming a coalition of 122 civil organizations and launching a campaign that led to the passage of an information access law in 2000.

[17] As David Flaherty, former Information Commissioner of British Columbia, Canada, once noted ironically: politicians simply love the idea of freedom of information – *before* and *after* they are in power.

[18] The Swedish Constitution consists in four fundamental laws, one of them is the so-called 'Freedom of the Press Act', which in fact is a FOI law.

an entire system of codified information rights and freedoms, a brand new legal branch was created, which entwined the complete legal system with a logic that was slightly different from that of the traditional branches, such as the areas of public and private law.[19]

Similarly, not every country reaches the stage of setting up independent institutions for monitoring the implementation of the law. But even in countries that have reached this stage, the efficiency and the public perception of these institutions can occasionally display wide variations. In countries, where either the institution as a whole, or its current leader, or perhaps just the occasional reactions and statements issued by the leader, draw public criticism (not from the counter-interested parties, whose power positions, political or business interests are threatened by the implementation of data protection or FOI laws but from civil society or the profession), we are likely to encounter the stirrings of professional or civil disapprobation, which could lead to the intervention by radical civil organizations. Actually, the latter phenomenon is a rather paradoxical one, since these are essentially two manifestations of the same type of 'legal protection' organization, which from time to time undertake the same tasks. For example, the Hungarian Commissioner's statements concerning CCTV issues provoked some civil organizations into nominating him for one of the prizes of the Big Brother Awards[20], the Audience Prize, which he received in 2004.[21]

Although data protection and freedom of information have run a similar course in history, the pace of development has been different at the international level. Thanks to Sweden and also to the influence Sweden wielded in the Nordic countries[22], FOI had an early start; however, in terms of the number of countries that took over the idea and codified their own FOI Acts, the development was slow. Then, beginning with the early 1990s, it picked up some speed and eventually finished very strongly, thanks to the new democracies, which launched a wave of legislation after the turn of the millennium.[23] The codification of information privacy, understood in the modern

---

[19] For example, at present Hungary has nearly 1000 acts and regulations that contain provisions on data protection and the processing of personal data.

[20] The negative prize invented by Privacy International that has been adopted in several countries.

[21] This case aroused animated debate among NGOs and activists. Is it legitimate for civilian advocates to resort to such measures to censor the official guardian of informational rights? And what does this criticism really reflect? The opinion of society on the whole, or the views of a handful of hard-line activists? Of course, no one should reasonably expect a civilian organization to dedicate itself to all-out impartiality or to consistently choose the golden mean. The voice of an NGO is generally a radical voice, crying out from a marginal, minority position against an injury perceived in a disturbed equilibrium – this is in fact the essence of its social mission. In the case at hand, however, the minority was certainly not an easily dwarfed one, for the panel consisted in renowned professionals and public figures. They may not have acted as the mouthpiece of some 'official' consensus but each of them certainly provided an authentic, one-person representation of the opinion formed by various social and professional groups.

[22] Finland, being a part of the Kingdom of Sweden, first introduced the Swedish FOI Act; it enacted its own law in 1951.

[23] See Alasdair Roberts' impressive chart (Roberts 2006, p. 16.)

sense, started later[24], it had a few bumper years in terms of the number of countries joining but at the moment it seems to be yielding ground to other legislative priorities. There are probably more FOI Acts around globally (approximately 70), than there are privacy or data protection acts (about 55), although their enumeration is rather difficult because of discrepancies, of both form and content. (These estimates are based on the annual global reports of EPIC[25] and Privacy International[26], as well as on the registries of international organizations). At the same time, there are more Privacy/Data Protection Commissioners (approximately 45), than Information Commissioners (approximately 22); their number can be estimated by the attendance figures of their annual conferences.

18.3.2 Common Solutions

With all their similarities and dissimilarities, information privacy and FOI are mutually interrelated and mutually interdependent concepts. Among the formulas designed to handle simultaneously the issues that have emerged in connection with marking the boundaries of these two areas and defining their detailed regulation, there exist a few tested models, which are internationally recognized as successful.

One such model is the joint, or at least interrelated, legislation of the two areas. In Canada's Provinces and Territories[27], legislation passed combined acts and these laws have proven their viability for many years now. The main advantage of regulating these areas in a combined act is that in this way the boundaries of the legal conflicts between the two information rights are clearly drawn, thus precluding the possibility of playing off one against the other: in other words, it makes it impossible to justify the curbing of one right in the name of the other. In the case of the new European democracies, Hungary chose the Canadian model in drafting its own combined data protection and freedom of information (DP&FOI) act. In addition to the necessity to harmonize the two areas to be regulated, Hungary was also motivated by certain political considerations in its decision: the experts drafting the legislation did not want to run the risk of the Parliament's approving the bill in one of the areas and rejecting it in the other, in an area that concerned constitutional rights and, therefore, required a two-third majority – in other words, the opposition's cooperation.

---

[24] The earliest piece of modern data protection legislation was enacted in the German province of Hessen in 1969; it was followed by Sweden's Data Act of 1973 and the US Privacy Act passed in 1974.

[25] Privacy and Human Rights, published by the Electronic Privacy Information Center (1999–2006).

[26] Freedom of Information Around the World (Banisar 2006).

[27] With the exception of New Brunswick, similar joint laws – largely promulgated in the 1990s – are applied in all the Provinces and Territories. In addition to these pieces of legislation, which originally were only applied to the public sector, many of the Territories introduced new, separate Privacy Acts, which already reflected the concept of the new, federal Privacy Act and had their effects also extended to the data controllers in the private sector.

The other way to resolve the problem is to assign the task of independent supervision for both areas either to the same person or body. Those countries and sub-national territories, which opted for the combined act, appointed a joint, independent agency for the supervision of both areas. However, the practice of setting up joint supervisory agencies has been spreading even in countries, which legally regulate the framework and guarantees of information privacy and FOI in separate laws – mainly as a result of the positive examples set by similar institutions functioning elsewhere. Naturally, having a joint supervisory body is more cost-effective, as only one office needs to be set up and run for the Commissioner or the Ombudsman, instead of two but this is not the only advantage. In those instances, when the Commissioner's or the Ombudsman's statement, recommendation or verdict is sought in connection with issues concerning the grey areas of the overlap, there are clear advantages in both the practical realization of uniform interpretation and the quasi case law consequence in both areas, not to mention the advantages that lie in avoiding the situation, where the two independent supervisors of the two areas come to diametrically opposite conclusions. To demonstrate the reciprocal effects that old and new democracies can occasionally exert on each other, it is worth mentioning the example of Germany and Hungary: in establishing its new system of information rights, Hungary borrowed the German model based on informational self-determination; as for the advantages of joint supervisory agencies, the various federal states in Germany had been encouraged by the Hungarian experiences before setting up their own institutions.[28]

There are further joint possibilities in education: not just in regular school education but also in the formal and informal education of citizens, data controllers, public officials, journalists and IT experts. In today's strongly specialized world, these actors have a tendency to view these two areas as isolated, depending on which one of the two rights' realization or limitation happens to be in their interest at that moment. Developing an understanding of the joint system of information rights helps these actors in acquiring, or at least learning, the norms of lawful and ethical behaviour, even when their momentary interests seem to dictate otherwise.

It is interesting to note that a certain convergence seems to exist among those civil organizations and movements, which were originally active in one of these two areas. This convergence can be discovered in two areas: one is the cooperation among organizations engaged in the propagation of information privacy and FOI, as manifested both in the mutual support they lend to each other's actions and campaigns and in the establishment of coalitions; the other is the civil organizations' tendency to broaden the scope of their interests, mutually extending their activities to the other sphere. An example of the latter is EPIC, which has, in the course of the

---

[28] The hearing of the Hungarian DP&FOI Commissioner in the Brandenburg legislation in December 1997 played a crucial part both in the creation of Brandenburg's FOI legislation and in the establishment of the institution of joint parliamentary commissioner; Brandenburg's example was soon followed by Berlin and Schleswig-Holstein (for more details, see Dix 2001).

last few years, gradually extended its interest to other areas of information rights, such as free speech, open government and freedom of information. The situation is similar with Privacy International (partly due to personal factors but also thanks to the expansion of structural concepts), which has been active also in freedom of expression and FOI.[29] Another relevant example is the Access to Information Program (AIP) in Bulgaria, which deserves a fair share of the credit in connection with the passage of the Bulgarian access law, the education of the public officials and the monitoring of the FOI-related cases[30] and in the last few years it also turned its attention to the protection of personal data.

18.4 Neighbouring Areas

From the viewpoint of privacy, the requirements of self-determination over and protection of, personal data can, in certain cases, be curtailed not only by FOI but also by some of its neighbouring areas. By way of a brief demonstration, we mention two such areas in the following.

18.4.1 Freedom of Information and Freedom of Expression

According to a well-known concept, freedom of information and freedom of opinion and expression both belong to the common family of 'communication rights': each of them traces its origin to the same ancestry in communication law. From the viewpoint of this concept the realization of this fundamental communication right is limited by information privacy. There are, however, other comprehensive theories, which place privacy itself among the communication rights, together with democratic media governance, participation in one's own culture, linguistic rights, rights to enjoy the fruits of human creativity, to education, peaceful assembly and self-determination.[31]

Most concepts are in agreement on the point that freedom of information constitutes one of the preconditions of freedom of opinion and expression; in specific, they concur in the view that unfettered access to information that provides the basis of opinions is indispensable to people's freedom to form their own views. By way of a grotesque historical counter-point, we should mention the example of the Soviets' campaign for liberalization during Glasnost: after the long decades of censorship and self-censorship, it finally became possible to criticize everything and everybody, while essential information about the fundamental processes behind the scenes continued to be inaccessible to the average citizen. In other words, while there was

---

[29] Among other things, it publishes its comprehensive annual report, the Global Survey.

[30] See Szekely (2007a).

[31] See, for example: Assessing communication rights: A handbook (CRIS 2005).

freedom of information in the West, there was freedom *without* information in the Soviet Union.[32]

Without denying the interconnection and structural interdependence of FOI and FOE, the author does not subscribe to the idea of a universal *communication* right. For example, the notion of 'communication' cannot be applied to the freedoms of religion and conscience and in any case, it is better to talk about *information* rights than about communication rights. Communication forms only one branch of the information operations[33] , the practicing of which may be accompanied by rights and freedoms.

At the same time, the concept of freedom of expression vis-à-vis information privacy is relatively easily manageable, both in the public thinking and within the law. The associated concepts are well-established; the legal and procedural rules related to freedom of expression have a long tradition in civil law and in some cases in criminal law, also; and it is a familiar terrain for judges. By contrast, freedom of information represents a branch of law that stems from a relatively new area of constitutional law; its interpretation in the judicial practice has not yet been firmly established and, therefore, the quasi case law of the independent monitoring institutions plays a major role.

18.4.2 Archives and Privacy

In the case of archives, it is not only the freedom to access data and documents that can clash with the protection of privacy but also the freedom to do scientific research. In their daily work, researchers of recent history routinely experience difficulties in trying to obtain free access to the archives on legal grounds related to the protection of privacy. The archives store large quantities of documents, which contain information about persons either positively identified or easily identifiable. In view of the fact that the (data protection) rules relating to the protection of information privacy only apply to living persons, this issue, complete with its legal and ethical aspects, could not have emerged in connection with people living in the 19th century or before: the personal data of the individuals mentioned in those documents have by now become part of history – and therefore also come under the freedom of scientific research. By contrast, documents dated from the 20th or 21st century mainly belong to a 'grey zone': neither the archivist nor the researcher can be certain whether these persons are still alive. To make things worse, several legal systems offer provisions for the temporary protection of information related to the deceased in legal constructions, which are codified outside the protection of information privacy or personal data; also, the data related to the deceased can usually be associated with other persons, too (for example, a widow or other family members) and, therefore, these are also regarded as *their* personal data.

---

[32] 'Freedom of Expression Minus Access to Information Equal "Glasnost"' (Sirotkin 1997). See also Szekely (2006).

[33] For example, the generation, recording, storage, processing and reproduction of information.

In the majority of European countries, archival law – in tune with the archivists' concept, which primarily focuses on documents, rather than on the data they contain – has tried to resolve this complicated situation by specifying a general restriction period[34], which must pass before the documents are made available for research. On top of that, the archival laws in some of the countries set a separate restriction period for documents containing personal data. And to make the situation even more complicated, these definitions of the restriction period usually list a number of exemptions, which neither the law nor the archivists can get around: consent to doing research in the documents by the person concerned (or his/her surviving relatives) overrules the restriction period. Similarly, those documents, which prior to their transfer to the archives, according to the FOI rules, have been publicly accessible, could not be barred from public access afterwards, regardless of whether or not they contained personal data (for example, personal data concerning public figures).

While the above-mentioned problems undoubtedly affect the traditional, 'historical' archives, too, the impact they have on the modern archives is far greater. The dramatic processes, which (sometimes visibly and sometimes concealed by the traditional institutional mechanisms) have led to fundamental changes in archival practices and institutions, as well as in the accessibility of archived data and documents, raise further questions about the relationship between information privacy and accessibility. The new archival paradigm of the present era[35], the vision of global accessibility, is accompanied by new techniques and practices. The *post-custodial archives* no longer admit documents in their material form and therefore they cannot exert direct control over their use. According to the concept of the *document life-cycle management*, every document is 'archivable' from the moment of its creation (even though only a fragment of them ever make it to an archive) and therefore the same rules should apply to their handling throughout their life-cycle. Mass digitization, along with the documents that are originally produced in a digital format, offer the possibility of unlimited copies and accessibility through the Internet. According to the notion of *distributed storage*, digital format data and documents will be stored in thousands and millions of computers connected to the Internet, making use of their continuously changing memory capacity available at the moment. This is capped by a vision outlined by the biggest Internet service providers (in the author's view, it is more of an illusion than a vision, both as far as its philosophy and its practicability are concerned), whereby in principle *all* information will be archivable, preservable *indefinitely* and usable *anywhere, at any time* through digital technology.

---

[34] The various European countries specify the general restriction period between 10 and 100 years, with 30 years being the most widespread. For more details, see: Kecskemeti and Szekely (2005).

[35] The ramifications of a change of paradigm in the archival practice have been explored in numerous publications, including (Cook 1997). The author of this paper has drawn up a new catalogue of the various paradigms, arranged according to their most important features, with an emphasis on information. See Szekely (2007b) (in Hungarian).

The scope of the present paper does not allow us to do more than simply outline the problems and describe the present conditions. But even so, we can conclude as much as this: archival legislation and practice failed to meet expectations on two counts. First, in the realm of traditional archives it failed to come up with detailed regulations and practical procedures, which do not place impossible demands on researchers of recent historical documents on the one hand and which do not lower the level of protection in the case of personal data on the other; and second, in the realm of networked digital technology it failed to offer practical solutions regarding the possibilities and problems of archiving and accessibility.

18.5 Common Danger: Restrictions in the Post-9/11 Era

Along with other information rights and freedoms, information privacy and FOI were obliged to endure severe limitations in the period beginning with the symbolic choice of date: September 11, 2001. In the case of privacy, the continuous surveillance of citizens, i.e., the wiretappings and the analyses of personal communication, became general on the grounds of references to national security; and respecting FOI, the range of public information, which had previously been freely accessible, was narrowed down and the practice of classifying documents became broader, also on ground of national security (Roberts 2006; see also Fischer 2007).

However, the reasons put forward to justify the limitations and especially its proposed scale, could and must, be questioned. The phenomenon characterized with the help of metaphors such as surveillance society or the Panopticon has a harmful effect on the life of democratic societies not only on account of infringing our formal rights and unfavourably rearranging the power relations in the field of information but also because of eroding our existing values. From the British sociologist Clive Norris' analysis it becomes clear that the sociological phenomenon referred to as 'risk society' shows up in the ideology of crime-fighting and crime prevention with a modified meaning and in a distorted sense: according to their interpretation, *crime* is no longer inherently associated with *sin*, which means that its handling is relegated to a statistical problem, losing its original value content. In other words, everyone is a potential criminal and the only thing that stops people from committing a crime is the relatively high risk of apprehension. In turn, permanent surveillance can keep the risk of apprehension high; but if we assume that the only thing that stops the people doing the surveillance from committing a crime (for example, against those who are under surveillance) is the high risk of their apprehension, then they too, should be placed under surveillance and so forth. This is the logic that forms one of the ideological foundations of the surveillance society. Even when it produces good statistical results in the area of crime-fighting, this concept exerts a harmful effect on the value system of society, as well as on the distinction between normal and abnormal behaviour and on the handling of penal justice and rehabilitation.[36]

[36] See for example the Chapter 'Critical Criminology' of the Literature Review prepared for the UrbanEye project (McCahill and Norris 2002)

Similarly, a secretive state exerts a harmful influence on society not simply on account of infringing our formal rights and unfavourably rearranging the power relations in the field of information but also because of the shaky grounds on which the restrictions are justified. As Alasdair Roberts has pointed out (Roberts 2007), it is not true that the extent of national security risk is inversely proportional to the volume of the information that is freely accessible – in some instances quite the opposite is true: a broadly informed public can reduce the national security risks.

There are numerous observers who question the claim that the serious restrictions actually began after September 2001.[37] They point out that the monitoring of people's private life, which is achieved through the use of modern information and communication technologies now available in surveillance and which is aided by the privacy-invasive structure of Internet services forming an integral part of our everyday life, had begun much earlier. '9/11' only provided the ideological justification; in other words, it exploited the political and public mood for the purpose of legislating further restrictions and securing for the risk industry huge contracts and vast sums of money in development funding.

Naturally, in an emergency situation it is possible to restrict information rights and freedoms – just as well as any other rights and freedoms – in a manner that is both legal and legitimate; in fact, since the rights and freedoms are not absolute, this is not even preconditioned by an emergency situation. But in an emergency situation, such as the fight against terrorism, the restrictions should be implemented in the same manner that applies to any temporary limitations of other rights. The main criterion of such a limitation is reversibility. Just as a curfew or the ban on the right to assemble can be lifted after the danger has passed, so the guarantees to the information rights should be restored to their former level after the threat has expired. Nevertheless, there are very few signs to suggest that the legislative bodies of the various countries or the industry controlling the handling of information would want to do that. In theory, the reversibility of FOI stands a better chance in this regard, since as soon the documents have been declassified, the information hitherto withheld from the public will at once return to the freely accessible domain. By contrast, the processes concerning information privacy seem irreversible. Once a piece of personal data have entered the all-pervading, networked information system, where it would be analysed and shared by various non-public government (and, through outsourcing, private) organizations without the knowledge or the consent of the data subjects, the latter will have practically no chance at all to contact each and every one of the various data controllers and data processors in order to discover, modify, delete or control information about themselves.

---

[37] ACLU's coalition letter to the US Attorney General on alerting privacy issues was signed in May 2001 (ACLU 2001); Amitai Etzioni in a post-9/11 study reported on Carnivore and other privacy-invasive electronic surveillance technologies introduced before September 2001 (Etzioni 2002); even the open letter of leading US constitutional lawyers, published in the New York Review of Books in February 2006 (Bradley et al. 2006), which criticized the warrantless electronic surveillance programmes introduced after 2001 from a legal point of view, confirmed the existence of the problem since the late 1970s.

18.6 How to Restrict Informational Rights: The Need for a Checklist

One could write a great deal about the relationship between information privacy and FOI, about the complex network, which encompasses various other rights and freedoms, as well as ideals and values, concerning the fields of information and communications. In this paper, the author has made an attempt to demonstrate that. Hopefully, this brief review has made it clear that the two concepts are, if not exactly friends, at least no foes of each other, either. In any case, the post-9/11 restrictions and the common threat to both types of information rights (and also to a number of kindred rights and freedoms) have ushered all of them to the same camp.

This common threat makes it necessary to find the common ground, the common criteria, on the basis of which information and communication rights and freedoms can be restricted in a democratic society. Naturally, such criteria already exist and the constitution of numerous countries records them, with the detailed rules and regulations being scattered about in their legal systems. But the decision-makers, who have ordered these restrictions and who, partly due to their direct interests and partly out of a shared conviction, consider the legal articles too abstract and the human rights advocates as a hindrance to their work, are usually unable and unwilling to interpret these scattered pieces of legislation as a group. Similarly, those who implement these decisions, or those who lend technological assistance in this, may come to conclude that their task in our highly specialized world and under the great social scheme of the division of labour, could be no other than the preservation of security and the protection of the community's values against the stronger side of the individual and that the noble end to fulfil this role justifies the means of eroding the information rights and the values behind them.

In the author's opinion, the human rights advocates, the civil organizations and the experts of the field should all do away with the practice of merely saying 'no' to the people who order or execute, or simply work in the service of implementing, the anti-terrorist measures, thus remaining on the defensive against them. They should also be able to prescribe the type of circumstances and the actual conditions, under which the curtailment of the information rights is *acceptable*. Neither the decision-makers, nor the executors, nor the auxiliary staff are prepared or motivated to carry out a detailed analysis of the factors that should limit them in executing their primary function. One of the reasons why their decisions have restrictive effects is quite frequently the fact that they either do not take into account the specific interconnections and system of criteria of the information rights, or only consider them at a far too general level. What seems to be needed is a simple, brief and well-structured document, some sort of a checklist, which clearly lists the conditions that decision-makers, along with everyone else, who executes these decisions or assists in their implementation, should take into account in the case of an emergency. The task of drafting such a checklist should befall on human rights advocates and people with specialist knowledge; then, at the next stage of the debate, they should engage the persons responsible for restricting the information rights, thus finalizing the elements of the list jointly. After this, the people who are involved in the curtailment of either information privacy or FOI can be held to account in the matter of compliance with the resulting document (even when it only carries the weight of a recommendation), with the hope that the restrictions will always be kept to the extent that is both necessary and sufficient and that they will be done in a reversible manner, on the basis of legally and morally justifiable arguments.

References

ACLU (2001). Coalition Letter to Attorney General Ashcroft on Privacy Issues, May 2, 2001. American Civil Liberties Union, Center For Democracy And Technology, Electronic Privacy Information Center, Electronic Frontier Foundation, Free Congress Foundation, Law Enforcement Alliance Of America. http://www.aclu.org/privacy/spying/15076leg20010502.html Accessed 24 February 2009.

Banisar, D. (2006). *Freedom of Information Around the World 2006. A Global Survey of Access to Government Information Laws.* London: Privacy International. http://www.privacyinternational.org/foi/foisurvey2006.pdf Accessed 24 February 2009.

Bradley, C. et al. (2006). On NSA Spying: A Letter to Congress. *New York Review of Books,* Volume 53, Number 2, February 9, 2006. http://www.nybooks.com/articles/18650

Communication Rights in the Information Society (CRIS) (2005). *Assessing communication rights: A handbook.* CRIS Campaign. http://www.crisinfo.org/pdf/ggpen.pdf Accessed 24 February 2009.

Cook, T. (1997). What is Past is Prologue: A History of Archival Ideas Since 1898, and the Future Paradigm Shift. *Archivaria,* 43 (Spring 1997). http://journals.sfu.ca/archivar/index.php/archivaria/article/viewFile/12175/13184 Accessed 24 February 2009.

Crane, P. S. [1967] (1999). *Korean Patterns.* Royal Asiatic Society Korea Branch, by Seoul Press, 1999.

Dix, A. (2001). The influence of Hungarian Freedom of Information legislation abroad – The Brandenburg example and experience. In Majtenyi, L. (Ed.), *The Door Onto the Other Side.* [Bilingual edition] (pp. 231–238). Budapest: The Office of the Parliamentary Commissioner for Data Protection and Freedom of Information.

Electronic Privacy Information Center (EPIC) (1999–2006). *Privacy and Human Rights: An International Survey of Privacy Laws and Developments.* Washington, DC: Electronic Privacy Information Center.

Etzioni, A. (2002). Implications of Select New Technologies for Individual Rights and Public Safety. *Harvard Journal of Law & Technology,* Volume 15, Number 2 Spring 2002. http://jolt.law.harvard.edu/articles/pdf/v15/15HarvJLTech257.pdf Accessed 24 February 2009.

Fischer, W. (2007). Bush Administration Ramps up Secrecy. *Atlantic Free Press,* Monday, 10 September 2007. http://www.atlanticfreepress.com/content/view/2363/81/ Accessed 24 February 2009.

Kecskemeti, Ch. and Szekely, I. (2005). *Access to archives. A handbook of guidelines for implementation of Recommendation No. R (2000) 13 on a European policy on access to archives.* Strasbourg: Council of Europe Publishing.

Louis, C. (2006). Freedom of Information is the flipside of Data Protection. http://www.rechtsanwalt-louis.de/foia_&_data_protection_law.htm. Accessed 24 February 2009.

McCahill, M. and Norris, C. (2002). Literature Review, UrbanEye project, Working Paper No. 2, March 2002. http://www.urbaneye.net/results/ue_wp2.pdf Accessed 24 February 2009.

Pitt-Payne. T. (2007). Freedom of Information and Data Protection: Creative Tension or Implacable Conflict? A Paper for the Franco-British Lawyer's Society Conference, Inn of Court Northern Ireland 27/28 April 2007. http://www.franco-british-law.org/pages/ENG/publications/documents/Pitt-Payne.pdf Accessed 24 February 2009.

Roberts, A. S. (2001). Structural pluralism and the right to information. *University of Toronto Law Journal*, 51.3 (July 2001), 243–271.
Roberts, A. S. (2006). *Blacked out: Government Secrecy in the Information Age*. New York: Cambridge University Press.
Roberts, A. S. (2007). Transparency in the Security Sector. In Florini A. (Ed.), *The Right to Know. Transparency for an Open World*. New York: Columbia University Press.
Schou, C. D. et al. (2002). *Comprehensive Information Assurance Dictionary (Draft)*. National Information Assurance Training and Education Center, Idaho State University. http://security.isu.edu/NIATECV30d.pdf Accessed 24 February 2009.
Singleton, S. (2002). The Freedom of Information Versus the Right to Privacy. A Pro-Market Framework for Arizona. *Arizona Issue Analysis 171*, May 24, 2002. http://www.goldwaterinstitute.org/Common/Files/Multimedia/35.pdf Accessed 24 February 2009.
Sirotkin, S. (1997). Access to Public Information. In Fridli, J., Toth, G. A. & Ujvari, V. (Eds.), *Data Protection and Freedom of Information* (pp. 46–53). Budapest: Hungarian Civil Liberties Union.
Szekely, I. (2006). Freedom of information or freedom without information? The place of Hungary in the Central and Eastern European region. In Peterfalvi, A. (Ed.), *Ten years of DP&FOI Commissioner's Office*. [Bilingual edition] (pp. 261–280). Budapest: The Office of the Parliamentary Commissioner for Data Protection and Freedom of Information.
Szekely, I. (2007a). Central and Eastern Europe: Starting from Scratch. In Florini, A. (Ed.), *The Right to Know. Transparency for an Open World*. New York: Columbia University Press.
Szekely, I. (2007b). The four archival paradigms [A négy archívumi világkép]. *Információs Társadalom*, 2007. Vol. VII, No. 3, 15–46 (in Hungarian).
Theale Medical Centre (2007). Data Protection versus Freedom of Information and how it affects making an appointment. http://www.thealemedicalcentre.com/data_protection.htm Last updated 10 January 2007. Accessed 24 February 2009.

Chapter 19
Privacy Protection on the Internet: Risk Management and Networked Normativity

Pierre Trudel

19.1 Introduction

In cyberspace's present form, particularly with respect to Web 2.0 applications, the conditions in which personal information circulates have changed. The Internet is now encompassing almost all aspects of social life. Yves Poullet observes that the Internet promotes dual globalisation: first, with respect to the international aspect of networks and their convergence and, second, with respect to the fact that all activities are transformed into digital information.[1]

Given such globalisation,[2] simple exegesis of state law will not suffice to describe the legal framework protecting privacy in cyberspace. Despite the global nature of the network, assessments and values are different in the various cultural milieus in which rules apply.[3] Some phenomena modulate accepted norms and prevent their application across the network. Such phenomena prevent application of rules that could be taken out of context with respect to the situation or cultural substrate in which they apply. One such phenomenon seems to be legal risk: stakeholders' assessment of the concrete possibility that a statute or other rule will be applied to their activities explains why, though the Internet is a global network, no one feels complied to obey all pieces of national legislation that could in theory apply.[4]

Philippe Amblard notes that a characteristic of Internet regulation is that the normative process is multifaceted, which tends to promote the social effectiveness of

P. Trudel (✉)
Faculty of Law, Centre de recherche en droit public, Université de Montréal, Montreal, QC, Canada
e-mail: pierre.trudel@umontreal.ca

[1] Yves Poullet, 'Mieux sensibiliser les personnes concernées, les rendre acteurs de leur propre protection,' [2005] 5 *Revue Lamy Droit de l'immatériel*, 47, note 66.

[2] Here, the word is used to refer to the growing interconnection of economies and societies resulting from the development of information technologies. Cynthia Ghorra-Gobin, *Dictionnaire des mondialisations*, (Paris: Armand Colin, 2006), p. 185.

[3] Jack Goldsmith and Tim Wu, *Who Controls the Internet? Illusions of a Borderless World*, (New York: Oxford University Press, 2006), Chapter 9, 'Consequences of Borders.'

[4] For a legal risk analysis methodology, see Franck Verdun, *La gestion des risques juridiques*, (Paris: Éditions d'organisation, 2006), pp. 39 ff.

S. Gutwirth et al. (eds.), *Reinventing Data Protection?*
DOI 10.1007/978-1-4020-9498-9_19, © Springer Science+Business Media B.V. 2009

living law in contrast with 'the positivist artificiality of state law.'[5] After describing various models of Internet regulation, Michel Vivant observes that 'it is indeed of regulations, in the plural, that we should speak, of forms of regulation that should be identified so as to combine them effectively.'[6]

According to a number of theorists, we need to speak of multi-regulation and of co-existence on the network of different types of regulation with different purposes and different methods but equal legitimacy.[7] Regulation of activities occurring on the Internet can be seen as a kind of network. Thomas Schultz notes that cyberspace is an interesting laboratory for contemporary legal phenomena.[8] Privacy regulation has to be examined with a view to the flows of normativity that underlie the law that is in fact applied in cyberspace.

Seen from the point of view of a network, privacy protection on the Internet can be expressed as active normativity resulting from risk management decisions made by regulators and stakeholders. In other words, on the Internet, users and other stakeholders manage risk. Through stakeholders' decisions and behaviour, norms created in nodes generate risks that are spread to stakeholders' counterparts and partners. Sources of norms cannot claim sovereignty over cyberspace but they have complete power to establish rules that generate risks for stakeholders.

The scope and effectiveness of privacy protection on the Internet result from risk management decisions. Users and other stakeholders have to decide whether they accept risks to privacy and how they will transfer them, if applicable. Governments can take measures to increase or limit risks facing cybernauts under their jurisdiction. However, for stakeholders on the Internet, government legislation appears as yet another risk to be managed. Legislation and other norms, such as technical standards, can both increase and decrease risks to stakeholders' privacy and other interests.

19.2 Privacy on the Internet

The Internet is a theatre of many situations in which invasion of privacy can occur.[9] Privacy has to be protected in accordance with users' legitimate expectations while at the same time we have to take into account the fact that users are necessarily

---

5 Philippe Amblard, *Régulation de l'Internet l'élaboration des règles de conduite par le dialogue internormatif*, (Brussels: Bruylant, 2004), No. 80 [our translation].

6 Michel Vivant, 'Internet et modes de régulation,' in Étienne Montero, *Internet face au droit*, (Brussels: Story Scientia, 1997), 215, p. 229 [our translation].

7 Thomas Schultz, *Réguler le commerce électronique par la résolution des litiges en ligne*, (Brussels: Brulant, 2005), p. 162. Schultz reports on the points of views of the Mission interministérielle français sur l'Internet and the French Conseil supérieur de l'audiovisuel. He describes the findings of Marc Maesschalck and Tom Dedeurwaerdere, 'Autorégulation, éthique procédurale et gouvernance de la société de l'information,' in Jacques Berleur Christophe Lazaro and Robert Queck, *Gouvernance de la société de l'information*, (Brussels: Bruylant- Presses Universitaires de Namur, 2002), 77–103.

8 Thomas Schultz, 'La régulation en réseau du cyberspace,' [2005] 55 *R.I.E.J.*, 31, p. 32.

9 Paul M. Schwartz, 'Internet Privacy and the State,' [2000] 32 *Connecticut L. Rev.*, 815–947; Fred H. Cate, 'Principles of Internet Privacy,' [2000] 32 *Connecticut L. Rev.*, 877–896.

involved to various degrees in public life and therefore engage in activities that concern other people. Like the physical environment, cyberspace has both public and private spheres and legitimate expectations of privacy should therefore vary depending on the context.

Police surveillance is often referred to as a possible threat to privacy on the Internet. Yet, in all countries with privacy legislation, the forces of law and order have powers authorizing them to obtain information likely to prevent or solve crimes. Thus, privacy protection with respect to possible abuses by the police is not an issue specific to cyberspace. Certainly, the accumulation and persistency of information on the Internet make it possible to create directories that could be made available to the police. This is one of the web's risks. However, the police's right to exact such information is essentially a problem that has to be solved by regulating the police not the Internet.

Some Internet interactions are public while others presuppose privacy. In order to establish protection that balances all basic rights, we have to take into account the fact that public and private situations lie along a continuum. In cyberspace, nothing is purely public or strictly private, just as nothing is completely black or white. The degree to which a situation is public or private varies according to the context and circumstances. This is how we have to approach the right to privacy. However, the approach flowing from personal data protection law is far from sufficiently shaded to ensure the balance that has to be maintained between the public and private spheres.

19.2.1 Personal Data Protection

Privacy protection on the Internet is often confused with personal data protection law. Nicola Lugaresi notes that 'protection of privacy is often adjusted to meet the needs of personal data protection.'[10] Certainly, personal data protection law is a facet of privacy protection[11] but privacy has many hues and covers both more and less than the notion of personal data.

The all-encompassing nature of the notion of personal data has its origin in a need for a simple definition of information about people that should be protected. In order to circumvent problems involved in teasing out what has to remain secret in order to respect the right to privacy, a notion was chosen that conflates 'information that identifies an individual' with 'information about an individual's private life' and personal data protection law has been structured around the principle that the whole set is confidential. This has resulted from a desire to get around the difficulties flowing from the contextual nature of privacy. While it is clear that some data concerning individuals is private, it is also clear that not all is. Apparently in

[10] Nicola Lugaresi, 'Principles and Regulations about Online Privacy: 'Implementaion Divide' and Misunderstanding in the European Union,' TPRC 2002 Working Paper No. 42, online at: < http://papers.ssrn.com/sol3/papers.cfm?abstract_id=333440 >

[11] Raymond Doray, 'Le respect de la vie privée et la protection des renseignements personnels dans un contexte de commerce électronique,' in Vincent Gautrais, Ed., *Droit du commerce électronique*, (Montréal: Éditions Thémis, 2002), p. 303–361.

the quest for standards guaranteeing fair[12] personal data collection and processing practices, the nuances that had until then described the concept of privacy were left behind and instead measures were adopted that prohibit the circulation of any data on individuals. This slide has obscured the fact that the right to privacy is not the only right relating to the Internet. It has to be weighed against other rights and freedoms.[13]

It is well-known that public figures have less privacy than other people. Public figures are people who, through their own free will or owing to special circumstances, participate in activities that take place in public or who seek to win public trust or attention. Such figures include government representatives, artists, athletes, leaders of organizations and professionals who intervene in the public space. Though it is essential to democracy, this distinction is often ignored in application of personal data protection laws.

For example, if one participates in a public sports competition, it is supposed that one agrees to comply with the rules. Information relevant to ensuring the probity of sports competitions should be public. Unfortunately, strict application of some principles of personal data protection law tends to favour a conception of privacy that leaves little room for transparency and accountability. For example, in an opinion rendered in June 2005, the CNIL criticized the publication of a directory of over 1000 racing cyclists who had admitted to or tested positive for doping.[14]

The case of a list of notaries published on the Internet is another illustration of the excessiveness of some applications of personal data protection law. A blacklist of notaries was published but the targeted notaries were not given the opportunity to object to publication of their names and addresses. This was found to contravene the French statute on data protection. In a January 11, 2007 decision, the Bourges Court of Appeal upheld the criminal court of Bourges' July 5, 2006 conviction of the European Defence League for the Victims of Public Notaries. The League, which has now been disbanded, had authorized its Secretary-General to create and publish a web site on its behalf. The site was critical of some notaries and on the home page it said that the profession of a public notary 'puts clients at great risk.' This statement was accompanied by a list of 2500 notaries and a note to the effect that 'the fact of appearing in the European Defence League for the Victims of Public Notaries' list implies no prejudice or pre-judgment. It simply means that the League has a file concerning one or more of the notary's clients.' Some public notaries who objected to having their competency and honesty questioned wrote to the site to have

[12] Joel R. Reidenberg, 'Setting Standards for Fair Information Practice in the U.S. Private Sector,' [1995] 80 *Iowa L. Rev.*, 497; Spiros Simitis, 'Reviewing Privacy in an Information Society,' [1987] 135 *U. Pa.L.Rev.*, 707.

[13] Pierre Trudel, 'La protection de la vie privée dans les réseaux: des paradigmes alarmistes aux garanties effectives,' [2006] 61 *Annales des télécommunications*, 950–974, p. 957.

[14] CNIL, Suite à l'information donnée sur son site par l'intéressé lui-même, la CNIL confirme qu'elle a mis en demeure le responsable de ce site de cesser la publication d'un annuaire du dopage, News Release, June 30, 2005, < http://www.cnil.fr/index.php?id=1843&news[uid]=271&cHash=a9b6482b22 >.

their names withdrawn. However, the League's Secretary-General refused because the publication was meeting the objectives for which it was designed. The case was submitted to the French *Commission nationale sur l'informatique et les libertés* (CNIL), which introduced an action against the League. The CNIL considered that the League had violated the right to object for legitimate reasons to having one's personal information processed, as set out in section 38 of the statute on informatics and freedoms. The Bourges criminal court and Appeal Court both ruled in favour of the Commission's point of view.[15]

Clearly, as it is now applied, personal data protection law can oppose legitimate criticism of individuals with respect to their public activities and restrict circulation of information not related to an individual's private life.[16] Yet, privacy protection on the Internet should reflect the social dimensions of activities that take place there, rather than favour an approach incompatible with transparency and public criticism. Human dignity is not protected by *de facto* prohibiting criticism of people's actions and behaviour.

19.2.2 The Right to Privacy

It is important to identify approaches able to provide regulations that protect privacy effectively in network spaces. Unlike the all-encompassing notion of personal data or information, the concept of privacy includes recognition of reference points reflecting the constraints of life in society. It is thus better equipped to deliver concepts that can ensure a balance among all of the basic rights that have to be protected.

Web 2.0 applications require greater user involvement as producers and suppliers of information. They make it all the more necessary to seek a theory that can situate privacy protection in a cyberspace environment that is slipping further and further away from prefabricated categories and theories inherited from a time when computer technology was seen by a certain elite as the realm of surveillance.

The right to privacy is sometimes depicted as an overriding right to be protected from an infinity of constraints flowing from social life. This has been taken to such an extreme that, in order to evade the requirements of balance that flow from the right to privacy, we have come to use the notion of 'protection of personal life' to justify regulations inspired by people's desires to control information that displeases them.

Yet, unless it is seen as the right that eclipses all others, the right to privacy is simply a rampart guaranteeing human dignity in infinitely variable contexts. Understood

---

[15] *Gisèle N., Ligue européenne de défense des victimes de notaires / Ministère public*, Cour d'appel de Bourges 2ème chambre Arrêt du 11 janvier 2007, < http://www.legalis.net/jurisprudence-imprimer.php3?id_article=1903 >

[16] Flora J. Garcia, '*Bodil Lindqvist*: A Swedish Churchgoer's Violation of the European Union's Data Protection Directive Should Be a Warning to U.S. Legislators,' [2005] 15 *Fordham Intell. Prop. Media & Ent. L.J.*, 1206–1244.

in this way, the right to privacy is a fuzzy notion that refers to shifting thresholds of compatibility depending on time and location.[17]

The meaning of the right to privacy varies depending on the era and culture. Its content varies according to the circumstances, the people concerned and the values of the society or community.[18] Generally, private life includes things relating to love and sex, health, family life, one's home and even religious, political and philosophical opinions. Private information may also include an individual's sexual orientation, anatomy and intimate life. Private life is presented as an area of activity that is specific to a person and that he or she can close off from others.[19] It is also generally accepted that a public figure's personal life can in some circumstances be more restricted than that of an average citizen.[20] However, on the Internet, there are situations when one is in a public situation. You cannot publish your profile on the Internet and expect to run no risks.

In order to establish that there has been a violation of privacy, it has to be determined whether the disclosure of information or intrusion concerns an aspect of private life. Private life covers certain types of information that are, in principle, related but it can also vary depending on the person's position and circumstances. The concrete content of private life varies from person to person, according to the position they have in society and other circumstances. Taking the context into account is inherent to the notion of private life. It makes it possible to identify the borders of private life according to the circumstances, particularly in relation to an individual's participation in community life.[21]

19.2.2.1 Areas of Varying Degrees of Privacy

Privacy varies depending on the context. On the Internet, as elsewhere, the degree of privacy varies according to many factors. There are different situations that delimit the extent of privacy and weighing the requirements of human dignity against the legitimate information needs of others leads to recognition that some spaces and information are public. Indeed, this is taken into account in legal systems through various concepts and standards. For example, in Canadian criminal law, notions such as reasonable expectation of privacy are used to circumscribe situations in which the right to privacy and other imperatives apply.[22]

---

[17] Jean-Louis Halperin, 'L'essor de la 'privacy' et l'usage des concepts juridiques,' *Droit et Société*, 61/2005, 765, p. 781.

[18] Pierre Trudel and France Abran, *Droit du public à l'information et vie privée: deux droits irréconciliables?*, (Montréal: Thémis, 1992).

[19] Bernard Beignier, 'Vie privée et vie publique,' Sept. 1995 124 *Légipresse* 67–74.

[20] André Bertrand, *Droit à la vie privée et droit à l'image*, (Paris: Litec, 1999).

[21] Patrick A. Molinari and Pierre Trudel, 'Le droit au respect de l'honneur, de la réputation et de la vie privée: aspects généraux et applications,' Barreau du Québec, *Application des chartes des droits et libertés en matière civile*, (Cowansville: Éditions Yvon Blais, 1988), 211.

[22] *Regina* v. *Dyment*, [1988] 2 S.C.R. 417. The *Dyment* decision recognized that the right to privacy has an information-based aspect. See Karim Benyekhlef, *La protection de la vie privée dans les échanges internationaux d'information*, (Montréal: Éditions Thémis, 1992), p. 29.

Thus, depending on the context, there are different spheres of privacy. The spheres vary over time, space and circumstances. The relationships in which people are involved mean that those they interact with have different interests in different information. For example, one's spouse has a legitimate interest in knowing some aspects of one's private life but the next door neighbour does not. Likewise, employers have an interest in knowing some kinds of information about their employees for certain purposes but not for others.

The different interests in knowing are limits on privacy. When there are legitimate interests or when conditions exist that open the way to such interests, the right to privacy must give way. Legitimate interests to know what is going on restrict the right to privacy.

This can be illustrated by thinking about the information protected by the right to privacy as being located in concentric circles. Such circles delimit the information that can remain private and thereby also identify which information can circulate legitimately. Such information may not necessarily match what we consent to make available. Kayser shows that consent is not an appropriate concept for explaining the legitimacy of circulation of personal information. He writes that it is inaccurate to postulate that people tacitly consent to investigation and disclosure since 'a person who leaves private life to engage in a public activity does not think about consenting to disclosure of the activity. He or she thinks even less about authorizing research into his or her public activities.' He adds:

"The explanation has the greater defect of being inaccurate because, if it described reality, people would be able to express opposition to investigation and disclosure of their public activities. They would even be able to oppose the production and publication of images showing them engaged in such activities. However, they do not have that power."[23]

Doctrine has focused on describing the circle of privacy in relation to public life.[24] There is abundant case law examining the criteria for determining whether a situation is public or private.[25] Thus, as soon as one engages in a public activity, one leaves private life behind. Unless we completely abandon freedom of expression, we cannot extend privacy protection to claim a veto over information relating to public life.

---

[23] *Pierre Kayser,* La protection de la vie privée par le droit, *3rd Edition, (Paris: Economica-Presses universitaires d'Aix-Marseille, 1995), No. 134 [our translation].*

[24] See in particular Frederick Schauer, 'Internet Privacy and the Public-Private Distinction,' [1998] 38 Jurimetrics, 555–564; Daniel Solove, Marc Rotenberg and Paul M. Schwartz, *Information Privacy Law,* 2nd Edition, 2006; François Rigaux, *La protection de la vie privée et des autres biens de la personnalité*, (Brussels: Bruylant; Paris: LGDJ, 1990); Emmanuel Dreyer, 'Le respect de la vie privée, objet d'un droit fondamental,' *Communication commerce électronique*, May 2005, pp. 21–26.

[25] The French case law is analysed by Pierre Kayser, *La protection de la vie privée par le droit*, 3rd Edition, (Paris: Economica-Presses universitaires d'Aix-Marseille, 1995). See also Nathalie Mallet-Poujol, 'Vie privée et droit à l'image: les franchises de l'histoire,' *Légicom*, 1994/4, 51.

There are also situations that do not belong to public life but involve a third party's interest in knowing. For example, the right to privacy can be limited by children's right to know their origins, which can extend to knowing the identity of their biological parents. Owing to the imperatives of a job, an employer can have a legitimate interest in knowing some information that would otherwise belong to an employee's private life. However, for people located outside of the family circle or employment relationship, the information remains confidential.

An individual's choices also determine whether a piece of information is public or private. Choices differ from person to person and according to the context. For example, it may be considered natural to confide more in an intimate friend than in an employer. This explains why a piece of information can circulate legitimately inside a family or circle of friends, or even among co-workers, though a violation of privacy would occur if it circulated more broadly.

On the Internet, it is possible to make some information available to some people but not to others, for example, various functionalities make it possible to authorize different levels of disclosure of information on social networking sites.

Thus, the scope of privacy can be seen as composed of public, semi-public and semi-private spaces. This reflects the multiplicity of information-sharing circles associated with different areas of life, such as family and work. In the circles, information is public or private to varying degrees.

The way privacy is delimited is also determined by information-sharing circles flowing from specific events. Even when they have no public position, people can find themselves in the public eye when they are involved in public events. Such limited time-dependent circles make it possible to establish a 'right to social oblivion.'[26]

Violation of the right to social oblivion illustrates the relationship between the right to privacy and other people's right to know. The violation involves disclosing information that used to be known in the past but giving it a temporal and spatial scope different from that flowing from the initial disclosure. What is considered a violation and punished is disclosing it again, which is seen as unjustified in the context. Thus, the legitimacy of a right to social oblivion is dependent on assessment of the context in which the information is disclosed. Social oblivion is a right when it is judged unreasonable to disclose the information. In such cases, disclosure is found to be a violation, in other words, something that a reasonable person would not have done in similar circumstances. Context of disclosure is thus a very important factor in determining whether disclosure is legitimate.

The scope of the right to privacy is thus a function of the interest in disclosure. The purposes and interest in disclosure have to be identified. The premise is that the mere existence of a piece of information is not sufficient to making its disclosure legitimate. This shows the importance of the process of determining the interest in

---

[26] Catherine Costaz, 'Le droit à l'oubli,' *Gazette du palais*, 26 and 27 July 1995, p. 2; See also Roseline Letteron, 'Le droit à l'oubli,' *Revue de droit public*, 1996, 385 and François Petit, 'La mémoire en droit privé,' *Revue de la recherche juridique*, 1997-1, 17.

knowing. The scopes of the right to privacy and the right to disclose are determined by that process.

19.2.2.2 Interest in Knowing

Logically, not everything about an individual belongs to his or her private life. The right to privacy concerns information that affects an individual's independence and ability to exercise control over information concerning intimate relationships and life choices. However, as soon as an individual does things that concern others, his or her private life is necessarily constrained by their legitimate interests.

The democratic conception of privacy postulates that people holding public office or doing jobs that solicit public trust generally have a greater duty of transparency. People involved in public events, whether of their own free will or involuntarily, also have to expect a more restricted private life, at least as long as the event in question lasts. On the Internet there are public places and events. Visiting such places and participating in such events bring benefits but there are also accompanying risks and drawbacks.

The right to privacy varies in scope depending on the weight given to human dignity and other values in different relational contexts. For example, the right to privacy in the workplace depends on factors such as work requirements, confidentiality and level of trust.

As a legal standard, the notion of an interest in knowing has more than one meaning. Legal standards require us to examine what is acceptable in the context in which the decision applies. A standard is a flexible norm based on an intentionally underdetermined criterion.[27]

The various meanings of standards are established through different processes ranging from courts and professional fora to more fuzzy channels, such as common sense and ethical reflexes. Every meaning given to the notion can be seen as legitimate in some way. This is why it becomes the focal point when different interest groups in civil society come into conflict. It is rare that there is consensus on a definition. When there is unanimity, it is often easier to define the scope and limits of rights and duties in a more detailed manner a priori. However, when there is no unanimity, it is easier to state a rule by referring the interpreter to an assessment of the interest in knowing. This supposes recourse to a standard that can guide decision-makers. Thus, the meaning of the notion of interest in knowing emerges out of the history of concrete situations.[28]

The meaning of the notion of the interest in knowing is also defined through loose systems such as morals, ideology, common or generally accepted beliefs, ideas and fantasies more or less widespread in civil society, in short, through the common

[27] André-Jean Arnaud, Ed., *Dictionnaire encyclopédique de théorie et de sociologie du droit*, 2nd Edition, (Paris: LGDJ, 1993), p.581.

[28] Pierre Trudel, 'L'intérêt public en droit français et québécois de la communication,' in Emmanuel Derieux and Pierre Trudel, *L'intérêt public, principe du droit de la communication*, (Paris: Éditions Victoire, 1996), 179–189.

sense of the time and morality revealed in the body social as a whole. No source of law, not even legislation, can have a definitive effect on the conceptions and points of view that spontaneously combine, conflict and merge. Refining the arguments, concepts and views involved in determining what the public has a right to know or legitimate interest in knowing requires maintaining a healthy environment in which different ideas can challenge one another.

Seen in this way, the right to privacy is an individual's right to exercise control over information concerning something that does not belong to public space or that others do not have a legitimate right to know. It does not have universal scope. Its extent and meaning necessarily flow from examination of the limits entailed when there is an interest in knowing.

19.2.2.3 The Diversity of Circles of Friends on the Internet

The Internet is not uniform: it contains spaces of many different kinds. Some are more risky than others for the privacy of people who visit them. For example, social networking web sites make it possible for people to meet and connect through social networks. Sites such as *MySpace* (http://www.myspace.com) and *LinkedIn* (http://www.linkedin.com/) offer online services that allow people to get together. Such sites can be used to make friends, create professional relationships, publicize music groups, meet people who share the same interests, find old classmates, etc. One need only choose the site that meets one's needs and register to be potentially linked with millions of people.

The registration form generally enables users to create a basic profile containing their name, home town and occupation. Next, users can add more details, photographs, résumés and information on their interests. The information is located in a personal space.

In order to be linked with other people, users enter contact information into their address books. This requires searching for people who are already members of the site and inviting them to contact you. Users can also contact people who are not members, suggest they register and invite them to become friends. Some sites let you import a list of contacts from an existing email address so that you can send invitations to all the people on the list. When people join the site, they in turn bring in their friends and so the network grows.

The different circles of friends are protected in various ways, such as through technical barriers and a priori security. However, since this type of activity exists on the Internet, in other words, since users can decide to display certain pieces of personal information, we have to postulate that on the Internet there is information belonging to collective life in addition to that belonging to private life. In contrast, what we do on the Internet, our connection data and key words we have used are a priori private and generally should not be made public.

The different places on the Internet and the power of some information processing functions mean that cyberspace engenders greater risks that have to be managed. For example, the danger of information compiling and search engine capacities has often been noted.[29] Information, even public information, can be found more easily and then compiled so as to deduce private information. This changes the scale of threats to privacy on the Internet.

19.2.3 The Internet Changes the Scale of Risk

On the Internet, spatial and temporal reference points change and those applying in a less networked world are inadequate. Stakes unknown in the physical world arise with great acuity in networked space.[30] The OECD's *Report on the Cross-Border Enforcement of Privacy Laws* notes that increased circulation of information, particularly on the Internet, increases risks to privacy.

Larger volumes of cross-border flows at higher speeds, reaching broader geographical areas, transferring alpha-numeric, voice and image data among an ever-greater multiplicity of actors is likely to increase the number and cost of privacy breaches borne by individuals and organizations.[31]

Risk to human dignity occurs on different scales. Circles of privacy are redrawn, shifted and re-centred.

There is a spatial shift: physical space seems to dissolve in cyberspace. The location where information is situated now has little impact on its accessibility. As soon as a document is available on a server, it can be found using general Internet search tools or other specialized tools. Distance in space and the passage of time seem to have much less impact on the real availability of information.

The Internet makes publication routine and information can easily be published outside of legitimate circles, thus the increased risk. Naturally, cyberspace is made up of both public and private spaces but the reference points that distinguish between private and public have been blurred. Belgum notes that:

"Personal data, such as address, phone number, income, property value and marital status have always been available to those willing to dig. The Internet can make it possible for a much wider class of persons – essentially all Internet users – to gain access to similar types of personal information at little or no cost."[32]

The Internet changes the spatial scale used to assess privacy risks. Outside the networked world, gaining access to a piece of information can be very difficult. On the Internet, it seems that much information is within the reach of a simple search engine query. Solove observes:

---

[29] Daniel J. Solove, 'Access and Aggregation: Public Records, Privacy and the Consitution,' [2002] 86 *Minn. L. Rev.*, 1137–1218.

[30] Frederick Schauer, 'Internet Privacy and the Public-Private Distinction,' [1998] 38 *Jurimetrics* 555.

[31] OECD, *Report on the Cross-Border Enforcement of Privacy Laws*, (Paris: OCDE, 2006), p. 8, <http://www.oecd.org/dataoecd/17/43/37558845.pdf>.

[32] Karl D. Belgum, 'Who Leads at Half-time?: Three Conflicting Visions of Internet Privacy Policy' [1999] 6 *Rich. J.L. & Tech.* 1.

"Until recently, public records were difficult to access. For a long time, public records were only available locally. Finding information about a person often involved a treasure hunt around the country to a series of local offices to dig up records. But with the Internet revolution, public records can be easily obtained and searched from anywhere."[33]

Access to court records is emblematic of the quantitative and qualitative changes generated by the Internet. As Natale M. Gome-Velez says:

"Providing Internet access to court records increases exponentially the availability of court records, including any sensitive information they contain. Examples of sensitive information that might be found in court records include: social security numbers, home addresses, names of minor children, financial account numbers and medical information."[34]

There is also a temporal shift. The persistency of information entails that it can last longer than the circle in which it was legitimate. For example, it may be legitimate for a piece of information to be available to the public owing to a current event but archiving and virtual permanent availability on the Internet could go beyond what is necessary to report the news.

Information compiling capacities make it possible to create deposits of information on people and those deposits can be used by both the police and wrongdoers. In short, now that information can be found effortlessly, there is no default privacy protection. This means we have to reassess the arguments used to determine whether one is in public or private.

All of these changes to the scope of what is at stake in terms of privacy show that the level of risk entailed by networked circulation of information has also changed. The scope of the new risks to privacy transforms the reasons underlying laws. While it used to be taken for granted that the level of risk to privacy remained low or easy to control, as the Internet has spread, qualitative and temporal changes to the scale mean that there are greater threats. This explains the calls for stronger privacy protection when information processing environments are set up.

19.3 Risk Management Through Networks

Faced with the quantitative and qualitative changes in risks to privacy, there is a big temptation to call for stronger legislation. There is even a tendency to want to give the right to privacy such priority that other rights, such as the right to transparent public process, are limited. However, regulators have to deal with cyberspace's

---

33 Daniel J. Solove, 'Access and Aggregation: Public Records, Privacy and the Constitution,' [2002] 86 *Minn. L. Rev.*, 1137–1218, p. 1139.

34 *Natalie M. Gomez-Velez, 'Internet Access to Court Reports- Balancing Public Access and Privacy,' [2005] 51* Loyola L.Rev., *365–438, p. 371.*

special characteristics. The most effective way to ensure better privacy protection is to increase the risks to those who endanger it.

The normative framework of the Internet can be viewed in relation to the risks that the technology seems to entail. Internet privacy regulation is a set of decisions pertaining to management of risks that are perceived by stakeholders in the network.

Risk as a social construction is assessed differently depending on the time and cultural, political and social context.[35] Ideas about the dangers and potential of technologies help construct collective perceptions of their risks and benefits. Perceptions vary over time; they are not always the same. They are also dependent on the social context and law and other norms flow largely from varying perceptions reflecting social and historical contexts.

Internet stakeholders assess the risks that a measure or rule presents for their activities. The decision to comply with one rule but not others flows from an assessment of legal risks. The risk potential of laws of different legal orders is assessed by stakeholders in relation to various factors, such as real possibility of legal action, ownership of assets in the country in question, the desire to win trust and the concern to behave like a 'good citizen.' These factors are components in analyses used by stakeholders to orient their risk management strategies.

19.3.1 Risk

Regulation of the Internet is justified largely by the perceived risks of poorly regulated use. Maryse Deguergue points out that risk can be classified as an axiological notion describing reality while at the same time passing a value judgment on it, which makes it possible to establish legal rules.[36]

The diverging and converging perceptions of Internet risks help to construct reasons that form the foundations for legal rules designed to provide a framework for how the Internet operates. Risk forecasting, management, sharing and transfer are among the primary concerns of legal systems. Ulrich Beck explains:

"Modern society has been transformed into a risk society [...] because the fact of discussing risks produced by society itself, the fact of anticipating and managing them, has gradually become one of its main concerns."[37]

With respect to the Internet, normativity is motivated largely by the desire to reduce, manage and spread risk flowing from availability of information. Generally, risk is seen as a social object. Yvette Veyret says that 'risk as a social object is defined as the perception of danger. Risk exists only in relation to an individual, social or professional group, community or society that perceives it [...] and deals

---

[35] Christine Noiville, *Du bon gouvernement des risques*, (Paris: PUF, les voies du droit), 235 p.

[36] Maryse Deguergue, 'Risque,' in Denis Alland and Stéphane Rials, *Dictionnaire de la culture juridique*, (Paris: Quadridge, Lamy, PUF, 2003), p.1372.

[37] *Ulrich Beck, 'Risque et société,' in Sylvie Mesure and Patrick Savidan,* Le dictionnaire des sciences humaines, *(Paris: Quadrige, PUF, dicos poche, 2006), p. 1022 [our translation].*

with it through specific practices. Risk does not exist when there are no people or individuals who perceive or could be affected by it.'[38] Risk does not exist in a vacuum; it necessarily flows from a social context.

Naturally, protection of information belonging to private life depends on relationships between risks. The consequences of information circulation are not necessarily known by stakeholders when information is put into circulation. It is often the agglomeration of information that is considered dangerous. For example, a harmless piece of personal information can be published and then combined with other information and this can lead to disclosure of something private about an individual. In such a situation, the person concerned has consented to the disclosure or the public nature of the situation has brought the information out of the field of private information but there is nonetheless a violation of privacy.

Once acknowledged, risk entails an obligation to take precautions. Indeed, legal risk flows from situations in which there could be a violation of the rights of others. Even though they are different, there is a close link between technological and legal risk. When technological risk is proven, it almost always entails an obligation to take it into account and behave accordingly. Likewise, legal risk can result from non-compliance with laws or other obligations. Hypothetically, legal risk arises in situations in which individuals can be blamed.

Those who take part in cyberspace activities do so to a greater or lesser degree depending on the amount of risk to which they are aware of exposing themselves.

19.3.2 Networked Normativity

Risk management is part of a networked regulation process.[39] Networks are the result of interactions among people who find themselves linked. Networking supposes interconnected environments uniting stakeholders, regulators and the bodies playing a role in governance of the Internet.[40] In the spaces created by networks, namely, cyberspace, normativity is developed and applied according to a network

---

[38] Yvette Veyret, 'Les risques,' *Dossier des images économiques du monde*, FEDES, cited by Franck Verdun, *La gestion des risques juridiques*, (Paris: Éditions d'organisation, 2006), p. 11 [our translation].

[39] Katherine J. Strandburg, Gabor Csardi, Jan Tobochnik, Peter Érdi and Laszlo Zalanyi, 'Law and the Science of Networks: An Overview and an Application to the 'Patent Explosion,' [2006] 21 *Berkeley Technology L.J.*, 1293–1351; Andrea M. Matwyshyn, 'Of Nodes and Power Laws: A Network Theory Approach to Internet Jurisdiction through Data Privacy,' (2003) 98 *Nw.U.L.Rev.*, 494–544; Avitai Aviram, 'Regulation by Networks,' [2003] *Brigham Young U. L.Rev.*, 1180–1238; Lior Jacob Strahilevitz, 'Asocial Networks Theory of Privacy,' [2005] 72 *U. Chi.L.Rev.*, 919–988.

[40] Manuel Castells, *La société en réseaux. L'ère de l'information*, (Paris: Fayard, 1998); François OST and Michel de Kerchove, *De la pyramide au réseau: pour une théorie dialectique du droit*, (Brussels: Publications des facultés universitaires Saint-Louis, 2002).

model.[41] Renaud Berthou sees the Internet as 'a factor for development of a multiplicity of network processes.' While it is not the only cause of network development in law creation in post-modern times, it is a major instrument of change.[42]

In a network, stakeholders manage risks and seek to limit them or transfer them to others. For example, operators of social networking sites publish warnings so that users will consciously accept the risks flowing from putting their personal profiles online. Other stakeholders may consider establishing mechanisms to obtain consent for personal data processing so as to limit risk entailed by enforcement of national personal information protection laws.

Regulations can flow from technological standards, management norms and legal rules. There is no reason to consider that legal or other norms are always dominant. In fact, various sets of regulation-producing norms compete with one another: technological, market and legal standards are not always consistent. In some situations, legal references are absent from debates over what are seen as essentially management or technological issues. In other contexts, technology is bridled by law.

Government and other players can increase the risks involved in some forms of behaviour and activities, or reduce the risk associated with safe action. For example, when strict legislation is adopted against certain practices, the risk associated with those practices increases. In the case of legitimate activities, the government can signal and even limit risks to stakeholders. While government seems to have lost power in cyberspace, it generally still has strong influence over bodies located on its territory as well as over those that could be targeted by legislation indirectly.

In a network, every stakeholder able to set conditions has the ability to increase the risk of others. Thus, a government can impose duties on citizens living on its territory. The latter then have to manage the resulting risk. They will seek to ensure that their partners comply with the obligations that they themselves are required to fulfil and for which they are responsible.

In sum, the system of regulation is designed to re-establish balance between risks and precautions. It has to encourage all stakeholders to minimize the risks flowing from situations over which they have some control and to maximize the risk incurred by stakeholders who choose to behave in ways that are harmful or unduly increase risks to legitimate users. Privacy protection on the Internet belongs to this approach.

19.3.2.1 The Many Relations Among Norms

The Internet can be seen as a world made up of normativity nodes and relays that influence one another. What is at stake is not whether law, technology or self-regulation provides the best protection for privacy. Effective normativity results

---

[41] Pierre Trudel, 'Un 'droit en réseau' pour le réseau: le contrôle des communications et la responsabilité sur internet,' in INSTITUT CANADIEN D'ÉTUDES JURIDIQUES SUPÉRIEURES, *Droits de la personne: Éthique et mondialisation,* (Cowansville: Éditions Yvon Blais, 2004), pp. 221–262.

[42] Renaud Berthou, *L'évolution de la création du droit engendrée par Internet: vers un rôle de guide structurel pour l'ordre juridique européen*, PhD thesis, Université de Rennes I, Rennes, July 2, 2004, p. 373 [our translation].

from dialogue among stakeholders and their ability to relay norms and principles. In order to learn which norms govern an environment connected to the Internet, we have to identify the nodes in which they are stated.[43] For example, a state sets out legislation that is obligatory on its territory. Relays both connect and separate nodes. For example, to manage risk adequately, a company governed by the laws of Québec has to require parties with whom it signs contracts to protect personal data in accordance with Québec law. In virtue of other legal relationships, the same company may have to comply with European legislation. Co-contractors also have to comply with contract terms and technical standards.

Thus a way to strengthen privacy protection is to establish a set of measures designed to reinforce one another so as to limit risks to the privacy of cybernauts engaging in licit activities. The strategy has to be deployed in a network: stakeholders have to comply with rules and be encouraged to relay the requirements to those they influence.

In risk management, government measures will be more effective if they are accompanied by dynamic surveillance and enforcement policies wherever possible. Legislation that is notoriously not applied will be perceived as entailing lower risk.

For stakeholders in cyberspace, responsibility law that is set out and enforced by the state is an important part of the framework structuring actions and circumscribing obligations. Indeed, both collective and individual stakeholders adopt rules of conduct in order to manage risk and limit responsibility. This entails relaying the requirements set out in nodes of normativity. In every environment, the principles stated in such nodes, such as statutes and widely accepted principles, are relayed through micro- and self-regulation.

The network structure of cyberspace law makes it possible to describe the many relationships among the different orders of norms applying on the web. The risk management paradigm provides an explanatory hypothesis concerning the effectiveness of norms. Rules' effectiveness seems to be a function of their ability to promote optimal management of the risk that they permit stakeholders to identify, since the risk concerns both the danger justifying the norm itself and the sanctions and other constraints it engenders.

19.3.2.2 Norms are Proposed, Imposed and Relayed

In a network, many different relations can be seen between norms. Norms are proposed and even imposed in various nodes of normativity, which both compete with and complement one another. Relays between norms ensure rules are applied effectively because they make them explicit and disseminate the norms and their consequences.

---

[43] Pierre Trudel, 'Un 'droit en réseau' pour le réseau: le contrôle des communications et la responsabilité sur Internet,' in INSTITUT CANADIEN D'ÉTUDES JURIDIQUES SUPÉRIEURES, *Droits de la personne: Éthique et mondialisation*, (Cowansville: Éditions Yvon Blais, 2004), pp. 221–262.

A number of relationships can be identified among norms. In most cases, there is obligation: national legislation is compulsory for a person located in that country and that person necessarily has to relay the obligations flowing from the legislation or else suffer the consequences. This shows the degree of risk flowing from effective legislation. If legislation is not enforced, it will be perceived as generating negligible risk. This also shows how important it is to limit the number of laws. If legislation is adopted but enforcement resources are not provided, the law will be feeble.

In other situations, indirect application of norms flowing wholly or partially from other legal orders can be seen as a risk. For example, European directives affect not only member countries but also the obligations of stakeholders in countries with strong relationships with European nationals. This also applies in the case of American legislation: people running sites in other countries often consider that it is a good practice to comply with American laws because they hope to do business with Americans.

Regulation of Internet use thus often results from both the national law of the country where a site is based and the law of bodies that influence other sources of norms.

Some sources of normativity produce norms and coordination processes while others function like spaces of negotiation and balancing in which regulations are applied through a dialogue with other sources of normativity. For example, it is often following invitations from international organizations that states are led to spread norms contained in their legislation. This occurred in the case of the *Convention on Cybercrime*[44], which has been promoted by European Council and is open to signing by other countries.

Finally, when we engage in an activity on the Internet, we generally have to consider the possible risks entailed by failure to comply with many different kinds of norms. While the legislation of the country where we are located automatically applies, we may also have to cope with other legal, technical and customary rules that flow from the broad expanse of sources of norms.

19.4 Conclusion

On the Internet, users manage risks: they accept them or transfer them, limit or minimize them. It results that in practice, privacy protection on the Internet is regulated through risk management.

The risk management approach shows that what is at stake is not so much whether legislation or self-regulation should be used to protect privacy, as if one excluded the other. On the contrary, understood as a set of risks to be managed, Internet regulation has to be seen as a set of various kinds of norms that are necessarily relayed through many different networked processes. The incentive to relay

---

[44] COUNCIL OF EUROPE, *Convention on Cybercrime*, Budapest, 23 November 2001 < http://conventions.coe.int/Treaty/EN/Treaties/Html/185.htm >

the requirements of a rule so as to oblige others to comply depends on whether the rule generates risks that are seen as significant by those concerned.

Norms flowing from technical standards either increase or limit risks to privacy. Government and other regulators can also expand or shrink risk. Risk management decisions taken in nodes with enforcement capacity create norms that are in turn relayed to other actors. Governments can impose obligations that limit risks to privacy. On the Internet, such measures are generally treated by stakeholders as risks to be managed and transferred to co-contractors or other partners.

Cyberspace is an interconnected whole composed of interacting nodes of normativity. It is made up of spaces in which norms applying to users are enforced wholly or partly. A set of systems of norms are discussed and applied in cyberspace. In addition to government and private regulations, there are processes designed to provide frameworks for activities that cannot be regulated entirely by territory-based law. Technology and related constraints are also sources of norms in networks.

All of the norms on the Internet can be described according to a network model. Internet activities are thus governed by a networked normativity, the effectiveness of which is largely a function of norms producers' ability to create sufficient risk for other stakeholders so as to motivate them to manage the risk. It is as if the network were a vast environment in which stakeholders generate the risks that they perceive and then produce obligations that they spread to those with whom they are in virtual contact.

Privacy protection develops and functions according to a network model. Stakeholders can increase, transfer and limit risks. The effectiveness of regulation is a function of the real ability to increase the risk of those engaging in dangerous activities and to manage the risk of legitimate users. The more we understand about the relations between the various risk management processes, the greater our chances of achieving effective privacy regulation on the Internet.

Towards a New Generation of Data Protection Legislation

Herbert Burkert

Both the call for change as a leitmotiv of the contributions in this volume and the title of this contribution imply dissatisfaction with the present situation. Data protection, it seems, has reached a state in which there is a significant and even troublesome difference between data protection legislation and practices on the one side and, on the other side, the concepts and values once associated with privacy as expressed in fundamental documents as e.g., in Article 8 of the European Convention on Human Rights.

Alienation

This is not an issue of terminology. There seems to be a predominance of the usage of "privacy" in the US American context, while in the European context "data protection" may be used more often, within these texts, the terms "privacy" and "data protection" have largely been used interchangeably throughout and this interchangeability reflects common usage certainly on the international level.

Rather, this is about alienation – not totally uncommon in other areas of legislation either – an alienation developing over time between what had been assumed as basic values and principles at the outset of a legislative programme and what practices, interpretations and legislative modifications have been made out of these values and principles over time.

Why is this alienation felt now?

The title, if read cynically, may provide an answer: Perhaps we are already at the dawn of a new generation of data protection legislation, with laws continuously extending purpose and storage time of existing personal data collections, allowing new sharing and matching procedures, creating new multipurpose data collections, now euphemistically called "data fusions"[1] restricting rights of data

H. Burkert (✉)
Research Centre for Information Law, University of St. Gallen, Switzerland
e-mail: herbert.burkert@unisg.ch

[1] Data fusion centres have been mandated by the (US) Homeland Security Act of 2002 and the Intelligence Reform and Terrorism Prevention Act of 2004 (Intelligence Reform Act). Further

subjects, moving closer and closer to the psychological and biological qualities and quantities of what constitutes the essence of "data subjects".

Alienation might also result from dissatisfaction about practices and disappointment with those to whom data protection had expressly been entrusted. Have data protection agencies been showing enough resistance against such legislative changes? Have they settled too early for political compromise? Have they set their priorities in the right order? Have they become too bureaucratic instead of concentrating on the "real" issues? There is – after forty years of experiences with such institutions – still no basic consensus, even within such relatively homogeneous "normative spaces" like the European Union, on whether such an agency should have a political mandate at all, or whether we have best to envisage it as a sort of competition agency watching the "market" of privacy, intervening only at such instances when this market seems to be failing.

Constructive Responses and Their Chances

Against this background it is almost surprising to find in this volume so many constructive suggestions on how to improve the current situation. These contributions can be roughly grouped into three categories[2]: the reformers, trusting that only minimal change is necessary, the reformists, arguing for more fundamental changes often of a conceptual and/or structural nature and reengineers, i.e., those who focus on (new) technical supplements to legislation, whether reformed or revised. Reformers e.g., would reflect on ways to better adapt data protection regulations to the new demands of a networked world, connecting not only individuals and organizations but increasingly objects with in-built complex reactions. Reformists would e.g., emphasize that basic assumptions like e.g., the separation between the public and the private sector can no longer be taken for granted, that more definite limits need to be set to avoid that privacy values continue to erode with every new balance of interest, that more comprehensive privacy evaluation approaches need to be taken into account before new information systems are being implemented. Reengineers would e.g., recall and enlarge upon privacy enhancing technologies and technological designs that could exist without any personal data at all, or which would have inbuilt privacy defence mechanisms. These categories do not necessarily apply to individual contributors or contributions. Very often authors would provide

details: United States Government Accountability Office, Report to Congressional Committees: Homeland Security. Federal Efforts Are Helping to Alleviate Some Challenges Encountered by State and Local Information Fusion Centres. GAO-08-35, Washington D.C, October 2007.

[2] About these categories: Burkert, Herbert (2007). Changing Patterns – Supplementary Approaches to Improving Data Protection. A European Perspective. In: *Technology, Law and Privacy*, ed. Lisa Austin; Arthur A .J. Cockfield; Patrick A. Molinari, 243–258. Toronto: Canadian Institute for the Administration of Justice.

suggestions that could be grouped into all three categories. The terms are therefore meant to be merely descriptive and to provide a heuristic structure.

Against this background and now re-reading the title of this contribution constructively rather than cynically it can be assumed that a new generation of data protection legislation will adopt many such suggestions from all three categories. However, to predict which of these suggestions is, of course, a different matter. Legislation is not only about inducing change, about setting a normative path for further developments: While legislation does influence social change, legislation itself is subjected to the environment which it seeks to change. We are observing a reciprocal process and the legislative evolution resulting from such dynamics does not follow a rational, predictable path. Laws evolve, their interpretations and practices change within a complex ecological environment of political forces, socioeconomic and technological change and value changes.

From this perspective then, while no precise predictions can be made, it can at least reasonably be assumed that those suggestions for restructuring data protection will have the best chance of being adopted, which are the most responsive to social change and the concerns this change evokes.

Four such dimensions of change may be identified that would guide the "evolutionary selection" for the new generation of data protection laws:

(a) *Globalization* will lead to a (geographical) extension of such data protection regimes. The legal mechanisms used will depend on the geographical areas to be covered: We will see more international conventions and treaties, including the modification of exiting ones with a new generation of transpositions into national and local rules. These international regimes will have to compete with bilateral agreements, on national and regional levels, addressing (mostly sectoral) data protection issues directly or being embedded in agreements on international private or public sector cooperation, rules that will vary in the degree to which they will be binding across industries and services within the global economy.
(b) Further *differentiations in the (private) service sector* will lead to a stronger demand for predictability both by service operators and consumers alike and again locally as well as internationally: Normative typologies of acceptable practices in the various services sectors will (continue to) receive more prominence. Individual contractual solutions will concentrate on specific deviations from such models; such deviations might, however, still be considerable.
(c) Public sector services and "universal services" provided by non-public sector providers will continue to amalgamate into *hybrid services*. Being complex and seeking to remain flexible, primarily efficiency oriented data quality requirements and post-processing transparency rules will gradually substitute limitations of purpose, sharing and matching in such areas.
(d) The *physical integration* of services into objects and operational environments will emphasize the role of technical standards of information handling for such devices.

> However, as the developments described under (c) most clearly indicate, none of these trends would as such *necessarily* lead to a material and substantive strengthening of privacy in the traditional understanding of the concept and thus help to overcome the alienation diagnosed above. Rather there is the continuing danger that we would see a continuation of a competition for efficiency under the umbrella of data protection terminology.

This trend assessment then provokes another question: If even these constructive contributions will have to go through a filter of what is technologically, economically and socially acceptable, before being integrated into a new generation of data protection legislation, what then will remain of the "normative" potential of privacy? If there is indeed such a strong impact of the environment on legislative processes, are we not at a stage, as indicated at the beginning of this contribution, when the environment has already started to change – so to speak – the "genetic code" of privacy legislation to an extent that it is no longer recognizable as such, that indeed a new species of data protection law is evolving that might best be described as "personal data systems legislation", legitimizing the implementation and operation of comprehensive personal information systems, with all the constructive efforts put forward in this volume at best leading to an optimization of data quality and processing efficiency?

Structural Defects of Data Protection Legislation

Even if we concede that legislation is not only changing the world but that the life-cycle of regulations is at least also dependent on how its subject area is evaluated under changing political circumstances, we would still want to believe that there is a certain type of legislation that tends to be more resistant to changes in the economic, social and political environment. Such legislation is usually closely related to what constitutes the basic values and structures of a society, in legal terms, the constitutional norms. While not being part of the constitution in a strict formal sense such legislation might be called "constitutional neighbouring legislation" because it serves as a direct transmission of constitutional norms and often expressly so. Data protection legislation would certainly belong into this category. Why then is data protection legislation not more value resistant, forming society rather than, as it has to be assumed, being formed by society's changing concerns?

Data protection legislation conceived as a defence of constitutional values at a time of technological change has been – so to speak – born with two defects that at the same time constitute part of its key elements. These two structural elements are consent and "legislative override" (i.e., the possibility to deviate from basic principles if the legislature should decide to do so with a formal law) and they are increasingly showing their destructive potential.

Both elements are not uncommon as legislative devices: Consent reflects a key axiom of private autonomy, legislative override is a key axiom in democratic systems. In the context of data protection, however, they are both an expression of political compromise rather than an expression of fundamental principles. It should be remembered that while we in Europe might want to think of the time after the European (general) Data Protection Directive and before 2001 as the Golden Age of data protection legislation, this time had not been that golden at all. We tend to forget that it had e.g., taken almost two decades for the European Union to move from the first data protection initiatives of the European Parliament (then even not yet elected directly) to the Directive, not to speak of the Directive's full implementation in the Member States that even today is still an issue of dispute. We tend to forget the political battles that had been fought in Europe over e.g., the extension of data protection to the private sector. In short we tend to forget that data protection legislation, even at its "heydays" has always been the result of political strive and compromise. It is this continuous strive for compromise that had left data protection regulations with consent and legislative override as exit mechanisms open for political adjustments to renegotiate previous political compromise at any time.

Of course, both principles are embedded within cautionary restraints:

There has been a long debate on the true value of consent, a debate that at least has restricted the use of consent rules in the public sector. This change, however, can only be regarded as a limited success in view of the blurring borderline between what constitutes the public and the private sector and in view of its still extensive use in the consumer area.

"Legislative override" should only apply – at least for those countries that are subject to the European Convention on Human Rights – under the restrictions set by Article 8 of the Convention, namely if such legislative change is necessary within a democratic society. This restriction, however, in a sort of implicit "division of labour" no longer seems to serve as an inherent principle guiding *law makers* and even among courts it seems to have been left exclusively to courts of last resort either on the national level or even only to the Strasbourg Court. And even then this restriction only helps in individual cases and always only very belatedly.

The Essence of Data Protection Legislation?

Legislatures having provided such inroads like consent and legislative override, leaving restrictions to the courts and only to those of last resort and the restrained practices of the courts themselves nurture a more fundamental suspicion:

Data protection (privacy protection) may not only be about protecting a perhaps old fashioned and perhaps too rigid and too inflexible socio-psychological concept of the "self". Data protection legislation may even not only be about the right to informational self-determination (or at least co-determination) in an age of local, regional, national and international social and economic dependencies but data protection (privacy protection) may also – and perhaps essentially so – be about the distribution of power within and between societies, addressing conflicts of power in such constellations by reframing them as informational and communicative power conflicts. Data protection (privacy) legislation – in this understanding – would then seek to de-legitimize asymmetries of information distribution and aim at more equitable distribution patterns in the interest of individual freedoms and democratic participative structures. Arguing about data protection legislation – again from this perspective – is to continue to discuss age old fundamental social conflicts in a modern technology mode at a time when discussing such conflicts in terms of antagonisms of industrial organization, class, race, gender and regional differences of development is no longer considered to be adequate.

This reading of data protection legislation might explain why there is what Stefano Rodotà in this volume has identified as "schizophrenia" with regard to data protection: There is a general consensus demonstrated again and again in national and international legal documents, in political statements, in organizational assessments and in the appreciation by individuals when asked about their opinions that "data protection" and "privacy" are important values in society. Whenever, however, under the surface of largely consensual privacy language legislation seems to be touching upon existing patterns of informational distribution between individuals and organizations, between the citizens and the state, between consumers and providers of services and goods, between states and regions, between privileged and less privileged social groups, there is resistance. "Other" concerns are invoked and data protection legislation is being transformed to safeguard and to continue to harness exclusively power amplifications provided by information and communication technology for those who are already enjoying organizational and structural advantages. While "data protection" legislation has initially been – as everybody agrees – a misnomer, it now gradually turns into "information distribution protection" legislation and is suddenly becoming less of a misnomer.

Consequences

Consenting to this analysis we cannot expect too much from data protection legislation, even from a new generation of data protection legislation or at least not from data protection legislation alone. The core of the problem then seems to reside in the structural rifts in the distribution and control of power in our democratic societies, conflicts that have sharpened with the power enhancing capabilities of the modern information and communication technologies. Within this new environment e.g., the relationship between courts, the executive and the legislature has to be reassessed. In these terms, resignation of privacy rights in the name of security e.g., is not just about allowing changes of storage time and purpose, allowing new sorts of data collection and sharing but it is about resigning further informational power to the executive without sufficient counterbalances from either the legislature or the courts.

Within the limitations of this contribution it may almost seem futile to speculate why these ongoing structural transformations of our democratic societies have not (yet?) received more resistance on this more fundamental level. One possible reason may be – echoing here e.g., Ulrich Beck's reflections on today's risk societies[3] – that

[3] Beck, Ulrich 1986. *Risikogesellschaft. Auf dem Weg in eine andere Moderne*. Frankfurt am Main: Suhrkamp.

our societies because of their increasing complexities and interdependencies have created an asymmetrical risk situation where small interventions result in potentially large repercussions, which are then answered with asymmetrical distributions of informational power granting all kinds of "executive" organizations (including their public/private hybrids) informational supremacy to meet such risks. In such situations there seems to be an increased willingness to hand over information in exchange for better protection notwithstanding the paradoxical consequence that the individual risk would still have to be absorbed individually. This transformation process would mirror the long historical processes in which the democratic state has obtained the legitimized "monopoly of force" from societal residues of power, albeit against the price of a restraining structure of individual rights, procedural and institutional guarantees. It would seem then that in the current transformation process of transferring informational power, which is more complex because the role of the state itself is changing, the appropriate ensemble of individual rights, procedural and institutional guarantees has not yet fully evolved. Within such a conceptual framework we would then also have to discuss to what extent information and communication technology have also served or at least will serve as power enhancement tools for (non-organized) individuals and "third sector" organizations and to what extent we can expect from such groups effective attempts at re-balancing informational power distribution in our democratic societies.

Conclusion

At the current stage at least it seems that – within the limited context of this contribution – constructive suggestions of this volume cannot and perhaps even should not inspire too much optimism that any of these suggestions even if implemented would fundamentally help to restore the core values of privacy. In this situation, between the Scylla of cynicism and the Charybdis of unfounded optimism data protection *legislation* may indeed not be the solution but rather a part of the problem and we might have to recognize that for solutions we have to turn elsewhere even if it implies a continuation of the Privacy Odyssey.

Taking such a position is certainly awkward at a time when globalization has made us painfully aware of the synchronicity of the asynchronous: While e.g., in Europe we have the luxury to evaluate our experiences with data protection, pondering on their reduction to merely symbolic legislation, there are other countries which, over decades now, have strived but not yet achieved to enact data protection laws at all. However, this global mission might even be in greater danger if the experiences of those who have experienced data protection legislation are not carefully reviewed. Otherwise such global attempts will end in frustration discouraging both newcomers and those with data protection legislation experience alike.

Looking elsewhere would imply to re-read data protection legislation and the resistance it meets as a conflict about distributing informational power in our societies. It would imply to look at the structural safeguards our democracies provide for checks and balances, enlarging the social forces to be included into such a rebalancing process. A new generation of data protection legislation would then not only require that legislators take the demands of a democratic society, as a society based on the concepts of "pluralism, tolerance and broadmindedness"[4] seriously already at the *stage of legislation* but that the normative framework as such in which legislators, courts, administrators and social groups operate is considered as to which extent it still reflects a democratic society that can legitimately and effectively make such demands work.

[4] See most recently the interpretation of "necessity in a democratic society" with further references at European Court of Human Rights, Grand Chamber, Case of Lindon, Otchakovsky-Laurens and July v. France (Applications nos. 21279/02 and 36448/02). Judgment of 22 October 2007 at 45.

Printed in the United Kingdom by
Lightning Source UK Ltd., Milton Keynes
140840UK00002B/15/P

9 781402 094972